# OBJECTIVE-C AND iOS PROGRAMMING: A SIMPLIFIED APPROACH TO DEVELOPING APPS FOR THE APPLE iPHONE AND iPAD

## ARSHIA KHAN

CENGAGE
Learning·

Australia • Brazil • Japan • Korea • Mexico • Singapore • Spain • United Kingdom • United States

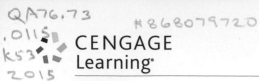

### Objective-C and iOS Programming: A Simplified Approach to Developing Apps for the Apple iPhone and iPad
### Arshia Khan

Product Director: Kathleen McMahon

Senior Product Manager: Jim Gish

Senior Content Developer: Alyssa Pratt

Development Editor: Ann Shaffer

Product Assistant: Gillian Daniels

Content Project Manager: Jennifer Feltri-George

Art Director: Cheryl Pearl, GEX

Compositor: Integra

Copyeditor: Jeri Freedman

Proofreader: Lisa Weidenfeld

Indexer: Sharon Hilgenberg

Cover Designer: GEX Publishing Services

Cover image credit:
©kornik/Shutterstock

Objective-C® is a trademark of Apple Inc., registered in the U.S. and other countries. iOS is a trademark or registered trademark of Cisco in the U.S. and other countries and is used under license.

Additional credits:

© iStockphoto/GlobalP
© iStockphoto/GlobalP
© iStockphoto/GlobalP
© iStockphoto/Milax
© iStockphoto/benjikat
© iStockphoto/ingret
© iStockphoto/midwi
© iStockphoto/midwi
© iStockphoto/midwi
© iStockphoto/midwi
© iStockphtoto/German
© iStockphoto/stock_art
© iStockphoto/German
© iStockphoto/Lori Lee Miller
© iStockphoto/revjake

For product information and technology assistance, contact us at **Cengage Learning Customer & Sales Support, www.cengage.com/support**.

For permission to use material from this text or product, submit all requests online at **cengage.com/permissions**. Further permissions questions can be e-mailed to **permissionrequest@cengage.com**.

Library of Congress Control Number: 2013950529

ISBN-13: 978-1-285-18705-1

**Cengage Learning**
200 First Stamford Place, 4th Floor
Stamford, CT 06902
USA

Cengage Learning is a leading provider of customized learning solutions with office locations around the globe, including Singapore, the United Kingdom, Australia, Mexico, Brazil, and Japan. Locate your local office at: **www.cengage.com/global**

Cengage Learning products are represented in Canada by Nelson Education, Ltd.

Purchase any of our products at your local college store or at our preferred online store: **www.cengagebrain.com**

Some of the product names and company names used in this book have been used for identification purposes only and may be trademarks or registered trademarks of their respective manufacturers and sellers.

Microsoft product screenshots used with permission from Microsoft Corporation.

Unless otherwise credited, all art and tables © 2015 Cengage Learning, produced by Integra.

Cengage Learning reserves the right to revise this publication and make changes from time to time in its content without notice.

Printed in the United States of America
1 2 3 4 5 6 7 17 16 15 14

# Brief Contents

# Contents

iv

v

# Preface

This book provides a basic foundation in the exciting field of iOS app development. With the advent of smartphones, applications have shifted to the mobile platform, promising ease and practicality, and a huge potential for further growth. So it makes sense for programmers to develop expertise in this area to increase their marketability. As the popularity of Apple devices continues to grow, professionals trained in iOS programming will be especially employable.

## Approach

To learn how to create iOS apps, you first need to learn how to program in Objective-C, the language underlying iOS. Most books on the market are specific either to Objective-C programming or iOS programming, making it difficult to teach app development in the course of one semester. This single book covers the necessary topics in *both* Objective-C and iOS programming, so students can get right to work creating iOS apps.

Numerous books on Objective-C and iOS programming are available, but none take the simplistic approach offered by this book, which includes abundant screenshots, examples, review questions, Programming Exercises, Hands-On Labs, and Business Case Studies, along with complete solutions.

To use this book successfully, no prior knowledge of iOS development is required. However, it would be helpful to have knowledge of at least one object-oriented programming language. New programmers should be also able to use this book, assuming an instructor is available to offer help when necessary.

Because this is an introductory book, it does not touch on higher level techniques that would be affected by the latest version of iOS in use. Thus, although the screenshots and code samples in this book were created using iOS 6, they are compatible with iOS 7, and should remain compatible with subsequent versions of iOS.

### What This Book Is

This book introduces the concepts required to create simple apps that can run on Apple mobile devices, providing step-by-step guidance, with plentiful screenshots to allow you to check your work. Chapters 1-7 cover the relevant topics in Objective-C, walking you through the steps required to write simple Objective-C programs. Chapters 8-14 introduce you to full-blown iOS programming, stepping you through the process of designing and programming an app interface. Throughout this book, you write code and create app interfaces using Xcode, Apple's integrated development environment for iOS.

## What This Book Is Not

This is not a resource book. It is not designed for advanced iOS developers and hence does not cover advanced topics in iOS. After you've mastered the basics explained in this book, you can find more detailed information about iOS programming online.

# Organization and Coverage

Chapters 1 through 7 explain how to write simple programs in Objective-C. In Chapters 8 through 14, you use your new familiarity with Objective-C to develop iOS apps that can run on Apple mobile devices.

**Chapter 1** introduces iOS, explains Apple's two developer programs, and provides a guided tour of Xcode, the integrated development environment you will use to write Objective-C code. The chapter then walks you through the steps of writing, saving, and running a simple Objective-C program in Xcode.

**Chapter 2** covers variables and constants, data types, and arithmetic expressions.

**Chapter 3** introduces decision and conditional statements, which are statements that decide which part of a program will execute at any given time.

**Chapter 4** explores looping and repetition mechanisms such as the for, while, and do-while statements. It also explains how to nest one looping statement inside another.

**Chapter 5** covers the fundamental programming concept of functions, which makes it possible to make a program modular, separating code based on tasks.

**Chapter 6** focuses on the Foundation Framework, which is unique to Objective-C. It discusses the utility classes that Apple has provided in an attempt to create consistency in all the domains of the language.

**Chapter 7** examines some object-oriented programming concepts, such as classes and objects, encapsulation, instantiation, methods, and inheritance.

**Chapter 8** examines the iOS platform, exploring the basics of iOS programming and the architecture of iOS. This chapter introduces controls, IBOutlets and IBActions, while explaining how to create a simple app interface.

**Chapter 9** focuses on using storyboards and creating apps that allow the user to pass data between multiple view controllers.

**Chapter 10** deals with transitions without using storyboards, and passing data from view 1 to view 2 with and without delegates.

**Chapter 11** teaches how to display data in the form of lists using table views, with and without storyboards.

**Chapter 12** introduces tab bar controllers and picker view controllers, with and without storyboards.

**Chapter 13** explores the process of adding images, sound, and video to apps. To complete the examples and exercises in this chapter, students need to download the necessary data files from the CengageBrain.com home page.

**Chapter 14** discusses various means of creating apps that can store and retrieve data.

**Appendix A** explains how to use the debugger.

# Features of the Book

Each chapter in *Objective-C and iOS Programming: A Simplified* includes the following features:

- *Objectives*—This bulleted list of major topics covered in the chapter serves as a useful study aid.

- *Step-by-Step Instructions*—Numbered steps walk you through the process of creating apps. These steps include full-color code examples and specific instructions explaining exactly how to interact with the Xcodes interface.

- *Screenshots*—Plentiful screenshots allow you to check your work as your follow the chapter's numbered steps.

- *Conceptual figures and tables*—Diagrams clarify programming concepts and tables give you at-a-glance summaries of useful information.

- *Key terms*—Important terms are formatted in bold.

- *Hands-On Lab*—This detailed, step-by-step lab walks you through the process of creating an app that incorporates all the major concepts covered in the chapter examples. Like the chapter examples, the Hands-On Lab includes plentiful screenshots to help you check your work.

- *Summary*—This end-of-chapter list recaps the programming concepts and techniques covered in the chapter so that you have a way to check your understanding of the chapter's main points.

- *Exercises*—Multiple-choice and true/false questions encourage you to review key concepts covered in the chapter.

- *Programming Exercises*—These programming problems require the student to use the techniques and concepts explained in the chapter to create a variety of apps. Students are encouraged to work through the problems and have instructors check their work against the solution files.

- *Business Case Study*—This continuing exercise, which builds on work done in preceding chapters, focuses on building and expanding on a useful business-related app in Chapters 1 through 7, and a medical-related app in Chapters 8 through 14.

## Student Resources

Source code for the in-chapter examples and Hands-On Labs in *Objective-C and iOS Programming: A Simplified Approach to Developing Apps for the Apple iPhone and iPad* are available at *www.cengagebrain.com*. A set of data files are also provided for Chapter 13.

## Software and Hardware Used in This Book

To complete the steps and exercises in this book, you will need the following:

- An Intel-based Mac running Mac OS X Snow Leopard or later
- A user ID as a registered apple developer or as a member of the iOS developer program.
- iOS SDK (Software Development Kit), the software development environment designed by Apple for iOS
- Chapter 13 data files downloaded from *www.cengagebrain.com*

Chapter 1 describes the various options for downloading the iOS SDK. A free version is available, with some restrictions, as explained in Chapter 1. The screenshots in this book were created using Xcode version 4.6.3 on a Mac with OS X version 10.8.4. However, since this is an introductory book, it does not cover topics that will be affected by the release of new iOS versions. In other words, this book should continue to be current through subsequent versions of iOS. Also, Apple will continue to support older versions as new versions are released.

Note that you do not need an iPhone, iPad or other Apple device to use this book, because the apps you create can run on a software-based simulator instead.

## For the Instructor

This book can also be used in a one- or two-semester format, with the Objective-C programming language taught first and iOS programming taught second. Ideally, students will have already learned an object-oriented programming language before using this book, but with help from an instructor, a new programmer can also be successful with this book.

At the College of St. Scholastica (CSS), where the author teaches, students use this book in a class on Objective-C and iOS programming for mobile devices. It has been used in a classroom setting and in online courses. In the classroom setting, CSS students have access to a Mac lab, with the development tools already installed.

***Instructor Companion Site.*** This collection of book-specific lecture and class tools is available online and provides everything you need for your course in one place, at *sso.cengage.com*. Access and download PowerPoint presentations, images, an instructor's manual, and more.

***Instructor's Manual.*** The electronic Instructor's Manual follows the book chapter-by-chapter to assist in planning and organizing an effective, engaging course. The manual includes learning objectives, chapter overviews, lecture notes, teaching tips, ideas for classroom activities, and additional resources. A sample course syllabus is also available.

*Test Bank.* This book is accompanied by Word-based test banks for each chapter that offer True/False and Multiple Choice questions.

*PowerPoint Presentations.* This book comes with PowerPoint slides for each chapter. They're included as a teaching aid for classroom presentations, to make available to students on the network for chapter review, or to be printed for classroom distribution. Instructors can add their own slides for additional topics or customize the slides by adding any of the figures from the book.

*Solution files.* Solution files are provided for all Hands-on Labs, Exercises, Programming Exercises and Business Case Studies.

*Source code.* The source code for this book's programs is provided for students. In addition to being available online through *sso.cengage.com*, it's available for students through *www.cengagebrain.com*.

# Acknowledgements

*Objective-C and iOS Programming: A Simplistic Approach to Developing Apps for the Applie iPhone and iPad* has been successfully delivered with the hard work and hours of devotion from a very determined group of professionals. Thank you to the folks at Cengage—specifically Jim Gish, Senior Product Manager; Alyssa Pratt, Senior Content Developer; Michelle Ruelos Cannistraci, Senior Content Developer; Jennifer Feltri-George, Content Project Manager; Christine Myaskovsky, Rights Acquisitions Specialist; Jeri Freedman, copyeditor; Lisa Weidenfeld, proofreader; and Susan Pedicini, MQA tester. Also many thanks to Indumathy Gunasekaran, Project Manager at Integra Software Services, and Ann Shaffer, Developmental Editor, at Shaffer Technical Editing.

Thank you to the reviewers of this book: Rafael Azuaje, Sul Ross State University; Paul Norrod, Lorain County Community College; Andy Poe, Northern Michigan University; Michael Saelee, Illinois Institute of Technology; Michael Shafae, California State University, Fullerton.

Thank you to my beautiful kids, Danish Imtiaz, Rana Imtiaz, and Nabiha Imtiaz, who tolerated me spending extended hours day and night on this book. I am grateful to them for their patience and understanding while their mom sat writing in her bedroom. Thanks to my mom, Afzalunnisa Begum, for her help and support, especially with the cooking and taking care of the kids, as I was busy writing and editing.

A special thank you to my son, Danish Imtiaz, who helped research and explore some of the topics covered in the book in addition to testing some of the apps and the end-of-chapter exercises and solutions. Also thank you to my students, Eric Hiller, Joel Poualeu, and Rishika Dhody, who helped with the end-of chapter exercises and solutions.

Thanks to my late Dad, Abdul Hafeez Khan, who instilled the drive to persevere through thick and thin.

Finally, thank you to my darling husband, Imtiaz Mohamed, for his patience, support, and understanding while the lonely writing process took over our lives. I can't think of anyone but him with whom I would take the journey of life.

# Launching and Getting Started

In this chapter you will:

- ◎ Learn about the iOS platform
- ◎ Explore the requirements for creating iOS apps
- ◎ Prepare to register with Apple as a developer
- ◎ Learn about Xcode and the iOS SDK
- ◎ Write a simple Objective-C program in Xcode
- ◎ Learn about the Xcode Debugger

iOS is a mobile operating system developed by Apple for use on the iPhone, iPad, and iPod. To develop iOS apps, you need the following:

- An Intel-based Mac running Mac OS X Snow Leopard or later.

- A user ID as a registered Apple developer or as a member of the iOS developer program. You will learn more about these two developer options later in this chapter.

- The ability to program in Objective-C, which is the programming language used to create iOS applications.

- iOS SDK (Software Development Kit), the software development environment designed by Apple for iOS, which includes the following:

  ○ The integrated development environment Xcode, in which you can write, test and develop Objective-C code.

  ○ iOS Simulator, which allows you to test an app as if it were running on an iPhone or iPad.

  ○ Cocoa Touch, which is the programming framework of Objective-C and therefore iOS. A programming framework is the underlying platform for a programming language, providing, among other things, code libraries, tool sets, and more.

This chapter introduces you to iOS, explains the two developer programs, and provides a guided tour of Xcode, the integrated development environment you will use to write Objective-C code. The chapter then walks you through the steps of writing, saving, and running a simple Objective-C program in Xcode. You will use the skills you learn in this chapter to write more complicated Objective-C code in Chapters 2 through 7. Starting in Chapter 8, you will use your new familiarity with Objective-C to learn to develop apps that can run on Apple's mobile devices.

Note that you do not need an iPhone, iPad, iPod, or other mobile device to learn iOS programming. Instead, you will use the iOS Simulator, built into Xcode, to mimic a mobile device running your apps.

## Introduction to iOS

The iOS mobile operating system, which was initially called the iPhone Operating System (iOS), is developed and distributed by Apple. It is used by developers around the world to create mobile applications, or apps, which are then made available to users via Apple's App Store. The App Store is built into OS X Mountain Lion, Apple's most recent operating system. According to Apple, the App Store is the world's largest entertainment store with more than 800,000 apps. These apps have been tested for malware by Apple before they are made available for sale in the App Store. The possibilities for apps are limitless, providing infinite opportunities for development.

The iOS platform has a very powerful foundation derived from OS X, the operating system originally designed for the Mac, sharing technologies such as the kernel, networking sockets, and the programming frameworks. Like OS X, iOS is written in Objective-C. Cocoa Touch, the programming framework of OS X and iOS, includes interactive Multi-Touch technologies that allow a developer to create applications that respond to the user touching a device's screen. Like OS X and iOS, Cocoa Touch is implemented in Objective-C. For this reason, it is essential to learn Objective-C. Objective-C is the language for programming in the iOS environment.

Objective-C is an object-oriented programming language that runs at very fast speeds while employing dynamic runtime. Objective-C is an offshoot of the procedural programming language C. In essence, if you add object-oriented programming to C, you get Objective-C. Any C code will work in an Objective-C program and will be compiled by Objective-C. Another important aspect of Objective-C is that, unlike most other programming languages, methods in Objective-C are sent rather than called or invoked.

Most of the C programming language syntax applies to Objective-C as well. Hence the C programming language concept of headers files translates into the concept of @interface and @implementation files. The @interface file holds the instance variable, properties, and method declarations, whereas the @implementation file holds the method implementations. All the properties are also synthesized in this file. The @interface file has a suffix of .h and the @implementation file has a suffix of .m.

## Registering as a Developer

Apple provides a tremendous amount of support for writers of iOS apps, with documentation on programming and other help for programmers. In order to gain access to these supports, you need to register with Apple. When registering, you have two options: registered Apple developer and iOS developer. To complete the exercises in this book, you need to register as one or the other.

### Registering as an Apple Developer

Registering as an Apple developer is the simplest option. You simply register with Apple, without having to pay any fee. However, you are required to have an Apple ID (just as you would to purchase music or apps in the iTunes Store). Registering as an Apple developer gives you access to developer resources such as online documentation and tutorials, and also allows you to download Xcode for free. However, iOS simulator is not fully functional for Apple developers. Features such as the camera and video recording cannot be tested in iOS Simulator and, instead, must be tested on an actual device.

To register as an Apple developer, go to https://developer.apple.com/programs/register/

### Registering as an iOS Developer

Registering as an iOS developer has multiple advantages over registering as an Apple Developer. One of the advantages is that it permits the developer to test the apps on devices and sell the apps in the App Store. Unlike the Registered Apple Developer Program, the Registered iOS Developer Program offers additional features such as the ability to transfer the app to a device, as well as sell the app in the App Store.

4

You can choose from three different iOS developer programs: the iOS Developer Program, the iOS Developer Enterprise Program, and the iOS Developer University Program. The iOS Developer Program is the one best suited for individuals and costs $99 a year. The iOS Developer Enterprise Program is designed for organizations and costs $299 a year. The iOS Developer University Program is designed for educational purposes and is free.

You can complete the exercises in this book as a registered Apple developer. However, if you are a student, your instructor may have set up iOS Developer University accounts for your entire class. Check with your instructor to make sure you understand which option you should use. The iOS Developer University Program is the preferred option.

To register as an iOS developer, go to https://developer.apple.com/support/ios/

## An Introduction to Xcode and the IOS SDK

As explained earlier, Xcode is the integrated development environment in which you create applications for iOS. The power of Cocoa Touch is also integrated into Xcode, making it easy to develop animation, networking, and other powerful touch features.

Xcode is actually just one part of a larger development application known as the **iOS Software Development Kit**, or **IOS SDK**. In addition to Xcode, the iOS SDK includes the compiler for the Objective-C language, a debugger, an interface builder, and the iOS Simulator. This chapter assumes that you have already downloaded and installed Xcode using the instructions provided in Appendix A at the end of this book. When you download Xcode, you actually download the entire iOS SDK.

When you start Xcode, you see the interface shown in Figure 1-1.

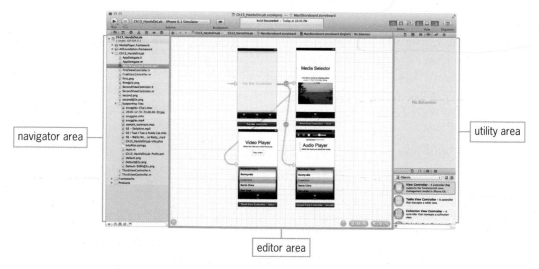

**Figure 1-1**   Xcode workspace
Copyright © 2014 Apple®. All Rights Reserved.

The Navigator area is where you can navigate through the files in a project. As you'll see later in this chapter, you actually type and edit Objective-C code in the editor area. Starting in Chapter 8, you will use the tools in the utility area to create user interfaces for iOS apps. For now, you can ignore that part of the Xcode workspace.

Starting in Chapter 8, you will use iOS Simulator to mimic the execution of your apps on an iPhone. Figure 1-2 shows an app running on an iPhone in iOS Simulator.

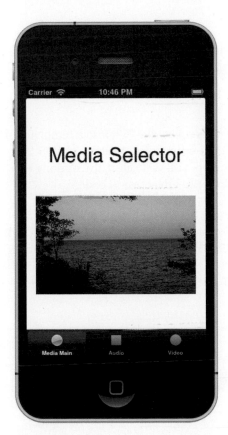

**Figure 1-2**   iPhone app running in iOS Simulator
Copyright © 2014 Apple®. All Rights Reserved. Photo courtesy Arshia Khan.

# Creating and Running a Project in Xcode

You are now ready to create a new project in Xcode. The following steps walk you through the process.

**To create a new project in Xcode:**

1. Click the Xcode icon in the dock or find Xcode in the list of applications. When Xcode starts, you see a welcome window. If Xcode has previously been used on your computer, you will see a list of existing projects. In this case, however, you want to start a new project. See Figure 1-3.

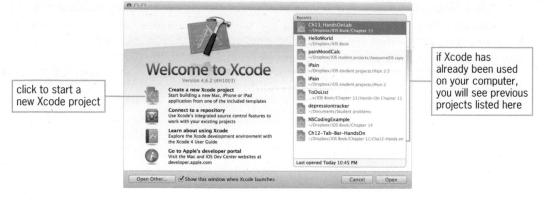

click to start a
new Xcode project

if Xcode has
already been used
on your computer,
you will see previous
projects listed here

6

**Figure 1-3**  Xcode welcome window

2.  Click the **Create a new Xcode project** button. This opens the "Choose a template for your new project" window, which gives you several options for creating an iOS application or an OS X application. In the next step, you will select the options that will allow you to use the Command Line tool to write Objective-C code.

3.  In the left pane, under "OS X," select **Application**. You might wonder why you are selecting OS X here instead of iOS. The reason is that you will be using the command-line tool to run the Objective-C compiler in OS X in Chapters 1–7.

4.  In the upper-right pane, select **Command Line Tool**. At this point, your screen should match Figure 1-4.

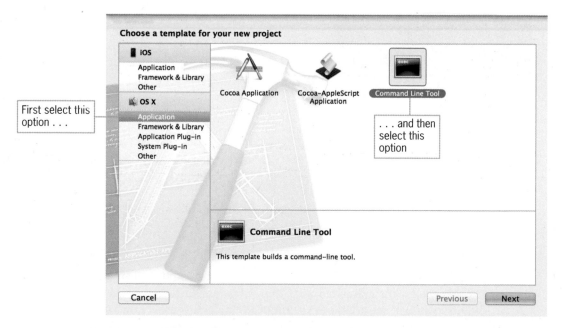

First select this
option . . .

. . . and then
select this
option

**Figure 1-4**  Selecting a template for the new project

5. Click **Next**. Now you see the "Choose options for your new project" window. Here you can provide a name for your project, the name of your organization, and the company identifier. A typical entry for the Company Identifier is "edu" or "com."

6. For the product name, enter **addTwoNumbers**; for the organization name, enter your school's initials. For the company identifier, enter **edu**.

7. For the Type, select **Foundation**. When you are finished, your screen should include the options shown in Figure 1-5.

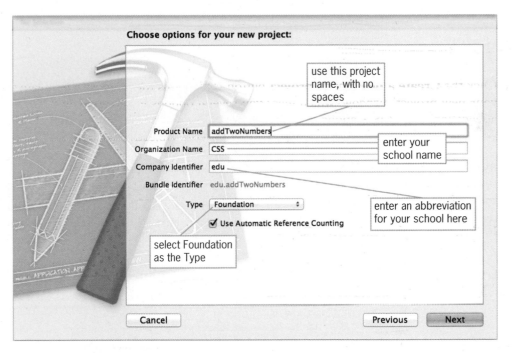

**Figure 1-5**   Choosing options for your new project

8. Click **Next**. The Save As dialog box opens, where you can either navigate to an existing folder or click the New Folder button, type a name for the new folder, and press return and then click the Create button. When you are finished saving, you see the Xcode workspace, as shown in Figure 1-6.

**Figure 1-6**    Xcode workspace with addTwoNumbers project open

9. In the navigator area on the left side, click **main.m** to display the source code for the main method in the editor area. Xcode automatically generates the following code:

```
//
//  main.m
//  AddTwoNumbers
//
//  Created by Arshia Khan on 5/7/17.
//

#import <Foundation/Foundation.h>

int main(int argc, const char * argv[])
{

    @autoreleasepool {

        // insert code here ...
        NSLog(@"Hello, World!");

    }
    return 0;
}
```

This auto generated code starts with comments containing the name of the program, copyright information, and the date the project was created, followed by an `import` statement that imports the foundation library. You will not need to use this statement in Chapters 1–7, but for convenience we will leave it there. Following the `import` statement is the `main` function, where the program execution starts. The first statement in the `main` function is `@autoreleasepool`, which handles memory management. You'll learn more about this in later chapters. At this point, although we do not need this statement, we will leave it in the program since it does no harm to include it. Any code you will write goes between the curly braces of the `@autorelease` statement. An `NSLog` statement that outputs the statement "Hello World" is always autogenerated in any new program.

To get some practice interacting with Xcode, you will now enter and run some Objective-C code. At this point, you do not need to understand the code. However, if you are an experienced programmer, you probably will understand it. In any case, your goal is simply to gain some practice working in the Xcode environment.

**To enter and run some Objective-C code in Xcode:**

1. Delete the `NSLog` statement and type the following code in the curly braces of the `@autoreleasepool` statement. When you are finished, your screen should match Figure 1-7.

```
int x, y;
x = 10;
y = 12;

NSLog(@"The sum of x and y is: %i", x+y);
```

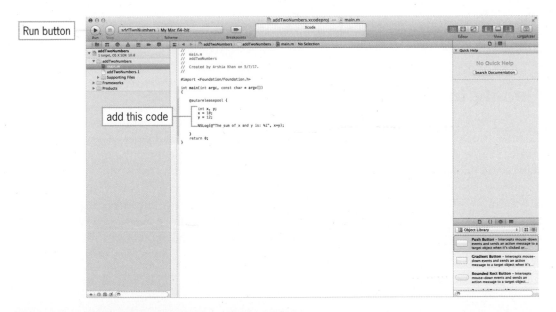

**Figure 1-7**   addTwoNumbers project with new code

2.  Click the **Run** button. The sum of the two numbers, 10 and 12, is displayed in the output window in the bottom-right corner of the workspace, as shown in Figure 1-8.

**Figure 1-8**    Output of addTwoNumbers program

You are finished with the project, so you can close it. You don't need to save it first, because Xcode automatically saves a program when you run it.

3.  Click **File** in the menu bar, and then click **Close Project**.

## Getting to Know the Debugger

The Xcode has a built-in debugger that lets you walk through a program's code. You can activate the debugger by clicking on any line of code to add a break point. The next time you run the code containing a break point, the execution of statements will stop at the point where the debugger was added. Figure 1-9 shows a break added to some code, and Figure 1-10 shows the debugger activated when the app containing the break point is run. When code execution reaches a break point, you have the option of stepping into, stepping over, or stepping out of the code, or continuing execution. The window in the lower-left corner displays the variables, their data types, and the contents. As the debugger steps through the code, the contents of the variables can be monitored.

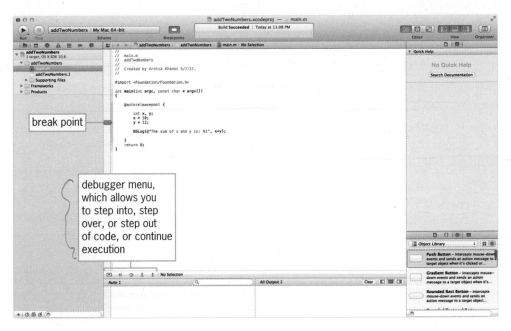

**Figure 1-9** Break point added to code

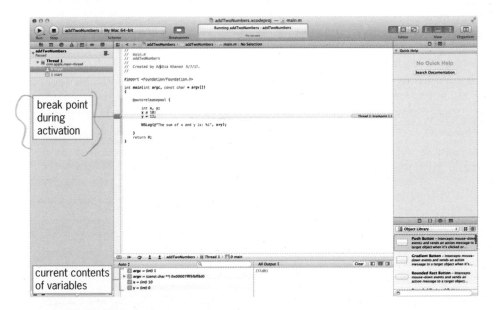

**Figure 1-10** Debugger activated

Not all programmers like to use debuggers when writing code. However, some programmers rely on them heavily. If you are interested in using the debugger while working on the examples and exercises in this book, consult Appendix B for more details.

## Summary

- To program in iOS, you will need a Mac running OS X Snow Leopard or later, Xcode, knowledge of Objective-C, knowledge of iOS, and membership in one of Apple's developer programs.

- You can complete the exercises in this book using a registered Apple developer account, or an iOS Developer University account. Check with your instructor to make sure you understand which option you should use. The iOS Developer University Program is the preferred option.

- iOS is the operating system that runs on Apple's mobile devices. The iOS platform is derived from OS X, the operating system originally designed for the Mac. Objective-C is the language of development for the iOS platform. Objective-C is mostly C with the addition of object-oriented features.

- Cocoa Touch, the programming framework of OS X and iOS, includes interactive Multi-Touch technologies that allow a developer to create applications that respond to the user touching a device's screen.

- iOS SDK is a software development kit that provides the tools you need to create iOS apps. Among other things, iOS SDK includes Xcode, iOS Simulator, and Cocoa Touch.

- Xcode is a powerful integrated environment that you can use to write Objective-C code and to create iOS apps.

- iOS Simulator allows you to run an app on a simulated version of a real device.

- You can activate the debugger by clicking on any line of code to add a break. The debugger is covered in more detail in Appendix B.

## Exercises

1. To develop iOS apps you will need an Intel-based Mac running Mac OS X Snow Leopard or later. If this statement is false, explain why.

   a. True
   b. False

2. The main programming language for iOS applications is Java. If this statement is false, explain why.

   a. True
   b. False

3. Cocoa Touch provides the Multi-Touch technologies used in iOS apps. If this statement is false, explain why.

   a. True
   b. False

4. Xcode is the integrated development environment in which iOS applications are developed. If this statement is false, explain why.

   a. True
   b. False

5. Describe the three iOS developer programs.

6. Name one advantage of the iOS Developer Program over the Apple Developer Program.

7. What is iOS Simulator?

8. List the features of iOS that cannot be tested with Xcode Simulator if you are a registered Apple developer.

9. Briefly describe the following elements of Xcode:

   a. Navigator area
   b. Editor area
   c. Utility area

10. Explain how to activate the debugger.

# CHAPTER 2

# Data Types and Arithmetic Expressions

In this chapter you will:

◎ Work with variables and constants

◎ Use the NSLog method to output data

◎ Use the Scanf method to read user input

◎ Learn about basic and derived data types

◎ Learn how to define a new data type with enumerations

◎ Use the preprocessor to create custom statements

◎ Create arithmetic expressions

# Variables and Constants

Programming is mainly data manipulation. This data can take many forms, including numbers, individual alphabetic characters, strings of alphabetic characters, and numbers with specific decimal precision. The purpose of the program you are creating drives the type of data the program will have to manipulate and store. To store data, a program requires placeholders, which can be either variables or constants. A **variable** placeholder holds data that changes as the program runs, whereas a **constant** placeholder holds data that have a fixed value. A variable has a data type and a name for identification.

Objective-C supports several types of data. As you should already know from your study of programming, data types help the compiler allocate memory for storage. For instance, one data type may use 1 byte, whereas another data type may use 2 bytes to store the same data. The data type also helps the programmer identify the possible tasks that can be performed on the data without generating errors. For example, numbers can be added, but strings are concatenated. (**Concatenation** is the process of combining strings to form a single string.) If you attempt to add two numbers with decimal places and then store it in a data placeholder that does not hold decimal places, the compiler will generate an error, indicating a loss of precision.

# NSLog and Scanf

Before we go on to discuss the various Objective-C data types, we'll pause to introduce the function that helps us print to the console and take user input. We'll then use this function in the examples that illustrate the various Objective-C data types.

NSLog is identified by Apple as an error log mechanism used to output data to the console. An optional output mechanism is the `printf()` function, but the `printf()` function is a C-based function, whereas NSLog not only is an Objective-C foundation function but also provides an extended set of functionality such as the option to format data using format specifiers. Format specifiers are tokens with the symbol % followed by a character that specifies a data type. For example, the data type `int` has d, i, or x as format specifiers.

NSLog takes one or more parameters in the form of a string with format specifiers. (Strings will be covered in Chapter 6.) The string with the format specifier starts with the @ symbol. Table 2-1 lists the format specifiers for commonly used data types. The % symbol is a placeholder for the actual value of the variable.

| Data type | Format specifier |
|---|---|
| int | %d, %i, %x (for hexadecimal) |
| char | %c |
| float | %f |
| double | %f |
| newline | \n |
| literally print symbol % | %% |
| pointer | %p |

**Table 2-1**    Data types and corresponding format specifiers

In Example 2-1, the NSLog statement prints Hello All! This is Chapter 2. The format specifier for the variable chapter specifies its location and the format in which it should be printed. The \n in the NSLog statement is the newline character, which causes a new line to be inserted.

Note that the numbered examples include line numbers, to make it easier to discuss the code.

## Example 2-1

```
1  #import <Foundation/Foundation.h>
2
3  int main(int argc, const char * argv[])
4  {
5      @autoreleasepool
6      {
7          int chapter = 2;
8          NSLog(@"  \nHello All!, This is Chapter %d", chapter);
9      }
10     return 0;
11 }
```

**Output for Example 2-1**

```
2017-07-29 23:10:27.812 Example2.1[99816:403]
Hello All!, This is Chapter 2
```

The scanf function uses the format specifiers in the same manner as NSLog and reads user typed input. Each argument maps to its corresponding format specifier in the string. In Example 2-2, the first NSLog statement prompts the user for a number. The next statement is a scanf statement whose first argument is a format specifier that indicates the type of argument the user can enter. The next argument is the name of the variable in which the user number will be stored. The variable name in the argument should always have an & symbol.

*double*
*%.1f*

Note that for code that requires the user to enter data that will be stored as a **double**, you cannot use the %f format specifier. Instead, you have to use %lf. This is because %f implies that the input will be a float, which takes up 4 bytes of storage space whereas a double takes up 8 bytes. In order to make scanf recognize the double as a **double**, and so accept the input, you need to add the lowercase l (that is, the lowercase letter L).

## Example 2-2

```
1   #import <Foundation/Foundation.h>
2
3   int main(int argc, const char * argv[])
4   {
5       @autoreleasepool
6       {
7           int num;
8           NSLog(@"  \nPlease enter a number\n");
9           scanf("%d", &num);
10          NSLog(@"\nThe number you entered is %d", num);
11      }
12      return 0;
13  }
```

### Output for Example 2-2

```
2017-07-29 23:25:22.573 Example2.2[99935:403]
Please enter your a number
6
2017-07-29 23:25:26.390 Example2.2[99935:403]
The number you entered is 6
```

# Basic Data Types

Now that you are familiar with the NSLog and Scanf functions, we can launch into our discussion of the most commonly used data types in Objective-C.

## Type *int*

The int data type is used to store an integral—that is, a whole number that does not have a decimal point. In Example 2-3, score is defined as an int and assigned a value of 85, whereas age, which is also defined as an int, is initialized to 56. In Example 2-3, the NSLog function prints the values of score and age to the console as evident in the output following the example.

## Example 2-3

```
1   #import <Foundation/Foundation.h>
2
3   int main(int argc, const char * argv[])
4   {
5       @autoreleasepool
6           {
7               //variable declarations
8       int score = 85;
9       int age = 56;
10              NSLog(@"\n score = %d and age = %d", score, age);
11          }
12      return 0;
13  }
```

**Output for Example 2-3**

```
2017-07-27 16:55:27.284 Example 2.3[92453:403]
score = 85 and age = 56
```

## Type *char*

The char data type is used to store a single character. The char value is stored in single parentheses. In Example 2-4, grade has a type of char and is initialized to C. The type for last is also char and it is initialized to Z. The char data type uses 8 bits of space for storage. In Example 2-4, the NSLog function prints the values of grade and last to the console.

## Example 2-4

```
1   #import <Foundation/Foundation.h>
2
3   int main(int argc, const char * argv[])
4   {
5       @autoreleasepool
6         {
7           //variable declarations
8           char grade = 'c';
9           char last = 'Z';
10          NSLog(@" \n grade = %c and last = %c", grade, last);
11        }
12      return 0;
13  }
```

**Output for Example 2-4**

```
2017-07-27 22:07:59.451 Example2.4[92677:403]
grade = c and last = Z
```

## Type float

A number with decimal places is called a real number. The **float** data type is used to store real numbers. In Example 2-5, the data type for **percent is float**, and it has a constant value of 5.013, whereas **area** is also a **float** and has a constant value of 65.28. The storage space utilized by float is 32 bits. In Example 2-5, the **NSLog** function prints the values of **percent** and **area** to the console.

## Example 2-5

```
1   #import <Foundation/Foundation.h>
2
3   int main(int argc, const char * argv[])
4   {
5      @autoreleasepool
6        {
7            //variable declarations
8            float percent = 5.013;
9            float area = 65.28;
10           NSLog(@" \npercent = %f and area = %f", percent, area);
11       }
12      return 0;
13   }
```

**Output for Example 2-5**

```
2012-07-27 22:18:09.748 Example2.5[92868:403]
percent = 5.013000 and area = 65.279999
```

## Type double

A **double** is similar to a **float** but provides almost twice the precision, utilizing 64 bits of storage space. In Example 2-6, both the variables are of the type **double**. The variable **rate** is initialized to 5.013, whereas **speed** is initialized to 67.54. In Example 2-6, the **NSLog** function prints the values of **rate** and **speed** to the console.

## Example 2-6

```
1   #import <Foundation/Foundation.h>
2
3   int main(int argc, const char * argv[])
4   {
5      @autoreleasepool
6        {
7            //variable declarations
8            double rate = 5.013;
9            double speed = 67.54;
```

```
10              NSLog(@" \nrate = %f and speed = %f", rate, speed);
11          }
12      return 0;
13      }
```

**Output for Example 2-6**

```
2017-07-27 22:29:38.793 Example2.6[92974:403]
rate = 5.013000 and speed = 67.540000
```

## Derived Data Types

Various combinations of the basic data types can be used to create more complex data types, which are called **derived data types**. The following sections introduce some commonly used derived data types.

### Type *pointer*

The `pointer` type is a data type that points to the location where data is stored. In other words, it holds the memory location of the data type it is pointing to. In Objective-C code, a pointer is always preceded by an asterisk character and a space. The * symbol in Objective-C creates a pointer and also dereferences it, meaning it extracts the value the pointer is pointing to.

In the following example, an `int` variable called `value` is declared and assigned a value of 5.

```
int value = 5;
```

An integer pointer variable called `ptrValue` is then created, as follows:

```
int *ptrValue;
```

Next, the pointer variable `ptrValue` is pointed to the address of the location of the variable value. In this line of code, the & symbol before the variable value gives its address location:

```
ptrValue = &value;
```

We can then use the `NSLog` statement to print the pointer value. Notice in Example 2-7 that the `*ptrValue` is used as the argument in the `NSLog`. The * symbol dereferences the pointer, making it easy to print the value the pointer is pointing to.

Figure 2-1 illustrates the concept of a pointer variable.

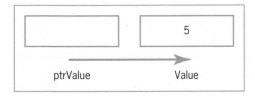

**Figure 2-1**   Pointer to the address of an `int` variable
© 2015 Cengage Learning

Example 2-7 provides a more complete example of how we might use a pointer variable.

In line 7, a variable called value is declared as an int and initialized to 5. In line 8, a pointer ptrValue is created by using the * symbol. In line 9, the pointer is pointed to the address of the value variable using the & address-of symbol.

Notice that, in the NSLog statement in line 10, the value of the pointer and its address is printed. The * symbol dereferences the pointer and NSLog prints the actual value of the pointer, whereas the variable itself, without the * symbol, causes NSLog to print the address of the pointer. Also note that the format specifier for the actual value of the pointer is d and that the format specifier for the pointer is p.

As you can see in the second part of Example 2-7, if you'd like to manipulate the actual value of the pointer or the value the pointer is pointing to, you need to use the * symbol. In line 13, for instance, the pointer is incremented by 6. Notice how the * symbol is used to dereference the pointer in order to increment the actual value it is pointing to.

## Example 2-7

```
1   #import <Foundation/Foundation.h>
2
3   int main(int argc, const char * argv[])
4   {
5       @autoreleasepool
6       {
7           int value = 5;
8           int * ptrValue;
9           ptrValue = &value;
10          NSLog(@"\nThe value of the pointer ptrValue is %d and the
11              address is %p",*ptrValue, ptrValue);
12  //Now if you would like to add 6 to the variable value
13          *ptrValue = *ptrValue + 6;
14          NSLog(@"\nThe new value of the pointer is  %d and the address
15          is %p", *ptrValue, ptrValue);
16      }
17      return 0;
18  }
```

### Output for Example 2-7

```
2017-07-31 04:10:58.668 Example2.7[2041:403]
The value of the pointer ptrValue is 5 and the address is
0x7fff6506989c
2017-07-31 04:10:58.672 Example2.3.2.1 [2041:403]
The new value of the pointer is  11 and the address is
0x7fff6506989c
```

Combine data

## Type *struct*

The **struct** type is a combination of several data types that creates a new custom data type. It provides a means to group various data types. A remnant of the original ANCI C language, before object oriented programming was introduced, the **struct** type is a static version of a class. In Example 2-8, **int**, **float**, and **char** data types are combined to create the ball **struct**. In essence, the various data types are the properties of *ball*.

## Example 2-8

```
1  #import <Foundation/Foundation.h>
2  int main(int argc, const char * argv[])
3  {
4      @autoreleasepool
5      {
6          struct ball
7          {
8              int num;
9              float size;
10             char color;
11         };
12
13         struct ball b;
14         b.num = 2;
15         b.color = 'F';
16         b.size = 3.0;
17         NSLog(@" \nnum = %d, color = %c and size = %f",
18         b.num, b.color, b.size);
19     }
20     return 0;
21 }
```

### Output for Example 2-8

```
2017-07-29 17:57:41.120 Example2.8[98910:403]
num = 2, color = F and size = 3.000000
```

Individual data types in the structure can be accessed and populated independently as seen in the following statement from Example 2-8:

```
b.num = 2;
```

*Combine int & char*

Here the num variable in the ball structure is assigned a value of 2. In the following statement the color variable of the ball structure is assigned a value of 'F':

b.color = 'F';

In Example 2-9, the struct course has a combination of an int and a char data type.

The structure called course is created with the integer variable score and a char variable called grade. In lines 12 and 13 the variables score and grade are populated using the dot notation. The NSLog statement in Line 14 prints the values of the score and the grade, again using the dot notation. The dot notation is used to populate and retrieve the values of the variables in the structure.

## Example 2-9

```
1   #import <Foundation/Foundation.h>
2   int main(int argc, const char * argv[])
3   {
4       @autoreleasepool
5       {
6         struct course
7           {
8               int score;
9               char grade;
10          };
11          struct course math;
12          math.score = 92;
13          math.grade = 'B';
14          NSLog(@" \nscore = %d and grade = %c", math.score,
15          math.grade);
16      }
17      return 0;
18  }
```

**Output for Example 2-9**

2017-07-29 18:06:19.551 Example2.9[98986:403]
score = 92 and grade = B

# Enum

The Enum functionality in Objective-C allows the programmer to define a new data type with enumerations. The term **enumeration** means to define a range of values for a variable. These values can be specific to the use of the variable. Enum provides a means of associating a list of values with a variable.

For example, in Example 2-10, an enumerated data type called Month can have a list of individual months as its values.

# Example 2-10

```
1  #import <Foundation/Foundation.h>
2  int main(int argc, const char * argv[])
3  {
4      @autoreleasepool {
5          typedef enum {
6              Jan = 1,
7              Feb = 2,
8              March = 3,
9              April = 4,
10             May = 5,
11             } Month;
12         Month month = April;
13         NSLog(@"  \n The value of the Month April is %d", month);
14     }
15     return 0;
16 }
```

**Output of Example 2-10**

```
2017-07-29 16:29:42.303 Example2.10[98065:403]
The value of the Month April is 4
```

Note that enumerations are of integer type. If the values for the months were not assigned, the compiler would assign values starting at 0. In Example 2-11, the enumerations are *not* defined. Thus, the compiler defined them, starting with 0. As a result, April was assigned a 3 instead of a 4 as in Example 2-10.

# Example 2-11

```
1  #import <Foundation/Foundation.h>
2  int main(int argc, const char * argv[])
3  {
4      @autoreleasepool {
5          typedef enum {
6              Jan,
7              Feb,
8              March,
9              April,
10             May,
11             } Month;
12         Month month = April;
13         NSLog(@"  \n The value of the Month April is %d", month);
14     }
15     return 0;
16 }
```

**Output for Example 2-11**

```
2017-07-29 16:29:42.303 Example2.11[98065:403]
 The value of the Month April is 3
```

# Preprocessor: # define statement

The preprocessor is a special tool in Objective-C that helps you create custom statements. For example, one example of a preprocessor, the *#define* statement, is used to define constants and associate them with a unique name. In other words, it allows you to customize constants in a program. In Example 2-12, PERC_PASSED is defined as 95.0 and in subsequent uses of PERC_PASSED its value will be 95.0. The advantage of using constants is that, if the value of the constant needs to be changed, the programmer only needs to change it in one location rather than searching the entire program and modifying every instance.

## Example 2-12

```
1  #import <Foundation/Foundation.h>
2  #define PERC_PASSED 95.0
3  int main(int argc, const char * argv[])
4  {
5      @autoreleasepool
6      {
7        NSLog(@"  \nIf there are 20 students in a class, then the
8            number of students passed is %f", PERC_PASSED*20/100);
9      }
10      return 0;
11 }
```

**Output for Example 2-12**

```
2017-07-29 15:10:48.555 Example2.12[97494:403]
If there are 20 students in a class, then the number
of students passed is 19.000000
```

# Arithmetic Expressions

Expressions that contain operands and operators are called **arithmetic expressions**. An operand can be any integral or real number. The operators, on the other hand, can be divided into basic and compound assignment operators.

## Basic

Table 2-2 describes the basic assignment operators.

| Operator | Name | Function |
|---|---|---|
| + | plus | Add |
| − | minus | Subtract |
| * | mult | Multiply |
| / | div | Divide |
| % | mod | Modulus; finds the remainder after division |

**Table 2-2**    Basic assignment operators

In Example 2-13, the user is prompted for two numbers. The basic operators are implemented by adding, subtracting, multiplying, and dividing the two numbers. Line 7 declares the variables needed for storing the user-entered numbers and the results of the basic arithmetic operations. Lines 9 and 13 prompt the user for numbers, and lines 11 and 15 store these values in num1 and num2, respectively. Lines 19 through 38 perform the basic arithmetic operations, and lines 30 through 38 print the results of these operations.

Note that when used with integers, div gives the correct answer only if the remainder is zero. If there is a remainder, then the div will round down to the nearest integer.

## Example 2-13

```
1  #import <Foundation/Foundation.h>
2  int main(int argc, const char * argv[])
3  {
4      @autoreleasepool
5      {
6      //variable declarations for the calculations
7      int num1, num2, add, mult, div, sub = 0;
8      //Prompt the user for a number
9      NSLog(@"  \nPlease enter a number\n");
10     // Store the user-entered number in the num1 variable
11     scanf("%d", &num1);
12     //Prompt the user for a second number
13     NSLog(@"  \nPlease enter a second number\n");
14     // Store the user entered number in the num2 variable
15     scanf("%d", &num2);
16
17     // add the user-entered numbers and store the result in the
18     //variable called add
19     add = num1 + num2;
20     // subtract the user entered numbers and store the result in
21     //the variable called sub
22     sub = num1 - num2;
23     // multiply the user entered numbers and store the result in
24     //the variable called mult
25     mult = num1 * num2;
26     // divide the user entered numbers and store the result in the
27     //variable called div
28     div = num1 / num2;
29     //Print the sum of the user entered numbers
30     NSLog(@"\nThe sum of the numbers you entered is %d\n", add);
31  //Print the difference of the user entered numbers
32     NSLog(@"\nThe difference between the numbers you entered is
33         %d", sub);
34     //Print the product of the user entered numbers
35     NSLog(@"\nThe product of the numbers you entered is %d",
36         mult);
```

```
37      //Print the division of the user entered numbers
38      NSLog(@"\nThe division of the numbers you entered is %d",
39        div);
40      }
41      return 0;
42  }
```

**Output for Example 2-13**

2017-07-30 00:01:27.692 Example2.13[378:403]
Please enter a number
24
2017-07-30 00:01:33.099 Example2.13 [378:403]
Please enter a second number
15
2017-07-30 00:01:36.274 Example2.13 [378:403]
The sum of the numbers you entered is 39
2017-07-30 00:01:36.275 Example2.13 [378:403]
The difference between the numbers you entered is 9
2017-07-30 00:01:36.276 Example2.13 [378:403]
The product of the numbers you entered is 360
2017-07-30 00:01:36.277 Example2.13 [378:403]
The division of the numbers you entered is 1

# Modulus Operator

The modulus operator returns the remainder after division. Of all the basic operators, the modulus operator can be the trickiest, so it's helpful to study some uses of it. In Example 2-14, int b is assigned a value of 7. The modulus of b and 2, b % 2, returns 1, because when 7 is divided by 2, the quotient is 3 and the remainder is 1.

In line 2, x =10. Therefore,

x % 2  = 10 % 5

returns 0, because when 10 is divided by 5, the quotient is 2 and the remainder is 0.

In line 3, y =1. Therefore,

y % 2  = 1 % 2

returns 1, because when 1 is divided by 2, the quotient is 0 and the remainder is 1.

In line 4, z = 6. Therefore,

6 % 7

returns 6, because when 6 is divided by 7, the quotient is 0 and the remainder is 6.

In line 5, a = 105. Therefore,

105 % 2

returns 5, because when 105 is divided by 10, the quotient is 10 and the remainder is 5.

Note that the modulus operator only works on integers. In Example 2-14, if b, x, y, z, or a were a double, the compiler would print an error. Also note that the NSLog statements include two percent symbols (%%) in lines 13 through 17. The extra % is necessary to print the % symbol.

## Example 2-14

```
1  #import <Foundation/Foundation.h>
2  int main(int argc, const char * argv[])
3  {
4      @autoreleasepool
5      {
6      //variable declarations
7      int b = 7;
8      int x = 10;
9      int y = 1;
10     int z = 6;
11     int a = 105;
12
13     NSLog(@"  \n%d %% 2 is %d", b, b % 2);
14     NSLog(@"  \n%d %% 5 is %d", x, x % 5);
15     NSLog(@"  \n%d %% 2 is %d", y, y % 2);
16     NSLog(@"  \n%d %% 7 is %d", z, z % 7);
17     NSLog(@"  \n%d %% 10 is %d", a, a % 10);
18     }
19     return 0;
20 }
```

**Output for Example 2-14**

```
2017-07-29 12:49:45.810 Example 2.14[96521:403]
7 % 2 is 1
2017-07-29 21:06:25.448 Example 2.14 [99458:403]
10 % 5 is 0
2017-07-29 21:06:25.449 Example 2.14 [99458:403]
1 % 2 is 1
2017-07-29 21:06:25.450 Example 2.14 [99458:403]
6 % 7 is 6
2017-07-29 21:06:25.451 Example 2.14 [99458:403]
105 % 10 is 5
```

## Compound Assignment Operators

Table 2-3 describes the compound assignment operators.

| Operator | Name | Function | Example |
|---|---|---|---|
| = | Assign | Assign | a = 7.0 |
| ++ | Increment | Increment by 1 | a++ i.e a = a +1 i.e a = 8.0 |
| -- | Decrement | Decrement by 1 | a-- i.e a = a -1 i.e |
| += | Increment Assign | Add and assign | a += 3 i.e a = a + 3 |
| -= | Decrement Assign | Subtract and assign | a -= 4 i.e a = a - 4 |
| *= | Mult Assign | Multiply and assign | a *= 3 i.e a = a * 3 |
| /= | Div Assign | Divide and assign | a /= 2 i.e a = a / 2 |
| %= | Mod Assign | Find Modulus and assign | a %= 2 i.e a = a % 2 |

**Table 2-3**    Compound assignment operators

### Pre/Post Increment and Pre/Post Decrement Operators

The pre increment operator increments first and then performs other operations in the expression. For example, if x =5, then

```
++x* 2 =   (5+1)*2 = 12.
```

Whereas the post increment operator will perform the increment after the expression is evaluated. For example, if x = 5, then

```
x++*2 =   (5*2) +1 = 11;
```

The pre/post decrement works very similar to the pre/post increment. In a pre decrement example, if x =5, then

```
--x*2 = (5-1)*2 = 8
```

In a post decrement example where x =5,

```
x--*2 = (5*2) -1 = 9
```

The results for the pre and post operations are not the same, as you can see in Example 2-15. The user is prompted for two numbers, which are stored in variables num1 and num2. The pre/post increment and pre/post decrement operations are performed in lines 18, 23, 28, and 33, and the results of these operations, respectively, are displayed in lines 20, 25, 30, and 35.

## Example 2-15

```
1  #import <Foundation/Foundation.h>
2  int main(int argc, const char * argv[])
3  {
4      @autoreleasepool
```

```
5     {
6     //variable declarations
7     int num1, num2, add;
8     //Prompt the user for a number.
9     NSLog(@" \nPlease enter a number\n");
10    // Store the user-entered number in the num1 variable.
11    scanf("%d", &num1);
12    //Prompt the user for a second number.
13    NSLog(@" \nPlease enter a second number\n");
14    // Store the user entered number in the num1 variable.
15    scanf("%d", &num2);
16
17    // pre increment
18    add = num1 + 2*num2++;
19    //print the value
20    NSLog(@"\nThe sum of the numbers you entered in pre
21 increment is %d\n", add);
22    //post increment
23    add = num1 + 2*++num2;
24    //print the value
25    NSLog(@"\nThe sum of the numbers you entered in post increment
26 is %d\n", add);
27    //pre decrement
28    add = num1 + 2*num2--;
29    //print the value
30    NSLog(@"\nThe sum of the numbers you entered in pre decrement
31 is %d\n", add);
32    //post decrement
33    add = num1 + 2*--num2;
34    //print the value
35    NSLog(@"\nThe sum of the numbers you entered in post decrement
36 is %d\n", add);
37
38    }
39    return 0;
40 }
```

**Output for Example 2-15**

```
2017-07-30 00:36:45.262 Example2.15[656:403]
Please enter a number
4
2017-07-30 00:36:49.508 Ex Example2.15 [656:403]
Please enter a second number
6
2017-07-30 00:36:50.299 Example2.15 [656:403]
The sum of the numbers you entered in pre increment is 16
2017-07-30 00:36:50.301 Example2.15 [656:403]
The sum of the numbers you entered in post increment is 20
2017-07-30 00:36:50.302 Example2.15 [656:403]
The sum of the numbers you entered in pre decrement is 20
2017-07-30 00:36:50.302 Example2.15 [656:403]
The sum of the numbers you entered in post decrement is 16
```

*Compound Operators: Add and Assign (+=), and Subtract and Assign (−=)*

The add and assign operators are used in conjunction to add a value to a variable and assign this new value to the variable. If $A = 6$ and $B = 2$, then the expression A+=B would be evaluated as $A = 6 + 2 = 8$

Similarly, the subtract and assign operators, when used in conjunction, first subtract a value from a variable and then assign this new value to the variable.

For example, if $A = 4$ and $B = 1$, then the expression A− = B would be evaluated as $A = 4 - 1 = 3$

In Example 2-16, num1 = 2 and num2 = 3, num1 + = num2 on line 9 can be written as num1 = num1 + num2; hence, num1 = 2 + 3 = 5. Line 15 assigns 2 to num1. The (−=) operation on line 15 is the same as num1 = num1 − num2, hence num1 = 2 − 3 = −1.

## Example 2-16

```
1   #import <Foundation/Foundation.h>
2
3   int main(int argc, const char * argv[])
4   {
5     @autoreleasepool
6       {
7           int num1 = 2, num2 = 3;
8           //Add and assign
9           num1 += num2;
10          NSLog(@"\nThe result of the num1 += num2 = %d\n", num1);
11      // reassigning the original values to num1 and num2
12          num1 = 2;
13
14          //subtract and assign
15          num1 -= num2;
16          NSLog(@"\nThe result of the num1 -= num2 =  %d\n", num1);
17      }
18      return 0;
19  }
```

**Output for Example 2-16**

```
2017-07-31 00:42:57.158 Example2.15[1778:403]
The result of the num1 += num2 = 5
2017-07-31 00:42:57.161 Example2.15[1778:403]
The result of the num1 -= num2 =   -1
```

*Compound operators : Multiply and Assign (\*=), and Divide and Assign (/=) operators*

The mult and assign operators, when used in conjunction, multiply the two operands and then assign the result to the operand on the left. For example, if $A = 3$ and $B = 2$, then the expression A\*=B, which can be written as $A = A * B$, would be evaluated as

$A = 3*2 = 6$

Similarly the div assign operators, when used in a compound statement, divide the first operand by the second and assign the value to the first operator. For example, if A = 6 and B = 3, then the expression A/=B, which can be written as A = A / B, would be evaluated as

A = 6/2 =3

In Example 2-17, when num1 = 6.0 and num2 =4.0, the expression num1*= num2 in line 9 can be written as num1 = num1 * num2. Hence, num1 = 6.0 * 4.0 = 24.0

In the (/=) operation on line 12, the expression num1 /= num2; can be written as num1 = num1 / num2. Hence num1 = 24.0/4.0 = 6.000000, because num1 is now 24.0.

## Example 2-17

```
1   #import <Foundation/Foundation.h>
2
3   int main(int argc, const char * argv[])
4   {
5       @autoreleasepool
6   {
7           double num1 = 6.0, num2 = 4.0;
8           //multiply and assign
9           num1 *= num2;
10          NSLog(@"\nThe result of the num1 *= num2  %f\n", num1);
11          //divide and assign
12          num1 /= num2;
13          NSLog(@"\nThe result of the num1 /= num2  %f\n", num1);
14      }
15      return 0;
16  }
```

### Output for Example 2-17

```
2017-07-31 00:46:26.178 Example2.16[1820:403]
The result of the num1 *= num2  24.000000
2017-07-31 00:46:26.181 Example2.16[1820:403]
The result of the num1 /= num2  6.000000
```

## Compound operator : Modulus and assign (%=)

The modulus and assign compound operator implies the same as finding the modulus.

In other words, that A%= 2 is the same as A%2. In Example 2-18, line 8 evaluates the expression num1 %= num2. The result is the same as simply finding the modulus of the operand with the other operand. Replacing the variable names with the values in line 8, 6%4 has a remainder of 2.

## Example 2-18

```
1   #import <Foundation/Foundation.h>
2   int main(int argc, const char * argv[])
3   {
4       @autoreleasepool
5       {
6           int num1 = 6, num2 = 4;
7           //modulus and assign
8           num1 %= num2;
9           NSLog(@"\nThe result of the num1 %%= num2 is %d\n", num1);
10      }
11      return 0;
12  }
```

**Output for Example 2-18**

**2017-08-01 01:48:29.900 example2.4.3.3[4351:403]**
**The result of the num1 %= num2 is 2**

## HANDS-ON LAB

In this Hands-on Lab you will write a program that performs various operations with numbers and output results to the console. This practice lab implements most of the concepts covered in this chapter.

### VARIABLE DECLARATIONS AND INITIALIZATIONS

1.  Declare and initialize two variables named num1Int and num2Int, of type int to hold the user's input:

    ```
    int num1Int, num2Int;
    ```

2.  Initialize the variable. The program should prompt the user for input and store the user-entered numbers in num1Int and num2Int.

    ```
    //User prompts and variable initialization
    NSLog(@"Enter the first integer");
    scanf("%i", & num1Int);
    NSLog(@"Enter the second integer");
    scanf("%i", & num2Int);
    ```

### IMPLEMENTATION OF BASIC DATA TYPES

3.  Declare two variables, named num1Double and num2Double, of type double to hold the user's input.

    ```
    double num1Double, num2Double;
    ```

4. Prompt the user for input, and store the user-entered numbers in num1Double and num2Double.

```
//User prompts and variable initialization
NSLog(@"Enter the first floating point number");
scanf("%lf", & num1Double);
NSLog(@"Enter the second floating point number ");
scanf("%lf", & num2Double);
```

Note: The format specifier for a double will be %lf as explained in the NSLog and Scanf section earlier in this chapter.

5. Declare the variables addResult, subResult, and modResult of type int. Also, declare the variables multResult, and divResult of type double. These variables will hold the addition, subtraction, modulus, multiplication, and division operations, respectively, on the user-entered values.

```
int addResult, subResult, modResult;
double multResult, divResult;
```

## IMPLEMENTATION OF DERIVED DATA TYPES

6. Declare two pointers, *ptrAddResult, *ptrSubResult, of type int that point to the variables sum(addResult) and difference(subResult).

```
int *ptrAddResult;
int *ptrSubResult;
```

7. Declare one variable of type struct called birthdate with day, month, and year of type int.

```
struct birthdate
    {
        int day;
        int month;
        int year;
    };
```

8. Initialize the variables in the birthdate structure you just created with a fictitious birthday.

```
struct birthdate dob;
dob.day = 12;
dob.month = 04;
dob.year = 2000;
```

9. Declare an enum called operation with variables addition, multiplication, division and modulus.

```
typedef enum {
    addition = 1,
    multiplication,
    division,
    modulus
    } Operation;
```

10. Declare a variable for the enum you just created and name it myOperation. Select division as the operation.

```
Operation myOperation = division;
```

## ADDITION

11. Add the variables num1Int and num2Int and store the result in addResult and print the result.

```
addResult = num1Int + num2Int;
NSLog(@"The result of the addition of %d and %d is %d",
num1Int, num2Int, addResult);
```

## SUBTRACTION

12. Subtract numInt2 from numInt1 and store the result in subResult and print the result.

```
subResult = num1Int - num2Int;
NSLog(@"The result of the subtraction of %d from %d is
%d", num2Int, num1Int, subResult);
```

## MULTIPLICATION

13. Multiply the variables num1Double and num2Double and store the result in multResult and print the result.

```
multResult = num1Double * num2Double;
NSLog(@"The result of the multiplication of %f and %f
is %f", num1Double, num2Double, multResult);
```

## DIVISION

14. Divide the variables num1Double by num2Double and store the result in divResult and print the result.

```
divResult = num1Double / num2Double;
NSLog(@"The result of the division of %f and %f
is %f", num1Double, num2Double, divResult);
```

## MODULUS

15. Find num1Int modulus num2Int, store the result in modResult and print the result.

```
modResult = num1Int % num2Int;
NSLog(@"The result of the modulus of %d and %d
is %d", num1Int, num2Int, modResult);
```

## IMPLEMENTATION USING DERIVED DATA TYPES

16. Point *ptrAddResult to the memory address of addResult and *ptrSubResult to subResult.

```
ptrAddResult = &addResult;
ptrSubResult = &subResult;
```

17. Print the contents and the address of the pointers.

```
NSLog(@"\nThe value of the pointer ptrAddResult is %d and
the address is %p", *ptrAddResult, ptrAddResult);

NSLog(@"\nThe value of the pointer ptrSubResult is %d and
the address is %p", *ptrSubResult, ptrSubResult);
```

## IMPLEMENTATION OF COMPOUND OPERATOR

18. Increment by one the value of the integer that the pointer ptrAddResult is pointing to, and print the resulting value.

```
(*ptrAddResult)++;

NSLog(@"Incrementing the value of the ptrAddResult makes
the value %i ", *ptrAddResult);
```

19. Add 8 to the value of the ptrAddResult using the compound operator (+=), and print the resulting value.

```
(*ptrAddResult) += 8;

NSLog(@"Adding 8 using the (+=) operator to the value of
the ptrAddResult makes the value %i ", *ptrAddResult);
```

20. Subtract 5 from the value of the ptrSubResult using the compound operator (-=) and print the value

```
(*ptrSubResult) -= 5;

NSLog(@"Subtracting 5 using the (-=) operator from the value
of the ptrSubResult makes the value %i ", *ptrSubResult);
```

21. Multiply the value of MultResult by 3 using the compound operator (*=) and print the resulting value.

```
(multResult) *= 3;
NSLog(@"After multiplying the value of the multResult
using the (*=) operator the new value is %f ",
multResult);
```

22. Divide the value of `divResult` by 2 using the compound operator (`/=`), and print the resulting value

```
(divResult) /= 2;
NSLog(@"After dividing the value of the divResult
using the (/=) operator the new value is %f ", divResult);
```

23. Find the modulus of `modResult` and 2 using the compound operator (`%=`), and print the resulting value.

```
(modResult %= 2;)
NSLog(@"After finding the modulus using the (/=) operator
the value of the modResult is %i ", modResult);
```

24. Print your date of birth using the structure you created.

```
NSLog(@"Your date of birth is: %d/%d/%d", dob.day, dob.month,
dob.year);
```

## USING AN ENUM

25. Print an operation that thanks the user.

```
NSLog(@"Thank you for using operation %d", myOperation);
```

**Note:** The NSLog statements in the source code start with a \n. This is so that the output is generated on a new line.

## SOURCE CODE

The following is the complete source code for this lab.

```
#import <Foundation/Foundation.h>
int main(int argc, const char * argv[])
{
    @autoreleasepool {
        int num1Int, num2Int;
        //User prompts and variable initialization
        NSLog(@"\nEnter the first integer");
        scanf("%i", & num1Int);
        NSLog(@"\nEnter the second integer\n");
        scanf("%i", & num2Int);
        double num1Double, num2Double;
        //User prompts and variable initialization
        NSLog(@"\nEnter the first floating point number\n");
        scanf("%lf", &num1Double);
        NSLog(@"\nEnter the second floating point number\n ");
        scanf("%lf", &num2Double);
        int addResult, subResult, modResult;
        double multResult, divResult;
```

```
int *ptrAddResult;
int *ptrSubResult;
struct birthdate
{
    int day;
    int month;
    int year;
};
struct birthdate dob;
dob.day = 12;
dob.month = 04;
dob.year = 2000;
typedef enum {
    addition = 1,
    multiplication,
    division,
    modulus
} Operation;
Operation myOperation = division;
addResult = num1Int + num2Int;
NSLog(@"\nThe result of the addition of %d and %d is
        %d\n", num1Int, num2Int, addResult);
    subResult = num1Int - num2Int;
    NSLog(@"\nThe result of the subtraction of %d from %d is
        %d\n", num2Int, num1Int, subResult);
    multResult = num1Double * num2Double;
    NSLog(@"\nThe result of the multiplication of %f and %f
        is %f\n", num1Double, num2Double, multResult);
    divResult = num1Double / num2Double;
    NSLog(@"\nThe result of the division of %f and %f is
        %f\n", num1Double, num2Double, divResult);
    modResult = num1Int % num2Int;
    NSLog(@"\nThe result of the modulus of %d and %d is
        %d\n", num1Int, num2Int, modResult);
    ptrAddResult = &addResult;
    ptrSubResult = &subResult;
    NSLog(@"\nThe value of the pointer ptrAddResult is %d and
        the address is %p",*ptrAddResult, ptrAddResult);
    NSLog(@"\nThe value of the pointer ptrSubResult is %d and
        the address is %p",*ptrSubResult, ptrSubResult);
    (*ptrAddResult)++;
    NSLog(@"\nIncrementing the value of the ptrAddResult
        makes the value %i ", *ptrAddResult);
    ( *ptrAddResult) += 8;
    NSLog(@"\nAdding 8 using the (+=) operator to the value
        of the ptrAddResult makes the value %i ", *ptrAddResult);
    ( *ptrSubResult) -= 5;
    NSLog(@"\nSubtracting 5 using the (-=) operator from the
        value of the ptrSubResult makes the value %i ",
        *ptrSubResult);
    ( multResult) *= 3;
```

```
            NSLog(@"\nAfter multiplying the value of the multResult
                using the (*=) operator the new value is %f ",
            multResult);
            ( divResult) /= 2;
            NSLog(@"\nAfter dividing the value of the divResult using
                the (/=) operator the new value is %f ",
            divResult);
            modResult %= 2;
            NSLog(@"\nAfter finding the modulus using the (/=)
                operator the value of the modResult is %i ", modResult);

            NSLog(@"Your date of birth is: %d/%d/%d", dob.day,
                dob.month, dob.year);
            NSLog(@"Thank you for using operation %d", myOperation);
        }
    return 0;
}
```

## RESULTS

```
2017-08-01 01:00:17.611 Example[4069:403]
Enter the first integer
5
2017-08-01 01:00:22.512 Example[4069:403]
Enter the second integer
8
2017-08-01 01:00:23.822 Example[4069:403]
Enter the first floating point number
6.5
2017-08-01 01:00:27.308 Example[4069:403]
Enter the second floating point number
3.5
2017-08-01 01:00:30.531 Example[4069:403]
The result of the addition of 5 and 8 is 13
2017-08-01 01:00:30.533 Example[4069:403]
The result of the subtraction of 8 from 5 is -3
2017-08-01 01:00:30.534 Example[4069:403]
The result of the multiplication of 6.500000 and 3.500000 is
22.750000
2017-08-01 01:00:30.535 Example[4069:403]
The result of the division of 6.500000 and 3.500000 is 1.857143
2017-08-01 01:00:30.536 Example[4069:403]
The result of the modulus of 5 and 8 is 5
2017-08-01 01:00:30.536 Example[4069:403]
The value of the pointer ptrAddResult is 13 and the address
is 0x7fff6e30a884
2017-08-01 01:00:30.537 Example[4069:403]
The value of the pointer ptrSubResult is -3 and the address
is 0x7fff6e30a880
2017-08-01 01:00:30.538 Example[4069:403]
Incrementing the value of the ptrAddResult makes the value 14
2017-08-01 01:00:30.538 Example[4069:403]
Adding 8 using the (+=) operator to the value of the ptrAddResult makes
```

```
the value 22
2017-08-01 01:00:30.539 Example[4069:403]
Subtracting 5 using the (-=) operator from the value of the ptrSubResult
makes the value -8
2017-08-01 01:00:30.540 Example[4069:403]
After multiplying the value of the multResult using the (*=) operator
the new value is 68.250000
2017-08-01 01:00:30.543 Example[4069:403]
After dividing the value of the divResult using the (/=)
operator the new value is 0.928571
2017-08-01 01:00:30.544 Example[4069:403]
After finding the modulus using the (/=) operator the value of the
modResult is 1
2017-08-01 01:00:30.545 Example[4069:403] Your date of birth is: 12/4/2000.
2017-08-01 01:00:30.545 Example[4069:403] Thank you for using operation 3
```

41

## Summary

- The main purpose of programming is to manipulate data.

- NSLog is identified by Apple as an error log mechanism to output data to the console. NSLog takes one or more parameters in the form of a string with format specifiers such as the i, d, x for int; c for char; f for float; p for pointer; etc.

- The scanf function uses the format specifiers in the same manner as NSLog and reads user-typed input. Each input argument maps to its corresponding format specifier.

- Data types come in two forms: basic and derived.

- Some examples of basic data types are int, char, double, and float.

- Derived data types are a combination of the basic data types. Some examples of the derived data types are struct, typedef enum, and pointers.

- A preprocessor # define statement is a means of declaring a constant value that does not change throughout the program and can be given a unique name.

- An arithmetic expression is a combination of operands and operators. There are two kinds of operators: basic and compound. The basic operators are +, -, *, / and %. The compound operators are a combination of the basic operators. Examples of compound operators include: +=, -=, *=, /=, and %=.

- The modulus operator finds the remainder after the division of the two operands in the expression.

## Exercises

1. Which of the following is not a valid format specifier in Objective-C?

    a. %c

    b. %q

    c. %f

    d. %n

    e. %i

2. Which of the following is not a reserved word in Objective-C?

    a. `char`

    b. `double`

    c. `String10`

    d. `int`

    e. `float`

3. Review the following code and answer the questions below, using the line numbers for reference:

    ```
    1  int x = 45;
    2  int * y = &x;
    3  x ++;
    4  (*y)+=10;
    ```

    a. What is the value of y at line 4?

    b. What is the difference between the value of x and y at any given point?

    c. Write a line of code to print the memory address of the variable x.

4. Identify the error(s) in the following code:

    ```
    int x = 56;
    x++;
    x-=5;
    int *y = x;
    NSLog(@"The value of y is %i", y);
    ```

5. Explain the difference between the following declarations. Include examples in your explanation.

    a. `double *d` and `double d`

    b. `double d` and `float d`

6. Write the following simple statements as their equivalent compound statements

    a. `*c = *c + 5`

    b. `x = x + y + 2`

    c. `num = sum-3 * num`

7. Consider the following code:

```
typedef enum {
            Sunday,
            Monday,
            Tuesday,
            Wednesday,
            Thursday,
            Friday,
            Saturday,
                } Days;
        Days day = Sunday;
```

   a. What is the value of Sunday?

   b. Modify the code so that Wednesday will have a value of 2.

8. What is the difference between an **enum** and a **struct** datatype? Give an example of the use of each.

9. Identify and fix the error or errors in the following program:

```
int main(int argc, const char * argv[])
{

    @autoreleasepool {
        int GMT_time = 10, CST_time=10;

        int* state1 = &CST_time;
        CST_time += 5;
        NSLog(@"\nWhen the GMT time is %p o'clock, \nthen
                it is %i o'clock in Minnesota", GMT_time, state1);
    }
    return 0;
}
```

10. Modify the program in question 9 to get the GMT time from the user as a **double**. Calculate the display time in a different state based on the GMT time inputted.

# Programming Exercises

1.  Write a program that produces the following output, which contains the "obj," the abbreviation for "object," in asterisks.

```
**********************    ****              **********************
**********************    ****              **********************
****            ****      ****                              ****
****            ****      ****                              ****
****            ****      ****                              ****
****            ****      *********************              ****
****            ****      **********************             ****
****            ****      *****            ****              ****
****            ****      ****         ****  ****            ****
****            ****      ****         ****  ****  ****       ****
**********************    **********************   ****  ****
**********************    *********************        ************
```

2.  Using the following program, perform the following steps:

```
int main (int argc, const char * argv[])
{
    @autoreleasepool {
}
    return 0;
}
```

a.  Write an Objective-C statement that declares a variable called student of type struct with properties stdId, courseNum, assignment, test, and grade. The type of the properties should be int, int, double, double, and char respectively.

b.  Write an Objective-C statement that creates an object called currentStudent.

c.  Using the statement created in the previous step, write Objective-C statements that initialize stdId to 235, courseNum to 2123, assignment to 87.9, test to 96.2, and grade to A.

d.  Output the value of stdId, courseNum, assignment, test, and grade to the console.

3.  Consider the following program:

```
#import <Foundation/Foundation.h>
int main (int argc, const char * argv[])
{
    @autoreleasepool {
        double areaRec, perimeterRec, side, areaSquare,
perimeterSquare;
```

```
        double width = 36.67;
        double height = 25.2;
        areaRec = height * width;
        perimeterRec = (height + width) * 2;
        areaSquare = side * side;
        perimeterSquare = side * 4;
        NSLog(@"Rectangle height: %f", height);
        NSLog(@"Rectangle width: %f", width);
        NSLog(@"Rectangle area: %f", areaRec);
        NSLog(@"Rectangle perimeter: %f", perimeterRec);
        NSLog(@"Square side: %f", side);
        NSLog(@"Square area: %f", areaSquare);
        NSLog(@"Square perimeter: %f", perimeterSquare);
    }
    return 0;
}
```

Modify the program to get the width, height, and side from the user, make the calculations, and then output the result. Use a single NSLog and formatting identifier to output the result in the same format as above.

4. Write a program that prompts the user for a pay rate and total hours worked, producing the following output:

```
Pay Rate:$      //Outputs the value of the variable payRate
Hours Worked:            //Outputs the value of the variable
                         //hoursWorked
Salary:           //Outputs the value of the variable
                         //salary
Income Tax:              //Outputs the value of the variable
                         //iTax
Social Security Tax:  //Outputs the value of the variable
                         //ssTax
Net Pay:                 //Outputs the value of the variable
                         //pay
```

As you create the program, use the following information:

- The salary is the product of the pay rate and the hours worked.

- The income tax is 7% of the salary.

- The Social Security tax is 10% of the salary.

- The net pay is what is left after deducting the income tax and the Social Security tax.

5.  Write a program that prompts the user for a dollar amount and outputs the equivalent number of dollars, quarters, pennies, and nickels. For example, if the user input 12, the program's output would look like this:

```
12 dollars is 48 quarters
48 quarters is 120 dimes
120 dimes is 240 nickels
```

6.  Your uncle just opened a joint bank account for you and your sister. He made an initial deposit of $780. He gave you and your sister access to this money by giving you each distinct debit cards. You and your sister can also view your account statements online using different login information. Each of the accounts accesses the account amount via a distinct pointer. You and your sister modify the amount in the account via your respective pointers to the account amount. Your sister used 45% of this money for some personal purchases, and you used 65% of the remainder for your expenses. After these expenses, you add $100 to the account.

    Write a program that outputs:

    a.  The initial amount in the account

    b.  The amount shown online via your sister's user account

    c.  The amount shown online via your user account

    d.  Your sister's first expense and the amount you see left via your online account

    e.  Your first expense and the amount left in the account

    f.  The amount in the account after your deposit

7.  Modify the program you created in programming exercise 6. Your sister deposits 20% of her monthly salary into the account and spends 10% of her salary. Perform steps a through f.

    a.  Prompt for your sister's monthly salary and add her one month salary to the account.

    b.  Calculate your sister's deposit and spending.

    c.  Print your sister's salary, deposit amount per month. And her spending per month.

    d.  Compute the amount deposited by your sister over a period of one year and print the result.

    e.  Compute your sister's spending over a period of one year and print the result.

    f.  Print the final bank account total after your sister's deposits and spending over a period of one year.

# Business Case Study

You run a balloon business called Happy Days, which sells balloons for the birthdays, weddings, parties, and graduations.

You are creating an app that helps the user purchase balloons. Save the application as "BusinesscaseStudy". The first step in creating your app is recognizing the tasks your app will perform and identifying the variables needed to complete these tasks.

1. Create a list of tasks your app will perform. For example:

    o Select a balloon.

    o View a balloon.

    o Add balloon to the cart.

    o Complete the order

2. Declare variables for the balloon app application. For example:

    o An **enum** for the balloon type that can accommodate a different type of balloon for each of the four possible occasions (birthdays, weddings, parties, and graduations) with different prices for each.

    o An **int** to record the number of balloons ordered

    o A **struct** for order date with day, month, and year

    o A **double** variable to record the total price for the order

# CHAPTER 3

# Decisions and Conditions

In this chapter you will:

- ◎ Employ relational operators to create comparative statements
- ◎ Differentiate between assignment statements and tests for equality
- ◎ Learn to use control structures such as the `if-else`
- ◎ Creatively implement nested `if-else` statements
- ◎ Use the logical operators to combine two or more conditional statements
- ◎ Use the switch and ternary operators to create conditional statements

It would be nice if you could always predict what your programs had to do, because then you could write programs that simply ran through their code, line by line, with no variation. Writing such a program would be a relatively simple task. However, in the real world, your programs will often have to respond to varying conditions, branching off in different directions depending on user input and calculations involving changing data.

In this chapter, you will learn to write **decision statements**, which are statements that decide which part of a program will execute at any given time. You might use a decision statement to calculate a grade or decide if a person is underweight based on the body mass index.

When working with decision statements, you'll often use a **counter**, which is a variable that keeps track of, or counts, occurrences of a particular event. Counters are especially useful when you are learning about decision-making statements because they allow you to monitor a program's changing behavior based on user input. For example, you might create a program that increases, or increments, a counter by one if the user enters an even number, but, if the user enters an odd number, the program displays a message indicating that the number entered was not even. The algorithm for this example would be:

*Prompt the user for a number*
*If the user entered an even number*
*then increment the counter*
*else inform the user that the numbers entered is not even*

To translate this algorithm into an Objective-C program, you need to use an `if-else` statement. As you'll see in this chapter, the `if-else`, ternary operator, and `switch` statements are mainly used in Objective-C to perform decision making. All of these options require the use of relational operators, which we'll discuss next.

## Relational Operators

At the heart of any decision-making statement is the need to compare variables. For example, you might need to determine if a is greater than b, or if c is equal to d. The process of comparing variables is sometimes referred to as testing the relationship between variables. The operators that allow you to compare variables are known as **relational operators** or **comparison operators**. In this book, we will refer to them as relational operators. You can use relational operators to compare an integer with an integer, a floating point number with a floating point number, a single character with another single character, or a string with multiple characters. In each case, the result is Boolean—that is, either true or false.

The relational operators in Objective-C are listed in Table 3-1.

| Operator | Function |
|----------|----------|
| > | greater than |
| < | less than |
| >= | greater than or equal to |
| <= | less than or equal to |
| == | equal to |
| != | not equal to |

**Table 3-1**   Relational Operators

# Assignment and Test for Equality Operator

Before we discuss any conditional statements, we need to understand the difference between the assignment operator (=), which was introduced in Chapter 2, and the test for equality operator (==). The assignment operator (=) assigns a value to a variable and has no return value. For example, a = 6; means a is equal to 6. Likewise, label = 'C'; means the string label is equal to the character C.

The test for equality operator (==) is used to test for equality in a condition, and is used in if-else statements. It has a Boolean return type—that is, it returns either true or false. For example, a == 6; checks to see if a is equal to 6. Likewise, label == 'C'; means is the variable label is equal to the character C.

# if Statement

An if statement tests for a condition and allows the selection of a particular block of code based on the condition tested. The if statement facilitates control of execution of code offering more than one choice of flow of execution. For example, if(score >90) { grade = 'A'; } checks to see if score is greater than 90 and, if it is, assigns an 'A' to the variable grade. The assignment of 'A' to grade is only executed if the grade is greater than 90, offering a means of controlling the flow of execution.

# if-else Statement

An if-else statement is used to execute one chunk of code if a certain condition is true and another chunk of code if the condition is not true.

Since the if-else statement is a functionality that comes to Objective-C via the C language, true is equivalent to 1, while false is a 0, just as in the C language.

The syntax for the if-else statement is as follows:

**SYNTAX**

```
if (condition)
{
    //statements to be executed if the condition is satisfied
}
else
{
    // statements to be executed if the condition is not satisfied
}
```

Figure 3-1 depicts the if-else statement.

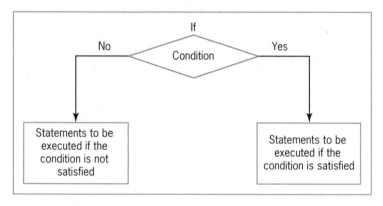

**Figure 3-1**   if-else statement
© 2015 Cengage Learning

Example 3-1 implements an if-else statement in Objective-C. Line 9 contains the following condition: num1%2 == 0. This statement computes the modulus (%) of variable num1 and num2. The modulus function in this statement is used to check if the number entered by the user is even or not by comparing the result of the modulus of num1 and 2 to zero. If the modulus is equal to zero then the number is divisible by 2, proving it to be an even number. Line 12 implements the else part of the if-else statement.

## Example 3-1

```
1  #import <Foundation/Foundation.h>
2  int main(int argc, const char * argv[])
3  {
4  @autoreleasepool
5  {
6      int num1;
```

```
7      NSLog(@"\nEnter a number.");
8      scanf("%d", &num1);
9      if (num1%2 == 0) {
10       num1++;
11    }
12     else {
13     NSLog(@"\nThe number you entered is not even.");
14          }
15    }
16   return 0;
17  }
18
```

The output for example 3.1 looks like this:

```
2012-08-04 13:04:11.079 example1.3.1[6303:403]
Enter a number.
3
2012-08-04 13:04:17.389 example1.3.1[6303:403]
The number you entered is not even.
```

Example 3-2 contains an if-else statement involving a relational operator, the greater than (>) operator. In this example, the user is prompted for two numbers, with the if-else statement used to find the larger of the two numbers. The logic of Example 3-2 goes like this: if num1 is greater than num2, then num1 is the greater of the two numbers, num1 and num2; otherwise, num2 is greater. The program then outputs the greater of the two numbers entered by the user.

## Example 3-2

```
1  int main(int argc, const char * argv[])
2  {
3  @autoreleasepool {
4     int num1, num2;
5     NSLog(@"\nEnter a number.");
6     scanf("%d", &num1);
7     NSLog(@"\nEnter another number.");
8     scanf("%d", &num2);
9     if (num1 > num2)
10    {
11       NSLog(@"\n %d is greater than %d", num1, num2);
12    }
13    else {
14       NSLog(@"\n %d is greater than %d", num2, num1);
15        }
16    }
17     return 0;
18  }
```

The output for example 3.2 looks like this:

```
2017-08-04 15:16:07.184 example3.2[6927:403]
Enter a number.
5
2017-08-04 15:16:11.529 example3.2[6927:403]
Enter another number.
2
2017-08-04 15:16:13.625 example3.2[6927:403]
 5 is greater than 2
```

# Nested if

Nested if statements are commonly used in programming to test one condition after another condition has been met or not met—that is, found to be true or not true. For instance, Example 3-3 compares two numbers to find the larger of the two numbers. The first if statement checks to see if num1 is larger than num2. If this condition is not met, then the second statement checks to see if num2 is larger than num1, nesting the second if in the first if as shown in Figure 3-2. This example doesn't address the possibility that the two numbers entered by user are equal.

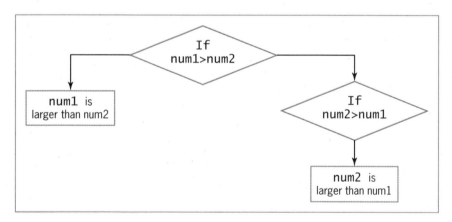

**Figure 3-2**   Illustration of nested if statement
© 2015 Cengage Learning

# Example 3-3

```
1  #import <Foundation/Foundation.h>
2  int main(int argc, const char * argv[])
3  {
4     @autoreleasepool {
5     int num1, num2;
6     NSLog(@"\nEnter a number.");
7     scanf("%d", &num1);
```

```
8      NSLog(@"\nEnter another number.");
9      scanf("%d", &num2);
10     if (num1 > num2)
11       {
12       NSLog(@"\n %d is greater than %d", num1, num2);
13       }
14     else if (num2 > num1)
15       {
16       NSLog(@"\n %d is greater than %d", num2, num1);
17       }
18     else
19       {
20       NSLog(@"\n %d is equal to %d", num2, num1);
21       }
22     }
23     return 0;
24  }
```

The output for example 3.3 looks like this:

**2017-08-04 15:35:14.027 example3.3[7041:403]**
**Enter a number.**
9
**2017-08-04 15:35:16.219 example3.3[7041:403]**
**Enter another number.**
9
**2017-08-04 15:35:17.828 example3.3[7041:403]**
 **9 is equal to 9**

Example 3-4 implements another nested if statement. This program calculates the grade of a student based on his or her score. In line 8, if the score is greater than 90, the student earns an A. In line 11, if the score is greater than 80, it would also be less than 90 since the first if tested to see if the score was greater than 90. Similarly, the score is tested if it is above 70 and less than 80, to earn a C in Line 15. Line 26 is executed if none of the above if statements is satisfied. The output shows the execution of this program with 78 as input, printing a C as the grade earned by the student.

## Example 3-4

```
1   #import <Foundation/Foundation.h>
2   int main(int argc, const char * argv[])
3   {
4       @autoreleasepool {
5       int score;
6       NSLog(@"\nEnter the score the student received.");
7       scanf("%d", &score);
8       if (score > 90) {
9          NSLog(@"The grade the student earned is A.");
10      }
```

```
11    else if (score >80)
12      {
13        NSLog(@"The grade the student earned is B.");
14      }
15    else if (score >70)
16      {
17        NSLog(@"The grade the student earned is C.");
18      }
19    else if (score >60)
20      {
21        NSLog(@"The grade the student earned is D.");
22      }
23    else
24      {
25        NSLog(@"The grade the student earned is F.");
26      }
27  }
28  return 0;
29  }
```

The output for example 3.4 looks like this:

**2017-08-04 23:45:48.803 example3.4[7299:403]**
**Enter the score the student received.**
78
**2017-08-04 23:46:06.657 example3.4[7299:403] The grade the**
**student earned is C.**

## Logical Operators

In essence, in Example 3-4, the score is being tested to see if it is within a certain range. The same program can be written using two conditions simultaneously in one if statement. Accomplishing this requires the use of compound relational operators, which are also called logical operators. The logical operators in Objective-C are listed in Table 3-2.

| Operator | Function |
| --- | --- |
| && | Both the conditions have to be true for the expression to be true. |
| \|\| | One of the conditions has to be true for the expression to be true. |
| ! | Negates or reverses the true/false condition |

**Table 3-2**    Logical Operators

Example 3-5 is an implementation of Example 3-4 using logical operators. Unlike in Example 3-4, line 11 is not part of the if statement that starts on line 8. Instead, Example 3-5 implements the condition from line 8 and 11 using the && logical operator. The first condition checks to see if the score is larger than 80, and the second condition checks to see if the score is less than 90. If both the conditions are true, the resulting expression will be true, which means if the score is above 80 and less than 90, the student earns a B. Similarly, line 16 combines two conditions that define a range from 70 to 80. In other words, if the score is above 70 and less than 80, the student earns a D. Unlike in Example 3-4, line 20 is not an else clause. Instead, it is a stand-alone if statement that tests to see if the score is below 60. One execution of this program with a score of 89 can be seen in the output, with the student earning a B.

## Example 3-5

```
1  #import <Foundation/Foundation.h>
2  int main(int argc, const char * argv[])
3  {
4  @autoreleasepool {
5  int score;
6  NSLog(@"\nEnter the score the student received.");
7  scanf("%d", &score);
8  if (score > 90)
9  {
10 NSLog(@"The grade the student earned is A.");
11 }
12 else if (score >80 && score <90)
13   {
14   NSLog(@"The grade the student earned is B.");
15   }
16    else if (score >70 && score <80)
17    {
18    NSLog(@"The grade the student earned is C.");
19    }
20     else if (score >60 && score <70)
21     {
22     NSLog(@"The grade the student earned is D.");
23     }
24      else if (score <60)
25       {
26        NSLog(@"The grade the student earned is F.");
27       }
28 }
29 return 0;
30 }
```

The output for example 3.5 will look like this:

```
2017-08-05 00:26:22.519 example3.5[7585:403]
Enter the score the student received.
89
2017-08-05 00:26:28.008 example3.5[7585:403]
The grade the student earned is B.
```

Consider another example of use of the logical operators, shown in Example 3-6. The program determines if the day entered is a weekday or a weekend. In this example, each day of the week has a value between 0 and 6. The user is prompted for a day of the week as an integer. The program then tests the day value to find out if the day entered is a weekend or a weekday. Line 9 implements the || logical operator to test if the day entered by the user is either a 5 or a 6—if so, the day is a weekend; otherwise, the day entered is a weekday. In the output, the day entered is a 4, which is a weekday.

## Example 3-6

```
1   #import <Foundation/Foundation.h>
2   int main(int argc, const char * argv[])
3   {
4       @autoreleasepool {
5       int day;
6       NSLog(@"\nEnter the day of the week as an integer value- for example
7           Monday would be a 0 and Tuesday would be 1 and so on.");
8       scanf("%d", &day);
9       if (day == 5 || day == 6) {
10        NSLog(@"This is a weekend day.");
11      }
12      else {
13        NSLog(@"This is a weekday.");
14      }
15  }
16  return 0;
17  }
```

The output for example 3.6 will look like this:

```
2017-08-05 00:51:13.023 example3.6[7683:403]
Enter the day of the week as an integer value- for example Monday would
be a 0 and Tuesday would be 1 and so on.
4
2017-08-05 00:51:19.326 example3.6[7683:403] This is a weekday.
```

## Switch

The switch statement is another decision-making tool offered by Objective-C. It is used to provide multiple options to make a decision. The switch statement can be used on integers, chars or a string of chars.

The syntax for the **switch** statement is as follows:

**SYNTAX**

```
switch(expression)
{
   case value1:
   //statements to be executed if this case is met
   break;
   case value2:
   //statements to be executed if this case is met
   break;
   case valuen:
   //statements to be executed if this case is met
   break;
   default:
   //statements to be executed if none of the above cases was met
}
```

The **switch** statement has cases with values to be tested against the expression in the **switch**. The term "switch" refers to the ability to change from one value to another. If a case is matched, then the statements within that case are executed. If a case contains a **break** statement, the program execution will exit the switch statement. Otherwise, if the case does not contain a **break** statement, the program keeps executing the remaining cases until it comes across a **break** statement. If none of the cases described in the **switch** are met, then the default will be executed.

In the previous day of the week example each day of the week has a value between 0 and 6. This can be implemented using an enum and a **switch** statement, as shown in Example 3-7. The enum, as in line 5, assigns the values to the days of the week, while the **switch** statement, as in line 20, tests it against the user entered value and prints out output indicating if the day of the week is a weekday or a weekend. Notice the default is executed only if none of the cases is met. In the output for Example 3-7, the program was first run with a 7 as the input. Since that is not a weekday value, the default (line 39) was executed in the **switch** and the output indicated that the user entered a number that is not a day of the week.

## Example 3-7

```
1  #import <Foundation/Foundation.h>
2  int main(int argc, const char * argv[])
3  {
4     @autoreleasepool {
5     enum weekday
6     {
7        monday = 0,
8        tuesday = 1,
```

```
 9       wednesday = 2,
10       thursday = 3,
11       friday = 4,
12       saturday = 5,
13       sunday = 6
14     };
15     enum  weekday day;
16     NSLog(@"\nEnter the day of the week as an integer value -- for
17       example, Monday would be a 0 and Tuesday would be 1 and so
18       on.");
19     scanf("%d", &day);
20     switch (day) {
21     case 1:
22       NSLog(@"This is a weekday.");
23     break;
24     case 2:
25       NSLog(@"This is a weekday.");
26     break;
27     case 3:
28       NSLog(@"This is a weekday.");
29     break;
30     case 4:
31       NSLog(@"This is a weekday.");
32     break;
33     case 5:
34       NSLog(@"This is a weekend day.");
35     break;
36     case 6:
37       NSLog(@"This is a weekend day.");
38     break;
39     default:NSLog(@"Not a correct day of the week.");
40     break;
41     }
42 }
43 return 0;
44 }
```

The output for example 3.7 looks like this

```
2017-08-05 01:36:10.109 example3.7[7885:403]
Enter the day of the week as an integer value -- for example, Monday
would be a 0 and Tuesday would be 1 and so on.
7
2017-08-05 01:36:13.857 example3.7[7885:403]
Not a correct day of the week.
```

Note that the switch statement is used to reduce the need for a complex nested if statements. Unlike in most popular languages, the switch in Objective-C works with most data types and has the ability to implement relational operators.

# Ternary operator

Objective-C offers another type of decision-making tool, called the conditional operator or the ternary operator, which means it has three operands. The syntax for the ternary operator is as follows:

**SYNTAX**

```
condition ? expression1 : expression2
```

Objective-C allows you to evaluate a condition, and based on the condition, choose the action you would like to perform. The compiler evaluates the condition. If the condition is true, the compiler executes expression1. Otherwise, it will execute expression2.

For example, suppose that, at a high school, students are allowed to take college-level classes only if their GPA is above 3.75. Line 9 in Example 3-8 implements this by using the ternary operator. Here 'a' means the high school student is allowed to take college-level courses, while 'n' means the student is not allowed to take college-level courses. In the ternary expression in line 9, the GPA is tested to see if it is above 3.75. If it is, then the switch value is 'a' and the case statement matching this will print a message indicating the student is allowed to take college-level courses as in line 10, while if the GPA is below 3.75 the switch will be a 'n' and the matching case in the switch will print that the student is not allowed to take college-level courses as in line 13. The output for Example 3-8 shows the output of the program run with a user input of GPA = 3.8. In this case, the student is allowed to take college-level courses because the GPA is above 3.75.

Note the switch can handle complex expressions for its switch expression as evident in the example 3.8 below

## Example 3-8

```
1   #import <Foundation/Foundation.h>
2   int main(int argc, const char * argv[])
3   {
4       @autoreleasepool
5       {
6       double GPA;
7       NSLog(@"Enter your GPA.");
8       scanf("%lf", &GPA);
9       switch ( GPA>3.75 ? 'a' : 'n') {
10        case 'a':
11          NSLog(@"You are allowed to take college level courses.");
12        break;
13        case 'n':
14          NSLog(@"You are not allowed to take college-level courses.");
15        break;
```

```
16        default: NSLog(@"More information is required to decide if you
17                    can take college-level courses.");
18        break;
19    }
20 }
```

The output for example 3.8 will look like this:

**2017-08-06 01:48:37.956 example3.8[10782:403] Enter your GPA.**
**3.8**
**2017-08-06 01:48:43.180 example3.8[10782:403]**
**You are allowed to take college-level courses.**

# Buffer Overflow with scanf When Reading a char

When a program reads a char, the char is stored in a buffer that is big enough to store one char. Occasionally there is a chance of buffer overflow—meaning the buffer can only take one char and the buffer already contains something from the previous time the code ran. If there was a character left from the previous time the code was run, then there is no space in the buffer to hold any more data, which in turn may cause premature termination of the program. For example, suppose your program reads

```
scanf("%c", &operation);
```

In this line, %c will read one char at a time, but if there is something else in the buffer from the previous running of the code, then input will not be accepted. One way of avoiding this is using the %s instead of the %c. As you'll learn in later chapters, %s is for strings.

Note the nested switch in the Hands-On Lab below.

## HANDS-ON LAB

In this exercise, you will program an ATM machine to do the following:

- Welcome the user to the ATM machine

- Prompt the user for the account number, and then use a switch statement to verify the account number and initialize the account balance.

- Prompt the user for the operation to be performed, using D for deposit and W for withdrawal (make sure you accommodate for data entry in lowercase)

- Use a ternary operator to ensure that the amount to withdraw is at least equal to the available account balance

For this program, the only valid account numbers and their balances are the following:

785415, $200

348721, $480

896531, $500

453927, $1000

## VARIABLE DECLARATION

1. Declare a variable account of type `int` to hold the user's account number; a variable operation of type `char` to hold the type of operation the user will perform; and variables `balance`, `deposit`, and `withdrawal` of type `double` to hold the `balance`, `deposit`, and `withdrawal` amount, respectively.

```
int account;
char operation;
double balance, deposit, withdraw;
```

## VARIABLE INITIALIZATION

2. Initialize the variable `balance` to 0.0:

```
balance = 0.0;
```

3. Welcome the user to the ATM, and prompt the user for an account number:

```
NSLog(@"\nWelcome to your ATM \nPlease enter your Account
number");
```

4. Initialize `account` with the user's entry:

```
scanf("%i", &account);
```

5. Use a `switch` statement to verify the account number entered by the user.

   Use the account numbers and balances defined earlier. Mark all other account numbers entered as invalid.

```
switch (account)
{
   case 785415:
      balance = 200.00;
   break;

   case 348721:
      balance = 480.00;
   break;

   case 896531:
      balance = 500.00;
   break;

   case 453927:
      balance = 1000.00;
   break;

   default:
   NSLog(@"Invalid account number");
   break;
}
```

6. For each of the cases in Step 5, do the following:

a. Print out the starting balance for the user:

```
NSLog(@"\nYour starting balance is %lf", balance);
```

b. Prompt the user to enter the desired operation type as a char, and store the user's entry in the variable *operation*:

```
NSLog(@"\nWhat will you want to do today? Enter D for Deposit,
        W for Withdrawal");
scanf("%s", &operation);
```

Use an if-else statement to handle the user's choice. Accommodate both lowercase and uppercase entries:

```
if (operation == 'D' || operation == 'd') {
//If the user is making a deposit, prompt the user to enter the
//amount to deposit and store this entry in the variable deposit.
NSLog(@"Enter the amount to deposit");
scanf("%lf", &deposit);
//Add this deposited amount the to balance and print out the new
//balance to the user.
balance += deposit;
NSLog(@"You deposited %lf. Your account balance is now %lf",
        deposit, balance);

}
```

c. Else, if the user is making a withdrawal, prompt the user for the amount to withdraw and store this entry in the variable *withdraw*:

```
else if(operation == 'W' || operation == 'w')
    {
    NSLog(@"Enter the amount to withdraw");
    scanf("%lf", &withdraw);
    }
```

d. Use a tertiary operator to ensure that the amount to withdraw is at least equal to the available account balance:

```
switch (balance < withdraw && balance >= 0.0 ? 'f' : 's')
    {
    case 'f':
    break;
    case 's':
    break;
    default:
    break;
    }
```

e. If the operation failed, that is, if the withdraw amount is greater than the available balance, notify the user that the balance is not up to the withdrawal amount and print the ending balance:

```
NSLog(@"You cannot withdraw %lf because you only have %lf in
       your account", withdraw, balance);
NSLog(@"Your account balance is %lf", balance);
```

f. Else, if the operation is successful, deduct the withdraw amount from the balance and print out the new balance:

```
balance -= withdraw;
NSLog(@"You have withdrawn %lf\n Your account balance is now %lf",
       withdraw, balance);
```

## SOURCE CODE

The source code for the entire program is as follows:

```
1  #import <Foundation/Foundation.h>
2  int main (int argc, const char * argv[])
3  {
4  @autoreleasepool {
5  int account;
6  char operation;
7  double balance = 0.0, deposit, withdraw;
8  NSLog(@"\nWelcome to your ATM \nPlease enter your
9         Account number");
10 scanf("%i", &account);
11 switch (account) {
12    case 785415:
13      balance = 200.00;
14      NSLog(@"\nYour starting balance is %lf", balance);
15      NSLog(@"\nWhat would you like to do today? Enter D for Deposit, W
16      for Withdrawal");
17      scanf("%s", &operation);
18      if (operation == 'D' || operation == 'd') {
19       NSLog(@"Enter the amount to deposit");
20       scanf("%lf", &deposit);
21       balance += deposit;
22       NSLog(@"You deposited %lf. Your account balance is now %lf",
23        deposit, balance);
24       }
25      else if(operation == 'W' || operation == 'w'){
26       NSLog(@"Enter the amount to withdraw");
27       scanf("%lf", &withdraw);
28       switch (balance < withdraw && balance >= 0.0 ? 'f' : 's')
29       {
30         case 'f':
31            NSLog(@"You cannot withdraw %lf because you only have %lf in
32            Your account", withdraw, balance);
33            NSLog(@"Your account balance is %lf", balance);
34            break;
```

```
35          case 's':
36              balance -= withdraw;
37              NSLog(@"You have withdrawn %lf\n Your account balance is now
38              %lf", withdraw, balance);
39          default:
40          break;
41      }
42      }
43  break;
44  case 348721:
45  {
46      balance = 480.00;
47      NSLog(@"\nYour starting balance is %lf", balance);
48      NSLog(@"\nWhat would you like to do today? Enter
49                  D for Deposit, W for Withdrawal");
50      scanf("%s", &operation);
51      NSLog(@"The value of operation is %c", operation);
52      if (operation == 'D' || operation == 'd') {
53          NSLog(@"Enter the amount to deposit");
54          scanf("%lf", &deposit);
55          balance += deposit;
56          NSLog(@"You deposited %lf. Your account balance is now %lf",
57              deposit, balance);
58          }
59      else if(operation == 'W' || operation == 'w'){
60          NSLog(@"Enter the amount to withdraw");
61          scanf("%lf", &withdraw);
62          switch (balance < withdraw && balance >= 0.0 ? 'f' : 's')
63          {
64              case 'f':
65                  NSLog(@"You cannot withdraw %lf because you only have %lf
66                      in your account", withdraw, balance);
67                  NSLog(@"Your account balance is %lf", balance);
68              break;
69              case 's':
70                  balance -= withdraw;
71                  NSLog(@"You have withdrawn %lf\n Your account balance is
72                      now %lf", withdraw, balance);
73              default:
74              break;
75          }
76      }
77      }
78  break;
79  case 896531:
80      balance = 500.00;
81      NSLog(@"\nYour starting balance is %lf", balance);
82      NSLog(@"\nWhat would you like to do today? Enter
83          D for Deposit, W for Withdrawal");
84      scanf("%s", &operation);
85      if (operation == 'D' || operation == 'd') {
86          NSLog(@"Enter the amount to deposit");
87          scanf("%lf", &deposit);
88          balance += deposit;
```

```
89        NSLog(@"You deposited %lf. Your account balance is now %lf",
90            deposit, balance);
91      }
92      else if(operation == 'W' || operation == 'w'){
93        NSLog(@"Enter the amount to withdraw");
94        scanf("%lf", &withdraw);
95        switch (balance < withdraw && balance >= 0.0 ? 'f' : 's')
96        {
97          case 'f':
98            NSLog(@"You cannot withdraw %lf because you only have %lf
99                in your account", withdraw, balance);
100           NSLog(@"Your account balance is %lf", balance);
101         break;
102         case 's':
103           balance -= withdraw;
104           NSLog(@"You have withdrawn %lf\n Your account balance is
105               now %lf", withdraw, balance);
106         default:
107         break;
108       }
109     }
110   break;
111   case 453927:
112    {
113    balance = 1000.00;
114    NSLog(@"\nYour starting balance is %lf", balance);
115    NSLog(@"\nWhat would you like to do today? Enter
116        D for Deposit, W for Withdrawal\n");
117     scanf("%s", &operation);
118     if (operation == 'D' || operation == 'd') {
119       NSLog(@"Enter the amount to deposit");
120       scanf("%lf", &deposit);
121       balance += deposit;
122       NSLog(@"You deposited %lf. Your account balance is now %lf",
123           deposit, balance);
124     }
125     else if(operation == 'W' || operation == 'w'){
126       NSLog(@"Enter the amount to withdraw");
127       scanf("%lf", &withdraw);
128       switch (balance < withdraw && balance >= 0.0 ? 'f' : 's')
129       {
130         case 'f':
131           NSLog(@"You cannot withdraw %lf because you only have %lf
132               in your account", withdraw, balance);
133           NSLog(@"Your account balance is %lf", balance);
134         break;
135         case 's':
136           balance -= withdraw;
137           NSLog(@"You have withdrawn %lf\n Your account balance is
138               now %lf", withdraw, balance);
139         default:
140         break;
141       }
142     }
143     }
```

```
144        break;
145        default:
146            NSLog(@"Invalid account number");
147        break;
148        }
149        }
150        return 0;
151  }
```

## RESULTS

**2017-08-08 22:38:29.560 example[12777:403]**
**Welcome to your ATM**
**Please enter your Account number**
453927
**2017-08-08 22:38:37.920 example[12777:403]**
**Your starting balance is 1000.000000**
**2017-08-08 22:38:37.921 example[12777:403]**
**What would you like to do today? Enter D for Deposit, W for Withdrawal**
d
**2017-08-08 22:38:40.113 example[12777:403] Enter the amount to deposit**
34
**2017-08-08 22:38:42.282 example[12777:403] You deposited 34.000000.**
**Your account balance is now 1034.000000**

# Summary

- Relational operators define a relation between two variables or expressions. The return is always a true or a false. The most common relational operators are >,<, ==, !=, >=, and <=.

- The difference between the = and the == relational operators is often misunderstood. The first, =, is an assignment operator, while == is a test of equality.

- The if-else statement one of the decision-making tool in Objective-C. In the if-else statement, if a condition is met, a certain number of lines of code are executed; otherwise, another set of lines of code is executed.

- Nested if-else statements have a series of if statements nested inside each other.

- The switch is an alternative to multiple nested if statements. The switch can be used in combination with an enum.

- The switch statement tests for an expression against two or more cases. If the conditions for none of the cases are met, the default is executed.

- The break in the `switch` statement terminates the `switch` statement. If a case does not have a break, then the cases following it will execute until the execution reaches either the end of the `switch` statement or another `break` statement.

- The ternary operator allows the program to evaluate a condition and, based on the outcome, choose which statements to execute. For example, consider the statement `condition ? expression1 : expression2`.
  In this example, if the condition is met, then expression1 will execute; if the condition is not met, then expression2 will execute.

## Exercises

1. For each of the following, indicate if the result is true or false.

   a. TRUE && FALSE

   b. FALSE || TRUE

   c. FALSE && FALSE

   d. !TRUE || FALSE

   e. TRUE || TRUE

   f. TRUE && TRUE

2. Evaluate the result of the following logical operations, given the indicated condition. Assume the variables `num1` and `num2` have been properly declared.

   a. `(num1 == 2 && num2 == 3)` given that num1 = 2 and num2 = 9

   b. `(num1 <= 4 && num2 >= -10)` given that num1 = 0 and num2 = -20

   c. `(num1 <= 12 || num2 >= 6)` given that num1 = 45 and num2 = 6

   d. `(num1 < 10 || num2 >= 1)` given that num1 = 0 and num2 = 1

   e. `(num1 <= 5 && num2 >= 4)` given that num1 = 0 and num2 = -20

3. What is the difference between the following statements?

   ```
   num1 = 2;
   num2 == 2;
   ```

4. For a and b, give the output.

   a. ```
   if(20 < 2*5)
       NSLog(@"I love programming");
   NSLog(@"I love Objective C");
   ```

   b. ```
   int num1= 5;
   if(!num1)
       NSLog(@"This is easy");
   if(num1)
       NSLog(@"This is easy too");
   else
       NSLog(@"I love doing this");
   ```

5.  Write a program that prompts the user for a gender and outputs *Boy* if the gender is 'M' or 'm' and *Girl* if the gender is 'F' or 'f'.

6.  Indicate whether the following statements are True or False

    a.  `Switch` statements can evaluate the integers, doubles, and Boolean.

        a.  True
        b.  False

    b.  The reserved word **break** is used to stop the execution in an associated `switch` statement.

        a.  True
        b.  False

    c.  Each case in a `switch` statement is followed by a colon immediately after the case value.

        a.  True
        b.  False

    d.  Both **if** statements and **else** statements always include a semicolon immediately after the condition.

        a.  True
        b.  False

    e.  An **if** statement is always paired with an **else** statement, and a `switch` statement always has a default case.

        a.  True
        b.  False

7.  Identify and correct the error(s) in the following lines of code:

```
if(s>=4);
    NSLog(@"The number is greater or equal to 4");
else (s<4)
    NSLog@"The number is not greater than 4");
```

8.  Consider the following code:

```
int input;
NSLog(@"Enter a number");
scanf("%i", &input);
switch(input) {
    case 0:
        input+=2;
```

```
    case 1:
    case 2:
      NSLog(@"input is: %i", input);
    break;
    case 3:
      input*=15;
      NSLog(@"input is: %i", input);
    break;
    case 4:
      input *=2;
      NSLog(@"input is: %i", input);
    default:
      input--;
      NSLog(@"input is: %i", input);
    break;
    }
```

The code is run three times, and each time the user enters one of the values below. What is the value of the variable input in each run?

a. 5

b. 10

c. 2

d. 0

9. Correct any errors in the following code:

```
int main (int argc, const char * argv[])
{
    @autoreleasepool {
    int first, second;
    NSLog(@"Enter an integer");
    scanf("%i", &first);
    NSLog(@"Enter another integer");
    scanf("%i", &second);
    if first < second
        NSLog(@"%i is less than %i", first, second);
    else;
        NSLog(@"%i is greater than %i", first, second);
    }
    return 0;
}
```

10. The program below contains errors. Find and correct them.

```
int main (int argc, const char * argv[])
{

    @autoreleasepool {
    double t, u, v, w;
    u = 21.2;
    if (u < 21)
      break;
    else if (u = 21){
      v = 12.65;
      w = 13.78;
      t = u-v * w;
      }
    else (u > 21) {
      v = 0.30;
      w = 2.21;
      t = v-w + u;
      }
    NSLog(@"The value of t is %f", t);
    }
    return 0;
}
```

# Programming Exercises

1. Using `switch` and `if-else` statements, write a program that outputs the number of days in a month. Your program should prompt the user for a year and the month as an integer in that year. Use this integer to output the number of days in that month in that year. If an invalid month is entered (that is, a number that is not between 1 and 12 inclusive), output the message: *Invalid month entered.* Consider leap years when calculating the number of days in February. Use the year 2000 as a base year.

2. Write a program that operates like a cashier. Prompt the user to enter the value of an item and the cash provided by the customer to purchase the item then compute the change owed the customer. Make sure the amount provided by the customer is greater than or equal to the cost of the item plus 5% tax. The program should allow decimal amounts. Your program should output the cost of the item the tax on the item the amount provided by the customer, and the change due to the customer.

3. A&B Company is hosting a promotion in which a customer gets $10 back for every $200 purchase. Write a program that prompts the user for a customer's total purchase and uses the ternary operator to determine if the customer is eligible for the promotion. Revise the program to include some additional calculations for a second

promotion: Customers who qualify for the first promotion and who spend more than $20 on organic food get an additional $2 back. Your program should prompt the user to enter the amount spent on organic food. Use either a `switch` statement or an `if-else` statement to handle the user's choice. (Remember that the amount spent on organic food cannot be less than the total spent.) Output the total amount spent by each customer as well as the amount each customer gets back after the purchase.

4. John Cooper is an American who just landed in France without any cash. He goes to an ATM in the airport and inserts his debit card. He sees the following message:

    *Bienvenue a votre distributeur automatique.*
    *To continue in English, press 1.*
    *Para continuar en español, prensa la 2.*

    John presses 1 and is prompted to enter the dollar amount of the money to retrieve. The machine then calculates the euro equivalent. John is then prompted to verify if the euro equivalent of his input is what he wants. If he accepts, the program dispenses the money, thanks John for using the ATM, and displays a Goodbye message. In either case, the program terminates and displays a goodbye message. Write a program that fulfills the preceding tasks (minus the money dispensation). Use the `define` statement to declare the unit conversion value.

5. Mary is in a checkout line at a local supermarket. After Jonah scans all her items, he asks if Mary would like to pay in cash, by credit card, or by debit card. He also explains that the store gives her a 10% discount if her total purchase is more than $50 and a 20% discount if the purchase is above $100. Jonah also explains that all senior citizens receive a 5% discount. Write a program that performs the necessary calculations, using at least one `if-else` statement. Your program should prompt the user for the total amount and handle the sales adequately—that is, it should make sure the user receives appropriate discounts. The program should also ensure the user has sufficient funds to purchase the goods. If not, the program should display a message indicating that the customer lacks sufficient funds. Make your program as realistic as possible.

6. Suppose a university has an honors program that applies a different grading standard than traditional, nonhonors classes. Table 3-3 shows the two grading scales.

| Points | Honors Grade | Traditional Grade |
| --- | --- | --- |
| >95 | A | A |
| >91 | B | A |
| >85 | C | B |
| >80 | F | B |
| >75 | F | C |
| >70 | F | F |

**Table 3-3**   Grade Scale for Honors and Traditional Classes

Write a program that uses logical operators to calculate the GPA. It should prompt the user for Test 1 for course 1, and Test 1 for course 2. The program should also prompt the user to enter the respective course type for each class (H for Honors and T for traditional). Assume the course type to be Honors if an invalid entry is made. The program should then use the test scores for each course to calculate the percentage score for each course and assign a grade according to the grading school shown in Table 3-3.

7.   A new phone company is offering great deals. Charges depend on the number of minutes used, with monthly charges calculated as follows:

- The first 40 minutes are free.

- The next 300 minutes are $0.40 per minute.

- Any minute after that is 0.10 per minute.

- The user has to pay a service fee of $5.00 each month.

Write a program that prompts the user for the number of minutes used in a month and calculates the amount due. The program should output both the user's input and the amount due.

8.   The phone company discussed in Exercise 7 has some new plans. The plans are as follows:

- Plan A: $25 per month for 0–250 minutes

- Plan B: $40 per month for 0–350 minutes

- Plan C: $50 per month for more than 350 minutes

- Plan D: Automatic Plan setting

According to plan D, the system automatically readjusts your plan depending on the number of minutes used. In other words, if 278 minutes are used, the system places the user on plan B for that month. For plans A and B, the amount for any additional minutes used is $0.30 per minute.

Write a program that performs these tasks. Your program should prompt the user for a choice of plan: 'A' for plan A, 'B' for plan B, 'C' for plan C, and 'D' for plan D. Make 'D' the default plan. The program should also prompt the user for the number of minutes used and calculate the amount due at the end of the month.

# Business Case Study

Revise the program you created in the Chapter 2 Business Case Study so that it does the following:

○ Prompt the user for a task/action.

○ Use an `if-else` statement to make a selection between the user entered choice of task. The possible tasks your program can perform are as follows:

- Select a balloon

- View a balloon

- Add a balloon to cart

- Complete the order

○ Using the `enum` statement you created in Chapter 2 for the various types of balloons you sell and their corresponding price as the value for the enumerations, create a `switch` statement that handles the choice of balloon type. Use the following as the cases:

- Birthday

- Wedding

- Party

- Graduation

○ For each of the cases, print the type of balloon the user selected and the task to be performed.

# CHAPTER 4

# Looping

In this chapter you will:

- ◎ Learn about the different forms of looping
- ◎ Distinguish between counter-controlled and condition-controlled loops
- ◎ Create for, while, and do-while loops
- ◎ Create nested for loops

## Types of Loops

Often a programmer needs to execute lines of code repeatedly. The mechanism of looping makes this possible. Objective-C allows for three main types of loops: the `for` loop, the `while`, and the `do-while` loop. These loops can be classified as counter-controlled or condition-controlled. If the number of iterations is known, then the counter-controlled loop is used, and if there is no knowledge of the number of iterations, then the condition-controlled loop is implemented.

How do you know if you need to include a loop in your program? A loop is usually necessary if a group of statements is to be executed repeatedly until a specific condition is met. It's helpful to start by examining an example that does *not* include a loop. We can then discuss how the example could be made more efficient through the introduction of a loop. Example 4-1 calculates the average score for a student in a semester.

## Example 4-1

```
1  #import <Foundation/Foundation.h>
2
3  int main(int argc, const char * argv[])
4  {
5      double subjectOne = 90;
6      double subjectTwo = 70;
7      double subjectThree = 65;
8      double avg = (subjectOne + subjectTwo + subjectThree)/3;
9      NSLog(@"The average score for the student is: %lf", avg);
10 return 0;
11 }
```

### Output for Example 4-1

**2017-03-19 20:52:48.298 ch4.1[9351:303] The average score for the student is: 75**

In Example 4-1, the average score for the three courses is calculated by dividing the sum of the three scores by 3. This approach is fine if you know for certain that you will only need to average three scores in the future. However, as you can see in Example 4-2, the introduction of a `for` loop makes it possible to average more or fewer scores. Note that if there is only one statement in the `for` loop, then there is no need for the braces that enclose the statements to be repeated.

## Example 4-2

```
1  #import <Foundation/Foundation.h>
2  int main(int argc, const char * argv[])
3  {
4      double sum = 0;
5      int numOfScores = 0;
```

```
6      double score = 0;
7      //Prompt the user for the number of scores.
8      NSLog(@"\nhow many scores would you like to add?");
9      scanf("%i", &numOfScores);
10
11   //The for loop below loops as many times as the number of scores.
12     for (int i = 0; i < numOfScores; i++)
13       {
14       NSLog(@"\nPlease enter a score"); //prompts the user for a score
15       scanf("%lf", &score); //stores the score in a variable score
16       sum+=score; // adds score to the sum
17       }
18
19     double avg = sum/numOfScores; // calculates the average score
20     NSLog(@"\nThe average score is %.2f", avg);//prints the average
21
22
23  }
```

**Output for Example 4-2**

```
2017-08-27 21:59:56.775 example[22258:403]
how many scores would you like to add?
5
2017-08-27 22:00:03.628 example[22258:403]
Please enter a score
45
2017-08-27 22:00:06.697 example[22258:403]
Please enter a score
34
2017-08-27 22:00:08.136 example[22258:403]
Please enter a score
67
2017-08-27 22:00:09.804 example[22258:403]
Please enter a score
23
2017-08-27 22:00:11.219 example[22258:403]
Please enter a score
56
2017-08-27 22:00:13.075 example[22258:403]
The average score is 45.00
```

# Counter-Controlled for Loop

The for loop is controlled by a counter that counts the number of times the loop is executed, meaning the loop is executed a fixed number of times. The for loop is also referred to as a counter-controlled loop, because its design is specific to the number of iterations in the loop, meaning the counter is equal to the number of iterations required. In Example 4-2, the number of repetitions was 5.

---

**SYNTAX**

```
for (counter initialization; counter test; counter
increment/decrement)
{
    // this line will be executed based on the counter;
}
```

---

The initializations for this type of loop are done in the loop declaration. For instance, consider Example 4-3, which calculates the average score for 10 courses. The counter i is initialized to *0* and then tested for termination condition. In this case, the counter is tested to see if it is less than *10*. If i<10, then i is incremented by one and the statements within the braces are executed as evident in Example 4-3.

## Example 4-3

```
1   #import <Foundation/Foundation.h>
2   int main(int argc, const char * argv[])
3   {
4       double sum = 0;
5       int counter = 0;
6       double score = 0;
7       for (int i = 0; i < 10; i++) {
8           NSLog(@"Please enter a score");
9           scanf("%lf", &score);
10          sum+=score;
11          counter++;
12      }
13      double avg = sum/counter;
14      NSLog(@"The average score is %.2f", avg);
15      return 0;
16  }
```

**Output for Example 4-3**

```
2017-03-19 20:54:03.616 ch4.1[9370:303] Please enter a score
34
2017-03-19 20:54:15.912 ch4.1[9370:303] Please enter a score
45
2017-03-19 20:54:20.383 ch4.1[9370:303] Please enter a score
56
2017-03-19 20:54:22.776 ch4.1[9370:303] Please enter a score
67
2017-03-19 20:54:27.016 ch4.1[9370:303] Please enter a score
78
2017-03-19 20:54:29.208 ch4.1[9370:303] Please enter a score
98
2017-03-19 20:54:32.688 ch4.1[9370:303] Please enter a score
69
```

```
2017-03-19 20:54:36.476 ch4.1[9370:303] Please enter a score
87
2017-03-19 20:54:38.768 ch4.1[9370:303] Please enter a score
65
2017-03-19 20:54:40.600 ch4.1[9370:303] Please enter a score
87
2017-03-19 20:54:42.384 ch4.1[9370:303] The average score is 68.60
```

Example 4-4 provides another instance of a for loop. This program finds the factorial of a number. The for loop is used to find the product of the numbers while decrementing the number.

## Example 4-4

```
1   #import <Foundation/Foundation.h>
2   int main (int argc, const char * argv[])
3   {
4       int num = 0;
5       int product = 1;
6       NSLog(@"\nEnter the number whose factorial you would like to know:
7   ");
8       scanf("%d", &num);
9       for (int i = num; i > 0; i--) {
10          product *= i;
11      }
12      NSLog(@"%i! is: %i", num, product);
13      return 0;
14  }
```

**Output for Example 4-4**

```
2017-03-19 20:56:42.439 ch4.1[9389:303]
Enter the number whose factorial you would like to know:
5
2017-03-19 20:56:44.194 ch4.1[9389:303] 5! is: 120
```

Although you are always encouraged to use curly braces, if there is only one line of code between the braces of a loop, the braces can be eliminated. The semicolon at the end of the statement will mark the end of the for loop statements to be repeated, as shown here:

```
for (int i = 0; i < 10; i++)
//all code in this line will be executed 10 times;
```

## break Statement

Occasionally the break statement is used to terminate a for loop from inside. For instance, in the average score example, if the score is negative, then the loop should terminate. This can be accomplished using a break statement as seen in Example 4-5.

## Example 4-5

```
1   #import <Foundation/Foundation.h>
2   int main(int argc, const char * argv[])
3   {
4       double sum = 0;
5       int counter = 0;
6       double score = 0;
7       for (int i = 0; i < 10; i++) {
8           NSLog(@"Please enter a score");
9           scanf("%lf", &score);
10          //If the user enters a negative score, we stop taking in the
11              scores and just print out the average so far
12          if (score < 0) break;
13          else{
14              sum += score;
15              counter++;
16          }
17      }
18
19      double avg = sum/counter;
20
21      NSLog(@"The average score is %.2f", avg);
22      return 0;
23  }
```

### Output for Example 4-5

```
2017-03-19 20:57:41.861 ch4.1[9400:303] Please enter a score
89
2017-03-19 20:57:48.668 ch4.1[9400:303] Please enter a score
67
2017-03-19 20:57:51.523 ch4.1[9400:303] Please enter a score
90
2017-03-19 20:57:54.291 ch4.1[9400:303] Please enter a score
87
2017-03-19 20:57:56.588 ch4.1[9400:303] Please enter a score
98
2017-03-19 20:57:58.508 ch4.1[9400:303] Please enter a score
43
2017-03-19 20:58:01.484 ch4.1[9400:303] Please enter a score
93
2017-03-19 20:58:06.275 ch4.1[9400:303] Please enter a score
67
2017-03-19 20:58:08.259 ch4.1[9400:303] Please enter a score
29
2017-03-19 20:58:10.555 ch4.1[9400:303] Please enter a score
65
2017-03-19 20:58:18.391 ch4.1[9400:303] The average score is 72.80
```

## continue Statement

Occasionally the program may call for stopping the execution of the current iteration and jumping to the next iteration. This can be accomplished using the `continue` statement. For instance, in the average score example if the score is equal to zero, then the loop should terminate. This can be accomplished using a `continue` statement, as shown in Example 4-6.

## Example 4-6

```
1   #import <Foundation/Foundation.h>
2   int main (int argc, const char * argv[])
3   {
4       double sum = 0;
5       int counter = 0;
6       double score = 0;
7
8       for (int i = 0; i < 10; i++) {
9           NSLog(@"Please enter a score");
10          scanf("%lf", &score);
11          counter++;
12          //If the user enters 0, we do not add it to the sum
13          if (score == 0)
14              continue;
15          else sum += score;
16      }
17      double avg = sum/counter;
18      NSLog(@"The average score is %.2f", avg);
19      return 0;
20  }
```

**Output for Example 4-6**

```
2017-03-19 20:59:45.812 ch4.1[9414:303] Please enter a score
67
2017-03-19 21:00:05.339 ch4.1[9414:303] Please enter a score
45
2017-03-19 21:00:06.780 ch4.1[9414:303] Please enter a score
89
2017-03-19 21:00:08.931 ch4.1[9414:303] Please enter a score
93
2017-03-19 21:00:11.267 ch4.1[9414:303] Please enter a score
54
2017-03-19 21:00:12.627 ch4.1[9414:303] Please enter a score
12
2017-03-19 21:00:14.155 ch4.1[9414:303] Please enter a score
94
2017-03-19 21:00:16.483 ch4.1[9414:303] Please enter a score
39
2017-03-19 21:00:17.979 ch4.1[9414:303] Please enter a score
47
2017-03-19 21:00:19.491 ch4.1[9414:303] Please enter a score
64
2017-03-19 21:00:21.707 ch4.1[9414:303] The average score is 60.40
```

## Condition-Controlled Loop

The condition-controlled loop works in two ways:

1.  It is executed only if a condition changes.

2.  It stops execution upon the satisfaction of a condition.

The `while` loop and the `do-while` loop can be classified as **condition-controlled** as well as **counter-controlled** loops, meaning the `while` loop and the `do-while` loop can each be implemented as a counter-controlled loop with a specific number of iterations or as a condition-controlled loop, where these loops can be executed based on a condition. The main difference between the `while` and the `do-while` loop is that the `while` loop is a pretest loop, meaning the condition is tested before the execution of the statements in the `while` loop. By contrast, the `do-while` is a post-test loop, meaning the `do-while` statements are executed at least once before the condition is tested.

## while Loop

A `for` loop is used when the number of iterations is finite and known. If you are unaware of the number of iterations required, you should use the `while` loop instead. The syntax for the `while` loop is:

```
SYNTAX
Initialization of a condition
while (condition)
{
...// statements to be executed
//condition changes facilitating the termination of the while
}
```

There are four main types of while loops:

1.  **Flag-controlled**—The loops continues until a Boolean variable changes its value.

2.  **Counter-controlled**—The loop continues until a counter variable attains a certain value, similar to the `for` loop.

3.  **Sentinel-controlled**—The loop continues until the user enters a predefined sentinel value to terminate the loop.

4.  **End-of-file-controlled**—The loop continues until the end of the file is reached.

If you are asked to calculate the average score of all the courses for a student, without knowing how many courses a student has taken, you can use a **flag-controlled while** loop. One approach to this problem is to test to see if the end of the courses has been reached.

This can be achieved by declaring a flag variable, which is a Boolean variable that tracks the end of courses as a Boolean that is either True or False. In Example 4-7, the Boolean variable controls the `while` loop. As soon as the value of this Boolean changes from `False` to `True`, the `while` loop ends.

## Example 4-7

```
1  int main (int argc, const char * argv[])
2  {
3  int numberofCourses = 0;
4  double input;
5  double total = 0;
6  double average;
7  BOOL lastCourse = FALSE; // boolean flag
8
9  NSLog(@"\nEnter the course score. When done, enter a negative
10 number"); //prompt the user for a termination number
11
12 while(!lastCourse){ //As long as user does not enter a negative
13 number, the while loop will continue.
14     printf("\nEnter the course score: ");
15     scanf("%lf", &input);
16     if(input >= 0){ //if input is a negative score, then add the score.
17       total += input;
18       numberofCourses++;// Increment the number of courses to find
19 average.
20     }
21     else
22     lastCourse = TRUE; // Boolean variable changes value when user
23 enters a negative score.
24 }
25 average = total/numberofCourses;//calculate average
26 NSLog(@"\nThe student average in %i courses is: %f", numberofCourses,
27 average); // print average
28 return 0;
29 }
```

### Output for Example 4-7

```
2017-08-27 22:41:55.643 example[22533:403]
Enter the course score. When done, enter a negative score

Enter the course score: 56

Enter the course score: 38

Enter the course score: -9
2017-08-27 22:42:19.334 example[22533:403]
The student average in 2 courses is: 47.000000
```

In Example 4-7, the condition is initialized before the start of the loop, and then the loop iteratively tests for the condition. As long as the condition is met, the statements within the loop are executed. As soon as the condition is not met, the execution jumps out of the loop. In Example 4-7, this occurs when the condition lastCourse turns true.

Now let's look at an example of a **sentinel-controlled while** loop. In Example 4-8, the sentinel value is 'Q'. If the user wants to stop counting the letters being entered, then the user must enter a 'Q'. The letter counter keeps track of the number of letters entered.

## Example 4-8

```
1  int main (int argc, const char * argv[])
2  {
3     char letter; // stores chars
4     int letterCount=0; // counts the characters entered by user
5
6     NSLog(@"\nEnter a letter, to quit enter a 'Q'");//prompts the user
7     scanf("\n%c", &letter);  // read the user entered char into letter
8
9     letterCount++; //increment counter
10
11    while (letter != 'Q' && letter != 'q') {    //sentinel value is Q
12        NSLog(@"\nEnter another letter"); //prompt the user for another
13 char
14        scanf("\n%c", &letter);  //store the char
15        letterCount++;   //increment counter to count the char
16    }
17
18    NSLog(@"\nThe number of letters entered are %i", letterCount);
19 //print
20
21 return 0;
22 }
```

### Output for Example 4-8

```
2017-08-27 22:56:03.886 example[22783:403]
Enter a letter, to quit enter a 'Q'
Q
2017-08-27 22:56:09.893 example[22783:403]
The number of letters entered are 1
```

Let's look at how we can implement the factorial problem from Example 4-4 that was written using a for loop. In Example 4-9, a while loop is used to solve the same problem. In this example, the counter variable is used to keep track of the number. This is an example of a **counter-controlled while** loop

## Example 4-9

```
1  #import <Foundation/Foundation.h>
2  int main (int argc, const char * argv[])
3  {
4      int num = 0; //stores the user input
5      int counter;  //used as a counter
6      long double result = 1;  //initializing the result for a factorial
7      NSLog(@"\nEnter the number for factorial"); //prompt the user for
8  a number
9      scanf("%d", &num);  //store the user entered number
10     counter = num;
11     while(counter > 0){
12         result = result * counter;
13         counter = counter -1;
14     }
15     NSLog(@"\nThe factorial of %i is: %Lf", num, result);
16     return 0;
17 }
```

**Output for Example 4-9**

**Enter the number for factorial**
**17**
**2017-05-19 20:56:16.172 Chapter4_InChapterExerc**
**The factorial of 17 is: 355687428096000.000000**

## do-while Loop

The do-while loop is a variation of the while loop. Although this is not a very popular looping mechanism, it comes in handy when you need to execute a set of instructions at least once before testing the condition.

**SYNTAX**

```
initialization of a condition
do
{
    // statements to be executed
//condition changes facilitating the termination of the while
}
while (condition);
```

Note the semicolon immediately following the while statement, indicating the end of the do-while syntax.

In Example 4-10, one student's average score is calculated first, and then the program tests to see if the last score was entered. The advantage of this approach is that it forces the user to enter at least one score per student.

## Example 4-10

```
1  #import <Foundation/Foundation.h>
2  int main (int argc, const char * argv[])
3  {
4  double score = 0;
5     double sum = 0;   // to hold the sum of the scores
6     int counter = 0;   // counter keeps track of the number of courses
7     BOOL lastCourse = NO; //indicates if last course
8     do{        //all the statements from here to the closing curly
9                     // brace are executed before the condition for the
10                    // last test score is made
11        NSLog(@"Please enter a score");
12        scanf("%lf", &score);
13        sum += score;
14        counter++;
15
16        if (counter == 10)
17          lastCourse = true;
18    }   //this is the last statement that will be
19        //executed before the test for the condition
20     while (!lastCourse);
21     double avg = sum/counter;
22     NSLog(@"The average for the 10 scores entered is: %.2f", avg);
23  return 0;
24  }
```

**Output for Example 4-10**

```
2017-03-19 21:06:19.576 ch4.1[9444:303] Please enter a score
56
2017-03-19 21:39:00.992 ch4.1[9444:303] Please enter a score
87
2017-03-19 21:39:02.648 ch4.1[9444:303] Please enter a score
98
2017-03-19 21:39:04.912 ch4.1[9444:303] Please enter a score
23
2017-03-19 21:39:06.256 ch4.1[9444:303] Please enter a score
42
2017-03-19 21:39:08.208 ch4.1[9444:303] Please enter a score
73
2017-03-19 21:39:10.192 ch4.1[9444:303] Please enter a score
82
2017-03-19 21:39:12.288 ch4.1[9444:303] Please enter a score
71
2017-03-19 21:39:14.463 ch4.1[9444:303] Please enter a score
94
2017-03-19 21:39:16.735 ch4.1[9444:303] Please enter a score
96
2017-03-19 21:39:18.575 ch4.1[9444:303] The average for the 10 scores
entered is: 72.20
```

In Example 4-11, the problem is to find the sum of the first 20 numbers. In this example, the variable counter keeps track of the numbers to be counted. The variable sum holds the sum of the numbers. The first number is added to zero and then the condition is tested.

## Example 4-11

```
1  #import <Foundation/Foundation.h>
2  int main (int argc, const char * argv[])
3  {
4      int sum = 0; //stores the sum of the numbers
5      int counter = 0;   //tracks the first 20 numbers
6
7      do{ //the statements between these curly brackets are executed
8          //once before the test for the while condition is made
9          sum += counter;
10         counter++;
11     }
12     while (counter <= 20); //condition for while
13     NSLog(@"The sum of the first 20 numbers is: %i", sum); //print sum
14 return 0;
15 }
```

**Output for Example 4-11**

```
2017-03-19 21:40:23.790 ch4.1[9486:303] The sum of the first 20
numbers is: 210
```

Example 4-12 implements the factorial problem from Example 4-4 using a do-while loop. The number for which you are calculating the factorial is stored in the variable factorial. The variable product holds the current factorial calculation and is multiplied with the next lower number in a do-while loop. Notice how the loop is executed once before the condition is tested. This means that, if you are calculating the factorial for 1, the loop would execute once, and then the condition would be tested and met. At that point, execution would jump out of the loop. The product variable that holds the factorial of the number is declared as a long double to accommodate large numbers.

## Example 4-12

```
1  #import <Foundation/Foundation.h>
2  int main (int argc, const char * argv[])
3  {
4      int num = 0;
5      long double product = 1;
6      int factorial; // stores the factorial number
7
8      NSLog(@"Please enter the number whose factorial you would like to
9  find: ");   //prompt for a number
10     scanf("%d", &num); // read it into num
11     factorial = num; //store num into factorial to print it at the end
```

```
12    do{
13        product *= num; //first multiply the number with 1
14        num--;        // then decrement the number
15    }
16    while (num > 0);  // now test to see if it has reached the end (0)
17    NSLog(@"%i! is: %Lf", factorial, product); // print the number and
18                                          //the factorial
19    return 0;
20 }
```

**Output for Example 4-12**

2017-05-19 20:44:25.961 Chapter4_InChapterExercises[1788:303] Please
enter the number whose factorial you would like to find:
62
2017-05-19 20:44:29.808 Chapter4_InChapterExercises[1788:303] 62! is:
31469973260387937525671402996393327390387578688777398582935178270660
1167307517200433152.000000

# Nested for Loop

The course grade examples so far related to calculating an average grade for one student who takes multiple courses. Now suppose you are asked to calculate the average score for three students in one class. In that case, you would use the code from Example 4-2 and run it for every student in the class. The repetition of the code can be accomplished using a nested for loop as shown in Example 4-13.

# Example 4-13

```
1  #import <Foundation/Foundation.h>
2  int main (int argc, const char * argv[])
3  {
4  double sum;  //sum of scores
5  double score;  //score input by user
6  double average;  // average for the courses
7  int noCourses; //  number of courses each student is taking
8  int noStudents; // number of students
9  int k;
10
11 NSLog(@"How many courses is each student taking?");// Prompts the user
12                                          //for number of courses.
13 scanf("%i", &noCourses); //saves it
14
15 NSLog(@"How many students are there?"); //Prompts the user for number
16                                          //of students.
17 scanf("%i", &noStudents);  // saves it
18
19 for (int i = 0; i < noStudents; i++) {  // This for loop loops through
20                                          //each student.
```

```
21      sum = 0;
22      score = 0;
23      average = 0;
24      k = i + 1; // Keeps track of the student number for the NSlog
25                 //statement.
26
27      for (int j = 0; j < noCourses; j++) { // This for loop loops
28                                            //through each course for
29                                            //one student at a time.
30          int i = j + 1;// Tracks the course number for each student
31                        //for the NSlog statement.
32          NSLog(@"\nPlease enter the score for the course number %i, for
33  the student number %i", 1, k);
34          scanf("%lf", &score);
35          sum += score;
36
37          }
38       average = sum/noCourses; //Calculates average for each student.
39
40      NSLog(@"\nThe average score for student number %i is %.2f", k,
41      average);// Prints average for each student.
42          }
43      return 0;
44  }
```

**Output for Example 4-13**

```
2017-03-19 21:43:14.680 ch4.1[9512:303] How many courses is each
student taking?
2
2017-03-19 21:43:20.133 ch4.1[9512:303] How many students are there?
2
2017-03-19 21:43:23.843 ch4.1[9512:303]
Please enter the score for the course number 1, for the student number 1
98
2017-03-19 21:43:42.103 ch4.1[9512:303]
Please enter the score for the course number 2, for the student number 1
79
2017-03-19 21:43:45.550 ch4.1[9512:303]
The average score for student number 1 is 88.50
2017-03-19 21:43:45.551 ch4.1[9512:303]
Please enter the score for the course number 1, for the student number 2
69
2017-03-19 21:43:48.271 ch4.1[9512:303]
Please enter the score for the course number 2, for the student number 2
79
2017-03-19 21:43:51.399 ch4.1[9512:303]
The average score for student number 2 is 74.00
```

In Example 4-14, nested looping is used to find the factorial for five different numbers. In this example, the first for loop goes through each of the five numbers at a time, while the nested for loop is used for calculating the factorial of each number. Notice the product variable is declared as a long double to accommodate large numbers

## Example 4-14

```
1   #import <Foundation/Foundation.h>
2   int main (int argc, const char * argv[])
3   {
4       for (int i = 0; i < 5; i++) { //First for loop- loops through one
5                                          number at a time
6       int num = 0;
7       long double product = 1;
8           NSLog(@"\nPlease enter the number whose factorial you would
9   like to know"); //prompt for a number
10          scanf("%i", &num);   //save in num
11
12          for (int j = num; j > 0; j--) product *= j; //Nested for loop
13                                  //calculates the factorial by multiplying
14                                  //numbers in descending order
15
16          NSLog(@"\n%i! = %Lf", num, product); //print the factorial
17      }
18  return 0;
19  }
```

### Output for Example 4-14

Notice how the factorial for each number is printed before the next number is requested from the user.

2017-05-19 20:37:43.080 Chapter4_InChapterExercises[1766:303]
Please enter the number whose factorial you would like to know
55
2017-05-19 20:37:46.280 Chapter4_InChapterExercises[1766:303]
55! = 12696403353658275924301844405547910612048885340572887946282875488103825408.000000
2017-05-19 20:37:46.281 Chapter4_InChapterExercises[1766:303]
Please enter the number whose factorial you would like to know
20
2017-05-19 20:37:50.520 Chapter4_InChapterExercises[1766:303]
20! = 2432902008176640000.000000
2017-05-19 20:37:50.521 Chapter4_InChapterExercises[1766:303]
Please enter the number whose factorial you would like to know
15
2017-05-19 20:37:53.920 Chapter4_InChapterExercises[1766:303]
15! = 1307674368000.000000
2017-05-19 20:37:53.921 Chapter4_InChapterExercises[1766:303]
Please enter the number whose factorial you would like to know
12
2017-05-19 20:37:57.368 Chapter4_InChapterExercises[1766:303]
12! = 479001600.000000
2017-05-19 20:37:57.369 Chapter4_InChapterExercises[1766:303]
Please enter the number whose factorial you would like to know
5
2017-05-19 20:37:59.008 Chapter4_InChapterExercises[1766:303]
5! = 120.000000

## HANDS-ON LAB

Create a program that simulates a cash register as follows:

- Welcome the customer to the store.
- Ask the customer if he has a purchase or return.
- If the customer has a purchase,
  - o Ask the customer for the value of the goods he is purchasing.
  - o Ask the customer for the cash he is providing.
  - o Display the change due to the customer.
- If the customer has a return,
  - o Ask the customer for the value of the goods he is returning.
  - o Display the cash due to the customer.

### VARIABLE DECLARATIONS

1. Declare two variables named task and change, of type char and double respectively, to hold the customer choice of task (purchase or return) and to hold the value returned when a Purchase is made or a Return is made:

   ```
   char task;
   double change;
   ```

2. Welcome the customer to the store:

   ```
   NSLog(@"\nWelcome to Khan's Cash register");
   ```

3. Prompt the customer for the type of transaction by specifying the choice of 'P' or 'p' for purchase and 'R' or 'r' for a return using an NSlog statement:

   ```
   NSLog(@"\nDo you have a [P]urchase or a [R]eturn?");
   ```

4. Save the customer-entered value in the task variable:

   ```
   scanf("%s", &task);
   ```

### DECISIONS

5. Depending on the choice made by the customer, process the purchase or the return. If the customer enters a 'P' or 'p', then process the purchase:

   ```
   //To process a purchase
      if((task =='P') || (task == 'p'))
         {
   ```

6. Declare two double variables to hold the price of the item to be purchased, and the cash the customer will hand over to the cashier:

   ```
   double price, cash;
   ```

7. Prompt the customer for the purchase price:

```
NSLog(@"\nEnter the value of goods you are purchasing");
```

8. Save the customer-entered value in the price variable created in Step 6:

```
scanf("%lf", &price);
```

9. Prompt the customer for the amount of cash he is providing, and save it in the cash variable:

```
NSLog(@"\nHow much cash are you providing");
    scanf("%lf", &cash);
```

10. Check to see if the customer offered enough cash. If not, ask for more.

```
while (cash < price)
    {
      NSLog(@"\nYou are a little short. Please enter the cash
        amount again");
```

11. Save the new customer-entered value in the price variable:

```
scanf("%lf", &cash);
        {
```

12. Find the difference between the price of the item and the cash offered by the customer, and return this in the method:

```
change = cash - price;
NSLog(@"\nThe change due is %lf", change);
        }
```

13. If the customer selects 'R' or 'r', then perform the return:

```
if((task =='R') || (task == 'r'))
      {
```

14. Declare a variable to hold the value of the item to be returned:

```
double value;
```

15. Prompt the customer for value of the returning goods, and save it in the value variable:

```
NSLog(@"\nPlease enter the value of goods to be returned");
    scanf("%lf", &value);

        change = value;
        NSLog(@"\nThe change due is %lf", change);
      }
```

16. After the execution of the Purchase method or the Return method, end the program by thanking the customer:

```
NSLog(@"=====================================================");
NSLog(@"\nThank you for shopping at Khan's Cash Register! Come again!");
}
```

## SOURCE CODE

```
#import <Foundation/Foundation.h>

int main(int argc, const char * argv[])
{
    @autoreleasepool {

//Declare variables
    char task;
    double change;
    double price, cash;

//Welcome the user and ask if they have a purchase or a return
    NSLog(@"\nWelcome to Khan's Cash register");
    NSLog(@"\nDo you have a [P]urchase or a [R]eturn?");
    scanf("%s", &task);

//To process a purchase
    if((task =='P') || (task == 'p'))
    {
        NSLog(@"\nEnter the value of goods you are purchasing");
        scanf("%lf", &price);

        NSLog(@"\nHow much cash are you providing");
        scanf("%lf", &cash);

      //If they did not provide enough cash
        while (cash < price)
        {
         NSLog(@"\nYou are a little short. Please re-enter the cash amount");
         scanf("%lf", &cash);
        }
        change = cash - price;

        NSLog(@"\nThe change due is %lf", change);
        }

//To process a return
    if((task =='R') || (task == 'r'))
    {
        NSLog(@"\nPlease enter the value of goods to be returned");
        scanf("%lf", &change);
        NSLog(@"\nThe change due is %lf", change);
    }

//Thank the user for using Khan's cashiering
NSLog(@"=====================================================");
    NSLog(@"\nThank you for shopping at Khan's Cash Register! Come again!");

    return 0;
}
```

**Output for Hands on lab**

```
2017-05-19 17:41:07.215 Chapter$_HandsOnEx[998:303]
Welcome to Khan's Cash register
2017-05-19 17:41:07.217 Chapter$_HandsOnEx[998:303]
Do you have a [P]urchase or a [R]eturn?
r
2017-05-19 17:41:10.407 Chapter$_HandsOnEx[998:303]
Please enter the value of goods to be returned
67.94
2017-05-19 17:41:17.136 Chapter$_HandsOnEx[998:303]
The change due is 67.940000
2017-05-19 17:41:17.136 Chapter$_HandsOnEx[998:303]
Thank you for shopping at Khan's Cash Register! Come again!
```

## Summary

- Looping provides an efficient means of executing a set of instructions repeatedly.

- There are two main types of loops: counter-controlled and condition-controlled.

- The for loop is a type of counter-controlled loop, in which the number of iterations is fixed.

- The while and the do-while are condition-controlled loops.

- The while loop tests for a condition and terminates when the condition is satisfied.

- The do-while loop is a variation of the while loop in which the set of instructions is executed at least once before the condition is tested.

- Nesting of for loops facilitates complex problem solving.

- The break statement is used to exit a loop.

- The continue statement enables the termination of an iteration in the middle of its execution and moving on to the next iteration.

## Exercises

1. Will the following code execute?

```
do
   sum += counter;
   counter++;
while (counter < 20);
   NSLog(@"The sum of the first 20 numbers is: %i",sum);
```

2. What is the output of the following code? Assume the variable i and the counters have been properly declared.

```
do
{
    i = 5;
    NSLog(@"The value of i is: %i",i);
}
while (counter < 10);
```

3. What is the output of the following code?

```
int main(int argc, const char * argv[])
{

    @autoreleasepool {

        for(int i = 10; i>0; i--)
        {
            NSLog(@"Objective- C programming is fun");
        }

    }
    return 0;
}
```

4. What is the output of the following code?

```
int i = 5;
while(i < 5)
{
    NSLog(@"***** I love Objective- C programming *****");
}
```

5. What is the output of the following code?

```
int i =3;
int j =2;

while(i <3)
    {
    while (j<2)
        {
        NSLog(@"***** I love Objective- C programming *****");
        NSLog(@"**********");
        }
    }
}
```

6. Write an Objective-C statement that use a loop to increment the value of an `int` variable i by 5.

7. Write Objective-C statements that prompt the user for a number and then computes the sum of the five numbers following this number.

8. Write a `for` loop that iterates five times while printing the user's ID

9. In the following code, how many times will the statement "*Objective- C programming is fun*" execute?

```
for (int i = 10; i>0; i--)
    {
        i--;
        NSLog(@"Objective- C programming is fun");
    }
```

10. Indicate whether the following statements are true or false. If the statement is false, explain why.

a. The `for` loop counter can be declared outside the for loop.

b. The `while` loop condition does not have to be initialized.

c. The `do-while` loop is used when you want to execute a set of instructions at least once.

## Programming Exercises

1. Create a program that prompts the user repeatedly for a temperature in Fahrenheit. The program should then convert the Fahrenheit temperature to Celsius. When the user enters -999, the program should terminate.

2. Create a program that calculates a student's average for a semester. The program does the following:

   • Prompts the user for the number of courses taken.

   • Prompts the user for the number of tests for each of the courses he or she took.

   • Prompts the user to enter a score for each test per course.

   • Calculates and prints the student's average score.

3. Write a program that prompts the user five times for a number. Each time the program should determine if the number is odd or even and then print a message indicating if the number is odd or even, depending on which is appropriate.

4. Write a program that prompts the user for two numbers at a time and then prints the least of the two numbers. The loop should terminate when the user enters -999 for the first number.

5. Prompt the user for 10 integers. The program should track all the numbers that are greater than 50 and print the count.

6. Write a program that prints the squares of numbers between 1 and 10.

7. Write a program that prompts the user for two numbers and then prints all the even numbers between these numbers.

8. Use a `while` loop to create a number guessing game.

   - The program should first generate a random number between 1 and 80.

   - The program should then offer the user ten tries at guessing the number.

   - If the user gets the number right, then he or she can either play again or exit.

   - If the user does not guess the correct number at the end of the 10 tries, he or she can either try again or exit.

   - The program should give the user a hint after each guess if the user should guess higher or lower.

9. Create a program that generates a rectangle of asterisks:

   - Prompt the user for a rectangle's length and width. Inform the user that these numbers cannot be greater than 5.

   - Use the user's input to generate a rectangle using asterisks (*). For example if the user enters 3 for length and 5 for the width, then the program should generate the following rectangle:

     *****

     *****

     *****

10. Modify the program for problem 9 so the program will also calculate the number of asterisks and print a message indicating whether the total number of asterisks is a prime number.

# Business Case Study

Building on the previous chapter's Business Case Study, in this chapter we will work on a way of giving the user control over terminating the program, while increasing the efficiency of the program by using `for` loops for task selection. We will use a sentinel value to terminate the program.

- Use a `while` loop with a Boolean variable to prompt the user for multiple tasks/actions. When the user is done using the program, he or she should terminate it using the Boolean variable

- Use a **for** loop to select multiple balloons, using the types in the following list:

  o Birthday

  o Wedding

  o Party

  o Graduation

- Use nested **for** loops to print the number of balloons selected by the user, and the total price.

# Functions

In this chapter you will:

◎ Declare, create, and call functions

◎ Distinguish between the scope of variables declared inside and out functions

◎ Declare prototypes

◎ Pass parameters to functions

Functions are a fundamental programming concept. They facilitate code modulation by grouping lines of code that are specific to a task. These chunks of code provide a means of dividing and conquering the code. Some of the benefits of functions are that they add modularity and provide code separation based on a task. The isolation of code into chunks also helps with debugging, making it easier to track and fix syntax errors as well as semantic/logic errors.

# An Introduction to Functions

A function consists of a declaration and a body. The declaration consists of three main parts: (1) the return type, which defines the type of data the function will return; (2) the function name, which is unique to each function; and (3) the parameters list in parentheses—that is, the data types that are passed to the function. The body of the function takes the data from the parentheses, does what it needs to do, and returns data of the type defined as the return type in the declaration. An example of a function is the `main` function, where the program execution starts. When you run a program, the compiler looks for the `main` function to start execution; if the `main` function is missing then nothing is executed.

The syntax of a function is as shown here:

```
SYNTAX
<Return_data_type> <function_name> (<arg1_data_type> <arg1>,
<arg2_data_type> <arg2>, ... );
```

The following list explains the parts of a function:

- `<Return_data_type>` specifies the type of data the function will return. If there is no value being returned, this is specified as `void`. By default, a function is assumed to return an `int`.

- `<function_name>` specifies the function's unique name, which is used to call the function. The name of each function should be unique. By default, a function is global and can be called from within the `main` function or any other function.

- `<arg1_data_type>` specifies the data type of the argument that is passed to the function. Each argument that is passed to the function should have a data type. These data types can be basic or derived.

- `<arg1>` specifies the name of the variable that is being passed to the function. Note that unlimited number of variables can be passed to a function.

Example 5-1 contains a function that displays a welcome greeting.

## Example 5-1

```
1   #import <Foundation/Foundation.h>
2   void welcome(void)
3   {
4       NSLog(@"\nGood Evening, how are you doing tonight?");
5   }
6
7   int main (int argc, const char * argv[])
8   {
9       @autoreleasepool {
10          welcome();
11      }
12      return 0;
13  }
```

**Output for Example 5-1**

```
2017-05-18 17:05:01.604
Chapter5_InChapterExercises[15227:303]
Good Evening, how are you doing tonight?
```

Line 2 is the function declaration. Because this function does not return anything, the first word in the declaration is void. Next is the unique name of the function, welcome. Inside the parentheses is where all the data types and the variables for the parameters that are passed to the function are declared. Since our function does not need any parameters, the parentheses merely contain the key word void. You do not have to even include the word void if you have no parameters to pass.

Line 4 is the body of the function. Here the function prints the welcome statement. The body can be as long as you want it to be. To make debugging your program easier, a function is designed to perform one specific task. Line 10 is where the function is called. At this point, execution jumps to the function itself. When the function is finished executing, execution comes back to the point where the call to the function was made in the main function.

## Prototype Declaration

The function can be placed either before or after the main function. The placement of the function with respect to the main function, where it is invoked, is critical, since the compiler scans the program from top to bottom, and if it comes across the function call before the declaration, then the compiler has to make an assumption regarding the function's return type. The compiler has to be made aware of the function in the program. This is done by creating a prototype of the function before the main function. The prototype is the declaration of the function, which contains the return type, the name of the function, and the parameters that are being passed to the function. Once the compiler is made aware of the existence of any functions and a call to a function is made, the compiler looks for it under the main function. Another way of making the compiler aware of the function is by creating and placing the function code before the main function. In Example 5-2, the program from Example 5-1 is rewritten with prototyping in line 2. Without this line, there would be a compiler error.

## Example 5-2

```
1  #import <Foundation/Foundation.h>
2  void welcome();
3  int main (int argc, const char * argv[])
4  {
5      @autoreleasepool {
6          welcome();
7      }
8      return 0;
9  }
10 void welcome()
11 {
12     NSLog(@"\nGood Evening, how are you doing tonight?");
13 }
```

**Output for Example 5-2**

```
2017-05-18 17:54:48.426
Chapter5_InChapterExercises[15358:303]
Good Evening, how are you doing tonight?
```

Now suppose you are asked to write a program that adds two numbers. Such a program would require three variables—two to hold the numbers to be added and a third to hold the result. This would be a simple program without much coding. Now, if you were asked to write a program that adds five numbers, you would have to create six variables. Such a program might still not be too lengthy. However, imagine writing a program that adds 100 numbers. In that case, you would be creating 101 variables, and probably feeling very frustrated because of the need to repeat so many lines of code. Certainly, you would begin looking for a shortcut to shorten your code.

Functions allow you this capability by creating a group of lines of code that can be called several times to perform a task that is done repeatedly. Consider Example 5-3, which adds five numbers.

**Note:** Objective C does not support function overloading.

# Example 5-3

```
1   #import <Foundation/Foundation.h>
2   int main (int argc, const char * argv[])
3   {
4       @autoreleasepool {
5           int num1, num2, num3, num4, num5, result;
6           NSLog(@"Enter first number to be added");
7           scanf("%d",&num1);
8           NSLog(@"Enter second number to be added");
9           scanf("%d",&num2);
10          result = num1 + num2;
11          NSLog(@"Enter third number to be added");
12          scanf("%d",&num3);
13          result = result + num3;
14          NSLog(@"Enter fourth number to be added");
15          scanf("%d",&num4);
16          result = result + num4;
17          NSLog(@"Enter fifth number to be added");
18          scanf("%d",&num5);
19          result = result + num5;
20          NSLog(@"\nThe sum of the 5 numbers is %d", result);
21      }
22      return 0;
23  }
```

**Output for Example 5-3**

```
2017-07-10 23:09:36.165 test[22329:303] Enter first number to be
added
3
2017-07-10 23:09:40.310 test[22329:303] Enter second number to be
added
2
2017-07-10 23:09:41.845 test[22329:303] Enter third number to be
added
1
2017-07-10 23:09:43.412 test[22329:303] Enter fourth number to be
added
5
2017-07-10 23:09:44.668 test[22329:303] Enter fifth number to be
added
6
2017-07-10 23:09:46.156 test[22329:303]
The sum of the 5 numbers is 17
```

Notice how the user is repeatedly prompted for a number, which is then added to the result. The repeated task, then, is adding two numbers. It's more efficient to write a function that adds two numbers, and that can be called anytime you need to add two numbers. In Example 5-4, the body of the function add is outside of the main function. The call to a function is made inside of the main function, but the actual code for the body of the function is never placed inside of the main function. Line 2 is the prototype declaration. The user is first prompted for a number, which is then stored in the variable called result. Next, the user is prompted to enter another number in a for loop. A call to the add function (line12) is also made in the for loop. The add method adds the result to the new number entered by the user. The add function (line 18), which is below the main function, returns an int data type and takes as parameters two int data types. In the body of the function, the numbers are added. In the main function, an int variable stands ready to hold the value returned by the add function.

## Example 5-4

```
1   #import <Foundation/Foundation.h>
2   int add (int n1, int n2);
3   int main (int argc, const char * argv[])
4   {
5       @autoreleasepool {
6           int num1, result;
7           NSLog(@"Enter first number to be added");
8           scanf("%d",&result);
9           for (int i = 0; i < 4; i++) {
10              NSLog(@"Enter another number to be added");
11              scanf("%d",&num1);
12              result = add(result, num1);
13          }
14          NSLog(@"\nThe sum of the 5 numbers is %d", result);
15      }
16      return 0;
17  }
18  int add (int n1, int n2)
19  {
20      return (n1 + n2);
21  }
```

### Output for Example 5-4

```
2017-05-18 17:58:29.860
Chapter5_InChapterExercises[15391:303] Enter first number to be added
87
2017-05-18 17:58:43.856
Chapter5_InChapterExercises[15391:303] Enter another number to be added
34
2017-05-18 17:58:46.740
Chapter5_InChapterExercises[15391:303] Enter another number to be added
45
2017-05-18 17:58:51.264
Chapter5_InChapterExercises[15391:303] Enter another number to be added
12
2017-05-18 17:58:53.594
Chapter5_InChapterExercises[15391:303] Enter another number to be added
45
2017-05-18 17:58:56.200
Chapter5_InChapterExercises[15391:303]
The sum of the 5 numbers is 223
```

# Return Type

The return type is the type of data the function will return when executed. This data type can be a basic data type, such as `int`, `char`, `double`, or `float`, or a derived data type such as `pointers`, `structures`, and `enums`. The called function should have a similar data type variable ready to hold the value the function will return. If the function does not return a value, then it is defined as void, as in Example 5-2.

Looking back to Example 5-4, the function that adds two numbers (line 18) returns an `int` data type. The `main` function includes an `int` variable called `result` that stands ready to accept the `add` function's return value. Functions can only return one value of the return data type.

# Passing Parameters

To perform the task for which it was created, a function may require data. The data can be passed to the function in parentheses after the function's name. You can pass as many parameters to a function as you wish. These parameters can be of any basic or derived data type. The parameters in the function definition are called the **formal parameters**; when the function is called, the **actual parameters** are passed to it. In Example 5-3, two `int` variables, n1 and n2, are the parameters passed to the function. In Example 5-5, the `main` function prompts the user for three numbers (line 7). The function `average` is then invoked on line 9. Execution then jumps to the `average` function (line 15) which calculates the average of the three numbers; execution then returns it to the `main` function (line 9), where the average is calculated and stored in the variable `avg`. Execution continues to the next line (line 10), which displays the result. The return type in this case is a `double`. The parameters that are passed to the function are of type `double` as well. Note that the parameters passed to the `average` function in line 15 are the formal parameters; the parameters passed to the `average` function in line 9 are the actual parameters.

## Example 5-5

```
1   #import <Foundation/Foundation.h>
2   double average(double n1, double n2, double n3);
3   int main (int argc, const char * argv[])
4   {
5       @autoreleasepool {
6           double n1, n2, n3, avg;
7           NSLog(@"Enter 3 numbers");
8           scanf("%lf" "%lf" "%lf", &n1, &n2, &n3);
9           avg = average(n1, n2, n3);
10          NSLog(@"The average of %lf  %lf  %lf is: %lf", n1, n2,
11                  n3, avg);
12      }
13      return 0;
14  }
15  double average(double n1, double n2, double n3)
16  {
17      return (n1 + n2 + n3)/3;
18  }
```

**Output for Example 5-5**

```
2017-05-18 18:01:18.985
Chapter5_InChapterExercises[15409:303] Enter 3 numbers
34
79
55
2017-05-18 18:01:28.729
Chapter5_InChapterExercises[15409:303] The average of
34.000000  79.000000  55.000000 is: 56.000000
```

# Implementing Functions in an Existing Program

Once you are comfortable using functions, you'll find many opportunities to use them to make a program more efficient. For example, consider the ATM machine program discussed in Chapter 3, which does the following:

- Welcomes the user to the ATM machine

- Prompts the user for the account number, uses a `switch` statement to verify the account number, and then initializes the account balance. For this program the only valid account numbers and their balances are:

| | |
|---|---|
| 785415 | $200 |
| 348721 | $480 |
| 896531 | $500 |
| 453927 | $1000 |

- Prompts the user to select a D for deposit or W for withdrawal (Make sure you accommodate for data entry in lowercase; this is good practice for validating data to ensure the program does not crash if the user enters lowercase.)

- Uses a ternary operator to ensure that the amount to withdraw is at least equal to the available account balance.

The ATM program presented in Chapter 3 required the repetition of several chunks of code multiple times. A much more efficient version, incorporating functions, is presented in Example 5-6. This example uses three functions: operationDecision, Deposit, and withdrawal.

Execution starts at the main function (line 6), which prompts the user for an account number (line 13). The operationDecision function is then invoked (line 23) in the switch statement (line 17). The operationDecision (line 78) function examines the user's input, and then calls either the Deposit function (line 96) or the withdrawal function (line 48), depending on the input. The switch statement (line 17) is used in the main function to decide which bank account to address and is also used in the withdrawal function to decide what action should be taken, depending on the account balance. The ternary operator is implemented in the switch condition (line 56) of the withdrawal function to ensure the amount withdrawn is not greater than the account balance.

Note that a function can call another function. In Example 5-6, the operationDecision function calls either the Deposit(line 87) or the withdrawal(line 91) function.

## Example 5-6

```
1  #import <Foundation/Foundation.h>
2  //prototype declarations
3  void Deposit (double balance);
4  void withdrawal (double balance);
5  void operationDecision(double balance);
6  int main (int argc, const char * argv[])
7  {
8  @autoreleasepool {
9  //variable declarations
10     int account;
11     double balance = 0.0;
12     //prompt the user for the account number
13     NSLog(@"\nWelcome to your ATM Machine\nPlease enter your
14 Account number");
15     scanf("%i", &account);
16     //switch on the account number
17     switch (account) {
18       case 785415:
19         balance = 200.00;
20         NSLog(@"\nYour starting balance is %lf", balance);
21         //invoke the operationDecision function to decide
22         //what operation the customer prefers
23         operationDecision(balance);
24         break;
25       case 348721:
26         balance = 480.00;
27         NSLog(@"\nYour starting balance is %lf", balance);
28         operationDecision(balance);
29         break;
30       case 896531:
31         balance = 500.00;
32         NSLog(@"\nYour starting balance is %lf", balance);
33         operationDecision(balance);
34         break;
35       case 453927:
36         balance = 1000.00;
37         NSLog(@"\nYour starting balance is %lf", balance);
38         operationDecision(balance);
39         break;
40       default:
41         NSLog(@"Invalid account number");
42         break;
43         }
```

```
44          }
45          return 0;
46      }
47  //withdrawal function- invoked by the operationDecision
48  void withdrawal (double balance)
49  {
50      double withdraw;
51      //prompt the user for the withdrawal amount
52      NSLog(@"Enter the amount to withdraw");
53      scanf("%lf", &withdraw);
54      //switch on the comparison of the balance with the
55      withdrawal amount
56      switch (balance < withdraw && balance >= 0.0 ? 'f' :'s')
57      {
58      //if withdrawal amount is greater than the deposit inform
59  customer
60          case 'f':
61            NSLog(@"You cannot withdraw %lf because you only
62                have %lf in Your account", withdraw, balance);
63            NSLog(@"Your account balance is %lf", balance);
64            break;
65          case 's':
66          //otherwise deduct the withdrawal amount from current
67  balance
68            balance -= withdraw;
69            //print current balance after withdrawal
70            NSLog(@"You have withdrawn %lf\n Your account balance is
71  now %lf", withdraw, balance);
72          default:
73            break;
74      }
75      }
76
77  //operationDecision function invoked by the main functiion
78  void operationDecision(double balance)
79  {
80      char operation;
81      //prompt the user for the type of operation
82      NSLog(@"\nWhat would you like to do today? Enter D for
83  Deposit, W for Withdrawal");
84      scanf("%s", &operation);
85      //invoke the deposit function if user entered d or D
86      if (operation == 'D' || operation == 'd') {
87          Deposit(balance);
88      }
89      //invoke the withdrawal function if user entered w or W
90      else if(operation == 'W' || operation == 'w'){
91          withdrawal(balance);
92          }
93      }
94
```

```
95   //The Deposit function invoked by the operationDecision function
96   void Deposit (double balance)
97   {
98       double deposit;
99       //prompt the user for the deposit amount
100      NSLog(@"Enter the amount to deposit");
101      scanf("%lf", &deposit);
102      //add the deposit amount to the current balance
103      balance += deposit;
104      //print the current balance
105      NSLog(@"You deposited %lf. Your account balance is now %lf",
106  deposit, balance);
107  }
```

**Output for Example 5-6**

```
2017-09-03 00:26:38.977 ex1[558:403]
Welcome to your ATM Machine
Please enter your Account number
785415
2017-09-03 00:26:52.701 ex1[558:403]
Your starting balance is 200.000000
2017-09-03 00:26:52.702 ex1[558:403]
What would you like to do today? Enter D for Deposit, W for
Withdrawal
w
2017-09-03 00:26:56.006 ex1[558:403] Enter the amount to
withdraw
48
2017-09-03 00:27:00.032 ex1[558:403] You have withdrawn
48.000000
Your account balance is now 152.000000
```

# Variable Scope

When working with variables and functions, you need to keep in mind the **scope**, or visibility range, of a variable. The scope of a local variable is within the set of curly braces in which it was declared. Global variables are declared outside of all the functions in the program, right after the import declarations. The scope of the global variables is limited to the entire program, meaning all the functions inside of this program can access this variable. Local variables, on the other hand, are seen only inside of the function they are declared in and are invisible to the rest of the program. The parameters of a function are local to the function, with values of the actual parameters passed to the function. The parameters of the function are live as long as the function is being executed. Once the function execution terminates the parameters turn invisible and cease to exist. The scope of the variables declared within a function is limited to the function itself.

Consider Example 5-7, which calculates the average growth of a tree in an apple orchard.

## Example 5-7

```
1  #import <Foundation/Foundation.h>
2  double diff (double n1, double n2);
3  double avg (double totalgrowth, double years);
4  double totalGrowth;   //growth in five years
5  int main(int argc, const char * argv[])
6  {
7  @autoreleasepool {
8      //declare variables
9      double initialHeight; //initial height of a tree in the
10     //apple orchard
11     double finalHeight; //final height of the tree after 5
12     //years
13     double avgGrowthPerYear;   //Average growth of an apple
14     //tree per year
15     //prompt for the initial height of the tree
16     NSLog(@"\nWhat is the initial height of the tree in feet");
17     scanf("%lf",&initialHeight);
18     NSLog(@"\nWhat is the final height of the tree in feet after
19  5 years");
20     scanf("%lf", &finalHeight);
21     totalGrowth = diff(initialHeight, finalHeight);
22     avgGrowthPerYear = avg(totalGrowth, 5.0);
23     NSLog(@"\nThe average growth of a tree in the apple orchard
24  is %lf feet", avgGrowthPerYear);
25     }
26     return 0;
27  }   // end of main function
28
29  double diff (double n1, double n2)     //diff function
30  {
31     double totalGrowth;
32     totalGrowth =   n2 - n1;
33     return totalGrowth;
34  }
35
36  double avg(double totalgrowth, double years) //avg function
37  {
38     return totalgrowth/years;
39  }
```

### Output for Example 5-7

A sample run of the above program is shown below
2017-09-01 19:21:52.740 ex[254:403]
What is the initial height of the tree in feet
6.7
2017-09-01 19:21:56.500 ex[254:403]
What is the final height of the tree in feet after 5 years
22.4

```
2017-09-01 19:22:01.400 ex[254:403]
The average growth of a tree in the apple orchard is
3.140000 feet
```

In Example 5-7, the difference between the initial height and the height after five years divided by 5 gives the average growth over a year (line 38). The variable `totalGrowth` (line 4) is a global variable, which means it is visible in the `main`, `diff`, and `avg` functions; this variable is live during the entire execution of the program. Variables `initialHeight` (line 9), `finalHeight` (line 11), and `avgGrowthPerYear` (line 13) are local to the `main` function and hence visible only inside of the `main` function. In other words, these variables are live only as long as the `main` function is being executed. The variable `totalGrowth` (line 31) is local to the `diff` function (line 29) and hence visible only inside of the diff function, making it live only during the execution of the `diff` function. As soon as the execution of the `diff` function terminates, the variable `totalGrowth` ceases to exist.

## HANDS-ON LAB

Consider a scenario in which we observe the work of a teller at a bank. Each time a customer approaches the teller, she finds out what the customer would like. Some customers need change—for example, quarters for parking meters—while others may want to withdraw or deposit money. The teller then proceeds to either open her cash register or enter the customer's account number for a deposit or withdrawal.

Create some accounts using the following account numbers and balance amounts:

23457, $5645.89

37678, $564.67

568298, $1235.35

Your program should welcome the customer and prompt the customer to enter one of the following numbers:

**1:** for deposit

**2:** for withdrawal

**3:** to check account balance

**4:** to get quarters for parking

### VARIABLE DECLARATIONS

1. Declare three `int` variables to hold the account numbers and three double variables to hold the balance for the respective accounts.

```
int account1 = 23457;
int account2 = 37678;
int account3 = 568298;
```

```
double balance1 = 5645.89;
double balance2 = 564.67;
double balance3 = 1235.35;
```

2. Welcome the customer and then ask what operation the customer would like to perform. Create a `switch` statement for the operation entered by the customer. The `switch` statement should invoke the function called `selection` that performs the specific task based on user selection.

```
@autoreleasepool {
int operation;
NSLog(@"Welcome to the bank!");
NSLog(@"\nEnter\n 1: for deposit,\n 2: for
withdrawal,\n 3: to check account balance,\n 4: to get
quarters for parking meters,");
scanf("%i", &operation);
switch (operation) {
    case 1:
      selection(1);
      break;
    case 2:
      selection(2);
      break;
    case 3:
      selection(3);
      break;
    case 4:
      change(4);
      break;
    default:
      break;
      }
}
    return 0;
}
```

## CHANGE DISPENSER

3. Create a function to prompt the suer for the amount to convert to change and print the number of quarters dispensed.

```
void change(int num){
    double amount;
    NSLog(@"Enter the amount to convert");
    scanf("%lf", &amount);
    if (num == 4 {
        NSLog(@"%i quarters dispensed", getCoins(amount));
    }
}
```

## TASK SELECTION

4.  Write a function called selection that handles options 1 through 4. This function should prompt the user to enter an account number. Write functions called deposit, withdrawal, and checkBalance that will assist the user in depositing, withdrawing, and checking the balance in the account. Call these functions from within the selection function depending on the operation entered by the user.

```
void selection(int num){
 int account;
 NSLog(@"Enter an account number");
 scanf("%i", &account);
 if (account == account1 || account == account2 ||
 account == account3) {
 if (num == 1) {
  double amt;
  NSLog(@"Enter the amount to deposit");
  scanf("%lf", &amt);
  deposit(account, amt);
  }
  else if (num == 2) {
     double amt;
   NSLog(@"Enter the amount to withdraw");
   scanf("%lf", &amt);
   withdrawal(account, amt);
   }
   else if (num == 3) {
     NSLog(@"The account balance is $%.2f",
          checkBalance(account));
   }
  }
 }
```

## DEPOSIT FUNCTION

5.  The function deposit should have an int parameter that represents the account number and a double parameter that indicates the amount to deposit in that account. The function should then add the deposit amount to the account balance.

```
void change(int num){
    double amount;
    NSLog(@"Enter the amount to convert");
    scanf("%lf", &amount);
    if (num == 4){
        NSLog(@" %i quarters dispensed", getCoins(amount));
    }
}
```

## WITHDRAWAL FUNCTION

6. The function withdrawal should have an `int` parameter that represents the account number and a `double` parameter that indicates the amount to withdraw from that account. The function should then deduct this amount from the account balance.

```
void change(int num){
    double amount;
    NSLog (@"Enter the amount to convert");
    scanf("%lf", &amount);
    if (num == 4){
        NSLog(@" %i quarters dispensed", getCoins(amount));
    }
}
```

## CHECKBALANCE FUNCTION

7. The function **checkBalance** should have an `int` parameter that represents the account number and that returns the account balance.

```
double checkBalance(int account){
  if (account == account1) {
    return balance1;
  }
  else if (account == account2) {
    return balance2;
  }
  else if (account == account3) {
    return balance3;
  }
  else
    return 0.0;
}
```

## GETCOINS FUNCTION

8. Declare another function called **getCoins**. This function should use the amount to change as a parameter and return the number of quarters by multiplying the amount by 100 and dividing by 25. It should have an `int` parameter greater than one and indirectly return the amount of quarters present in that `int` parameter.

```
int getCoins(double amt){
  if (amt > 1) {
    return amt*100/25;
  }
  else
    return 0;
}
```

## PROTOTYPING

9. Do not forget to prototype your functions

```
void selection(int num);
void deposit(int account, double amt);
void withdrawal(int account, double amt);
double checkBalance(int account);
void change(int num);
int getCoins(double amt);
```

## SOURCE CODE

```
#import <Foundation/Foundation.h>
void selection(int num);
void deposit(int account, double amt);
void withdrawal(int account, double amt);
double checkBalance(int account);
void change(int num);
int getCoins(double amt);

int account1 - 23457;
int account2 = 37678;
int account3 = 568298;
double balance1 = 5645.89;
double balance2 = 564.67;
double balance3 = 1235.35;

int main(int argc, const char * argv[])
{
@autoreleasepool {
  int operation;
  NSLog(@"Welcome to the bank!");
  NSLog(@"\nEnter\n 1: for deposit,\n 2: for
      withdrawal,\n 3: to check account balance,\n 4:to
      get quarters for parking meters");
  scanf("%i", &operation);
  switch (operation) {
    case 1:
      selection(1);
      break;
    case 2:
      selection(2);
      break;
    case 3:
      selection(3);
      break;
    case 4:
      change(4);
      break;
    default:
      break;
  }
```

```
    }
    return 0;
}

void change(int num){
    double amount;
    NSLog(@"Enter the amount to convert");
    scanf("%lf", &amount);
    if(num == 4){
      NSLog(@" %i quarters dispensed",getCoins(amount));
    }
}

void selection(int num){
    int account;
    NSLog(@"Enter an account number");
    scanf("%i", &account);
    if (account == account1 || account == account2 ||
        account == account3) {
      if (num == 1) {
        double amt;
        NSLog(@"Enter the amount to deposit");
        scanf("%lf", &amt);
        deposit(account, amt);
      }
      else if (num == 2) {
            double amt;
            NSLog(@"Enter the amount to withdraw");
            scanf("%lf", &amt);
            withdrawal(account, amt);
        }
        else if (num == 3) {
            NSLog(@"The account balance is $%.2f",
                checkBalance(account));
        }
    }
}

void deposit(int account, double amt){
    if (account == account1) {
        balance1 += amt;
         NSLog(@"The balance in the account is %lf", balance1);
    }
    else if (account == account2) {
        balance2 += amt;
         NSLog(@"The balance in the account is %lf", balance2);
    }
    else if (account == account3) {
        balance3 += amt;
         NSLog(@"The balance in the account is %lf", balance3);
    }

}
```

```
void withdrawal(int account, double amt){
    if (account == account1) {
        balance1 -= amt;
        NSLog(@"The balance in the account is %lf", balance1);
    }
    else if (account == account2) {
        balance2 -= amt;
        NSLog(@"The balance in the account is %lf", balance2);
    }
    else if (account == account3) {
        balance3 -= amt;
        NSLog(@"The balance in the account is %lf", balance3);
    }
}

double checkBalance(int account){
    if (account == account1) {
        return balance1;
    }
    else if (account == account2) {
        return balance2;
    }
    else if (account == account3) {
        return balance3;
    }
    else
        return 0.0;
}

int getCoins(double amt){
    if (amt > 1) {
        return amt*100/25;
    }
    else
        return 0;
}
```

**SAMPLE OUTPUT**

```
2017-06-02 00:16:03.285 chapter 5 hands on lab[12814:303]
Welcome to the bank!
2017-06-02 00:16:03.287 chapter 5 hands on lab[12814:303]
Enter
 1: for deposit,
 2: for withdrawal,
 3: to check account balance,
 4: to get quarters for parking meters
```

```
4
2017-06-02 00:16:05.881 chapter 5 hands on lab[12814:303]
Enter the amount to convert
4
2017-06-02 00:16:08.521 chapter 5 hands on lab[12814:303]
16 quarters dispensed
```

## Summary

- A function is a group of lines of code that are specific to a task.

- Functions add modularity, separate code based on task, and help with debugging by isolating chunks of code so that it is easier to fix syntax and semantic/logic errors.

- A function consists of a declaration and a body. The declaration consists of a return type (which defines the type of data the function will return), the function name (which is unique to each function), and the parameters list in parenthesis (which are the data types that are passed to the function). The body of the function takes the data from the parameters, does what it needs to do, and then returns data that is of the type defined as the return type in the declaration.

- The prototype is the first line of the function declaration.

- The scope of a variable is its visibility range in and out of a program. A variable's scope can be local or global. A variable is considered local if it is declared inside of a function, be it the `main` function or any other function. Its visibility is limited to the curly braces it is declared within. A variable is considered global when it is declared outside of all the functions in the program and right after the import declarations.

- A function can only return one value.

## Exercises

1. State whether each of the following function declarations is valid or invalid. If it is invalid, explain why.

   a. `int operation (double d, int s)`

   b. `double results (double num1, num2)`

   c. `resolve(int g);`

   d. `char greatest (char 's');`

   e. `int operation();`

   f. `char small(int num1, double num2, char num3);`

   g. `multiply(num1, num2);`

   h. `double operate;`

2. Mark each of the following statements as true or false.

a. Actual parameters are used in function declaration, while formal parameters are used in function calls.

b. Functions must have parameters. If none is needed, the parameters are replaced with the reserved word `void`.

c. A function may have no return type or several return types.

d. A global variable in a class can be accessed by any function in that class.

e. A global variable can only be modified in the `main` function but can be accessed by any function.

3. Given the following program:

```
double percentage(double s, double t, char u);
void welcome(void);
void goodBye(char y);
double percentage(double s, double t, char u)
{
    double result = s/t * 100;
    return result;
}
void welcome(void){
    NSLog(@"Hello World");
    NSLog(@"Welcome to our gender percentage calculator");
}
void goodBye(char y){
    NSLog(@"Thank you for using this function for the
    %c gender", y);
}
int main (int argc, const char * argv[])
{
    @autoreleasepool {
        char gender = 'F';
        int total = 263;
        int girlsTotal = 187;
        welcome();
        NSLog(@"The percentage of girls is %.2f",
                percentage(girlsTotal, total, gender));
        goodBye(gender);
    }
    return 0;
}
```

a. Define the formal and actual parameters of each function declared and used.

b. Define the return type of each of the functions used.

4. Write the following Objective-C functions:

   a. A function that prints the message "Welcome to Objective-C Programming"
   b. A function that has two `int`s as parameters and returns the larger of the two
   c. A function that has two `int`s as parameters and prints out the larger of the two
   d. A function that has two `int`s as parameters and returns and prints the larger of the two.
   e. A function that has two numbers as parameters and a char( '+', '*' or '-') as a parameter, for a total of three parameters. The function returns the value of the computation of the two numbers by the operation defined by the char parameter. The function returns zero for all invalid operations.

5. Indicate if the following statements are true or false

   a. Objective- C supports function overloading.
   b. A function declaration can only return one value.
   c. When a function is declared below the `main` function you have to prototype it.
   d. Public function can be called from anywhere.

6. In the following code segment, what is the value of `sum` after the program is executed?

```
#import <Foundation/Foundation.h>
int a = 20;
int add(int a, int b);

int main(int argc, const char * argv[])
{
    @autoreleasepool {
        NSLog(@"The sum is %d", add(a, 5));
    }
    return 0;
}
int add(int a, int b)
{
    a = 30;
    return (a+b);
}
```

7. Rewrite the program in Exercise 6 using a function that does not return a value.

8. Debug the following code segment:

```
#import <Foundation/Foundation.h>
void main(int argc, const char * argv[])
{
    @autoreleasepool {
        NSLog(@"The sum is %d", modulus(26, 5));
```

```
    }
    return 0;
}
int modulus(int a, int b)
{
    return (a%b)
}
```

9. Modify the modulus function in the program from Question 8 to calculate and return the average of a and b as well. Use pointers to accomplish this by passing a pointer as a parameter.

10. Debug the following code:

```
#import <Foundation/Foundation.h>
int high(int a, int b)
int main(int argc, const char * argv[])
    {
        @autoreleasepool {
        int a, b, c;
        NSLog(@"\nEnter 3 numbers");
        scanf("%d", &a);
        scanf("%d", &b);
        scanf("%d", &a);
        NSLog(@"\nThe highest number between %d, %d, %d is
%d", a,c, high(a,b,c));
        }
         return 0;
}
int high(int a, int b)
{
    if (a > b)
        return a;
    else
        return b;
}
```

# Programming Exercises

1. Create a program that functions like a calculator with the following operations: addition, subtraction, multiplication, division, and factorial. Each operation should be handled by a different function. Prompt the user for a number and an operator. If the operator chosen by the user is not factorial, then prompt the user for another number. Finally, compute the result of the operation and return the result to the user.

2. Using functions, solve Question 6 in the Programming Exercises in Chapter 3.

3. A British university has an honors program that uses the grading convention shown in Table 5-1.

| Points | U.S. university convention | British university convention |
|---|---|---|
| 95–100 | 4.0 | First |
| 90–94 | 3.67–3.33 | Upper Second |
| 85–89 | 3.32–3.66 | Lower Second |
| 80–84 | 3.0–3.31 | Third |
| 70–79 | 2.5–2.9 | Ordinary Pass |
| <70 | 0–2.49 | Fail |

**Table 5-1**   U.S. Grading Equivalent for Honors Grades.

Write a function to calculate the average score of students. This function should:

i.  Prompt the user to first enter the number of test scores to calculate the average.

ii. Prompt the user to enter as many test scores as the number of tests the user entered before.

iii. Prompt the user to enter his or her course types (U for U.S. courses and B for British courses). Assume the course type to be U.S. if no entry is made.

iv. Calculate the average and assign a corresponding U.S. GPA from the average and also list its British equivalent.

4. Write a program that converts a temperature from one scale to another. The program first prompts the user for a temperature and then prompts the user for the scale, Celsius, Fahrenheit, or Kelvin. The conversions are given below.

- $°C = (°F - 32) * 5/9$

- $°F = (°C * 1.8) + 32$

- $°K = °C + 273.15$

- $°C = °K - 273.15$

- $°F = 9/5 (°K - 273) + 32$

- $°K = 5/9 (°F - 32) + 273$

5. Assume a college provides an account in the cloud for each student. Each student is then allowed to create a numerical code to access his or her account. The code must have the following properties:

   i.   Be seven digits long

   ii.  Does not start with a numerical value

   iii. Includes at least one of the following special characters: #, $, -, _.

   Write a program that prompts the user for a code and uses a function to test if this code is valid. Your function should have a Boolean return type.

6. Lisa needs to work out to maintain her current weight. She can consume up to 1800 calories a day and not gain weight. If she consumes more than that, she has to burn off the extra calories by exercising. The number of calories she burns depends on the type and length of exercise she does. Table 5-2 lists the calories she burns in 30 minutes of five different forms of exercise.

| Type of Exercise | Calories burned |
| --- | --- |
| biking | 200 |
| walking | 150 |
| jogging | 300 |
| swimming | 250 |
| rollerblading | 250 |

**Table 5-2**   Calories burned in thirty minutes of exercise

Write a program that helps Lisa maintain her current weight. The program should do the following:

- Prompt Lisa for her calorie intake for the day and her type of exercise for the day.

- Run for a week at a time before Lisa restarts the program.

- Calculate the total calories and at the end of the week inform Lisa if she has gained, lost or maintained weight.

7. Consider the following program:

```
#import <Foundation/Foundation.h>

int main(int argc, const char * argv[])
{

    @autoreleasepool {

    int num = 0; //variable to store the number entered
    for (int i = 0; i < 5; i++)  { //loop for five iterations
```

```
NSLog(@"Enter a number: ");
scanf("%d", &num); //store the number entered in a variable

if (num%2 == 0) { //if num mod 2 == 0,then the number is even
        NSLog(@"%d is even", num);
    } else { //otherwise it is odd
        NSLog(@"%d is odd", num);
    }
}
}
return 0;
}
```

Modify this program to use a function that returns a Boolean to evaluate if the number entered by the user is odd or even.

8. Lori runs a pet store and would like to advertise her sale prices. Write a program that will first prompt Lori for the sale prices of pet grooming, dog food, kitty litter, and cat food, and then prints a list of prices and items surrounded by a frame of asterisks, as shown in Figure 5-1.

```
**********************************
*       Pet grooming    $40      *
*       Dog food        $21      *
*       Kitty litter    $15      *
*       Cat food        $20      *
**********************************
```

**Figure 5-1**    Output for Programming Exercise 8
© 2015 Cengage Learning

9. Write a function that calculates the number of days in a month. The program should prompt the user for the month and use enumerators to track the days of the month.

10. Rabbits reproduce in a Fibonacci sequence. Write a function that calculates the number of rabbits based on a number entered by the user. This number will provide the information for limiting the generation of the Fibonacci sequence, so it does not run forever.

# Business case study

Building on the previous chapter case study, organize the task selection into methods as follows

- Loop through the program continuously by prompting the user to enter "Y" to purchase another balloon or "N" to quit the program.

- Keep track of the number of balloons purchased and the total price, and print these at the end of the program.

- Create functions for the following tasks:

  - Select a balloon:

    - This function should process the purchase of a balloon selected by the user from the following options: birthday, wedding, party, and graduation.

    - Ask the user whether he or she would like to add this balloon to the order, and based on the user input, process the order.

    - Print the total number of balloons purchased and the total price.

  - View a balloon:

    - This function should display the price of the balloon from the collection for each occasion.

    - Ask the user whether he or she would like to add this balloon to the order, and based on the user input, process the order.

    - Print the total number of balloons purchased and the total price.

# CHAPTER 6

# Foundation Framework

In this chapter you will:

- ◎ Learn the ins and outs of Foundation framework
- ◎ Take a look at the Message syntax
- ◎ Learn the purpose of @autoReleasepool
- ◎ Create and edit NSString objects and methods
- ◎ Create and manipulate NSArray, NSDate, and NSDictionary objects

As evident in Figure 6-1, Ansi C and C++ have some overlapping concepts. C and C++ are also subsets of Objective-C.

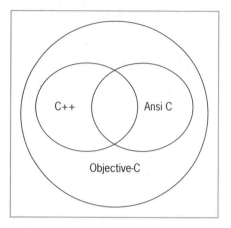

**Figure 6-1**  Concepts overlap in Ansi C, C++, and Objective-C
© 2015 Cengage Learning

So far in this book we have focused on programming concepts that Objective-C shares with the Ansi C language. Now we will focus on concepts that are unique to Objective-C. In particular, we will explore the framework, or infrastructure, on which the Objective-C programming language is built. That is, we will study the utility classes that Apple has provided in an attempt to create consistency in all the domains of the language. These utility classes are helper classes that are useful tools for programmers.

Objective-C is a superset of the Ansi C language, which is a procedural language. As discussed in Chapter 2, the Ansi C language contains a derived data type called a **structure** that holds a collection of data. An object is an extension of a structure in that it contains data as well as functions, called **methods**, which operate on this data. Invoking these methods in Objective-C is different than in other object-oriented methods.

## Message Invocation

In Objective-C, an object's method cannot be invoked by calling it. Instead, an object must pass a message to its method to invoke it. For example, a calculator object might have methods for adding, subtracting, multiplying, and dividing. The calculator method can invoke these methods by sending them messages.

The syntax for passing a message to a method is:

**SYNTAX**

```
[Object/receiver method/message]
```

The object is the receiver in this case and, as the name implies, it receives a message. In most object-oriented programming languages, an object's method is invoked by using the dot notation. For example, suppose you have an object called yorkie created from the dog class, and you need to invoke the method called run. The typical dot notation in an object-oriented language other than Objective-C would look like this:

```
yorkie.run();
```

In Objective-C, the run method of the yorkie object is invoked as follows:

```
[yorkie run]
```

Now suppose the run method has parameters as follows:

```
void run(int length)
{
    NSLog(@"The dog ran %i yards", length);
}
```

To pass it a length, the syntax would be:

```
[yorkie run:length]
```

You could also pass a constant as a parameter instead of the variable length. If the length were 12 the message syntax would be:

```
yorkie run:12]
```

Figure 6-2 illustrates the components of a method invocation in Objective-C.

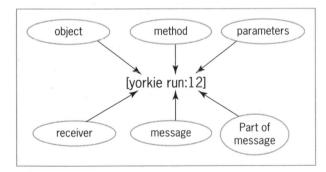

**Figure 6-2**  Components of a method invocation
© 2015 Cengage Learning

In **message nesting**, one message can be sent to another message, as follows:

```
[information getInfo:[name getName]];
```

Here, the output from [name getName] is used as the parameter for the message in the first message.

Note that the message syntax is usually used to invoke methods of an object. In the discussion of functions in Chapter 5, we did not use this message syntax to invoke the functions because the methods discussed in Chapter 5 were independent methods—that is, they were not part of a class.

# Introduction to the Foundation Framework

Now that you understand how objects communicate using messages, we will proceed with the Foundation framework, which forms the foundation of Objective-C and iOS programming. Figure 6-3 illustrates the role of methods in a framework. A set of methods makes up a class. A set of classes makes up a framework.

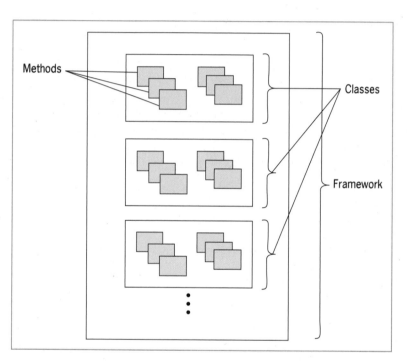

**Figure 6-3**    Constituents of a framework
© 2015 Cengage Learning

The **Foundation framework**, built on the premise of utility, support, consistency, independence of the operating system, and portability, forms the infrastructure of the Objective-C language. It is a library of classes and methods that provide language consistency and basic functionality for strings, numbers, arrays, dictionaries, dates, file systems, location and net services, and more. The Foundation framework includes a root object class called NSObject, which in turn provides support to some basic utility classes such as NSString, NSMutableString, NSArray, NSMutableArray, NSDictionary, NSMutableDictionary, NSDate, NSError, NSNetService, NSURL, NSNotification, and NSData. The NSObject class consists of subclasses that contain methods, which can be called upon to implement strings, arrays, date and time, URLs, net services, notifications, and more. It's left to the developers' discretion as to how to utilize these classes and methods to develop programs.

Not all Objective-C programming is done in the Foundation framework. So when you choose to implement the Foundation framework functionality, you must include the statement `#import <Foundation/Foundation.h>`.

In Objective-C, memory management—that is, the process of creating and releasing memory for objects-is crucial. One important memory management mechanism is `Autoreleasepool`.

## Autoreleasepool

When a data element is created, memory has to be allocated to store this data element. When that data is no longer needed, it is discarded, and any associations with the memory allocated to it also have to be discarded. Similarly, each time an object is created, memory is reserved for it, and when the object is no longer needed, the associated memory is discarded. In Objective-C, automatic reference counting (ARC) allows the compiler to use the `@autoreleasepool` to control the reservation and release of the memory for any object. This frees the developer from the burden of manual memory management. It works on the block of code placed in the curly braces following the statement `@autoreleasepool`, as shown in Example 6-1, lines 4 through 7. When `@autoreleasepool` is used, the compiler records the memory state. When the execution of the block of statements following the `@autoreleasepool` statement ends, the memory is cleared, all the objects are destroyed, and the memory returns to the state it was in before the execution of the block following `@autoreleasepool` (line 3).

## Example 6-1

```
1    int main(int argc, char *argv[])
2    {
3        @autoreleasepool
4        {
5            ....
6
7        }
8
9        return 0;
10   }
```

`@Autoreleasepool` implementation is required for the use of the classes in the Foundation framework. Some of the commonly used basic classes in the Foundation framework are `NSString`, `NSMutableString`, `NSArray`, `NSMutableArray`, `NSDate`, `NSDictionary`, and `NSMutableDictionary`.

## NSString

A string is an array of Unicode characters. The Unicode characters are a larger set of characters than the traditional alphabet character set. A string object is enclosed in double quotation marks and preceded by the @ symbol as seen below:

`@"This is my string object"`

Various operations can be performed on strings, such as comparing strings, finding a character in a particular location, finding a set of characters, searching for a character or set of characters, and many more. The Foundation framework of Objective-C provides the NSString class, which helps facilitate these operations.

An NSString object is **immutable** by default, which means it is defined when it is first created and cannot be changed subsequently. The NSMutableString, a subclass of NSString, supports the implementation of mutable strings.

The NSString class supports several methods; two of the basic ones are the length and characterAtIndex methods. The length method calculates the length of a string—that is, the total number of characters in a string. The characterAtIndex provides access to individual characters at a particular index position. Numerous string methods can be used to compare strings, find substrings, format strings, and more. To learn how these work, let us look at a simple version in Example 6-2, which declares a string (line 6), finds its length (line 9), finds a substring (line 12), converts the substring to lowercase (line 14), and prints the string in lowercase (line 15). Example 6-2 uses the methods length, substringFromIndex, and lowercaseString.

## Example 6-2

```
1   #import <Foundation/Foundation.h>
2
3   int main(int argc, const char * argv[])
4   {
5      @autoreleasepool {
6         NSString *str = @"Hello All";
7         NSString *substring;
8         int strLength;
9         strLength = [str length];
10        NSLog(@"\nYour string is %@ ", str);
11        NSLog(@"\nThe length of your string is %i", strLength);
12        substring = [str substringFromIndex:6];
13        NSLog(@"\nThe substring is %@", substring);
14        substring = [str lowercaseString];
15        NSLog(@"\nYour string in lower case is %@", substring);
16     }
17       return 0;
18  }
```

### Output for Example 6-2

```
2017-09-16 21:27:28.433 class[2231:403]
Your string is Hello All
2017-09-16 21:27:28.436 class[2231:403]
The length of your string is 9
2017-09-16 21:27:28.437 class[2231:403]
The substring is All
2017-09-16 21:27:28.438 class[2231:403]
Your string in lower case is hello all
```

In Example 6-3, the str1 and str2 objects are concatenated into str1. Notice that the NSString method used is stringByAppendingString. In this example str1 and str2 are declared (lines 6 and 7); str1 is then concatenated to a space (line 10), and lastly str1 is concatenated to str2 (line 11). Note when you append one string to another, as in Example 6-3, you are creating a new string.

## Example 6-3

```
1    #import <Foundation/Foundation.h>
2
3    int main(int argc, const char * argv[])
4    {
5        @autoreleasepool {
6            NSString *str1 = @"Programming in Objective-C";
7            NSString *str2 = @"is fun!";
8            NSLog(@"\nYour first string is %@", str1);
9            NSLog(@"\nYour second string is \n%@", str2);
10           str1 = [str1 stringByAppendingString:@" "];
11           str1 = [str1 stringByAppendingString:str2];
12           NSLog(@"Your new string after appending is\n %@", str1);
13       }
14       return 0;
15   }
```

### Output for Example 6-3

```
2017-09-16 22:06:45.359 class[2708:403]
Your first string is Programming in Objective-C
2017-09-16 22:06:45.362 class[2708:403]
Your second string is
is fun!
2017-09-16 22:06:45.363 class[2708:403] Your new string after appending is
Programming in Objective-C is fun!
```

As mentioned earlier, the NSString object creates an immutable string, meaning you cannot edit it. For instance, if you have a NSString object "Hello", you cannot change it to "Hi". Although you can append one NSString object to another to create a new NSString, you cannot delete or modify any individual characters in a string. If you would like to edit a string, you would have to create a mutable string using the NSMutableString object, as seen in Example 6-4. NSMutableString is a subclass of the NSString class. In this example, a string is inserted in another string (line 13) by declaring the first string as a NSMutableString (line 6).

## Example 6-4

```
1    #import <Foundation/Foundation.h>
2
3    int main(int argc, const char * argv[])
4    {
5        @autoreleasepool {
6            NSMutableString *str;
7            NSString *str1 = @"Programming in Objective-C";
8            NSString *str2 = @"is fun! ";
9            NSLog(@"\nYour first string is %@", str1);
10           NSLog(@"\nYour second string is \n%@", str2);
11           //populate mutable str by replacing it with str1
12           str = [NSMutableString stringWithString:str1];
13           [str insertString:str2 atIndex:12];
14           NSLog(@"Your new string after appending is\n %@", str);
15       }
16       return 0;
17   }
```

**Output for Example 6-4**

```
2017-09-16 22:22:59.545 class[2840:403]
Your first string is Programming in Objective-C
2017-09-16 22:22:59.548 class[2840:403]
Your second string is
is fun!
2017-09-16 22:22:59.549 class[2840:403] Your new string after appending is
Programming is fun! in Objective-C
```

## NSArray

An array is an ordered collection of data. It holds multiple variables that are accessed by their index value. The index of an array starts at 0 and ends at the total number of elements minus 1. The NSArray in the Foundation framework inherits from the NSObject and handles immutable arrays; in other words, the arrays created by NSArray cannot be edited. The NSMutableArray class, a subclass of the NSArray, handles the mutable or dynamic arrays. The NSArray class offers a number of methods that assist in the creation, comparison, initialization, querying, searching, finding, sending messages, and sorting of arrays, as well as many more functions related to arrays. Two of the most common methods are count, which returns the number of elements in the array, and objectAtIndex, which returns the value of the data at a particular index.

## Array Creation

Anytime we deal with an array, we have to use looping to populate, access or edit any of its values. The simple array program in Example 6-5 creates and populates an array and then prints its values. First, an array called myArrayNames is created and populated with string objects (line 9). A variable called myArrayNamesLength is declared (line 7) to store the number of elements in the array using the method count (line 12). A for loop (line 15) is then used to print the values (line 16) of the array using the method objectAtIndex (line 17).

## Example 6-5

```
1   #import <Foundation/Foundation.h>
2
3   int main(int argc, const char * argv[])
4   {
5   @autoreleasepool {
6   //create a variable to store the length of the array
7    int myArrayNamesLength;
8   //Create an array using arrayWithObjects method
9    NSArray *myArrayNames = [NSArray arrayWithObjects:@"Chocolate",
10  @"Vanilla", @"Raspberry", @"Blueberry", nil];
11  //Find the length of the array and print it
12   myArrayNamesLength = [myArrayNames count];
13   NSLog(@"\nmyArrayNames has %i elements", myArrayNamesLength);
14  //print the contents of the array
15   for (int i = 0; i < myArrayNamesLength; i++) {
16      NSLog(@"\nThe element at index %i is %@", i, [myArrayNames
17             objectAtIndex:i]);
18      }
19  }
20      return 0;
21  }
```

### Output for Example 6-5

```
2017-09-17 23:27:22.594 class[3910:403]
MyArrayNames has 4 elements
2017-09-17 23:27:22.597 class[3910:403]
The element at index 0 is Chocolate
2017-09-17 23:27:22.598 class[3910:403]
The element at index 1 is Vanilla
2017-09-17 23:27:22.599 class[3910:403]
The element at index 2 is Raspberry
2017-09-17 23:27:22.600 class[3910:403]
The element at index 3 is Blueberry
```

## Create a Mutable Array from an Immutable Array

Example 6-6 demonstrates the creation of a mutable array from an immutable array. A NSArray called myArrayNames is created and populated (line 7) with four names. A NSMutableArray called myMutableArray is created and populated with the immutable array, myArrayNames (line 11). The length of the mutable array is evaluated by sending a message to the count method (line 14). A for loop (line 17) is implemented to print (line 18) the values of the myMutableArray by sending a message to the objectAtIndex method (line 19).

## Example 6-6

```
1  #import <Foundation/Foundation.h>
2
3  int main(int argc, const char * argv[])
4  {
5  @autoreleasepool {
6  int myArrayNamesLength;
7  NSArray *myArrayNames = [NSArray arrayWithObjects:@"Anita",
8  @"Nagma", @"Rishika", @"Joel", nil];
9  //Create a mutable array from an immutable array using the
10 //arrayWithArray method
11 NSMutableArray *myMutableArray = [NSMutableArray arrayWithArray:
12 myArrayNames];
13 //find the length of the mutable array and print it
14 myArrayNamesLength = [myMutableArray count];
15 NSLog(@"\nmyMutableArray has %i elements", myArrayNamesLength);
16 //print the contents of the mutable array
17 for (int i = 0; i < myArrayNamesLength; i++) {
18     NSLog(@"\nThe element at index %i is %@", i, [myMutableArray
19          objectAtIndex:i]);
20     }
21 return 0;
22 }
23 }
```

### Output for Example 6-6

```
2017-09-19 18:35:53.740 class[8219:403]
myMutableArray has 4 elements
2017-09-19 18:35:53.743 class[8219:403]
The element at index 0 is Anita
2017-09-19 18:35:53.744 class[8219:403]
The element at index 1 is Nagma
2017-09-19 18:35:53.744 class[8219:403]
The element at index 2 is Rishika
2017-09-19 18:35:53.745 class[8219:403]
The element at index 3 is Joel
```

## Array Insertions and Additions

The elements of a NSArray cannot be deleted, and no new elements can be inserted in the array. If you would like to delete and insert elements anywhere in the array, you would need to implement the NSMutableArray. The NSMutableArray is a subclass of the NSArray. Two of the commonly used methods for insertions and additions are insertObject:atIndex and addObject. Example 6-7 demonstrates these method implementations.

In this example, a NSArray is created and populated with string objects (line 7). A NSMutableArray is then created and populated with the objects from the NSArray (line 11).

Next, the length of the NSMutableArray is evaluated (line 15), stored in the myArrayNamesLength int variable, and printed (line 16). Next, the addObject method is implemented in order to add a new object ("Console") to the NSMutableArray (line 18). The length of the NSMutableArray is evaluated again (line 20), stored in the myArrayNamesLength variable, and printed (line 21). Next, the insertObject method is implemented (line 24) to insert the object ("Plant") at index 2 in the NSMutableArray, and the length of the array is calculated (line 27) and printed (line 28). Finally, the contents of the NSMutableArray are printed using the for loop (lines 31 through 34).

## Example 6-7

```
1  #import <Foundation/Foundation.h>
2
3  int main(int argc, const char * argv[])
4  {
5  @autoreleasepool {
6    int myArrayNamesLength;
7    NSArray *myArrayNames = [NSArray arrayWithObjects:@"Table",
8  @"Chair", @"Couch", @"Lamp", nil];
9    //Create a mutable array from an immutable array using the
10 arrayWithArray method
11   NSMutableArray *myMutableArray = [NSMutableArray arrayWithArray:
12 myArrayNames];
13
14   //find the length of the mutable array and print it
15   myArrayNamesLength = [myMutableArray count];
16   NSLog(@"\nmyMutableArray has %i elements", myArrayNamesLength);
17   //add a new object to the mutable array
18   [myMutableArray addObject:@"Console"];
19   // find the length of the array again and print it
20   myArrayNamesLength = [myMutableArray count];
21   NSLog(@"\nmyMutableArray after adding an object has %i
22   elements", myArrayNamesLength);
23   //insert a new object at a particular index
24   [myMutableArray insertObject:@"Plant" atIndex:2];
25   // find the new length of the array again after the insertion
26   and print it
27   myArrayNamesLength = [myMutableArray count];
28   NSLog(@"\nmyMutableArray after insertion has %i elements",
29   myArrayNamesLength);
30   //print the contents of the array
31   for (int i = 0; i < myArrayNamesLength; i++) {
32       NSLog(@"\nThe element at index %i is %@", i,
33                   [myMutableArray objectAtIndex:i]);
34     }
35   return 0;
36 }
37 }
```

**Output for Example 6-7**

```
2017-09-19 18:47:32.180 class[8378:403]
myMutableArray has 4 elements
2017-09-19 18:47:32.183 class[8378:403]
myMutablArray after adding an object has 5 elements
2017-09-19 18:47:32.185 class[8378:403]
myMutableArray after insertion has 6 elements
2017-09-19 18:47:32.186 class[8378:403]
The element at index 0 is Table
2017-09-19 18:47:32.186 class[8378:403]
The element at index 1 is Chair
2017-09-19 18:47:32.187 class[8378:403]
The element at index 2 is Plant
2017-09-19 18:47:32.188 class[8378:403]
The element at index 3 is Couch
2017-09-19 18:47:32.189 class[8378:403]
The element at index 4 is Lamp
2017-09-19 18:47:32.190 class[8378:403]
The element at index 5 is Console
```

## Array Deletions

Some of the commonly used methods for deletions are removeObjectAtIndex, removeLastObject, removeObject, removeObjectIdenticalTo, and removeAllObjects. Example 6-8 demonstrates implementations of these methods. In this example, a NSArray is created and populated with string objects (line 8). A NSMutableArray is created and populated with the objects from the NSArray (line 13). Next, the length of the NSMutableArray is evaluated (line 16), stored in the myArrayNamesLength int variable and printed (line 17). Next, the removeObjectAtIndex method is implemented to remove the object at index 2 of the NSMutableArray (line 19). The length of the NSMutableArray is evaluated (line 21) again, stored in the myArrayNamesLength variable, and printed (line 22). Next, the removeObject method is implemented to remove the first occurrence of an object identified by a given string ("Lynx") in the NSMutableArray (line 25), the length of the array is evaluated (line 29), and it is printed (line 30). Next, the removeObjectIdenticalTo method is implemented to remove all occurrences of an object identified by a given string ("Lion") in the NSMutableArray (line 33), the length of the array is evaluated (line 36) and then printed (line 37). Next, the removeLastObject method is implemented to remove the last object in the NSMutable Array (line 40), the length of the array is evaluated (line 43), and it is printed (line 44). Next, the removeAllObjects method is implemented, which deletes all the objects from the NSMutableArray (line 47). Finally, the contents of the NSMutableArray are printed using the for loop (lines 54 and 57).

## Example 6-8

```
1  #import <Foundation/Foundation.h>
2
3  int main(int argc, const char * argv[])
4  {
5
6  @autoreleasepool {
7  int myArrayNamesLength;
8  NSArray *myArrayNames = [NSArray arrayWithObjects:@"Lion",
9  @"Mountain Lion", @"Cheetah", @"Leopard",@"Cougar", @"Tiger",
10 @"Bobcat",@"Jaguar",@"Lynx", nil];
11 //Create a mutable array from an immutable array using the
12 //arrayWithArray method
13 NSMutableArray *myMutableArray = [NSMutableArray arrayWithArray:
14                                  myArrayNames];
15 //find the length of the mutable array and print it
16 myArrayNamesLength = [myMutableArray count];
17 NSLog(@"\nmyMutablArray has %i elements", myArrayNamesLength);
18 //delete the 3rd element of the mutable array
19 [myMutableArray removeObjectAtIndex:2];
20 // find the new length of the array after deletion and print it
21 myArrayNamesLength = [myMutableArray count];
22 NSLog(@"\nmyMutableArray after deletion has %i elements",
23              myArrayNamesLength);
24 //delete the first occurrence of an object
25 [myMutableArray removeObject:@"Lynx"];
26
27 // find the new length of the array after another deletion and
28 print it
29 myArrayNamesLength = [myMutableArray count];
30 NSLog(@"\nmyMutableArray after another deletion has %i
31      elements", myArrayNamesLength);
32 //delete all occurrences of an object
33 [myMutableArray removeObjectIdenticalTo:@"Lion"];
34 // find the new length of the array after another deletion and
35 print it
36 myArrayNamesLength = [myMutableArray count];
37 NSLog(@"\nmyMutableArray after another deletion has %i
38      elements", myArrayNamesLength);
39 //delete the last object in the array
40 [myMutableArray removeLastObject];
41 // find the new length of the array after another deletion and
42 print it
43 myArrayNamesLength = [myMutableArray count];
44 NSLog(@"\nmyMutableArray after another deletion has %i
45      elements", myArrayNamesLength);
46 //delete all objects from the array
47   [myMutableArray removeAllObjects];
48 // find the new length of the array after another deletion and
49 //print it
50  myArrayNamesLength = [myMutableArray count];
51  NSLog(@"\nmyMutableArray after another deletion has %i
```

```
52                      elements", myArrayNamesLength);
53  //print the contents of the array
54    for (int i =0; i < myArrayNamesLength; i++) {
55        NSLog(@"\nThe element at index %i is %@", i,
56            [myMutableArray objectAtIndex:i]);
57            }
58  return 0;
59  }
60  }
```

### Output for Example 6-8

```
2017-09-19 19:36:57.166 class[8590:403]
myMutableArray has 9 elements
2017-09-19 19:36:57.169 class[8590:403]
myMutableArray after deletion has 8 elements
2017-09-19 19:36:57.170 class[8590:403]
myMutableArray after another deletion has 7 elements
2017-09-19 19:36:57.171 class[8590:403]
myMutableArray after another deletion has 6 elements
2017-09-19 19:36:57.172 class[8590:403]
myMutableArray after another deletion has 5 elements
2017-09-19 19:36:57.173 class[8590:403]
myMutableArray after another deletion has 0 elements
```

## Array Sorting

One of the main purposes of storing the variables in an ordered set as an array is the ease of sorting and searching through the set. Objective-C provides several methods associated with the NSArray class that makes sorting easy. One such method is sortedArrayUsingSelector, which uses a comparator to sort the array in ascending order. The sorting depends on the chosen comparator. In our case, the comparator used is a case-sensitive compare. Example 6-9 creates a NSMutableArray, populates it with the names of trees (line 7), and then creates a NSArray to hold the sorted array (line 21). A variable of type int is created (line11) to store the length (line 12) of the array, which can be used in the two for loops (lines 16 and 26) to count the number of times to loop. The sortedArrayUsingSelector is used to sort the array (lines 23 and 24), and the sorted array is then printed (line 27).

## Example 6-9

```
1   #import <Foundation/Foundation.h>
2
3   int main(int argc, const char * argv[])
4   {
5   @autoreleasepool {
6   //create a mutable array using the arrayWithObjects method
7   NSMutableArray *myMutableArray = [NSMutableArray
8   arrayWithObjects:@"Elm", @"Pine", @"Cedar", @"Alder",
9   @"Beech",@"CrabApple", @"Cypress",nil];
10  //find the number of elements in the array
11  int myArrayNamesLength;
```

```
12  myArrayNamesLength = [myMutableArray count];
13  NSLog(@"\nmyMutableArray has %i elements",
14  myArrayNamesLength);
15  //print the contents of the original array
16  for (int i = 0; i < myArrayNamesLength; i++) {
17  NSLog(@"\nThe element at index %i is %@", i, [myMutableArray
18          objectAtIndex:i]);
19  }
20  //Declare a new NSArray to hold the sorted array
21  NSArray *mySortedArray;
22  //Use the sortedArrayUsingSelector method to sort the array
23  mySortedArray = [myMutableArray
24  sortedArrayUsingSelector:@selector(caseInsensitiveCompare:)];
25  //print the contents of the sorted array
26  for (int i = 0; i < myArrayNamesLength; i++) {
27  NSLog(@"\nThe element at index %i is %@", i, [mySortedArray
28          objectAtIndex:i]);
29  }
30  return 0;
31  }
32  }
```

**Output for Example 6-9**

```
2017-09-18 18:12:21.473 class[7096:403]
myMutableArray has 7 elements
2017-09-18 18:12:21.476 class[7096:403]
The element at index 0 is Elm
2017-09-18 18:12:21.477 class[7096:403]
The element at index 1 is Pine
2017-09-18 18:12:21.478 class[7096:403]
The element at index 2 is Cedar
2017-09-18 18:12:21.480 class[7096:403]
The element at index 3 is Alder
2017-09-18 18:12:21.481 class[7096:403]
The element at index 4 is Beech
2017-09-18 18:12:21.482 class[7096:403]
The element at index 5 is CrabApple
2017-09-18 18:12:21.484 class[7096:403]
The element at index 6 is Cypress
2017-09-18 18:12:21.486 class[7096:403]
The element at index 0 is Alder
2017-09-18 18:12:21.487 class[7096:403]
The element at index 1 is Beech
2017-09-18 18:12:21.487 class[7096:403]
The element at index 2 is Cedar
2017-09-18 18:12:21.488 class[7096:403]
The element at index 3 is CrabApple
2017-09-18 18:12:21.489 class[7096:403]
The element at index 4 is Cypress
2017-09-18 18:12:21.491 class[7096:403]
The element at index 5 is Elm
2017-09-18 18:12:21.492 class[7096:403]
The element at index 6 is Pine
```

143

## NSDate

The NSDate class is an abstract class that helps create, compare, and calculate time intervals. This is a very handy class that not only provides date functionality but also time functionality. In Example 6-10, an NSDate object called today is created (line 7), populated with the date (line 7), and printed (line 9).

## Example 6-10

```
1  #import <Foundation/Foundation.h>
2
3  int main(int argc, const char * argv[])
4  {
5  @autoreleasepool {
6  //Create a date object
7          NSDate *today = [NSDate date];
8  //Print the date object
9          NSLog(@"\nToday's date and time are %@", today);
10      return 0;
11 }
12 }
```

**Output for Example 6-10**

```
2017-09-18 19:25:58.782 class[7254:403]
Today's date and time are 2017-09-19 00:25:58 +0000
```

In Example 6-11 two dates are compared. First, today is created (line 7) as an NSDate object. Another NSDate object, otherDate, is created (line 8) with the contents of a string that is a date and is in the format of YYYY-MM-DD HH:MM:SS ±HHMM. The ±HHMM portion of the format provides the time difference between the GMT and the time zone you are using. The NSComparisonResult is used to compare the today and the otherdate objects (line 13). The NSComparisonResult is a Foundation framework method that holds the value of a comparison (line 13). A switch (line 15) is used to analyze the result of the comparison of today and otherdate. The various possibilities for the case values in the switch are NSOrderedAscending (line 19), which means today is before otherdate; NSOrderedDescending (line 22), which means today comes after otherdate; and NSOrderedSame (line 16), which means today is the same as otherDate.

## Example 6-11

```
1  #import <Foundation/Foundation.h>
2
3  int main(int argc, const char * argv[])
4  {
5      @autoreleasepool {
6  // Create today and other dates for comparison
7      NSDate *today = [NSDate date];
```

```
8      NSDate *otherDate = [NSDate dateWithString: @"2021-03-24
9  10:45:32 +0600"];
10         // Print today's date and time
11     NSLog(@"\nToday's date and time are %@", today);
12  //create a variable to hold the result of the comparison
13     NSComparisonResult result = [today compare:otherDate];
14  //use the switch to analyze the result of the comparison
15     switch (result) {
16       case NSOrderedSame:
17            NSLog(@"The dates are same");
18            break;
19       case NSOrderedAscending:
20            NSLog(@"Today comes before otherdate");
21            break;
22       case NSOrderedDescending:
23            NSLog(@"Today is after otherdate");
24            break;
25       default:NSLog(@"Invalid dates");
26            break;
27     }
28     return 0;
29  }
30  }
```

**Output for Example 6-11**

```
2017-09-18 22:04:02.322 class[7663:403]
Today's date and time are 2017-09-19 03:04:02 +0000
2017-09-18 22:04:02.323 class[7663:403] Today comes before otherdate
```

# NSDictionary

The NSDictionary supports a data set that includes key-value pairs, meaning every key will have a corresponding value. A key-value pair is like having two parallel arrays attached to each other, with the corresponding indices aligned, meaning the index for a specific key will have a value at the same index. If a key has an index 3, then its corresponding value will be at index 3. The keys are unique and are not repeated, whereas the values themselves are not required to be unique. Figure 6-4 illustrates the key-value pair correspondence concept. Just like arrays and strings, dictionaries can be immutable or mutable. The immutable dictionaries cannot be edited, whereas the mutable dictionaries can be edited. By default, NSDictionary is immutable. Its mutable version, NSMutableDictionary, is a subclass of NSDictionary.

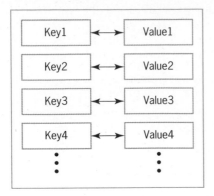

**Figure 6-4**  Key-value pair correspondence
© 2015 Cengage Learning

Example 6-12 demonstrates the creation of a dictionary (line 7) using the
`dictionaryWithObjectsAndKeys` method (line 8), which enters the key
and values directly in the dictionary. Notice that the `for` statement (line 11)
scans the dictionary for the keys (lines 13 and 14).

## Example 6-12

```
1  #import <Foundation/Foundation.h>
2
3  int main(int argc, const char * argv[])
4  {
5  @autoreleasepool {
6  //create a dictionary using the dictionaryWithObjects method
7  NSDictionary *myDictionary = [NSDictionary
8         dictionaryWithObjectsAndKeys:@"Apple", @"1",@"Banana",
9         @"2",@"Cherries", @"3", @"Orange", @"4", nil ];
10 //Print the dictionary
11 for(id key in myDictionary)
12    {
13      NSLog(@"\nmyDictionary contains object: %@ and key: %@",
14           key, [myDictionary objectForKey:key]);
15    }
16 return 0;
17 }
18 }
```

**Output for Example 6-12**

```
2017-09-19 23:18:52.083 class[9154:403]
myDictionary contains object: 3 and key: Cherries
2017-09-19 23:18:52.086 class[9154:403]
myDictionary contains object: 1 and key: Apple
2017-09-19 23:18:52.086 class[9154:403]
```

myDictionary contains object: 4 and key: Orange
2017-09-19 23:18:52.087 class[9154:403]
myDictionary contains object: 2 and key: Banana

---

In Example 6-13, a dictionary is created from two NSArrays, called myKeyArray and myValueArray (line 13). The dictionaryWithObjects method (line 14) populates myKeyArray (created in line 7) with the keys, and myValueArray (created in line 10) holds the values that are associated with the keys of the NSDictionary. The objectForKey (line 18) method is used to print the contents of the dictionary (line 17).

---

## Example 6-13

```
1  #import <Foundation/Foundation.h>
2
3  int main(int argc, const char * argv[])
4  {
5  @autoreleasepool {
6  //Create an array to hold the key
7  NSArray *myKeyArray = [NSArray arrayWithObjects:@"1", @"2", @"3",
8  @"4", @"5", nil];
9  //Create an array to hold the values
10 NSArray *myValueArray = [NSArray arrayWithObjects:@"Violin",
11 @"Piano", @"Guitar", @"Bass", @"Flute", nil];
12 //Create a dictionary from the above arrays
13 NSDictionary *myNSDictionary = [NSDictionary
14         dictionaryWithObjects:myKeyArray forKeys:myValueArray];
15 //Print the dictionary
16 for (id key in myNSDictionary) {
17     NSLog(@"\nmyNSDictionary holds Key: %@  Value: %@", key,
18         [myNSDictionary objectForKey:key]);
19         }
20 return 0;
21 }
22 }
```

### Output for Example 6-13

```
2017-09-19 23:16:24.114 class[9116:403]
myNSDictionary holds Key: Flute  Value: 5
2017-09-19 23:16:24.117 class[9116:403]
myNSDictionary holds Key: Bass  Value: 4
2017-09-19 23:16:24.118 class[9116:403]
myNSDictionary holds Key: Violin  Value: 1
2017-09-19 23:16:24.119 class[9116:403]
myNSDictionary holds Key: Guitar  Value: 3
2017-09-19 23:16:24.120 class[9116:403]
myNSDictionary holds Key: Piano  Value: 2
```

---

As mentioned earlier, dictionaries can be immutable or mutable. The immutable dictionaries cannot be edited and no new key-value pairs can be added to them. If you would like to add or edit key-value pairs in a dictionary, you need to create a mutable dictionary. In Example 6-14, a mutable dictionary is created and then a key-value pair is added to it using the dictionaryWithObjectsAndKeys method (line 8). The contents of this dictionary are printed in line 15.

## Example 6-14

```
1  #import <Foundation/Foundation.h>
2
3  int main(int argc, const char * argv[])
4  {
5  @autoreleasepool {
6  //Create a Mutable dictionary
7  NSMutableDictionary *myDictionary = [NSMutableDictionary
8       dictionaryWithObjectsAndKeys:@"Apple", @"1",@"Banana",
9       @"2",@"Cherries", @"3", @"Orange", @"4", nil ];
10 //Add an element to the mutable dictionary
11 [myDictionary setValue:@"Blueberries" forKey:@"5"];
12 //Using a for loop print the contents of the dictionary
13 for(id key in myDictionary)
14     {
15       NSLog(@"\nmyNSDictionary contains object: %@ and key: %@",
16            key, [myDictionary objectForKey:key]);
17     }
18 return 0;
19 }
20 }
```

**Output for Example 6-14**

```
2017-09-19 23:27:15.966 class[9257:403]
myNSDictionary contains object: 3 and key: Cherries
2017-09-19 23:27:15.969 class[9257:403]
myNSDictionary contains object: 1 and key: Apple
2017-09-19 23:27:15.969 class[9257:403]
myNSDictionary contains object: 4 and key: Orange
2017-09-19 23:27:15.970 class[9257:403]
myNSDictionary contains object: 2 and key: Banana
2017-09-19 23:27:15.971 class[9257:403]
myNSDictionary contains object: 5 and key: Blueberries
```

## HANDS-ON LAB

You have recently been hired as the assistant manager of a small printing company. Your first job is to calculate the next paycheck for the company's six employees. On your first day of work, you are provided with two arrays: one containing the names of all the employees and the other containing the hourly rate of each employee. Every week, the general manager also gives you an array containing the number of hours worked by each of the six employees during that pay period. You now need to write a program that can print the following for each employee:

- Employee's name

- Employee's total pay for that pay period

- Date and time when the pay was calculated

Use a dictionary to calculate the pay for each employee and output the dictionary's key-value pair, as well as the date and time this calculation was made.

## ARRAY CREATION AND POPULATION

1.  Declare three NSArrays named employees, rate and hoursWorked.

    ```
    NSArray *employees = [NSArray arrayWithObjects:
                                    @"Jones Marken",
                                    @"Cynthia Kari",
                                    @"Dexter Hanes",
                                    @"Marcus Bright",
                                    @"Jenna Champel",
                                    @"Alex Meyers",
                                    nil];

    NSArray *rate = [NSArray arrayWithObjects:
                          [NSNumber numberWithDouble:27.89],
                          [NSNumber numberWithDouble:34.89],
                          [NSNumber numberWithDouble:25.78],
                          [NSNumber numberWithDouble:29.67],
                          [NSNumber numberWithDouble:26.8],
                          [NSNumber numberWithDouble:28.99],
                          nil];

    NSArray *hoursWorked = [NSArray arrayWithObjects:
                                    @"36.00",
                                    @"39.00",
                                    @"40.00",
                                    @"49.50",
                                    @"38.50",
                                    @"40.00",
                                    nil];
    ```

Values in mutable dictionaries are stored as objects. For that reason, we store the double variables as NSNumber objects for later use in the mutable dictionary.

## DICTIONARY CREATION AND POPULATION

2.  Because the rate is fixed, we will use the employees array and the rate array to form the dictionary. The dictionary key is the employee name. Its value is the rate. Because the value changes during each pay period, we use a mutable array.

    ```
    NSMutableDictionary *dictionary = [NSMutableDictionary
    dictionaryWithObjects:rate forKeys:employees];
    ```

## VARIABLE DECLARATIONS

3. Create variables that will be used to access components of the dictionary to calculate total pay.

```
NSArray *keys = [dictionary allKeys];
id aKey;
double pay;
NSString *formatPay;
```

## PAY CALCULATION

4. Loop through each value of the dictionary and calculate the pay from the dictionary key (employee name) and the hoursWorked array provided during each pay period.

```
   //Loop through each element of the dictionary
for (int i = 0; i < [employees count]; i++) {
  //Get the key id by index
  aKey = [keys objectAtIndex:i];
    //Calculate the pay
  pay = [[rate objectAtIndex:i] doubleValue] *
       [[hoursWorked objectAtIndex:i] doubleValue];
    //Format the pay to 2 decimal places and store it as a string.
    formatPay = [NSString stringWithFormat:@"%.2f", pay];
    //Update the value in the dictionary for that key
    [dictionary setValue:formatPay forKey:[NSString
              stringWithFormat:@"%@", [employees
              objectAtIndex:i]]];

}
```

5. Create and initialize a variable to hold the date on which the calculations are made.

```
            //Get the current date
            NSDate *today = [NSDate date];
            //Get the date format
            NSDateFormatter * formatDate =
[[NSDateFormatter alloc] init];
            //Get the time format
            NSDateFormatter * formatTime =
[[NSDateFormatter alloc] init];
             //Format the date and time
            [formatDate setDateStyle:NSDateFormatterMediumStyle];
            [formatTime setTimeStyle:NSDateFormatterMediumStyle];
             //Store the date and time as a string
            NSString *date = [formatDate stringFromDate:today];
            NSString  *time = [formatTime stringFromDate:today];
```

## USE A FOR LOOP TO PRINT THE DICTIONARY'S CONTENTS

6. Output the name of each employee in the dictionary with its corresponding pay, as well as the date and time this pay was calculated. Use the format specifier \t to use tabs to format the output.

```
NSLog(@"\nName\t\t\t\tPay\t\t\tDate, Time");
    for (id key in dictionary) {
        NSLog(@"\n%@\t\t$%@\t%@, %@", key, [dictionary
            objectForKey:key], date, time);
        }
```

## SOURCE CODE

```
#import <Foundation/Foundation.h>

int main(int argc, const char * argv[])
{

    @autoreleasepool {

        NSArray *employees = [NSArray arrayWithObjects:
                        @"Jones Marken",
                        @"Cynthia Kari",
                        @"Dexter Hanes",
                        @"Marcus Bright",
                        @"Jenna Champel",
                        @"Alex Meyers",
                        nil];

        NSArray *rate = [NSArray arrayWithObjects:
                        [NSNumber numberWithDouble:27.89],
                        [NSNumber numberWithDouble:34.89],
                        [NSNumber numberWithDouble:25.78],
                        [NSNumber numberWithDouble:29.67],
                        [NSNumber numberWithDouble:26.8],
                        [NSNumber numberWithDouble:28.99],
                        nil];

        NSArray *hoursWorked = [NSArray arrayWithObjects:
                        @"36.00",
                        @"39.00",
                        @"40.00",
                        @"49.50",
                        @"38.50",
                        @"40.00",
                        nil];

        NSMutableDictionary *dictionary = [NSMutableDictionary
dictionaryWithObjects:rate forKeys:employees];

        NSArray *keys = [dictionary allKeys];
        id aKey;
        double pay;
```

```
        NSString *formatPay;

        for (int i = 0; i < [employees count]; i++) {
            aKey = [keys objectAtIndex:i];
            pay = [[rate objectAtIndex:i] doubleValue] *
[[hoursWorked objectAtIndex:i] doubleValue];
            formatPay = [NSString stringWithFormat:@"%.2f", pay];
            [dictionary setValue:formatPay forKey:[NSString
stringWithFormat:@"%@", [employees objectAtIndex:i]]];

        }

        NSDate *today = [NSDate date];
        NSDateFormatter * formatDate = [[NSDateFormatter alloc] init];
        NSDateFormatter * formatTime = [[NSDateFormatter alloc] init];
        [formatDate setDateStyle:NSDateFormatterMediumStyle];
        [formatTime setTimeStyle:NSDateFormatterMediumStyle];
        NSString *date = [formatDate stringFromDate:today];
        NSString  *time = [formatTime stringFromDate:today];

        NSLog(@"\nName\t\t\t\tPay\t\t\tDate, Time");
        for (id key in dictionary) {
            NSLog(@"\n%@\t\t$%@\t%@, %@", key, [dictionary
objectForKey:key], date, time);
        }
    }
    return 0;
}
```

**SAMPLE OUTPUT**

```
2017-09-25 20:52:07.653 Chapter 6 Hands ON[17492:403]
Name          Pay      Date, Time
2017-09-25 20:52:07.653 Chapter 6 Hands ON[17492:403]
Alex Meyers      $1159.60 Sep 25, 2017 8:52:07 PM
2017-09-25 20:52:07.654 Chapter 6 Hands ON[17492:403]
Dexter Hanes      $1031.20 Sep 25, 2017, 8:52:07 PM
2017-09-25 20:52:07.655 Chapter 6 Hands ON[17492:403]
Jones Marken      $1004.04 Sep 25, 2017, 8:52:07 PM
2017-09-25 20:52:07.656 Chapter 6 Hands ON[17492:403]
Cynthia Kari      $1360.71 Sep 25, 2017, 8:52:07 PM
2017-09-25 20:52:07.657 Chapter 6 Hands ON[17492:403]
Marcus Bright      $1468.67  Sep 25, 2017, 8:52:07 PM
2017-09-25 20:52:07.658 Chapter 6 Hands ON[17492:403]
Jenna Champel      $1031.80  Sep 25, 2017, 8:52:07 PM
```

## Summary

- The Foundation framework, as the name suggests, forms the infrastructure of the Objective-C language.

- In Objective-C, you invoke methods by passing a message to the method.

- The `@autoreleasepool` statement facilitates the compiler's handling of memory management. It frees the developer from allocating and releasing objects.

- `NSString` is a predefined class in the Foundation framework that handles strings that are immutable. The `NSMutableString` class handles mutable strings.

- The `NSArray` class handles arrays that are immutable. The `NSMUtableArray` class handles arrays that can be edited—that is, arrays that you can alter by adding or deleting elements.

- The `NSDate` object provides date and time functionality, including methods for finding the current date and time or the interval between two times.

- The `NSDictionary` object is an Objective-C version of the enumerated type. It stores a key-value pair. If you need the ability to edit a dictionary, you can use the `NSMutableDictionary` object, which lets you either insert or delete dictionary items.

## Exercises

1. State which of the following message calls are valid. If invalid, explain why.

   a. `this.length();`

   b. `[str lowercaseString];`

   c. `[str substringFromIndex 10];`

   d. `[myStr stringByAppendingString:"Hello World! "];`

   e. `NSArray * movies = [NSArray: nil, nil, nil, nil, nil];`

   f. `NSMutableArray *myMutableArray = [NSMutableArray arrayWithArray: movies];`

   g. `NSString* arrayCount = [myMutableArray count];`

2. Mark each of the following statements as true or false. Correct the false statements.

   a. The Foundation framework has a root object class called `NSString` that provides support to some basic utility classes such as `NSArray` and `NSDictionary`.

   b. All Objective-C programming is done in the Foundation framework.

   c. In Objective-C, methods can be invoked by calling them using the dot notation.

d. Two `NSString` objects can be concatenated using the `stringByAppendingString` method.

e. A string created using the `NSString` object is immutable by default.

f. The indices of an array start at 1.

g. The `count` method provided for `NSArray` gives the value of the last index.

h. The `NSDictionary` stores data in key-value pairs.

3. Write functions that have the following characteristics:

a. Has a word and a sentence as parameters, counts the number of occurrences of the word in the sentence, and then outputs the result.

b. Has an array of numbers as a parameter and returns the highest number in the array.

c. Has a dictionary and a value as a parameter, and returns the number of keys sharing that same value in the dictionary.

d. Has a dictionary as a parameter and returns the first key with no value in the dictionary.

e. Has a dictionary as a parameter and outputs all the values of the dictionary as a string, with each value separated by a comma.

4. Use the following code to answer Questions a through h, below:

```
NSString *s = @"I like Programming in Objective C";
NSArray *stringArray = [s componentsSeparatedByString:@" "];
NSString * newString1 = [s substringFromIndex:7];
NSString * newString2 = [s substringWithRange:NSMakeRange(7,7)];
NSString *newString3 = [s substringWithRange:NSMakeRange(22,9)];
NSString *newString4 = [newString2 stringByAppendingFormat:@"
                            %@", newString3];
NSString *newString5 = [NSString stringWithFormat:@"%@ %@",
                            newString3, newString2];
NSString *newString6 = [stringArray objectAtIndex:3];
NSString *newString7 = [s description];
NSString *newString8 = [stringArray description];
```

What is the value of each of the following variables?

a. newString1

b. newString2

c. newString3

d. newString4

e. newString5

f. newString6

g. newString7

h. NewString8

5. Define the following terms:

   a. Foundation framework
   b. Object
   c. `@autoreleasepool`

6. Write the Objective-C method calls described below:

   a. Create a `NSArray`, and then copy it into an `NSMutableArray`. `NSString str1` holds the first name and `NSString str2` holds the last name.
   b. Create a `NSString` object, `str3`, that contains both the first name and last name. `NSString` is a static object. Transform this object so that the word "and" is inserted at the third character. For example, if the value of the `NSString` object is `"TomJerry"`, after the transformation its value will be `"TomandJerry"`.

7. What's the output for the following code:

```
#import <Foundation/Foundation.h>
int main(int argc, const char * argv[])
{
    @autoreleasepool {
        NSString *string = @"We are geniuses!";
        NSString *substring;
        int strLen;

        strLen = [string length];

        NSLog(@"\nYour string is %@ ", string);
        NSLog(@"\nThe length of your string is %i", strLen);
        substring = [string substringFromIndex:7];
        NSLog(@"\nThe substring is %@", substring);
        substring = [string uppercaseString];
        NSLog(@"\nYour string in upper case is %@", substring);

    }
    return 0;
}
```

8. What is the value of `str` in the following code?

```
#import <Foundation/Foundation.h>
int main(int argc, const char * argv[])
{
    @autoreleasepool {
        NSString * str1 = @"Santa Barbara has ";
        NSString *str2 = @"beautiful houses";
```

```
            str1 = [str1 stringByAppendingString:str2];
            NSString* str = [str1 substringFromIndex:6];
        }
        return 0;
    }
```

9.  Write statements that accomplish the following tasks:

    a. Declare an array called `movies` and initialize it with the strings: `Twilight`, `Safe House`, `Prison Break`, `Internship`, `Mission Impossible`

    b. Print out the 3rd element of the array (with index 2).

    c. Convert the array to a mutable array called `mutMovies`.

    d. Delete the 4th element of the array (with index 3).

    e. Convert all array elements to uppercase.

    f. Reinitialize the 5th element of the array (with index 4) to "24".

    g. Declare another array called `prices` and initialize it to 24.00, 13.50, 12.99, 6.70, 7.99.

    h. Declare a dictionary using the array `mutMovies` as the keys and the array `prices` as values.

    i. Print the value and key for each position in the dictionary.

10. Given the following code

    ```
    NSSting *s = "Welcome to my world";
    NSArray * arr =  [[NSArray arrayWithObjects:@"Java", @"Php",
    @"Objective-c", nil]];
    ```

    Describe the function of the following lines of code, and give an example of how they can be used with the variable above. Include the result of the operation.

    a. `[s UPPERCASE];`

    b. `[s LOWERCASE];`

    c. `[s substringFromIndex:11];`

    d. `[arr length]`

    e. `[arr objectAtIndex:2]`

# Programming Exercises

1.  Suppose that the last two digits of a student ID number indicate the student's major, and that the following is a list of sample student ID numbers: JHGUS01, PHYBO02, GFIKH98, JGFTB54, RBWKG87, and HGTVN77. Write a program that prints an ID number and major for each student. Here is the list of major codes:

    - 01 Undecided

    - 02 English

    - 03 Biochemistry

- 98 Chemistry

- 54 Economics

- 87 Computer Science

- 77 Mathematics

2. Create a NSArray containing the following names: John, Bella, Stephanie, Leonardo, Michelangelo, Tom, Brad. All of these students have recently been awarded their doctorates. Update this array so that the word Dr. is prefixed to the names—for example, Dr. John, Dr. Bella, and so on. Print this array.

3. Create objects to store both a person's first and last name, and another object to store the person's middle name. Insert the middle name, which is the second object, between the first and last name of the first object so that the person's full name (first, middle and last) is now in a new third object. Print the person's three initials—that is, the first letter of the first, middle, and last names. Next, print the alternate initials-that is, the last letter of the first name, the last letter of the middle name, and the last letter of the last name.

4. Tom, a teacher at an elementary school, has organized an after-school recreation class. He asks you to create a program that will allow him to track which students attend the class. The class only accepts 15 students each day. Use an array to store the names, and print them alphabetically.

5. Revise the program from Programming Exercise 4 so that, in addition to storing the student's name, the program also stores the activity each student participates in. Assume that each student's name will be unique, and use an NSDictionary object in your solution.

   The possible activities are:

   - basketball

   - floor hockey

   - arts

   - checkers

6. Create a NSArray that stores the following five birth dates:

   - 27 September, 1988

   - 14 October, 1996

   - 23 July, 1991

   - 17 October, 1995

   - 25 December, 1991

   Calculate the age for a person born on each of these dates and print the ages from youngest to oldest.

7. Create an array containing the following words: Penny, Sheldon, is, faints, an, when, awesome, giving, friend, speeches. Use a single for loop to:

   a. Concatenate all the even entries and print the resulting NSString with appropriate spacing.

   b. Concatenate all the odd entries and print the resulting NSString with appropriate spacing.

   c. Insert the string "a WiFi stealer and" as an NSString at index 9 in the string that is holding the even entries and print the resulting string with appropriate spacing

8. Dr. Bikovsky creates a secure password for himself every year by arranging the names of his graduating doctorate students in ascending order and using the fifth letter from each name. For student names that are shorter than five letters long, he appends as many asterisks as necessary, for a total of five characters. The NSArray contains John, Bella, Stephanie, Leonardo, Michelangelo, Tom, Brad as the names of his graduating students this year. Print his password.

9. Write a program that outputs letters A through Z in a 5-by-5 square. (One line will have six letters.)

   a. The program should then prompt the user to compose a word or sentence with the letters displayed.

   b. Create an array whose elements are the individual letters in the word.

   c. The program should then output the user input as follows:
      1. Convert the entry to lowercase characters.

      2. Convert the entry to uppercase characters.

      3. Convert every other letter of the word to uppercase and the rest of the letters to lowercase.

      4. Include number of letters in the entry.

10. A palindrome is a word, phrase, number, or other sequence of units that can be read the same way in either direction, regardless of punctuations. One example of a palindrome is *step on no pets*. Write a program that prompts the user for an input, string or integer. Then write a program that determines if the input is a palindrome.

## Business Case Study

Building on the Business Case Study in Chapter 5, do the following:

- Create a NSMutableDictionary to hold the type of balloon and its price.

- Create a date object to print the current date.

- Create a NSString for the names of the customers.

- Use nested for loops to print the user-selected balloons and the tasks/actions performed.

# Object-Oriented Programming

In this chapter you will

- ◎ Create classes and objects
- ◎ Differentiate between class and instance methods
- ◎ Create @interface and @implementation files
- ◎ Use messages to communicate with objects
- ◎ Create properties
- ◎ Synthesize properties so the compiler can generate the setter and getter methods
- ◎ Create default and custom initializers
- ◎ Create description methods that can be used to print an object
- ◎ Apply inheritance to classes in Objective-C

Thus far we have learned some procedural concepts in Objective-C programming. Now it's time to examine some object-oriented programming concepts, such as encapsulation, instantiation, objects, and methods. In a procedural language, the programmer thinks in terms of problems, then proceeds to solve the problem by writing code that solves the problem step-by-step. By contrast, in object-oriented programming, we first think in terms of the objects required to perform specific tasks and then create mechanisms for implementing these objects using the appropriate data types and functions.

## Encapsulation, Objects, Instances, and Methods

Object-oriented programming is built on the concept of **encapsulation**, which is a process of combining data elements, as well as a set of functions that are operational on these data elements, to create a robust, secure object. Encapsulation allows the programmer to limit access to the data within a class in a manner that provides the most feasible data security and protection. Objects are an extension of the concept of structures. Structures combine a set of data elements in one unit. Objects not only combine data elements, but also the operations/functions performed on these data elements.

An **object** is an instance of a class. A **class** creates a description of the data and the operations on this data for the object. A class is similar to a blueprint of a building, whereas the building is the object. Another analogy is that of a template or a prototype that can create multiple instances called objects. Creating an instance or an object from a class is like taking a snapshot of the class in the time continuum.

To think of it another way, an object is something that can be visualized, such as a Yorkshire puppy, whereas a class is an abstract concept. If you say a particular Yorkshire puppy is a type of dog, the class is dog and the instance of the Dog class (that is, the object derived from the Dog class) is a particular Yorkshire puppy. A class consists of data members and a set of operations/functions. The operations/functions are constructors and methods. A function, when created in a class, is called a method.

**Constructors** are special types of methods that facilitate the creation of objects. See the UML diagram in Figure 7-1. The left-hand part of the figure depicts a generic UML diagram for a class. It consists of a name, some data attributes, constructors to create objects/instances of the class, and methods that operate on the data attributes. The right-hand part of the figure is an example UML diagram of a Dog class. The data members, or attributes, of the Dog class are breed, height, color, and age, while the operations on these variables (barking, wagging tail, whining) would either access or manipulate these variables.

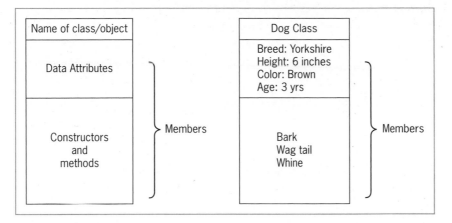

**Figure 7-1**   UML Diagram of a generic class and a specific example, the Dog class
© 2015 Cengage Learning

# Instance and Class Methods

A function in a class is called a **method**. There are two main types of methods in an Objective-C class: class methods and instance methods. Methods that can only be invoked after the instantiation of a class are called **instance methods**. The methods that can be executed irrespective of the instantiation of the class are called **class methods**. The instance methods are identified by a minus (–) sign before the method name, whereas class methods are identified by a plus (+) sign, as seen in the following code:

```
1  -(void) bark;      //------Instance method
2  +(void) DogBark:(NSString*) dogName;      //------class method
```

Line 1 is an instance method called bark with no parameters. Line 2 is a class method called DogBark with dogName as a parameter.

**Note**: Instance variables are also called data members or attributes. Instance methods are also called method members of a class or an object.

## Method Declaration

In Java, a declaration would look as follows:

```
(returnType) methodNamePart1namePart2(datatype parameter1,
datatype parameter2...)
```

In Objective-C, methods are declared using the format shown in Figure 7-2.

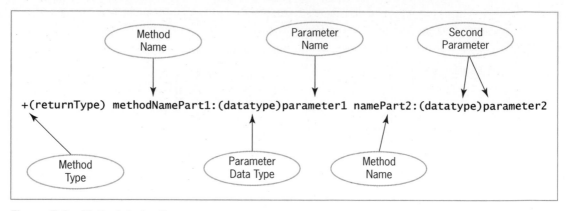

**Figure 7-2**    Method declaration
© 2015 Cengage Learning

In Objective-C, if a method has multiple parameters, then a long meaningful name can be given to the method and the name can be split into meaningful sections followed by a colon and then a parameter. A colon precedes each parameter. In essence, the method name is split into smaller sections, with meaningful names used to represent the parameters. This naming technique makes it easier for a developer to make sense of a declaration.

Let's look at an example of a method:

```
-(double) calculateBodyMass: (double) mass Weight(double): weight
```

In this example, the name of the method is `calculateBodyMassWeight`. This name is split meaningfully into two sections. Each section is followed by a colon and then the parameter. The first section, `calculateBodyMass`, corresponds to the parameter called `mass`. The second section, `Weight`, corresponds to the parameter called `weight`.

## Calling/Invoking Methods — Messaging

Calling, or invoking, methods in a class in Objective-C is done using the messaging system. In the traditional dot notation methodology that is used to invoke methods in a class, the name of the method follows the object name, with a dot in between, as seen in the following code:

```
yorkie.bark();
```

By contrast, an Objective-C message uses the following format:

```
[yorkie bark];
```

The `yorkie` is called the **receiver** and `bark` is called the **sender**. In other words, the object is the receiver and the method is the sender. Methods send and receive messages to and from the object, hence providing a means of communication with the object.

```
[receiver  sender];
```

Passing a parameter to the `yorkie` method would look as follows:

```
[yorkie bark:mimi];
```

Here mimi (the name of the dog) is the parameter to the bark method in the yorkie object. If you were to pass several parameters, the format would be as follows:

```
[yorkie bark:mimi anotherbark: lukas anotherbark: jojo];
```

Here the name of the method, barkanotherbarkanotherbark, has been split into smaller meaningful sections to allow for the parameters mimi, lukas, and jojo.

Syntactically, you could have written the preceding method with a shorter method name such as bark. In that case, the method call could look like this:

```
[yorkie bark: mimi :lukas :jojo];
```

However, the preceding statement is considered bad practice. Instead, you should have a section name for each parameter.

## Class Creation: @interface and @implementation

Before we delve any deeper into object-oriented programming concepts and examples, we need to learn about the @interface and the @implementation files, in addition to methods and the messaging mechanism.

When you create a class, you need to inform the compiler of the class's data members (also called instance variables) and the class's methods (also called operations). The instance variables and the method declarations are found in the **@interface file**, which is also known as the **header file**. Through the use of this file, Objective-C hides the implementation details of the code from the header declarations of the instance variables and the methods. That is, the declarations for the instance variables and the method headers go in the @interface file, with the actual implementation of the instance variables and the methods go in the **@implementation file**.

The @interface file has the extension .h, which is short for "header file." The first declaration in the @interface file is for the parent class. This is where the compiler learns about the class's inheritance information. The syntax for the @interface file is as follows:

```
SYNTAX

@interface myClass: parentClass
{
Instance variables also called data members.
}
Method declarations
@end
```

**Note:** In Objective-C, a variable and a method can have the same name.

Within the curly braces, the instance variables are declared the same way any other variables are declared. Following the instance variables are the method declarations, which only contain the headers for the methods. The actual code—that is, the implementation of the methods declared in the @interface file—goes in the @implementation file. The syntax for the @implementation file is as follows:

**SYNTAX**

```
@implementation myClass: parentClass
    Methods
@end
```

# Creating the @interface and @implementation Files

To create the @interface and @implementation files:

1. In the main menu, click **File ▶ New ▶ File**. This opens the "Choose a template for your new file" window.

2. In the left pane, under "iOS," click **Cocoa Touch**, and then click **Objective–C class**, as shown in Figure 7-3.

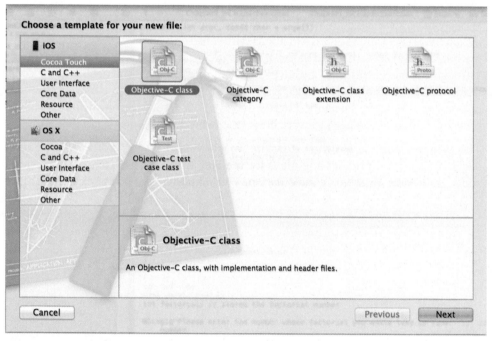

**Figure 7-3**    Choose a template for your new file window

3. Click the **Next** button. This opens the "Choose options for your new file" window.

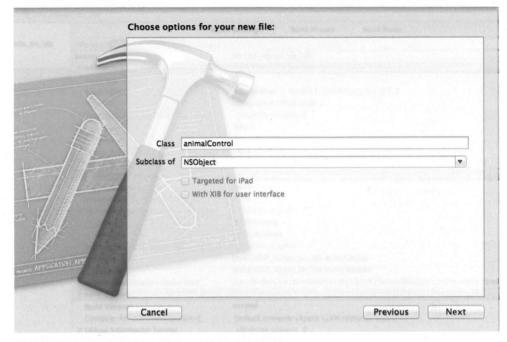

**Figure 7-4**   Choose options for your new file window

4.   In the Class box type **animalControl**, in the Subclass of box select **NSObject**, as shown in Figure 7-4, and then click the **Next** button.

## Creating a Simple Dog Class

In Examples 7-1, 7-2, and 7-3, the Dog class is created. The examples use three separate files. First, there's the @interface file, with the .h extension, which holds the instance variables and the method declarations for the class. Second, there's the @implementation file, with the .m extension, where the methods and the instance variables of the @interface file are implemented. Finally, there's the main file, where execution begins and the objects are created. The Dog class has breed, height, color, and weight as the instance variables and whine, bark, and wagtail as methods.

The @interface file has to be made known to the compiler and to the file that is creating an object from the class. For that reason, the @interface ( .h) file is imported into the @implementation file and the main function.

Example 7-1 contains the @interface file. In line 3, the Dog class inherits from the NSObject class:

## Example 7-1

```
1   //This is the @interface/header file called Dog.h
2   #import <Foundation/Foundation.h>
3   @interface Dog : NSObject
4   {
5       NSString *breed;
6       double height;
7       NSString *color;
8       double weight;
9   }
10  -(void) bark;
11  -(void) wagTail;
12  -(void) whine;
13
14  @end
15
```

The instance variables breed, height, color, and weight are declared in lines 5–8. Lines 10–12 contain the method declarations for bark, wagtail, and whine. The minus sign (-) before the method declarations indicates that the methods are instance methods. Notice how the instance variables are declared inside the curly brackets, whereas the methods are declared outside the curly brackets.

Next, in Example 7-2, we see the @implementation file, in which the methods bark (lines 6 through 9), wagtail (lines 11 through 14), and whine (lines 15 through 18) are implemented.

## Example 7-2

```
1   //This is the @implementation file called Dog.m
2   #import "Dog.h"
3
4   @implementation Dog
5
6   -(void) bark
7   {
8       NSLog(@"\nBow Wow … Bow Wow");
9   }
10
11  -(void) wagTail
12  {
13      NSLog(@"\nI like you");
14  }
15  -(void) whine
16  {
17      NSLog(@"\nEeeen… Eeeeen");
18  }
19  @end
```

Note that the header file has to be imported into the implementation file. This happens in line 3.

Example 7-3 shows the actual implementation of the methods in the `main` file.

## Example 7-3

```
1   //This is the main file called the main.m
2   #import <Foundation/Foundation.h>
3   #import "Dog.h"
4   int main(int argc, const char * argv[])
5   {
6
7       @autoreleasepool {
8
9           // create a yorkie object of the dog class
10          Dog *yorkie = [[Dog alloc] init];
11
12          //run the bark method
13          [yorkie bark];
14
15          // run the whine method
16          [yorkie whine];
17
18          //run the wag tail method
19          [yorkie wagTail];
20
21      }
22      return 0;
23  }
```

In the `main` function, the `yorkie` object is created from the `Dog` class by allocating and initializing the object (line 10). The methods `bark`, `whine`, and `wagtail` are invoked from the `main` function using the messaging mechanism in lines 13, 16, and 19, respectively. In other words the message of `bark`, `whine`, and `wagtail` are communicated to the `yorkie`, which is the object.

## Accessing Instance Variables

The mechanism that ensures that the instance variables are not accessible outside the class is called **abstraction**. Data in these variables can be accessed using the accessor/getter and mutator/setter methods. The accessor/getter methods get the value of the instance variables from the object, whereas the mutator/setter methods change or set the value of the instance variables in order to maintain abstraction and encapsulation.

Two of the getter methods for the `Dog` class are listed here:

```
1  -(NSString *) getBreed
2  {
3  return breed;
4  }
5  -(double) getHeight
```

```
6 {
7 return height;
8 }
```

**Note**: The getter methods only return the current value of the instance variable (lines 3 and 7).

Two of the setter methods for the **Dog** class are shown in Figure 7-5.

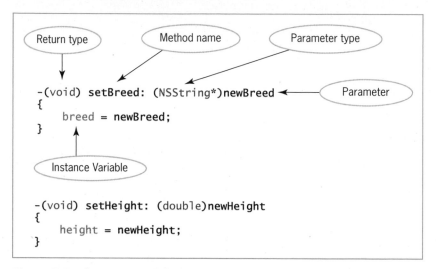

**Figure 7-5**   Setter methods for **Dog** class
© 2015 Cengage Learning

The setter methods set the instance variables to the value of the parameter; for example, in the **setBreed** method the parameter is **newBreed** and the instance variable **breed** is set to the new value passed to the method.

## Methods and Properties

The setter and getter methods, also known as the properties, are used to access instance variables. **Properties** provide access to the encapsulated data members of an object. In essence, properties are methods, or operations, on an object's data members.

Each instance variable can have a property associated with it, and with the @**property** directive used to set the property. You can specify properties individually in the code, or you can let the compiler generate them. There are two steps to having the compiler generate properties. The first step is to use the @**property** directive to declare the property. The second step is to use the @**synthesize** directive to autogenerate the setter and getter methods.

The syntax for the @property declaration is as follows:

169

**SYNTAX**

```
@property (optional attributes) dataType  instanceVariableName
```

The Dog class property directive for the first two instance variables is as follows:

```
@property NSString *breed;
@property double height;
```

The next step is to implement the property using the @synthesize directive. The syntax for the @synthesize directive is as follows:

**SYNTAX**

```
@synthesize instanceVariableName
```

The Dog class synthesize directive for the breed and height instance variables is as follows:

```
@property (getter = getBreed, setter = setBreed:) NSString *breed;
@property (getter = getHeight, setter = setHeight:) double height;
```

The @property directive gives the option of providing the names for the setter and the getter methods that the compiler will autogenerate. In this case, we have specified names that begin with the prefixes get and set.

The property generation code for the breed instance variable is shown in Figure 7-6.

```
-(NSString *) getBreed
{                          ⎫
    return breed;          ⎬ Getter Method
}                          ⎭

-(void) setBreed: (NSString*)newBreed
{                          ⎫
    breed = newBreed;      ⎬ Setter Method
}                          ⎭
```

**Figure 7-6**  Property generation code for the breed instance variable

## Initializers/Constructors

In an object-oriented programming language, initializers are similar to constructors in that they are used to instantiate (that is, to create) objects. The creation of an object is a two-step process:

1. Allocate memory for the object.

2. Initialize the instance variables of the object.

The syntax for object creation is shown in Figure 7-7.

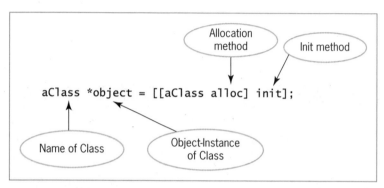

**Figure 7-7**    Format for object creation
© 2015 Cengage Learning

The allocation message is sent to the class. As a result, memory for the object is allocated. Next, the initialization message is sent to the object to initialize the object's instance variables.

## Default `init`

Objective-C classes ultimately inherit from the NSObject and hence have some common methods that can be used by all objects. One such method is the `init` method. The default `init` method initializes the instance variables of a class to nil or zero, depending on the variables' data type. When we created the yorkie dog object, we used the default `init` method, as shown here:

```
// create a yorkie object of the dog class
Dog *yorkie = [[Dog alloc] init];
```

In the yorkie object, the default `init` method initializes all the instance variables (breed, height, color, and weight) to null or zero, depending on the data type. Suppose we print the breed of the Yorkie object in the main function using the getBreed method, as follows:

```
//print the breed of the Yorkie
NSLog(@"The breed of the dog is %@",[yorkie getBreed]);
```

The output of this code would be null, as shown here, because the `init` method initialized the instance variable breed to null:

**2012-09-30 12:09:04.786 Chapter 7[3700:403] The breed of the dog is (null)**

# Custom `init`

You can create custom `init` methods that override the default `init` method. The syntax of an `init` method is as follows:

```
SYNTAX
-(id) init
{
    if (self == [super init])
        {
        //do the following
        }
    return self;
}
```

The super `init` is always called to ensure the instance variables of the parent class are initialized, where super `init` is the `init` method of the parent class. The term "parent class" is explained in the discussion of inheritance, later in this chapter.

Let's create a custom `init` method for the `Dog` class that initializes the `breed`, `height`, `weight`, and `color` of the `dog` object:

```
-(id) initwithbreed:(NSString *) newBreed
               :(double) newHeight
               :(NSString *) newColor
               :(double) newWeight
{
    if (self == [super init]) {
        [self setBreed:newBreed];
        [self setHeight:newHeight];
        [self setColor:newColor];
        [self setWeight:newWeight];

    }
    return self;
}
```

In this method, all the instance variables are initialized to specific values passed as parameters to the `init` method. Having specified the setter method names, we are able to use these names to invoke or send a message to the object, specifying the name of the setter methods for each of the variables.

Now let's create a new `Dog` object using the custom `init` method, with shihtzu as the `breed`, 8.0 as the `height`, White as the `color`, and 11.0 as the `weight`, as seen in the following code:

```
// create a shihtzu object of the dog class using the custom init
Dog *shihtzu = [[Dog alloc] initwithbreed:@"Shihtzu" :8.0
                                        :@"White" :11.0];
```

To print the breed and the height of the **dog** object, we use the following lines of code:

```
//print the breed and the height of the shihtzu dog
NSLog(@"The breed of the dog is %@ and the height is %.21f
            inches" ",[shihtzu getBreed], [shihtzu getHeight]);
```

The preceding statement sends the **getBreed** message and the **getHeight** message to the Shihtzu object. The **NSLog** statement then prints those values. The **%.21f** format specifier limits **height** to two digit significant digits. The output is as follows:

```
2017-09-30 12:14:35.868 Chapter 7[3817:403] The breed of the dog is Shihtzu
and the height is 8.00
```

## Using the description Method to Print an Object

The **description** method of the **NSObject** in the foundation framework offers a feature that allows you to print an object directly using the name of the object. This is similar to using the **toString()** method in Java. You first need to declare the **description** method in the **@interface** file and then create it in the **@implementation** file. Code placed in the body of the **description** method defines the object. When the name of the object appears in an **NSLog** statement, the **description** method is invoked and the string's contents, returned by the **description** method, are printed. For example, the **description** method for the **Dog** class would look like this:

```
-(NSString *) description
{
    NSString *objDescription = [NSString
stringWithFormat:@"\nBreed: %@ \nHeight: %.2f"
@"\nColor: %@\nWeight: %.2f",breed,height,color,weight];
    return objDescription;
}
```

**Description** methods can return a custom string that is formatted with a combination of the object's instance variables. In the preceding code, we used the **\n** newline character to print each of the instance variables on a new line. Also, the variables that are of type **double** are formatted to two decimal points.

Printing the **shihtzu** dog using **NSLog** would send the description method to the **shihtzu** object, as follows:

```
//print the shihtzu object that sends the description method to the
shihtzu object
NSLog(@"The description of the Shihtzu object is%@ ",shihtzu);
```

The output for this code is as follows:

```
2017-09-30 12:49:25.079 Chapter 7[4101:403] The description of the
Shihtzu object is
Breed: Shihtzu
Height: 8.00
Color: White
Weight: 11.00
```

**Note:** If no **description** method has been created, then printing the object directly by its name will print the object's memory location.

Figure 7-8 contains the UML diagram for the Dog class and its two objects, yorkie and shihtzu.

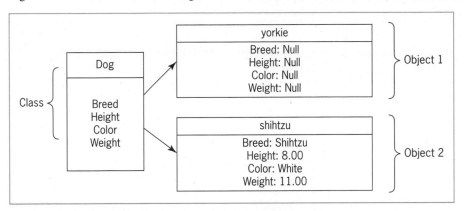

**Figure 7-8**    UML diagram for the Dog class and its two objects
© 2015 Cengage Learning

## Complete Code for the Dog Class

We're ready to put all the code together. Example 7-4 shows the complete @interface file.

### Example 7-4

```
1   #import <Foundation/Foundation.h>
2   @interface Dog : NSObject
3   {
4      NSString *breed;
5      double height;
6      NSString *color;
7      double weight;
8   }
9
10  -(id) initwithbreed:(NSString *) newBreed
11                    :(double) newHeight
12                    :(NSString *) newColor
13                    :(double) newWeight;
14
15  @property (getter = getBreed, setter = setBreed:) NSString
16  *breed;
17  @property (getter = getHeight, setter = setHeight:) double
18  height;
19  @property (getter = getColor, setter = setColor:) NSString
20  *color;
21  @property (getter = getWeight, setter = setWeight:) double
22  weight;
23
24  -(NSString *) description;
25  -(void) bark;
26  -(void) wagTail;
27  -(void) whine;
28  @end
```

173

Example 7-5 contains the implementation file for the Dog class.

## Example 7-5

```
1   #import "Dog.h"
2   @implementation Dog
3   @synthesize breed;
4   @synthesize height;
5   @synthesize color;
6   @synthesize weight;
7
8   -(id) initwithbreed:(NSString *) newBreed
9                      :(double) newHeight
10                     :(NSString *) newColor
11                     :(double) newWeight
12  {
13      if (self == [super init]) {
14          [self setBreed:newBreed];
15          [self setHeight:newHeight];
16          [self setColor:newColor];
17          [self setWeight:newWeight];
18
19      }
20      return self;
21  }
22
23  -(NSString *) description
24  {
25      NSString *objDescription = [NSString
26  stringWithFormat:@"\nBreed: %@"
    @"\nHeight: %.2f" @"\nColor: %@"
    @"\nWeight: %.2f",breed,height,color,weight];
27      return objDescription;
28  }
29
30  -(void) bark
31  {
32      NSLog(@"\nBow Wow … Bow Wow");
33  }
34  -(void) wagTail
35  {
36      NSLog(@"\nI like you");
37  }
38  -(void) whine
39  {
40      NSLog(@"\nEeeen… Eeeeen");
41  }
42
43  @end
```

Finally, Example 7-6 contains the main file for the Dog class.

## Example 7-6

```
1  #import <Foundation/Foundation.h>
2  #import "Dog.h"
3  int main(int argc, const char * argv[])
4  {
5
6      @autoreleasepool {
7
8          // create a yorkie object of the dog class using the
9  default init
10         Dog *yorkie = [[Dog alloc] init];
11
12         //print the breed of the Yorkie
13         NSLog(@"The breed of the dog is %@",[yorkie getBreed]);
14
15         // create a shihtzu object of the dog class using the
16  custom init
17         Dog *shihtzu = [[Dog alloc]
18  initwithbreed:@"Shihtzu" :8.0 :@"White" :11.0];
19
20         //print the breed and the height of the shihtzu dog
21         NSLog(@"The breed of the dog is %@ and the height
22  is %.2lf inches",[shihtzu getBreed], [shihtzu getHeight]);
23
24         //print the shihtzu object that sends the description
25  method to the shihtzu object
26         NSLog(@"The description of the Shihtzu object is%@",
27  shihtzu);
28
29         //run the bark method
30         [yorkie bark];
31
32         // run the whine method
33         [yorkie whine];
34
35         //run the wag tail method
36         [yorkie wagTail];
37
38     }
39     return 0;
40  }
```

The output for the program is shown here.

**Output for Examples 7-4, 7-5 and 7-6**

```
2017-09-30 15:56:33.853 Chapter 7[4503:403] The breed of the dog is (null)
2017-09-30 15:56:33.856 Chapter 7[4503:403] The breed of the dog is Shihtzu
and the height is 8.00 inches
```

```
2017-09-30 15:56:33.857 Chapter 7[4503:403] The description of the
Shihtzu object is
Breed: Shihtzu
Height: 8.00
Color: White
Weight: 11.00
2017-09-30 15:56:33.858 Chapter 7[4503:403]
Bow Wow … Bow Wow
2017-09-30 15:56:33.859 Chapter 7[4503:403]
Eeeen… Eeeeen
2017-09-30 15:56:33.860 Chapter 7[4503:403]
I like you
```

# Inheritance

**Inheritance** is an important feature of object-oriented programming that defines an "is-a" relationship between two classes. Classes in Objective-C ultimately inherit from the NSObject class. In other words, every Objective-C class *is a* NSObject.

Inheritance in programming is very similar to inheritance in real life. For example, a child may inherit facial features and mannerisms from parents. Similarly, a class can inherit attributes and operations from a parent class. The inheriting class is called the **child**. The class from which it inherits is called the **parent**.

The child class inherits the attributes and the operations of the parent class, but it can also have a set of attributes and operations of its own. Inheritance in Objective-C allows for inheritance only from a single parent, meaning an object cannot have two parents. Figure 7-9 emphasizes this point. However, a parent can inherit from another parent. In other words, as seen Figure 7-10, a child can inherit from another child.

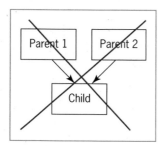

**Figure 7-9**   Inheritance from two parents is not allowed
© 2015 Cengage Learning

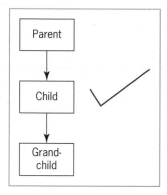

**Figure 7-10**   A child inheriting from another child is allowed
© 2015 Cengage Learning

**Note:** When we talk about a child class inheriting from a parent class, we sometimes also say that a child class is derived from the parent class.

## First Tier of Inheritance: Inheritance from NSObject

In this chapter we have so far looked at single level inheritance, in which all classes ultimately inherit from the NSObject.

Now we will drop one step lower in the hierarchy to examine how inheritance works with classes. We will learn about inheritance and apply it one level at a time.

As an example, we will discuss an imaginary class called iDevice, which holds features that are common to the iPhone and to iPadDevices such as the iPad. Note that this is just a conceptual example designed to illustrate characteristics of inheritance, and does not have any relation to real objects and classes in Objective-C.

In our example, iDevice inherits from the NSObject, and the iPhone and iPad inherit from the iDevice. The iPadMini inherits from the iPad as seen in Figure 7-11.

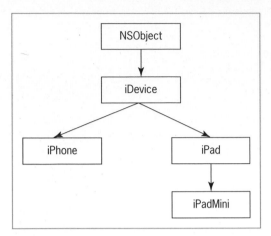

**Figure 7-11**    Conceptual example of an inheritance structure
© 2015 Cengage Learning

Now suppose the iDevice has length, width, and iName as instance variables and is a subclass of NSObject as defined in the @interface directive shown in Figure 7-12.

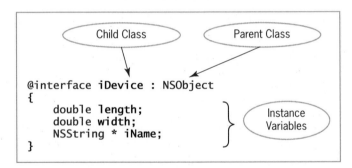

**Figure 7-12**    Interface file for the iDevice, a conceptual example
© 2015 Cengage Learning

Each of these variables has its corresponding properties evident in the following code:

```
@property double length, width;
@property NSString * iName;
```

These properties are synthesized in the implementation file shown here:

```
@implementation iDevice
@synthesize length, width;
@synthesize iName;
```

The iDevice objects can be created using either the default init method provided by the NSObject (which initializes all the instance variables to nil) or the custom init method shown in Example 7-7. In the custom init method, the instance variables of the iDevice are initialized (lines 7 through 9) to the new variable values only if the super (in this case the NSObject) is initialized (line 5).

## Example 7-7

```
1  -(id) initwithiDevice: (double) newLength
2                       :(double) newWidth
3                       :(NSString *) newiName
4  {
5      if (self ==[super init]) {
6
7      [self setLength:newLength];
8      [self setWidth:newWidth];
9      [self setIName:newiName];
10     }
11     return self;
12 }
```

In Example 7-8, an iDevice object is created in the main function. In line 3 of Example 7-8, memory is allocated and the init method is invoked to initialize the instance variables of the iDevice.

## Example 7-8

```
1  //create iDevice
2
3  iDevice * device1 =[[iDevice alloc]
4  initwithiDevice:11.00 :9.00 :@"iDevice"];
5
```

The description method in the implementation file in Example 7-9, which prints the instance variables of the iDevice object, is coded in line 2 through 7.

## Example 7-9

```
1  //description method
2  -(NSString *) description
3  {
4      NSString * objectString = [NSString stringWithFormat:@"\nThe
5  name of the idevice is %@:  \n\tThe length is %.2f and \n\twidth
6  is %.2f: ",iName,length,width];
7      return objectString;
8  }
```

The description method is invoked, and the object is printed as follows:

```
//print the device using the description method
NSLog(@"\nHello there! %@ ", device1);
```

179

## Second Tier of Inheritance: Inheriting from a Class

Continuing with our conceptual example, in the second tier of inheritance we find the iPhone class, which inherits from the iDevice. This child class, or subclass, inherits all the instance variables of the iDevice, as well as all the methods. The child class can have its own set of instance variables in addition to length, width, and iName, which belong to the iDevice class. Each of the instance variables of the iPhone has its own set of getter and setter methods, which are created using properties. These properties are then synthesized using the @synthesize directive so that the compiler can then autogenerate the setter and getter methods. The iPhone instance variable is shown in Example 7-10, along with its property. The @interface directive defines the iPhone as a subclass of iDevice in line 2. The iDevice.h has to be imported into the iPhone interface file (line 1) so the compiler is informed of the parent class –iDevice and hence can implement all the inheritance features. The property for the instance variable of the iPhone class is created in line 6.

## Example 7-10

```
1  #import "iDevice.h"
2  @interface iPhone : iDevice
3  {
4      NSString * feature;
5  }
6  @property NSString * feature;
```

In Example 7-11, the iPhone class is instantiated using the initializer. The init method first checks to see if the parent class (iDevice) is initialized (line 6) and then proceeds to initialize the instance variables that are local to the iPhone class (line 9).

## Example 7-11

```
1  -(id) initwithiPhone: (double) newLength
2                      :(double) newWidth
3                      :(NSString *) newiName
4                      :(NSString *) newFeature;
5  {
6      if(self == [super
7  initwithiDevice:newLength :newWidth :newiName])
8      {
9      [self setFeature:newFeature];
10     }
11     return self;
12 }
```

The iPhone object can be created in the main function, as seen in the following code:

```
//create an iPhone
        iPhone * device2 = [[iPhone alloc]
initwithiPhone:4.0 :2.75 :@"iPhone" :@"Cell Phone"];
```

The description method contains a description defined by the developer as seen in Example 7-12. This description is a string containing the instance variables of the iDevice and the iPhone (line 3).

181

## Example 7-12

```
1  -(NSString *) description
2  {
3      NSString * objectString = [NSString stringWithFormat:@"\nThis
4  device is the iPhone\nThe name of the idevice is %@: \n\tThe
5  length is %.2f \n\twidth is %.2f: \n\tThe feature
6  is: %@",iName,length,width, feature];
7
8      return objectString;
9  }
```

The NSlog statement in the main function simply states the name of the object. The description method is then executed, printing the object.

```
//print the device using the description method
NSLog(@"\nNow I am printing the device2 object %@ ", device2);
```

## Creation of Another Subclass at the Second Tier

The iPad class can be created similarly to the iPhone class. In Example 7-13, the iPad class has the instance variable type (line 6). The initwithiPad method (line 9) initializes the instance variables not only for the iPad class, but also for the iPhone class, which is a parent to the iPad class. The description method header is in line 14.

## Example 7-13

```
1  #import <Foundation/Foundation.h>
2  #import "iDevice.h"
3
4  @interface iPad : iDevice
5  {
6      NSString * type;
7  }
8  @property NSString * type;
9  -(id) initwithiPad: (double) newLength
10                     :(double) newWidth
11                     :(NSString *) newiName
12                     :(NSString *) newType;
```

```
13
14  -(NSString *) description;
15  @end
```

The implementation of the iPad class is shown in Example 7-14. This is very similar to the iPhone class. The methods initwithiPad (line 7) and the description (line 21 through 28) methods are implemented in this example.

## Example 7-14

```
1   #import "iPad.h"
2
3   @implementation iPad
4   @synthesize type;
5
6
7   -(id) initwithiPad: (double) newLength
8                      :(double) newWidth
9                      :(NSString *) newiName
10                     :(NSString *) newType
11  {
12      if (self == [super
13  initwithiDevice:newLength :newWidth :newiName])
14      {
15      [self setType:newType];
16      }
17      return self;
18  }
19
20  //description method
21  -(NSString *) description
22  {
23      NSString * objectString = [NSString stringWithFormat:@"\nThis
24  device is the iPad \nThe name of the idevice is %@: \n\tThe
25  length is %.2f \n\twidth is %.2f: \n\tThe type
26  is: %@",iName,length,width, type];
27      return objectString;
28  }
29  @end
```

## Third Tier of Inheritance

Third-level inheritance is similar to second-level inheritance. In Example 7-15, we create a subclass of the iPad class called iPadMini. The iPadMini class inherits all the instance variables of the iPad. It also inherits all instance variables of the iDevice class because the iPad inherits from the iDevice. This means the iPadMini will have length, width, iName, type, and the new instance variable, called sizePercentage (line 6). The @interface directive indicates that iPadMini inherits from the iPad class (line 4).

## Example 7-15

```
1  #import <Foundation/Foundation.h>
2  #import "iPad.h"
3
4  @interface iPadMini : iPad
5  {
6      double sizePercentage;
7  }
8
9  @property double sizePercentage;
```

In Example 7-16, the initwithiPadMini method sends the init method to the super class. That class's initializer then sends the init method to its super. In our example, the iPadMini sends the init method to the iPad. The init method of the iPad then sends the init method to its super, which is the iDevice.

## Example 7-16

```
1  -(id) initwithiPadMini: (double) newLength
2                        :(double) newWidth
3                        :(NSString *) newiName
4                        :(NSString *) newType
5                        : (double) newSizePercentage
6  {
7      if(self == [super
8  initwithiPad:newLength :newWidth :newiName :newType])
9      {
10     [self setSizePercentage:newSizePercentage];
11     }
12     return self;
13 }
```

The description method in Example 7-17 is very similar to the iPad description method. Although the iPadMini inherits from the iPad the description method, we create a new one for the iPadMini class so this method can print all its attributes, well as the attributes of the parent classes.

## Example 7-17

```
1  //description method
2  -(NSString *) description
3  {
4      NSString * objectString = [NSString stringWithFormat:@"\nThis
5  device is the iPadMini \nThe name of the iDevice is %@: \n\tThe
```

```
6    length is %.2f \n\twidth is %.2f: \n\tThe size percentage
7    is: %.2f",iName,length,width, sizePercentage];
8        return objectString;
9
10 }
```

The iPadMini object is created by invoking the init method, as shown in the following code:

```
//create a iPadMini
iPadMini * device4 = [[iPadMini alloc]
initwithiPadMini:5.50 :4.5 :@"iPadMini" :@"Mini Electronic Pad" :50.00];
```

The iPadMini object is printed using the NSLog statement, which automatically sends the description method to the iPadMini behind the scenes as shown here:

```
//print the device using the description method
NSLog(@"\nNow we are printing device4 %@", device4);
```

The UML diagram for our conceptual inheritance example is shown in Figure 7-13.

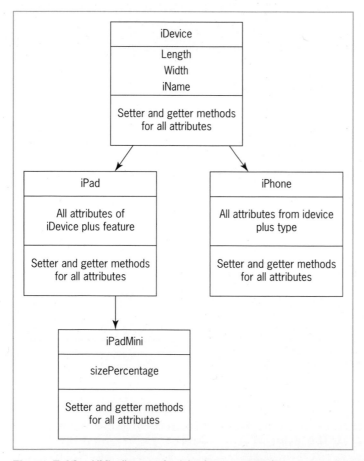

**Figure 7-13**   UML diagram for inheritance example
© 2015 Cengage Learning

Example 7-18 contains the complete @interface file for the iDevice class.

## Example 7-18

```
1   //The @interface file for the iDevice
2   #import <Foundation/Foundation.h>
3
4   @interface iDevice : NSObject
5   {
6       double length;
7       double width;
8       NSString * iName;
9   }
10
11  @property double length, width;
12  @property NSString * iName;
13
14  -(id) initwithiDevice: (double) newLength
15                       :(double) newWidth
16                       :(NSString *) newiName;
17
18  -(NSString *) description;
19
20  @end
```

Example 7-19 contains the @implementation file for the iDevice class.

## Example 7-19

```
1   //The implementation file for the iDevice
2   #import "iDevice.h"
3   @implementation iDevice
4   @synthesize length, width;
5   @synthesize iName;
6
7   -(id) initwithiDevice: (double) newLength
8                        :(double) newWidth
9                        :(NSString *) newiName
10  {
11      if (self ==[super init]) {
12
13      [self setLength:newLength];
14      [self setWidth:newWidth];
15      [self setiName:newiName];
16      }
17      return self;
18  }
19
20  //description method
21  -(NSString *) description
```

```
22  {
23      NSString * objectString = [NSString stringWithFormat:@"\nThe
24  name of the idevice is %@: \n\tThe length is %.2f and \n\twidth
25  is %.2f: ",iName,length,width];
26      return objectString;
27
28  }
29
30  @end
```

Example 7-20 contains the @interface file for the iPhone class.

## Example 7-20

```
1  //The @interface file for the iPhone
2  #import <Foundation/Foundation.h>
3  #import "iDevice.h"
4
5  @interface iPhone : iDevice
6  {
7      NSString * feature;
8  }
9  @property NSString * feature;
10
11  -(id) initwithiPhone: (double) newLength
12                    :(double) newWidth
13                    :(NSString *) newiName
14                    :(NSString *) newFeature;
15
16  -(NSString *) description;
17  @end
```

Example 7-21 contains the @implementation file for the iPhone class

## Example 7-21

```
1  //The @implementation file for the iPhone
2  #import "iPhone.h"
3  #import "iDevice.h"
4  @implementation iPhone
5  @synthesize feature;
6
7  -(id) initwithiPhone: (double) newLength
8                    :(double) newWidth
9                    :(NSString *) newiName
10                   :(NSString *) newFeature;
11  {
12      if(self == [super
13  initwithiDevice:newLength :newWidth :newiName])
```

```
14        {
15        [self setFeature:newFeature];
16        }
17        return self;
18  }
19
20  -(NSString *) description
21  {
22        NSString * objectString = [NSString stringWithFormat:@"\nThis
23  device is the iPhone\nThe name of the idevice is %@: \n\tThe
24  length is %.2f \n\twidth is %.2f: \n\tThe feature
25  is: %@",iName,length,width, feature];
26        return objectString;
27  }
28  @end
```

Example 7-22 contains the @interface file for the iPad class

## Example 7-22

```
1   //The @interface file for the iPad .
2   #import <Foundation/Foundation.h>
3   #import "iDevice.h"
4   @interface iPad : iDevice
5   {
6        NSString *type;
7   }
8   @property NSString *type;
9   -(id) initwithiPad: (double) newLength
10                    :(double) newWidth
11                    :(NSString *) newiName
12                    :(NSString *) newType;
13
14  -(NSString *) description;
15  @end
```

Example 7-23 contains the @implementation file for the iPad class

## Example 7-23

```
1   //The @implementation file for the iPad .
2   #import "iPad.h"
3   @implementation iPad
4   @synthesize type;
5
6   -(id) initwithiPad: (double) newLength
7                    :(double) newWidth
8                    :(NSString *) newiName
9                    :(NSString *) newType
```

```
10  {
11      if (self == [super
12  initwithiDevice:newLength :newWidth :newiName])
13      {
14      [self setType:newType];
15      }
16      return self;
17  }
18
19  //description method
20  -(NSString *) description
21  {
22      NSString * objectString = [NSString stringWithFormat:@"\nThis
23  device is the iPad \nThe name of the idevice is %@: \n\tThe
24  length is %.2f \n\twidth is %.2f: \n\tThe type
25  is: %@",iName,length,width, type];
26      return objectString;
27  }
28  @end
```

Example 7-24 contains the @interface file for the iPadMini class

## Example 7-24

```
1   //The @interface file for the iPadMini
2   #import <Foundation/Foundation.h>
3   #import "iPad.h"
4   @interface iPadMini : iPad
5   {
6       double sizePercentage;
7   }
8
9   @property double sizePercentage;
10
11  -(id) initwithiPadMini: (double) newLength
12                        :(double) newWidth
13                        :(NSString *) newiName
14                        :(NSString *) newType
15                        : (double) newSizePercentage;
16  //description method
17  -(NSString *) description;
18
19  @end
```

Example 7-25 contains the @implementation file for the iPadMini class

## Example 7-25

```
1   //The @implementation file for the iPadMini
2   #import <Foundation/Foundation.h>
3   #import "iPad.h"
4   @interface iPadMini : iPad
5   {
6       double sizePercentage;
7   }
8
9   @property double sizePercentage;
10
11  -(id) initwithiPadMini: (double) newLength
12                       :(double) newWidth
13                       :(NSString *) newiName
14                       :(NSString *) newType
15                       : (double) newSizePercentage;
16  //description method
17  -(NSString *) description;
18
19  @end
```

Example 7-26 contains the main function where the iPhone, iPad, and iPadMini objects are created.

## Example 7-26

```
1   #import <Foundation/Foundation.h>
2   #import "iDevice.h"
3   #import "iPad.h"
4   #import "iPadMini.h"
5   #import "iPhone.h"
6
7   int main(int argc, const char * argv[])
8   {
9       @autoreleasepool {
10
11          //create iDevice
12              iDevice * device1 =[[iDevice alloc]
13  initwithiDevice:11.00 :9.00 :@"iDevice"];
14
15          //print the device using the description method
16          NSLog(@"\nHello there! %@ ", device1);
17
18          //create an iPhone
19              iPhone * device2 = [[iPhone alloc]
20  initwithiPhone:4.0 :2.75 :@"iPhone" :@"Cell Phone"];
21
```

189

```
22              //print the device using the description method
23              NSLog(@"\nNow I am printing the device2 object %@ ",
24      device2);
25
26              //create an iPad
27              iPad * device3 = [[iPad alloc]
28      initwithiPad:11.00 :9.00 :@"iPad" :@"Electronic pad"];
29
30              //print the device using the description method
31              NSLog(@"\nNow I am printing the device3 object %@ ",
32      device3);
33
34              //create a iPadMini
35              iPadMini * device4 = [[iPadMini alloc]
36      initwithiPadMini:5.50 :4.5 :@"iPadMini" :@"Mini Electronic
37      Pad" :50.00];
38
39              //print the device using the description method
40              NSLog(@"\nNow we are printing device4 %@", device4);
41          }
42      return 0;
43  }
```

The output of the program is as follows.

**Output for Examples 7-18 to 7-26**

```
2017-10-01 17:48:03.082 Inheritance-Chapter7[8824:403]
Hello there!
The name of the idevice is iDevice:
    The length is 11.00 and
    width is 9.00:
2017-10-01 17:48:03.100 Inheritance-Chapter7[8824:403]
Now I am printing the dvice2 object
This device is the iPhone
The name of the idevice is iPhone:
    The length is 4.00
    width is 2.75:
    The feature is: Cell Phone
2017-10-01 17:48:03.102 Inheritance-Chapter7[8824:403]
Now I am printing the device3 object
This device is the iPad
The name of the idevice is iPad:
    The length is 11.00
    width is 9.00:
    The type is: Electronic pad
2017-10-01 17:48:03.103 Inheritance-Chapter7[8824:403]
Now we are printing device4
This device is the iPadMini
The name of the idevice is iPadMini:
    The length is 5.50
    width is 4.50:
    The size percentage is: 50.00
```

## HANDS-ON LAB

In this lab, you will create a class called `animalControl` that simulates the growth of an animal population. The population growth is affected by breeding and the spraying of insecticides. Breeding increases the population, whereas spraying of insecticides reduces the population.

- The `animalControl` class will have the following attributes
  - `animalName`
  - `population`
  - `insecticidePower`
  - `growthRate`

In the numbered steps that follow, you will:

- Create a custom `init` method called `initAnimalControl` with the following attributes: `animalName`, `population`, `insecticidePower`, and `growthrate`.

- Create a method called **breed** that increases the population by growth rate. For example, if the `population` is 20 and the `growth rate` is 0.3, then the invocation of the **breed** method should increase the `population` to 20*(1+ 0.3)= 26.

- Assume that the formula for calculating the `population` in the **breed** method is:
  `population = population*( 1 + growthRate);`

- Create a method named `SprayInsecticide`, which simulates spraying the population with insecticides. Spraying reduces the `population` by a percentage of the population specified by `insecticidePower`. For example, if the `insecticidePower` is 10, the spray method will reduce the `population` by 10%. If the `population` is 26, invocation of the `sprayInsecticide` method will reduce the `population` by 26*0.1 = 2.6, which means the new `population` would then be 26-2.6 = ~23.

- Assume that the formula for calculating population in the `SprayInsecticide` method is:

  `population = population*( 1 - insecticidePower/100);`

- Create an appropriate `description` method.

- Create a `main` function for the `animalControl` class that defines two animal objects. The first with an `animalName` "Termite", an `insecticidePower` of 5, a `population` of 40, and a `growthRate` of 0.5. The second animal object should have an `animalName` of "Roach", an `insecticidePower` of 8, a `population` of 200, and a `growthRate` of 2.5.

### CREATING THE @INTERFACE FILE

1. Create the `@interface` file, which contains the declaration for the `initAnimal Control` method. This method serves as the constructor for the `animalControl` class. The instance variables are declared in the curly braces. The properties are declared using the `@property` directive. Next follows the `description` method

declaration, which provides the capability of printing the object just by specifying its name in the NSLog statement.

```
//animalControl.h
    @interface animalControl : NSObject
    {
    NSString *animalName;
    double population;
    double insecticidePower;
    double growthRate;
    }

    -(id) initAnimalControl: (NSString*) theAnimalName
    : (double) thePopulation
    : (double) theInsecticidePower
    : (double) theGrowthRate;

    @property NSString *animalName;
    @property double population;
    @property double insecticidePower;
    @property double growthRate;

    -(NSString *) description;
    -(double) breed
    :(double) thePopulation
    : (double) theGrowthrate;
    -(double) sprayInsecticide
    :(double) thePopulation
    :(double) theInsecticidePower;
    @end
```

## CREATING THE @IMPLEMENTATION FILE

2.   Create the @implementation file for the animalControl class. The initAnimalControl method first checks to see if the parent class, which is the NSObject class, is initialized, and then proceeds to initialize the instance variables it contains by sending the setter methods to itself. The description method contains the information we want to print. In this case, we want to print the string that identifies the name of the animal, the population, the growth rate, the insecticide spray power, the population after breeding, and the population after the insecticide is sprayed.

```
//animalControl.m
#import "animalControl.h"

@implementation animalControl

@synthesize animalName, population, insecticidePower, growthRate;

-(id) initAnimalControl:(NSString *)theAnimalName
: (double) thePopulation
: (double)theInsecticidePower
:(double)theGrowthRate
```

```
{
if (self == [super init])
{
[self setAnimalName:theAnimalName];
[self setPopulation:thePopulation];
[self setInsecticidePower:theInsecticidePower];
[self setGrowthRate:theGrowthRate];
}
return self;
}

//description method
-(NSString *) description
{

NSString *objectString = [NSString stringWithFormat:@"\n The
animal's name is: %@\n\t with a population of %.2f\n\t with
insecticidePower of %.2f\n\t and growthRate of %.2f.\n Population
after breeding is %.2f\n\t and population after spraying
insecticide is %.2f", animalName, population, insecticidePower,
growthRate, [self breed:population:growthRate], [self
sprayInsecticide: population: growthRate]];
return objectString;
}

//breed method to breed the animals
-(double) breed
:(double) thePopulation
: (double) theGrowthrate
{
return (thePopulation*(1 + theGrowthrate));
}

//sprayinsecticide method to control the animal growth
-(double) sprayInsecticide
:(double) thePopulation
:(double) theInsecticidePower
{
return (thePopulation*(1-theInsecticidePower/100));
}

@end
```

## CREATING THE MAIN FUNCTION

3. The main file is where the execution starts, the objects are created, and the messages are sent. In the main function, sending the initAnimalControl method to the object creates the animal object. The object is then printed using the NSLog statements. This NSLog statement executes the parent's description method.

```
//Main Function
#import "animalControl.h"

int main(int argc, const char * argv[])
{

@autoreleasepool {

//create Termite
    animalControl *Termite = [[animalControl alloc]
      initAnimalControl:@"Termite" :40 :0.5:5];
    //print the Termite
    NSLog(@"\nThe first animal: %@", Termite);

//create Roach
    animalControl *Roach = [[animalControl alloc]
    initAnimalControl:@"Roach" :200 :2.5 :.8];
    //print the Roach
    NSLog(@"\nThe second animal: %@", Roach);
}
return 0;
}
```

**SAMPLE OUTPUT**

```
2017-07-20 00:07:20.386 Ch7_Hands_on_lab[2222:303]
The first animal:
 The animal's name is: Termite
     with a population of 40.00
     with insecticidePower of 0.50
     and growthRate of 5.00.
 Population after breeding is 240.00
     and population after spraying insecticide is 38.00
2017-07-20 00:07:20.387 Ch7_Hands_on_lab[2222:303]
The second animal:
 The animal's name is: Roach
     with a population of 200.00
     with insecticidePower of 2.50
     and growthRate of 0.80.
 Population after breeding is 360.00
         and population after sparaying insecticide is 198.40
```

# Summary

- Encapsulation is the process of combining data elements, as well as a set of functions that are operational on these data elements, to create a robust, secure object.

- Object-oriented programming is a programming concept that looks at programming in terms of objects that are instances of a class. It is based on the concept of encapsulation.

- There are two main types of methods in a class: class methods and instance methods. A class method does not need the class to be instantiated. The instance method needs an instance of the class to be executed. Instance methods are preceded by a minus (-) sign. Class methods are preceded by a plus (+).

- In Objective-C, headers and the implementation of the members of a class are typically defined in separate files. In simpler programs, it is possible to combine them into one file, but for larger programs, separate files are preferred.

- The `interface` file holds the declaration of the instance variables and the method declarations. An `@interface` file has a `.h` extension. The `@implementation` file, which holds the implementation of the methods declared in the `@interface` file, has a `.m` extension.

- Functions that are part of a class or an object are called methods. In Objective-C, methods are not invoked. Instead, the message of the method is sent to the object.

- Properties are a means of populating the instance variables of the class. The `@property` directive is used identify the properties.

- The `@synthesize` directive is used to have the compiler autogenerate the getter and setter methods of the properties.

- Initializers in Objective-C are similar to constructors in Java. They help create instances of the class.

- `Description` methods are very similar to `toString` methods in Java. They provide a means of printing what the developer chooses to from the set of instance variables of the object, in the form of a string.

- Inheritance facilitates the creation of subclasses that can inherit the attributes of the parent and have their own set of data members.

- Only single inheritance is allowed in Objective-C. In single inheritance, an object can inherit from one parent, but not from two parents.

# Exercises

1. A class named **brand** inherits from another class called **car**. Assume that **car** has three parameters declared in its constructor: **color** (string), **modelNum** (string), and **miles** (double). It also has a value-returning function named **getModelNum**, which returns the model of the car, a function called **setColor** that sets the color of the car and a function named **setMiles** that sets the miles of the **car**. The former function has no parameter but returns the model of the **car**, while the later function has a string parameter but no return.

   a. Write a statement that declares the class **brand** where **brand** inherits from the class **car**.

   b. Write a constructor of the class **car** that has no parameters and initializes all its variables to empty strings and 0.

   c. Write another constructor of the class **car** that has two parameters and initializes its variables to the value of these parameters

   d. Write a statement belonging to the class **brand** that declares an object, **first car** of the class **car**, using any of the constructors declared earlier.

   e. Write a statement similar to the one in Step d that creates another object, **secondCar**.

   f. Write a statement that prints the model number of **secondCar**.

   g. Write a statement that changes the color of **firstCar** to **blue**.

   h. Write a method, **func**, belonging to class **car**, that prints the value of all its variables.

   i. Write a statement that calls the function **func** to print the **color** and **model** number of **firstCar**.

   j. Write a statement that compares the color of **firstCar** and **secondCar** and returns **true** if they match and false otherwise.

2. The class, **apartment**, has several parameters: **name** (string), **address1** (string), **address2** (string), **city** (string), **state** (string), **zip** (string), **manager** (string), and **rating** (double). This class also has the following methods: **description**, which has no parameter and no return, and **title**, which has a parameter and no return. Write statements that create the **@interface** file for this class.

3. Ryan is new to Objective-C programming and just wrote the following code with errors. Find and correct Ryan's errors.

```
@interface myClass: parentClass
{
    -() identification;
    +() setTitle: NSString* title, int num;
    (int) identification;
    NSString* names;
}
```

4. A company just rented a new office painted in beige. This space has wooden flooring and an air conditioner for the whole office floor. The manager decides to subdivide this space into three offices. Describe how the principle of inheritance applies in this situation. List the parent and children, as well as the inherited properties.

5. Mark each of the following statements as true or false. Correct the false statements.

   a. Using encapsulation to provide security and protection is not feasible.

   b. Methods that can only be called after the instantiation of the class are known as the method members of a class or an object.

   c. A class is an instance of an object.

   d. The header declarations are found in the file with the .m extension.

   e. The Objective-C classes ultimately inherit from the NSObject.

6. Explain the following terms

   a. encapsulation

   b. inheritance

   c. object

   d. mutator methods

   e. properties

   f. initializers

7. Analyze the following code and answer the following questions:

   ```
   +(void) DogBark:(NSString*) dogName;
   ```

   a. Is this an instance method or a class method?

   b. What is the name of this method?

   c. Name the parameters of this method and state their data types.

   d. What does this method return?

   e. Write the code for making a call to this method (assume that dogName is Snowy).

8. Assume you are creating a class to describe food. Its attributes are: fat, calories, protein, and servingSize. The class contains a custom init method that gives a value of 10 to all the attributes. Describe the process of coding this class in terms of which aspects will be in the header file and which aspects of the class will be in the implementation file.

9. Given a set of classes, indicate which class is the parent and which is the child.

   a. Shape and Square

   b. Supervisor and Employee

   c. Elephant and Mammal

10. Write an algorithm for the following scenario: A bank mainly caters to customers who open savings accounts, but some customers also obtain loans. The bank has the following information about each savings account holder: first name, last name, savings account number, checking account number, Zip code, and Social Security number. The bank has the following information about each loan recipient: first name, last name, savings account number, checking account number, Zip code, Social Security number, loan amount, and the number of months for which the loan has been given.

# Programming Exercises

1. Create a program that contains a **course** class. Each course should have a name, instructor, and number. Many courses, but not all, also have labs. Each course that has a lab also has all of the properties of a **course**, as well as a list of lab materials. Include in your program four different **course** objects, two that contain a list of lab materials and two that don't have any lab materials. Give the user the option to choose the type of course to view.

2. Each order at restaurant named "Kabab" includes one or more of the following: an appetizer, a main course, chai, and a dessert. Each day, the chef prepares one appetizer and dessert, so the customer either orders the option for that day or declines that menu item entirely.

   For the main course, the customer can choose an entrée for $3.50. The customer can choose to order a main course or not. Also, all chai costs $3.00 (with free refills), and appetizers and desserts are $3.50.

   Write a program that prompts the user to select or decline an appetizer, main course, chai, and dessert. For the main course, the customer should have the option of choosing or declining the main course entirely. The program should output each order, showing the price for each item, as well as the total bill, including a 2% tax.

3. Survey questionnaires work a little bit like classes. You can think of the questionnaire as the parent class and a question as the child class. Mr. Maurice manufactures electronic devices and is looking to better satisfy his customers. For this purpose, he wants to create a questionnaire that he will use to survey five customers. He wants to ask the customers for their opinion about the color of a particular device, as well as about its weight, memory, and screen size.

   Each response is saved in an array. Mr. Maurice will then use this array to customize his next product. This next product will have the properties preferred by the majority of the surveyed customers. Create a program that accomplishes this.

   Your program should:

   • Use a **for** loop to create objects of the main class

   • Store each response to an array

   • Output the responses for Mr. Maurice to analyze.

4. A bookstore store just opened and needs polo shirts for its employees. Each shirt should display a quote from a famous author. The following are the quotes:

- After a storm comes a calm.

- Be kind whenever possible. It is always possible.

- Have faith in your abilities!

The quote can be located on the front or back of the shirt. For colors, the employee can choose between red, green, black and blue. The shirts come in small, medium, and large. Create a program that an employee can use to design his or her shirt. The program should allow the user to enter his or her name and gender, select the shirt color, and enter the desired quote, its location (that is, whether it should be printed on the front or the back), and the size. The system should store the order in an array. At the end of the day, the system should send all the information entered that day to the print shop so the shirts can be created. Write a program that accomplishes this task using the principles of inheritance. The information sent to the shop should look like this:

Total Number of orders

Order Summary

Order Number Name Gender Color Size Quote Location

5. Create a program that simulates a small ice cream shop that sells ice cream cones and milkshakes. Customers can choose from a variety of flavors and toppings. Ice cream cones are priced at $1.29 for small, $2.29 for medium, and $3.29 for large. Milkshakes are priced at $1.59 for small, $2.59 for medium, and $3.59 for large. Use inheritance to create both of the unique ice cream treats. The flavors options are: vanilla, chocolate, strawberry, mint, and cookie dough. The topping options are: Oreo, chocolate chips, brownie, pecans, chocolate, and caramel. Print the user's choices and the total price.

6. Write a program that contains a class that describes a place of business. This place should have the following attributes: place name, Zip code, address type (i.e., industrial or commercial). Create a main function that creates a myPlace object with the following attributes: place name, Atria; Zip code, 98765; and address type, commercial.

7. Create the program described in Programming Exercise 6, but make the following changes:

a. Create a custom initializer that sets the Zip code to 00000, the place name to placeA, and the address type to industrial.

b. Add a description method that prints the place name and address type when it prints the object.

8. Create an employee class that contains the following attributes: location, first name, last name, and employee number. The location attribute is of type place (the class created in Programming Exercise 7). When the main function is executed, an employee (for example, Jonathan Jones, with employee number 0975) should be created, whose location is the myPlace object created in Programming Exercise 7.

9. Create a **shoe** class to describe a **shoe** object that contains the following attributes: **color**, **length**, and **material**. Next, create a **boot** class that inherits from the **shoe** class and has the additional attribute of **height**. When the **main** function is executed, a **myBoots** object should be created and its attributes should be printed to the console. Assume that **myBoots** has a **color** of **brown**, has a **length of 15"**, is made up of suede, and is 2 feet tall. Use the getter method of the class to print out each of these values.

10. Modify the program from Programming Exercise 9 so that all of the attributes are properties and the getter and setter methods for each of the properties are autogenerated. Add a **generateDescriptor** method to the **shoe** class that concatenates the **length** of the shoe to its **color** (for example, 9black). Print the descriptor for the **myBoots** object.

## Business Case Study

Building on the Business Case Study from Chapter 6, create a class called **fun** with attributes of **date** and **occasion**. Create a subclass **balloon** with attributes of **size**, **color**, and **type** (halogen or not). Create the respective properties and description methods.

Create a **main** function that generates the following objects and their balloons.

- birthday
- wedding
- party
- graduation

# CHAPTER 8

# Working in the iOS Environment

In this chapter you will:

- ◎ Explore a brief overview of iOS platform and its frameworks
- ◎ Learn more about the iOS SDK and its components
- ◎ Learn to describe the architecture of iOS and the role of Cocoa Touch
- ◎ Outline the app life cycle
- ◎ Create a simple "Hello Universe" app
- ◎ Add labels, text fields and buttons to a view controller
- ◎ Create IBOutlet and IBAction connections

This book is designed to teach Objective-C and iOS programming. So far we have learned the fundamentals of Object-C language, which is the language of iOS programming. Now we will shift our focus to iOS programming. To understand iOS programming, you need to learn about Cocoa Touch, which is a significant part of iOS and uses Objective-C as its language of communication. We will start by examining the platform, exploring the basics of iOS programming and its elements and inspecting the architecture of iOS. We will learn about controls, `IBOutlet` and `IBAction` connections while creating a simple app.

# iOS Platform and Architecture

iOS is the operating system for Apple's mobile devices, such as the iPhone, iPad, and iPod. It is a means of communication between the hardware and the software on the apple mobile devices, connecting the hardware to the higher-level services provided by the devices.

The iOS architecture is divided into four layers of varying functionality and complexity. The lower layers provide services with the most basic functionalities, while the highest layer provides more complex services, incorporating object-oriented features, encapsulation, and abstraction of services. The layers are composed of frameworks, some of which access the hardware, forming the infrastructure for mobile apps.

## Frameworks

Frameworks form the infrastructure for each of these layers. A framework is a set of libraries and services, similar to Java libraries that assist in the development of apps. These frameworks contain methods that can be implemented by the developers. Some of the types of functionalities provided by the frameworks are data, user interface, location, graphics, motion, image, video, and media. Two of the most important frameworks are the Foundation framework, and the UIKit framework.

As discussed in Chapter 6, the Foundation framework offers development tools, such as `NSStrings`, `NSDictionaries`, and `NSData`. All of these objects inherit from the `NSObject` class. The UIKit framework provides tools for developing user interfaces. It is one of the most used frameworks in the entire family of frameworks provided by Apple. Any task that has to do with the user interface is handled by the UIKit framework. Likewise, any data input by the user or displayed on the screen is handled by the UIKit framework.

## Role of Cocoa Touch and iOS layers

The four layers of iOS are Cocoa Touch, Media, Core Services, and Core OS. Each of these layers is supported by a set of frameworks, such as the UIKit, Foundation, Game Kit, iAd Kit, and the iMap Kit. Figure 8-1 illustrates the architectural layers of iOS.

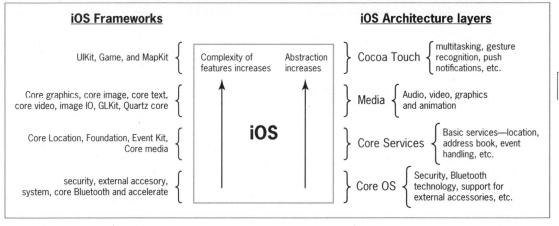

**Figure 8-1** iOS Architecture and frameworks
© 2015 Cengage Learning

Cocoa Touch plays a very significant role in iOS by providing some of the complex capabilities required for app programming, such as gesture recognition, animation, and multitasking. It forms the topmost layer in the iOS architecture and enforces encapsulation and abstraction by separating hardware complexities from program development. Cocoa Touch is built on the Model View Controller (MVC) design pattern, which separates the design logic and data from the actual interface design. This, in turn, enhances platform independance. As you learned in Chapter 1, the language of Cocoa Touch is Objective-C, with development done in iOS SDK, which also incorporates the Interface Builder.

The second layer in the iOS architecture, the Media layer, provides animation, graphics, video, and audio features.

The third layer is the Core Services layer, which supports services such as location information, motion, and event, as well as foundation services, such as the creation of NSString objects, NSNumbers objects, NSArrays objects, and NSDictionaries objects. The frameworks that support this layer include Core Location, Foundation, Event Kit, and Core Media.

The fourth layer, the Core OS layer, supports low level features such as security, Bluetooth technology, support for extrenal accessories, networking, and memory allocation.

Knowledge of the basic iOS layers, their functionality, and the frameworks that support these layers is essential to developing iOS apps.

# iOS Software Development Kit (SDK)

As you learned in Chapter 1, iOS SDK (Software Development Kit) is the software development environment designed by Apple for iOS. You also learned about some of its components in Chapter 1. A more complete list of components includes the following:

- The integrated development environment named Xcode, in which you can write, test and develop Objective-C code

- LLVM compiler, which is the built-in compiler in the iOS SDK

- Interface Builder, which provides the tools necessary to build interactive interfaces for the apps

- iOS Simulator, which allows you to test an app as if it were running on an iPhone or iPad

- Instruments, an analysis tool that helps the developer analyze an app's performance

- A supporting developer tool set, with documentation developers can use to learn more about the iOS SDK

Each of these tools is well integrated into Xcode, offering seamless transitions from code development to compiling to debugging to interface building to testing the app on the simulator and analyzing the performance of the app. These items are explained in more detail in the following sections.

## LLVM compiler

The LLVM compiler offers developers tools used to compile and debug code. The compiler also makes suggestions, detects errors, and corrects some errors as the developer types code. When you position the mouse pointer over a variable, it shows the variable's contents as the app is running.

## Interface Builder

The Interface Builder is a visual development tool that can be used to create the view controller the user interacts with. The view controller does not have direct access to the data elements; instead, it communicates with the view controller, which, in turn, has access to the data/model, sending messages from the user interface to the model and vice versa. The model is where all the data associated with the app resides and the view controller is where the code resides. When a button is pressed in the user interface, or view controller, a message is sent to the view controller. The view controller then accesses the model and returns the message to the view controller in the form of data or images, or any other functionality the user requested by pressing the button. Figure 8-2 shows the Interface Builder.

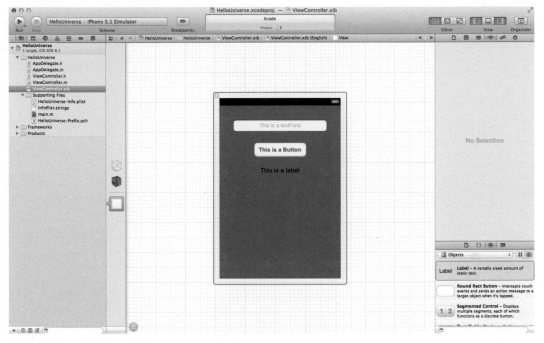

**Figure 8-2**  Interface Builder

# iOS Simulator

As you learned in Chapter 1, the iOS Simulator is used for testing apps. Before you use the iOS Simulator, you need to select the device you want to simulate. In this book, we will be using the iPhone, as shown in Figure 8-3. To select the iPhone simulator, you click the Scheme box at the top of the Xcode window, to the right of the Stop button, and then select the most recent version of iPhone. In Figure 8-3, iPhone 6.1 Simulator is selected. When you are ready to run your app, Xcode will run the app on the simulator you have selected. Xcode will continue to use that simulator until you select a new one. Since we will be using the iPhone simulator throughout this book, you need to select the iPhone simulator only once.

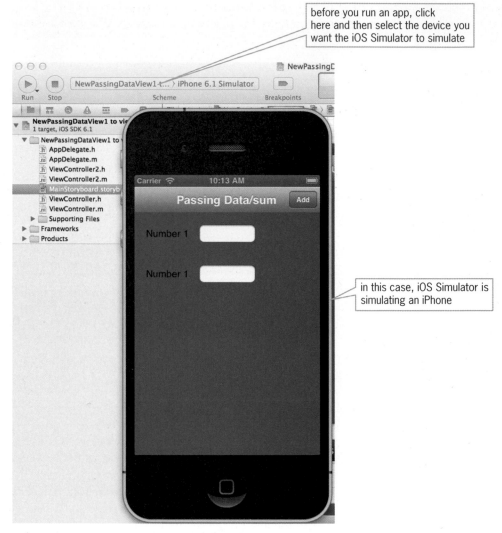

before you run an app, click here and then select the device you want the iOS Simulator to simulate

in this case, iOS Simulator is simulating an iPhone

**Figure 8-3**    App Running in iOS Simulator

Note that most functionality available on Apple devices is available in iOS Simulator. However, some functionality, such as location, phone capabilities, accelerometer, and the camera, are unavailable in the simulator.

## Instruments

Instruments is a development tool provided by the iOS SDK for testing the performance of an app. Mobile devices have limited resources and therefore require critical evaluation of performance so that apps do not consume unnecessary resources and slow the device.

Developers can use Instruments to make sure their apps do not exceed these limitations. Instruments is also useful in detecting memory leaks, in which memory allocations and releases are performed incorrectly.

## Development Support

Apple provides a large number of supporting documents and examples that you will find useful as you develop apps. This documentation support can be found at:

https://developer.apple.com/support/ios/.

# iOS App Life Cycle

When an iOS app starts, a UIApplication object is created. This UIApplication object then creates a UIWindow object and launches a UIView object within the UIWindow object. UIApplication then gets the UIApplicationdelegate running, which in turn manages the life cycle of the app by handling events such as startup, ending, phone calls and various notifications and alerts. The UIApplication is part of the UIKit framework, which provides the objects required for the user interface.

If the preceding paragraph is hard to grasp completely, don't worry. The app life cycle will become easier to understand as you create more apps. For now, the most important concept you need to understand is that there are two main components that are involved in the execution of an app. The first is the set of objects provided by the UIKit framework. The second is the code written by the developer to manage these objects. In the following code, when the user touches the app icon, the main method executes. That is, the UIApplicationMain loads the user interface and starts the event loop by creating the UIApplicationDelegate that manages the events. The Appdelegate and the view controller are created by the UIApplicationMain.

```
1  #import <UIKit/UIKit.h>
2  #import "AppDelegate.h"
3  int main(int argc, char *argv[])
4  {
5      @autoreleasepool {
6          return UIApplicationMain(argc, argv, nil,
7  NSStringFromClass([AppDelegate class]));
8      }
9  }
```

When the app starts, the UIKit, Foundation and CoreGraphics frameworks are automatically loaded by Xcode. This occurs because they are the most commonly used frameworks, and anything that is done in the Interface Builder would require these bare minimum frameworks. Figure 8-4 shows the list of currently active frameworks in Xcode.

**Figure 8-4**    Frameworks

## Views, View Controllers, IBOutlet Connections, and IBAction Connections

Before we begin creating an app, we need to take a moment to clarify some important terminology. A **view controller**, like the one shown in Figure 8-5, is the part of an app that displays data and translates input from the user (such as a word entered into a text field) into an action (such as entering that word into a database). In Xcode, the visual representation of the view controller is the rectangular image of the device's background (for instance, an iPhone's background or an iPad's background) that contains labels, buttons, text fields, and other controls. The term **view** refers to what you see in the view controller. A view can include labels, text fields, buttons, and lists of information, just to name a few possibilities. A view is also sometimes referred to as a **scene**, especially in a storyboard.

The views and controls on a view controller create interactivity between the user and the program. That is, they connect the view controller to the Objective-C logic.

208

**Figure 8-5** Control objects in a view controller

The interface objects are connected to the app's logic via connections. A **connection** is code that programmatically connects a control to the logic that allows it to perform a specific task. There are two main types of connections: `IBOutlet` connections and `IBAction` connections. Figure 8-6 illustrates this relationship.

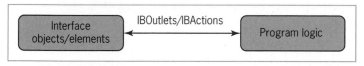

**Figure 8-6** Connection between the interface elements and program logic
© 2015 Cengage Learning

An `IBOutlet` connection is a control's instance variable. An `IBAction` connection is a control's instance method, which is triggered by the occurrence of an event, such as the pressing of a button. `IBOutlet` and `IBAction` connections are made in the `@interface` of the view controller. The implementation of the `IBAction` connection is done in the view controller's `@implementation` file.

## Creating and Using `IBOutlet` and the `IBAction` Connections

You can create `IBOutlet` and `IBAction` connections in the Interface Builder by a Control-drag operation—that is, you click a control in the view controller to select it, press and hold the Control key and the left mouse button simultaneously, and then use the mouse to drag the control from the view controller onto the interface file. This is sometimes known as a **Control-drag operation**.

Some controls, such as buttons, are event-based, which means they can trigger an event that creates an `IBAction` connection. Controls that are not event-driven, such as labels and text fields, create an `IBOutlet` connection instead. After the `IBOutlet` or `IBAction` connection is created in this way, code in your application can access the controls via the `IBOutlet` or the `IBAction` connection. For example, if you Control-drag a label called `newLabel` in a view controller, the code in your app connects to this label via the outlet in the following way:

`IBOutlet UILabel *newLabel;`

A Control-drag operation generates the `@ property` directive for each of the `IBOutlet` connections. It also generates the `@synthesize` directive, which instructs the compiler to generate the getter and setter methods for the control.

The Control-drag operation also generates the header for the action method or the variable in the `@interface` of the class and the implementation of the method or variable in the `@implementation` of the view controller. You then need to write the code for the task you want the program to perform when a particular event, such as the pressing of a button, occurs. The declaration of the `IBAction` connection looks like this:

`- (IBAction)myButton:(id)sender`

Notice the negative (–) sign before `IBAction`, which is necessary because `IBAction` is an instance method of the interface.

# iOS App Creation Process

To create an app, you create a new project in Xcode, open the Interface Builder, drag **interface objects**, or **controls**, such as labels, buttons, or text fields, onto the interface, or view controller, and then change the **attributes**, or **properties**, of the controls. For example, you might make a text field red by changing its color attribute to red. Next, you program the controls to make them do what you want. Finally, you run the app to test it.

In the following steps, we create a simple app with a single view application. The interface will eventually contain only one control: a label that displays the text "Hello Universe".

1. Open Xcode, and then click **Create a new Xcode project**. If Xcode is already open, then from the Xcode File menu, choose New ▶ New Project.

2. In the left pane of the Choose a template for your new project dialog, under "iOS," click **Application.**

3. In this chapter, we will first learn to work with a single view application (that is, an application with one view controller) before we move on to more complicated tasks associated with multiple view controllers. So, on the right, click **Single View Application**, as shown in Figure 8-7.

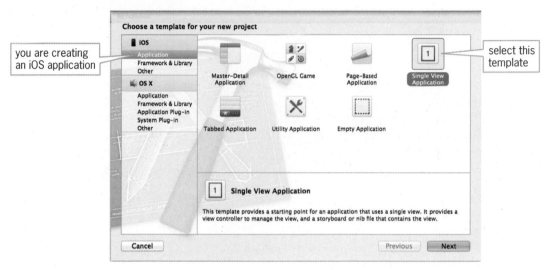

**Figure 8-7** Application type selection

4. Click the **Next** button. In the Choose options for your new project dialogbox, enter **HelloUniverse** as the Product Name, enter appropriate items in the Organization Name and Company Identifier boxes, make sure **iPhone** is selected in the Devices box, and then deselect the **Use Storyboards** check box. (You will learn the meaning of this check box in Chapter 9.) Make sure the option for Use Automatic Reference Counting is checked.

5. Click the **Next** button, and then save the project in the location of your choice. After you save the project, you see the screen shown in Figure 8-8. In the navigator area, on the left, you see several file names, including ViewController.h, ViewController.m, and ViewController.xib. The .xib file is the interface file. The ViewController.h and the ViewController.m files are the files that will hold the logic for the interface created in the .xib file. At this point, you do not need to worry about any other files you see in the navigator area.

**Figure 8-8**    Starting a new project

**6.** In the navigator area, on the left, click **ViewController.xib**, as shown in Figure 8-9. This opens the Interface Builder, displaying the project's one view controller in the editor pane, or canvas, as shown in Figure 8-10. Note the Object Library, in the lower-right corner of the screen. If the Object Library is not open on your computer, click **View ▶ Utilities ▶ Show Object Library** to display it. To see the objects in the Object Library, click the icon shown in Figure 8-10.

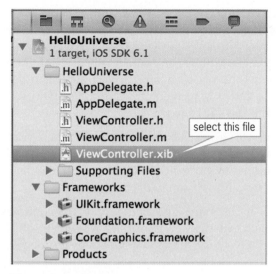

**Figure 8-9**  Navigator area

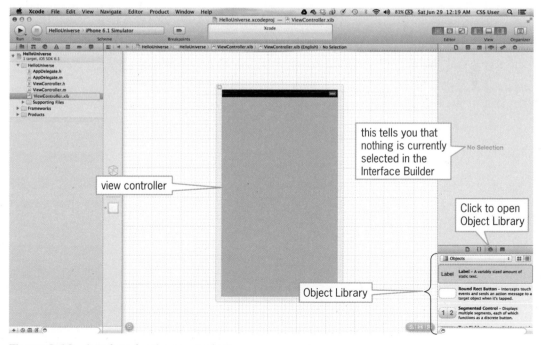

**Figure 8-10**  Interface for the new project

Each user interface, or view controller, has three associated files: **ViewController.xib**, **ViewController.h**, and **ViewController.m**. The **ViewController.xib** file, which is often simply referred to as the **nib** or **xib** file, actually contains the view controller. The ViewController.h is similar to the @interface file (.h), which contains the declarations of the instance variables and the methods. Likewise, the ViewController.m is similar to the @implementation file (.m), which contains the actual implementations of the instance variables and the methods that were declared in the @interface file.

At this point, the view controller is blank, as shown earlier in Figure 8-10. Now we are ready to add some controls to the view controller. We'll start by adding a label. We can accomplish this by dragging a label from the Object Library, in the lower-right corner of the xCode window, onto the view controller. After that, we can run our simple app.

In Figure 8-10, notice the words "No Selection" in the utility pane on the right. This indicates that the view controller is not currently selected. Once the view controller is selected (which you can do by clicking it), the utility pane will show all the functionality options for the view controller.

1.  Drag a label object from the Object Library on the lower-right side of the utility pane to the view controller. Center the label and then replace the existing text in the label with Hello Universe, as shown in Figure 8-11.

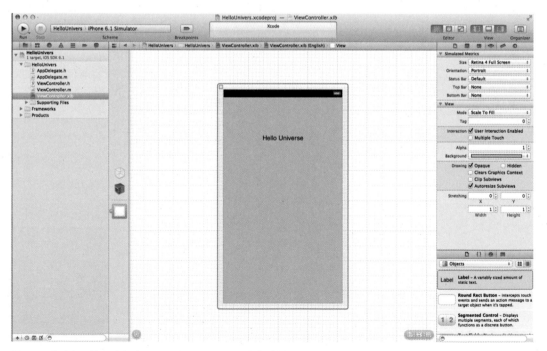

**Figure 8-11**    New label containing the text "Hello Universe"

2. Now you are ready to run the app in the iOS Simulator. But first, if you haven't already done so, you need to select the iPhone simulator. At the top of the Xcode window, to the right of the Stop button, click the Scheme box and then click the most recent version of the iPhone. If necessary, review Figure 8-3, earlier in this chapter, for clarification.

3. In the upper-left corner, click the **Run** button, as shown in Figure 8-12. The simulator appears, displaying the text "Hello Universe", as shown in Figure 8-13.

**Figure 8-12**   Run button and Stop button

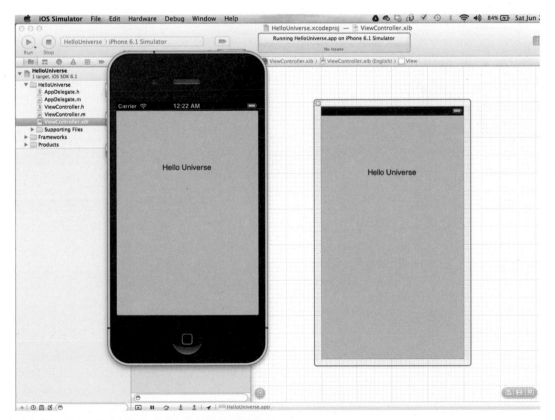

**Figure 8-13**   Simulator running the Hello Universe app

**4.** To stop the app from running, click the **Stop** button, as shown earlier in Figure 8-12.

In this chapter's Hands-On Lab, we will be using a label, a text field, and a button. In order to understand these controls it is essential to understand the `UIControl` class from which they are generated.

## UIControl Class

The `UIControl` class provides the control objects that offer interactivity to the user. The `UIControl` class sets and gets the attributes of the controls, dispatches the action messages to a target, draws the controls, and tracks the touches on a control. Figure 8-14 shows three commonly used control objects.

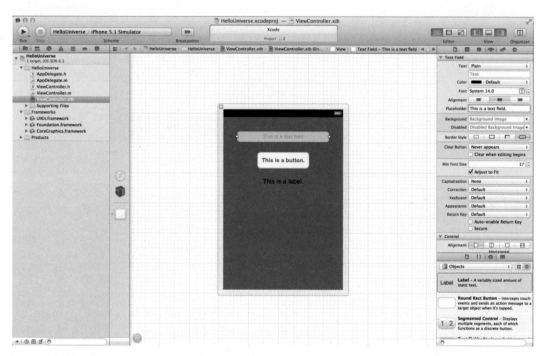

**Figure 8-14**    Three commonly used control objects

## UILabel Class

A label control object, like the one you added to the Hello Universe app, is an instance of the `UILabel` class. This type of control is traditionally used to provide information to the user. A label is a read-only interface object, meaning only the developer has access to its contents; the user can see it but cannot edit it. Hence the label is designed to ignore any touch events—indeed, it is designed to ignore any events. If you wanted a label to respond to an event, then you would have to change its setting to enable events.

# UIButton Class

A button control object is an instance of the UIButton class. The button is capable of intercepting touches; when it does so, it sends the action method to the target. The UIButton class inherits from the UIControl class and thus has access to the methods that send the action messages to the target.

# UITextField Class

A text field control object (sometimes called a text box) is an instance of the UITextField class. This type of control can be edited by the user and has an associated action method that is triggered when the user presses Enter after entering text. This action method can be programmed to perform a numerous tasks, such as searching for text, displaying additional text in a label or other control, and so on.

## HANDS-ON LAB

In this Hands-On Lab, we will create an app that has a text field, a label, and a button. When you run the completed app, the user should be able to type some text in the text field, click on the button, and then see that same text displayed in the label. We will drag the label, text field, and button from the Object Library. We will then change the attributes of some of these controls.

1. Create a new Xcode project that is an iOS application. Choose **Single View Application**, taking care to leave the Use Storyboards check box unchecked. Save the project as **myFirstApp** in the location of your choice.

2. Click the **ViewController.xib** file to display the blank view controller.

3. Make sure the Object Library is open, and then drag a label from the Object Library to the view controller, as shown in Figure 8-15. After you add a control to the view controller, you can change its appearance by changing its attributes. To do that, you need to make sure the attributes are visible at the top of the Utility pane.

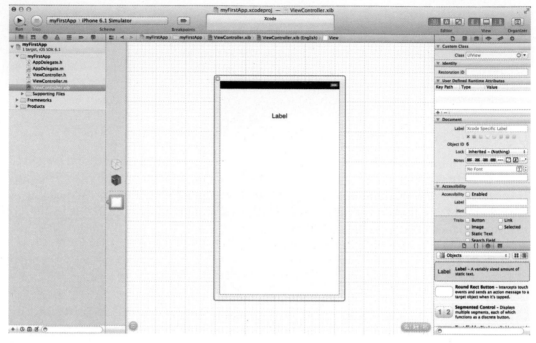

**Figure 8-15**    Label added to view controller

4.  Click the icon shown in Figure 8-16. Note that the Utility pane displays the attributes for the control that is currently selected in the view controller.

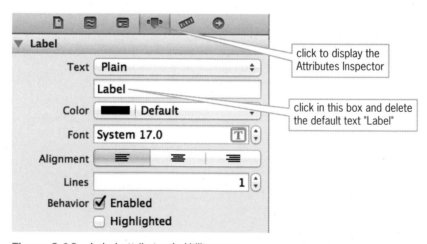

**Figure 8-16**    Label attributes in Utility pane

5. One attribute of a label is the text it contains. Right now, the label contains the default text "Label," but you want the label to be what the user enters in the text field when the app is run. That means you need to change the attributes to delete the default text. In the attributes in the utility pane, click the box shown in Figure 8-16, and then delete its contents.

6. Deselect the label by clicking outside it in the Interface Builder. At this point, you can no longer see the label, because it doesn't contain any text. This does not mean the label has disappeared. In the completed app, text will appear in the label when the user clicks a button.

7. Drag a text field from the Object Library onto the view controller, and then size it and position it roughly as shown in Figure 8-17. Note that in Figure 8-17 you are unable to see the label because there is no text in it. To size a text field control, drag a corner handle to increase or decrease the control's size. To position a control, left-click the control, hold down the mouse button, and drag the control to the desired location.

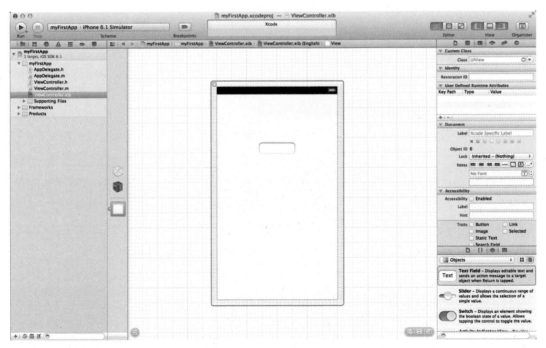

Figure 8-17   Correct size for text field

8. Now you need to specify the placeholder text that you want to be visible in the text field when the user first runs the app. You can do that by changing the text field's Placeholder attribute. Make sure the text field is still selected, and then, in the text field's attributes, click the **Placeholder** box and type **Enter your text here**, as shown in Figure 8-18. The new placeholder text, "Enter your text here" now appears in the text field. If necessary, widen the text field so you can see all of the placeholder text.

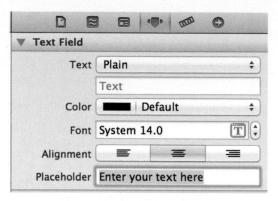

**Figure 8-18**    Text field with placeholder text

9.  Drag a round rect button from the Object Library to the view controller, double-click it, and type the text **Click Me!** Figure 8-19 shows the view controller with the label, button and text field. Here you are able to see the outline of the label only because it has been selected.

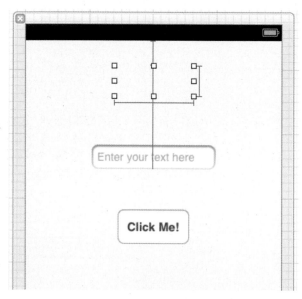

**Figure 8-19**    View with label, button, and text field

10. In addition to changing the attributes of the controls, you can also change the attributes of the view controller itself. To do that, you first need to make sure the view controller is selected. Click on the view controller in any open area where there are no controls to select the view controller and display its attributes. Now you can change one of these attributes, the background color.

11. In the view controller's attributes, click the up–down arrow in the Background box, as shown in Figure 8-20. This opens a menu with various color options.

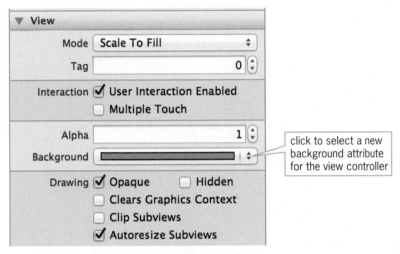

Figure 8-20    View controller's background Attribute

12. Click the red box, as shown in Figure 8-21. If you don't see red in the list of recently used colors, click **Other** (shown at the bottom of Figure 8-21) to open the Colors dialog, click the **Color Palettes** tab in the Colors dialog, make sure Apple is selected in the Palette list, click **Red**, and then close the Colors dialog. This changes the view controller's background color to red, as shown in Figure 8-22.

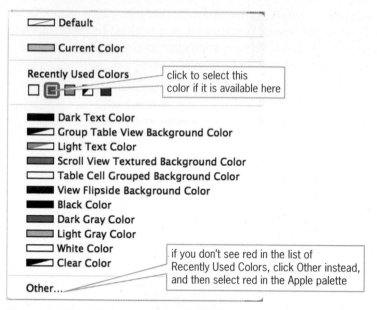

**Figure 8-21**    Red selected as the Background attribute

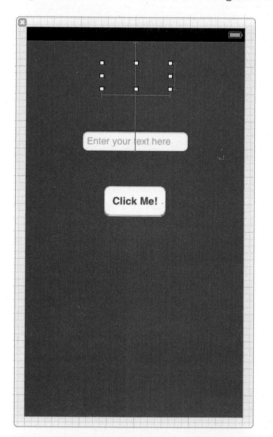

**Figure 8-22**    View controller with red background

13. To begin programming the controls on the view controller, we need to display the view controller file in the Assistant Editor pane. To accomplish this, click the icon shown in Figure 8-23. The Assistant Editor pane becomes visible, displaying the view controller and the respective interface file (in this case ViewController.h) simultaneously, as shown in Figure 8-23. Now you can begin programming the controls. You'll start with the label.

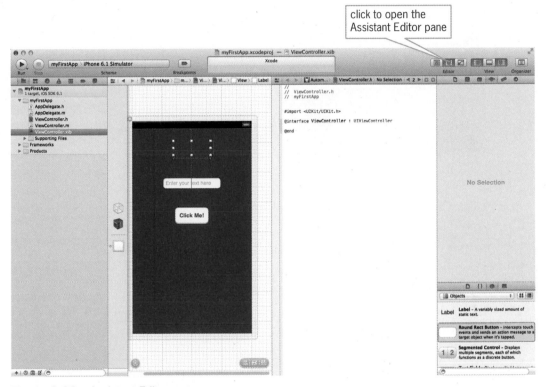

click to open the Assistant Editor pane

**Figure 8-23**   Assistant Editor pane

14. Select the label, press and hold the control button, and then drag from the view controller into the Assistant Editor pane, just below the @interface directive. This opens the dialog shown in Figure 8-24. Make sure **Outlet** is selected in the Connection box, and type **MyLabel** in the Name box.

Figure 8-24    Dialog for connecting the label control

15. Click **Connect**. This tells the compiler to generate the following code and display it in the Assistant Editor pane:

```
@property (weak, nonatomic) IBOutlet UILabel *MyLabel;
```

16. Next, Control-drag the text field into the Assistant Editor pane, right below the `@property` line created in the preceding step.

17. In the dialog, type **MyTextField** in the Name box, and make sure Outlet is selected in the Connection box. See Figure 8-25.

Figure 8-25    Dialog for connecting the text field control

18. Click **Connect**. The following code is generated by the compiler:

```
@property (weak, nonatomic) IBOutlet UITextField *MyTextField;
```

19. Next we need to create an IBAction for the button. To do this, control drag the button to the Assistant Editor pane, just below the @property line created in the preceding step.

20. In the dialog, select **Action** as the connection, as seen in Figure 8-26. In this case, you need to select Action because we are creating a connection for the button control, which is event-based, and therefore will create an IBAction. By contrast, for the label and the text field, we created an IBOutlet. The creation of the IBAction generates the following code:

```
- (IBAction)Click:(id)sender;
```

Figure 8-26   Dialog for connecting the button control

21. Review the code in the Assistant Editor pane. Your code should now look like this:

```
#import <UIKit/UIKit.h>
@interface ViewController : UIViewController
@property (weak, nonatomic) IBOutlet UILabel *MyLabel;
@property (weak, nonatomic) IBOutlet UITextField
*MyTextField;
- (IBAction)Click:(id)sender;
@end
```

22. In the navigator area, select the ViewController.m file. This displays the ViewController.m file in the Assistant Editor pane. Next, synthesize the label and text field by typing the following @synthesize directive in the ViewController.m file just below the @implementation directive.

```
@synthesize MyLabel;
@synthesize MyTextField;
```

23. Now we need to write the code that takes the contents of the text field and displays them in the label. In the ViewController.m file, find the Click method and type the following code, which sets the contents of the label equal to the contents of the text field when the user clicks the button. iOS has a set of predefined methods that you can use to retrieve data from controls. One such method that gets the contents of the control objects, such as the text field or the label, is the **text** method. Hence, we include the code object.text to get or set the contents of a control.

```
- (IBAction)Click:(id)sender {
    MyLabel.text = MyTextField.text;
}
```

24. Review the code in the Assistant Editor pane, and make sure it matches the following code. Note that the compiler automatically included a viewDidLoad method, which you can ignore for now. You'll learn more about it later.

```
#import "ViewController.h"
@interface ViewController ()
@end
@implementation ViewController
@synthesize MyLabel;
@synthesize MyTextField;
- (void)viewDidLoad
{
    [super viewDidLoad];

// Do any additional setup after loading the view
controller,typically from a nib.
}
- (void)didReceiveMemoryWarning
{
    [super didReceiveMemoryWarning];
    // Dispose of any resources that can be recreated.
}
- (IBAction)Click:(id)sender {
    MyLabel.text = MyTextField.text;
}
@end
```

25.   Run the app. The iOS Simulator appears, as shown in Figure 8-27.

**Figure 8-27**   App in the iOS simulator when you first run it

26.    Click in the text field and type **Hello!** as shown in Figure 8-28.

**Figure 8-28**    App after you type "Hello!" in text field

27. Click the button. The word "Hello!" is displayed by the label, as shown in Figure 8-29.

**Figure 8-29**   App Displaying "Hello" in the Label

28. Click the **Stop** button to stop the app.

## SOURCE CODE

The code for the **@interface** is as follows:

```
//
//  ViewController.h
//  myFirstApp
```

```
//

#import <UIKit/UIKit.h>

@interface ViewController : UIViewController
@property (weak, nonatomic) IBOutlet UILabel *MyLabel;
@property (weak, nonatomic) IBOutlet UITextField *MyTextField;
- (IBAction)Click:(id)sender;

@end
```

The code for the @implementation file is as follows:

```
//
//   ViewController.m
//   myFirstApp


#import "ViewController.h"

@interface ViewController ()

@end

@implementation ViewController
@synthesize MyLabel;
@synthesize MyTextField;

- (void)viewDidLoad
{
    [super viewDidLoad];

    // Do any additional setup after loading the view, typically
from a nib.
}


- (void)didReceiveMemoryWarning
{
    [super didReceiveMemoryWarning];
    // Dispose of any resources that can be recreated.
}


- (IBAction)Click:(id)sender {
  MyLabel.text = MyTextField.text;
}
@end
```

# Summary

- The iOS architecture can be divided into four layers: Cocoa Touch, Media, Core Services, and Core OS.

- Cocoa Touch plays a very significant role in iOS by providing some of the complex capabilities in app programming such as gesture recognition, animation, multitasking, and more.

- The Media layer provides the animation, graphics, video, audio, core graphics, core image, core text, core video, image IO, GLKit, Quartz core frameworks, and more.

- The Core Services layer supports services that are utilized by the operating system, such as location information, motion, event, and foundation services.

- Core OS layer supports low-level features such as security, Bluetooth technology, support for extrenal accessories, networking, memory allocation, threading, and more.

- When an iOS app starts, a `UIApplication` object is created, and this `UIApplication` object creates a `UIWindow` object and launches a `UIView` object in the `UIWindow` object.

- The `main` function invokes the `UIApplicationMain` object, which loads the user interface and starts the event loop by creating the `UIApplicationDelegate` object, which manages the events.

- UIKit, Foundation, and the core graphics frameworks are automatically loaded by Xcode since these are the most commonly used frameworks.

- Instruments is a development tool that the iOS SDK requires to test the performance of the app.

- iOS is used for testing apps, so that the developer does not have to test the app on the actual device.

- The Interface Builder is a visual development tool that can be used to create the view the user interacts with.

- A view controller is a visual interface that you can create using the Interface Builder in Xcode. A view controller mainly consists of interface elements, also known as **controls**, such as labels, text boxes, and buttons

- A label control object is an instance of the `UILabel` class. A label is a read-only interface object, meaning only the developer has access to the contents of this element. The user can see it but cannot edit it.

- A button control object is an instance of the `UIButton` class. A button is capable of intercepting touches; it then sends the action method to the target.

- A text field control object is an instance of the `UITextField` class. This type of control can be edited by the user and has an associated action method that is triggered when the user presses Enter after entering text. This action method can be programmed to perform numerous tasks.

## Exercises

1. Mark the following statements as true or false. Correct the false statements.

   a. The iOS architecture is made up of three layers.

   b. The higher levels of the iOS architecture are object oriented.

   c. Any data that will be input or displayed on the screen is handled by the Foundation framework.

   d. The goal of the Model View Controller is to increase dependency between design logic and interface design.

   e. Core services is the layer responsible for gesture recognition capabilities

2. Explain the following terms:

   a. UIKit

   b. Interface Builder

   c. Instruments

3. Describe each of the four layers of the iOS architecture: Cocoa Touch, Media, Core Services, and Core OS.

4. Describe the following items:

   a. Text field control

   b. Label control

   c. Button control

5. Describe the events that occur between when an iOS app starts and the delegate gets going.

6. Give an example of an `IBOutlet` and explain what an `IBOutlet` is.

7. Give an example of an `IBAction` and explain what an `IBAction` is.

8. Provide the code for the declaration of an outlet.

9. When an app starts, what frameworks are automatically loaded by Xcode?

10. What is the purpose of the UIKit?

## Programming Exercises

1. Create a concatenation app. This will be a modification of the Hands-On Lab. In the Hands-On Lab, the text entered in the text field was displayed in the label. Now ensure that every time that the button is clicked, the text in the text field is appended to the label. So if the user enters *Orange* in the text field and clicks the button, the text in the label would read *Orange*. Next, when the user enters *Apple* in the text field and clicks the button, the text in the label would read *Orange Apple*.

2. Create a number display app that includes the following:

- Two text fields in which the user can enter numbers
- Four buttons containing the text *Addition*, *Subtraction*, *Multiplication*, and *Division*
- One label that will display the result of the calculations. The user should be able to enter numbers in the text fields.

When the user clicks any button, the result should be displayed in the label. For example, if the user enters 5 and 6 in the text fields and then clicks the Addition button, the label should display 11. In case of any calculation errors (for example, if the user fails to enter one of the numbers), the label should display the word *ERROR*. Modify the background and add colors to the calculator to make it look more colorful and personalized.

3. Create a Fibonacci number generator app. A Fibonacci sequence starts with a 0 and 1, with each subsequent number the sum of the previous two numbers. The app should contain at least a text field, a label and a button. The user should input the amount of Fibonacci numbers that he or she wants to. For instance, if the user enters 3 in the text field and clicks the button, the label should display the first three Fibonacci numbers, as follows: 0, 1, 1.

4. Create a quote-of-the-day app. This app should contain at least one label and one button. Each time that the button is clicked, a new quote should appear in the label. One way of doing this would be to create an NSArray object that contains 10 quotes. Ensure that the same quote cannot appear consecutively. For instance, if a user clicks on the button and gets the quote, "An eye for an eye makes the whole world blind," the next time the user clicks the button, he or she should not get the same quote.

5. Create an area and perimeter calculator for a rectangle. The app should include two text fields: one for length and one for width. It should also contain two buttons: one to calculate the area and another to calculate the perimeter.

6. Create a program that lets the user choose among various ice cream choices. When a choice is made, the choice should appear in a label.

7. Create an app for elementary school students that allows a student to display either the formula for area of a square or the formula for the perimeter of a square. The formulas should appear in a label.

# Business Case Study

In this Business Case Study, you will begin creating a pain management journal that allows the user to record pain levels at various times during the day. You will continue working on this app in subsequent chapters. The completed app will contain multiple view controllers, so that the user can display a summary of pain levels in a separate view controller. By the end of Chapter 14, you will have a functional app.

To get started on the pain management app, create a single view app. Modify the background to show a gray color. Add a label that holds the title "Pain Tracker".

# CHAPTER 9

# Understanding and Creating User Interfaces

In this chapter you will:

◎ Learn about the UIKit framework and its role in the building of an app's interface

◎ Create apps using storyboards

◎ Add a navigation controller to an app

◎ Pass data between views

In Chapter 8, we learned how to create apps using the single view template, which provides a single view controller and the `viewController.xib` file. In this chapter, we learn how to create an app with multiple view controllers, using storyboards. We will create basic apps using interface elements, learn how to use storyboards , and explore how to pass data between views.

## UIKit Framework

The UIKit framework, illustrated in Figure 9-1, is the most important framework in the design and building of an interactive interface. It consists of a set of classes that begin with the prefix "UI." These classes manage the application object, event handling, windows, views, and all the controls that help create an interactive touch screen user interface. These classes, in turn, help create and manage windows, view controllers, and user interface elements.

Taken as a whole, these classes allow the developer to create an interactive, touch-sensitive app. The most commonly used classes are the `UIApplication`, `UIWindow`, `UIView`, `UIViewController`, `UIEvent`, `UITouch`, `UIResponder`, `UIButton`, `UILabel`, and `UITextField`.

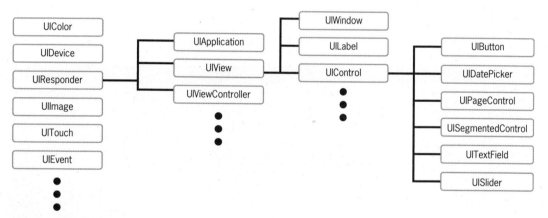

**Figure 9-1**    UIKit Framework
© 2015 Cengage Learning

## Storyboards

**Storyboarding** is a feature that allows the developer to work with all the view controllers in an app at one time. You drag and drop view controllers into the Xcode editor pane, or **Interface Builder canvas**, and then connect them via controls such as buttons, labels, and text fields.

Storyboards make it easy to understand the transitions, or **segues**, between views, giving you a broad overview of the app. A scene is a screen of content, which can be a view. As you will see later in this chapter, you can create a segue between views by control-dragging a control on one view onto another view.

When you have a large number of views displayed at one time, the Xcode window can get crowded. To avoid this problem, it's helpful to use a large monitor when working with storyboards. Note that you can also use the icon seen in Figure 9-2, which is located at the bottom-right corner of the editor pane in Xcode, to zoom in and out of a storyboard. The figures in this book show the screen at varying zoom levels, depending on what is being emphasized in the figure.

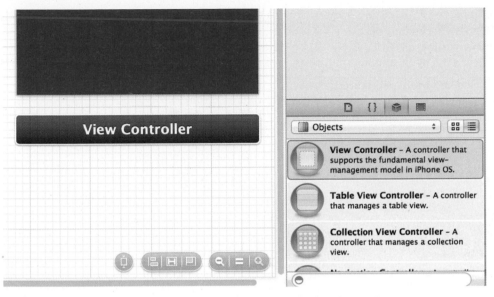

**Figure 9-2** Icons you can use to zoom in when using a storyboard

A bird's-eye view of an app is shown in Figure 9-3.

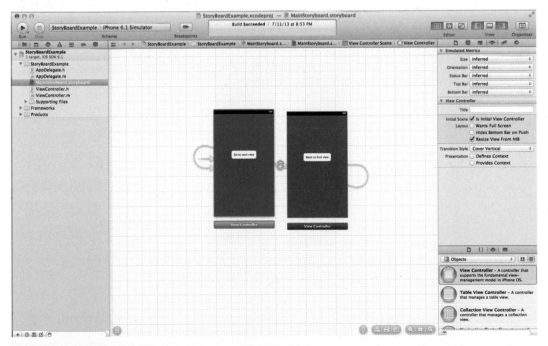

**Figure 9-3** Bird's-eye view of an app in storyboard

In the apps you created in Chapter 8, each view had its own .h, .m, and .xib files. With storyboards there is no need for individual .xib files; instead, there is a MainStoryboard. storyboard file as seen in Figure 9-4.

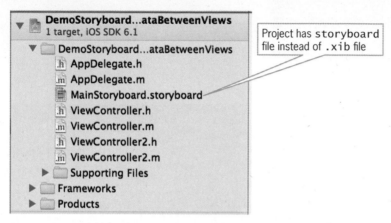

Figure 9-4   A storyboard file instead of a .xib file

## A Simple Transition Using Storyboards

It's time to get some practice with storyboards. We'll create an app with a simple transition between views.

1.  Start Xcode, and then click **Create a new Xcode project.**

2.  In the Choose a template for your new project window, select the **Single View Application** icon, as shown in Figure 9-5.

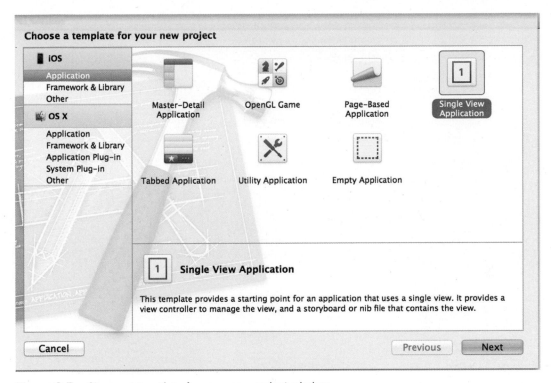

Copyright © 2014 Apple®. All Rights Reserved.

**Figure 9-5** Choose a template for your new project window

3. Click the **Next** button to open the Choose options for your new project window, and then select the options shown in Figure 9-6. Use **StoryBoardExample** as the Product Name, use the appropriate option for your school in the Company Identifier and Organization Name boxes, select **iPhone** in the Devices box, and then make sure the **Use Storyboards** and **Use Automatic Reference Counting** check boxes are selected, as shown in Figure 9-6.

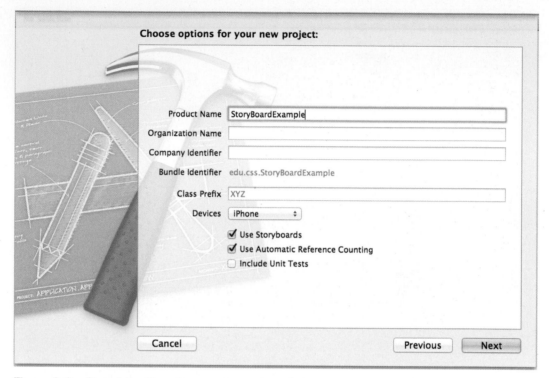

**Choose options for your new project:**

| | |
|---|---|
| Product Name | StoryBoardExample |
| Organization Name | |
| Company Identifier | |
| Bundle Identifier | edu.css.StoryBoardExample |
| Class Prefix | XYZ |
| Devices | iPhone |

☑ Use Storyboards
☑ Use Automatic Reference Counting
☐ Include Unit Tests

Cancel            Previous     Next

**Figure 9-6**    Choosing options for your new project window

4.  Click the **Next** button to choose a location to save the project, and then click the **Create** button. This will finish creating the project and open Xcode.

5.  Click the **MainStoryboard.storyboard** file name in the navigation area on the left-hand side of the screen. The project opens in the editor pane, with a single view visible. The arrow on the left side of the view controller tells you that this is the project's initial view. See Figure 9-7. The initial view is the view that you first see when the app starts to run. Xcode automatically generates these files for your project: AppDelegate.h, AppDelegate.m, MainStoryboard.storyboard, ViewController.h, ViewController.m. These files are seen in the navigation area.

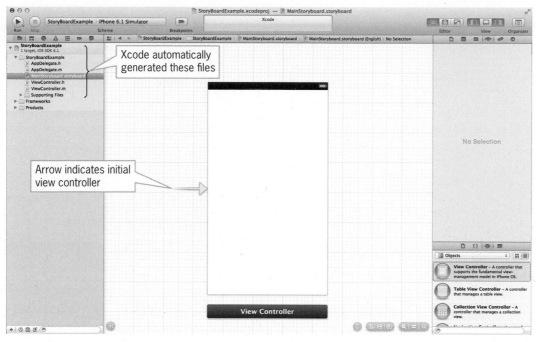

**Figure 9-7** A project's storyboard with a single view

6. If the Object Library is not open, open it now using the Xcode menu as follows: click **View ▶ Utilities ▶ Show Object Library**. The Object Library, as you remember from Chapter 8, is in the lower right of the screen, in the lower section of the utility pane. This is where you will select controls and then drag them to the view to build the interface.

7. From the list of objects in the Object Library, click on the View Controller box, hold down the mouse button, drag it onto the blue grid, which is the editor pane. This creates a new view controller as seen in Figure 9-8.

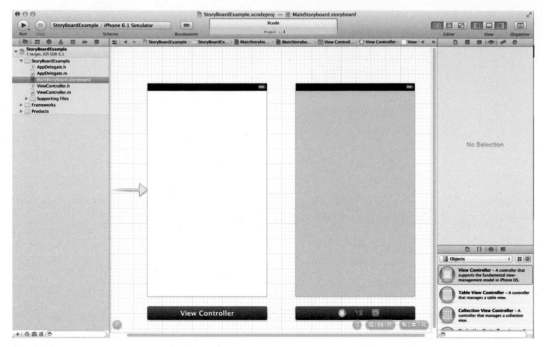

**Figure 9-8**   New view controller added to storyboard

**8.** Click the first view controller (the one on the left) to select it, change the background color to blue, and then change the background color for the second view controller to red. You learned how to select a new background color in Chapter 8.

**9.** Drag a Round Rect button from the Object Library onto the left view controller, double-click it, and type **Go to next view**.

**10.** Drag a Round Rect button from the Object Library to the right view controller, double-click it, and type **Back to first view**. At this point, your screen should match Figure 9-9. Now you are ready to create a connection, or segue. Your goal is to create a connection between the "Go to next view" button, and the right-hand view controller. That is, when the user clicks the "Go to next view" button, you want the right-hand view controller (the one with the red background) to appear.

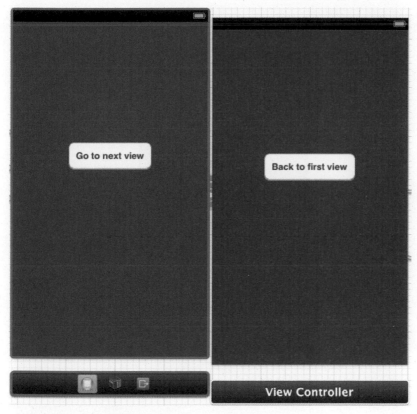

**Figure 9-9**  Two views with one button each

11. Press and hold the Control button while you drag the "Go to next view" button from the left view controller onto the right view controller. This displays a window with three options, as shown in Figure 9-10.

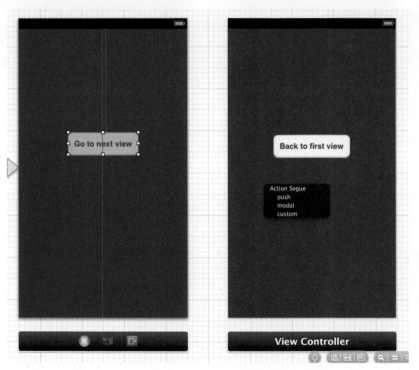

**Figure 9-10**    Three options for making a connection

The first option, push, is used with a navigation bar; you'll have a chance to use this option later in this chapter. The third option, custom, lets the developer code a custom connection. Right now you'll use the second option, modal, which is typically used for presenting a new view controller without a navigation controller. The new view controller in a modal segue is considered to be a child of the presenting view controller.

**12.**  Click **modal** to create the segue. The newly created segue is shown in Figure 9-11.

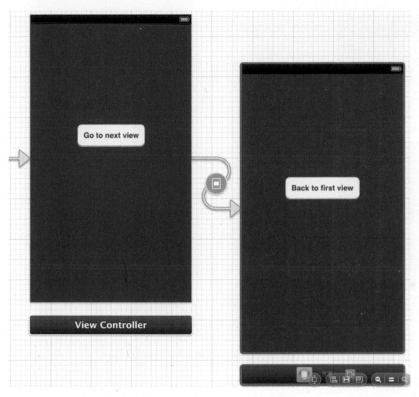

**Figure 9-11** Newly created segue

**13.** Next, you need to create a connection, or segue, between the "Back to first view" button and the left view controller (the one with the blue background). Press and hold the Control key, and then drag the "Back to first view" button from the right view controller to anywhere on the left view controller and select **modal**. This creates a second segue, as seen in Figure 9-12.

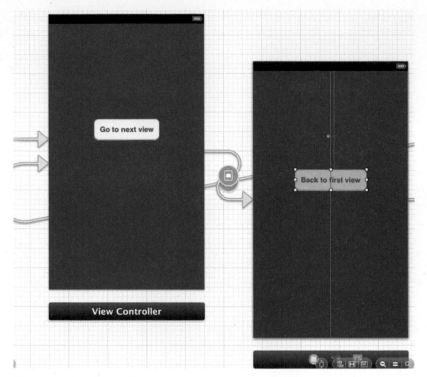

**Figure 9-12**    Second segue

14. Click the **Run** button in the upper-left corner of the Xcode window to run the app. The view with the blue background appears first, as seen in Figure 9-13.

    Note: If you have trouble getting a project to run, verify that all the code is correct. If it still won't run, close Xcode, reopen it, and then try running the project again.

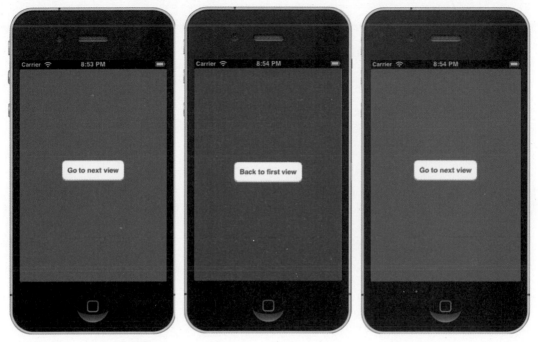

**Figure 9-13**   Running the app

15. Click the **Go to next view** button. This displays the view with the red background.

16. Click the **Back to first view** button. This redisplays the view with the blue background, shown earlier in Figure 9-13.

## Storyboard Example with Navigation Bars

In this example we will create a storyboard with two view controllers, each with a navigation bar. A **navigation bar** is a horizontal bar with buttons that the user can click to move among view controllers.

1. Create a Single View Application project named **navigationBarExample**. Make sure to select the **Use Storyboards** and the **Use Automatic Reference Counting** check boxes.

2. Click the **MainStoryboard.storyboard** file name in the navigation area on the left side of the screen. The project opens in the editor pane.

3. Now we will embed a navigation controller in the view controller. Select the view controller then on the menu click **Editor ▶ Embed In ▶ Navigation Controller**, as shown in Figure 9-14. Embedding a navigation controller adds a navigation bar at the top of the view controller as well as a navigation controller, as shown in Figure 9-15. The arrow to the left of the new navigation controller tells you that it is now the initial view controller. Note that if you want to make a view controller the initial view controller, you can adjust the setting shown in Figure 9-16. We will not be changing this setting now, but you should be aware that it is possible to do so.

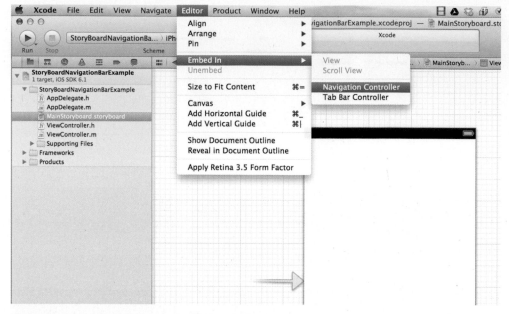

**Figure 9-14**  Embedding a navigation controller

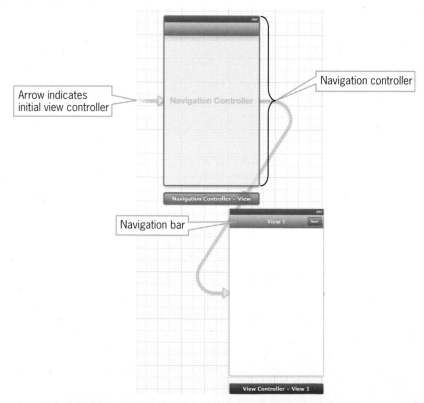

**Figure 9-15**  After embedding a navigation controller

**Figure 9-16** Setting to making a view controller the initial view

Copyright © 2014 Apple®. All Rights Reserved.

4. To add a title to the navigation bar, double-click in the center and then type **View 1**, as shown in Figure 9-17.

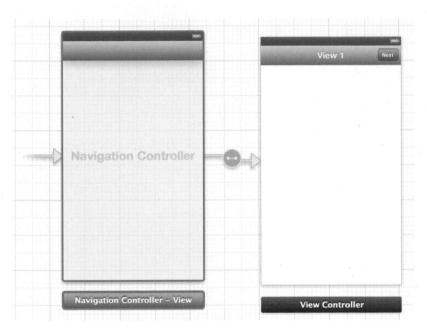

**Figure 9-17** Navigation bar with new title

Copyright © 2014 Apple®. All Rights Reserved.

5. Change the view's background color to black. This will make it easier to see the transition from one view to the next.

6. Add a second view controller, embed a navigation controller in it, and then add the title **View 2** to the navigation bar. At this point, your screen should match Figure 9-18. Note that the connections between the view controllers and the navigation controller were automatically generated when we embedded the navigation controllers.

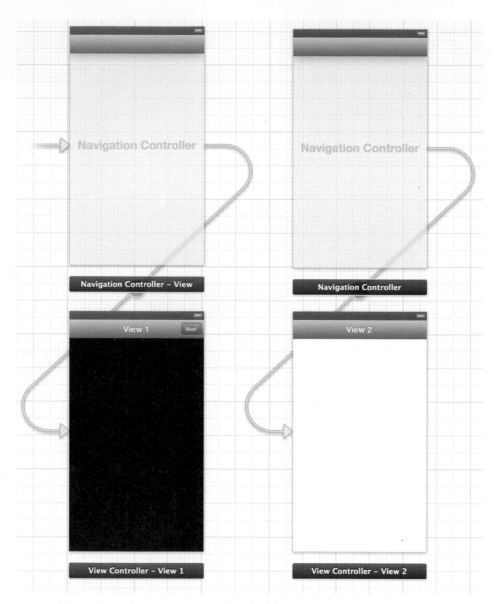

**Figure 9-18**   Second view controller with embedded navigation controller

7.  Now we need a button to initiate a transition. Drag a Bar Button Item from the Object Library on the lower-right corner of the utility window to the view controller with "View 1" in the navigation bar. You can search for the bar button in the Object Library by typing the initial few letters of the item you are searching in the search field, as shown in Figure 9-19.

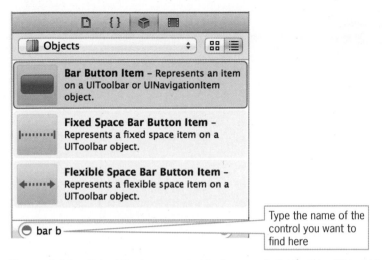

Type the name of the control you want to find here

**Figure 9-19** Searching for a control in the search field of the Object Library

Copyright © 2014 Apple®. All Rights Reserved.

8. Double-click the new **Bar Button Item**, and type **Next**.

9. Create a segue from the bar button on the first view controller to the second view controller using the push option. See Figure 9-20.

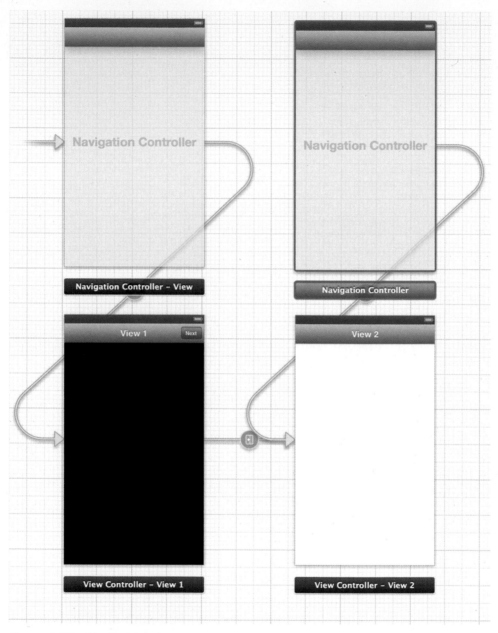

**Figure 9-20**    Newly created segue

10. Click the **Run** button to run the app, as shown in Figure 9-21. The first view, with the black background, is displayed.

**Figure 9-21** Running the app

Copyright © 2014 Apple®. All Rights Reserved.

11. Click the **Next** button to display the second view, with "View 2" as the title in the navigation bar, as shown in Figure 9-22. Note the "View 1" button in the navigation bar, which is automatically generated.

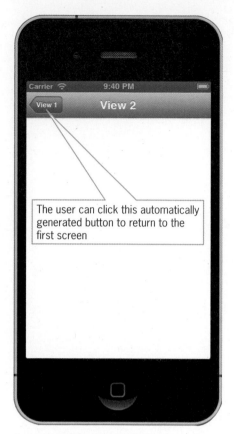

The user can click this automatically generated button to return to the first screen

**Figure 9-22**   View after clicking the Next button

Copyright © 2014 Apple®. All Rights Reserved.

**12.** Click the **View 1** button. The first view is displayed, as seen earlier in Figure 9-21.

# Passing Data Between Views

So far we have learned to transition from one view to another. Now we will learn to pass data between the views. In this example, we will create a storyboard project with two view controllers that passes data from the first view controller to the second view controller. This app will allow the user to enter two numbers and then touch Sum to display a new view that displays the sum in a label.

**1.** Create a **Single View Application** project. Make sure to select the **Use Storyboards** and the **Use Automatic Reference Counting** check boxes. Name this project **PassingDataBetweenViews**.

**2.** Embed a navigation controller in the view controller, and add the title **View 1** to the navigation bar.

**3.** Add another view controller, embed another navigation controller in this new view controller, and add the title **View 2** to the navigation bar. Since each view is required to be associated with the `ViewController.h` and `ViewController.m` files and we only have one set of `ViewController.h`, and `ViewController.m` files, we need to create another set of view controller files.

4. Create a set of `ViewController.h` and `ViewController.m` files by choosing **File ▶ New ▶ File** from the menu bar as seen in Figure 9-23. In the Choose a template for your new file dialog, select **Cocoa Touch** in the left column and then **Objective-C class**, as shown in Figure 9-24.

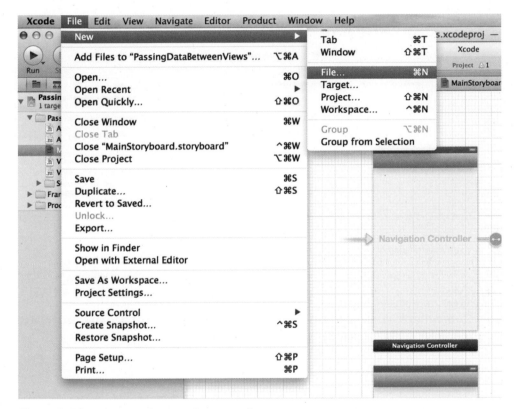

**Figure 9-23** Creation of a new view controller

256

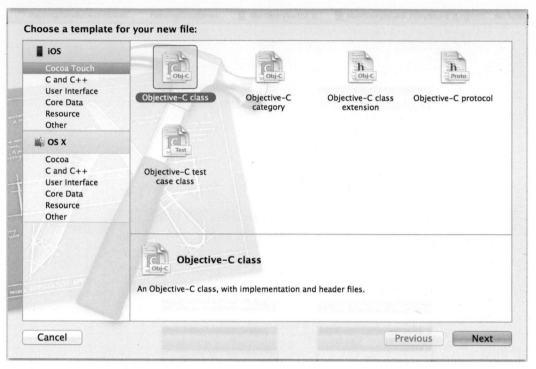

**Figure 9-24**    Choose a template for your new file

5.  Click **Next** to display the Choose options for your new file dialog. Enter
    **ViewController2** in the Class box, and, for the subclass, select **UIViewController** in
    the drop down menu, as shown in Figure 9-25.

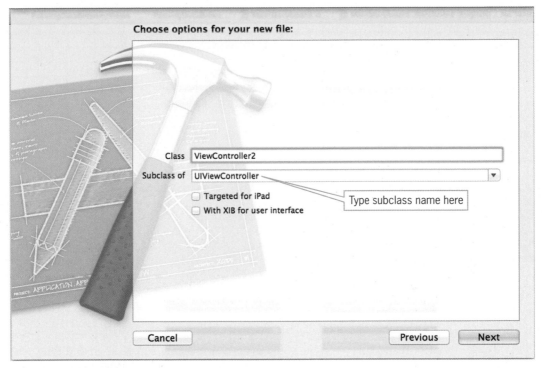

Figure 9-25    Selecting a class and a subclass

6.  Click **Next** and save the files in the project folder. This generates the `ViewController2.h` and `ViewController2.m` files as shown in Figure 9-26. Also notice that the files associated with View1 are called `ViewController.h` and `ViewController.m` as they were auto generated and renaming them would cause issues at this point.

Figure 9-26    `ViewController2.h` and `ViewController2.m` files

7. Select the `MainStoryboard.storyboard` file in the navigation area and then open the Assistant Editor pane as explained in Chapter 8 so you can see the view controller alongside its associated `ViewController.h` file.

8. Now you need to associate the newly added `ViewController2.h`, and `ViewController2.m` files with the second view. Select the newly added view controller, and then, in the utility area, select the Identity Inspector icon, as shown in Figure 9-27, to display the Identity Inspector.

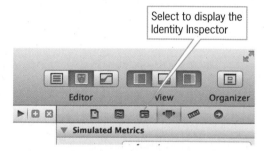

**Figure 9-27**    Identity Inspector icon
Copyright © 2014 Apple®. All Rights Reserved.

9. In the Identity Inspector, open the Class drop-down menu, scroll down and then select **ViewController2**. Figure 9-28 shows ViewController2 selected. Make sure you select the view controller by clicking in its top blue bar, near the battery icon. A blue line will appear around the controller, as shown in Figure 9-28, when the controller is selected.

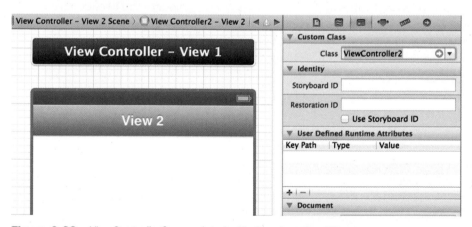

**Figure 9-28**    ViewController2 associated with the `.h` and `.m` files
Copyright © 2014 Apple®. All Rights Reserved.

Note that if you are not able to see this file, there could be two possible problems. One possibility is that you did not select the UIViewController as the subclass while creating the view controller classes. If you think that is the case, recreate these files using the correct options and remember to delete the files you chose not to use. The second possibility is that Xcode may not be recognizing the files yet. To resolve this you may have to close Xcode and reopen it.

10. Change the color of the first view to blue and the second view to green.

11. On the blue view controller's navigation bar, change the title to **Passing Data/Sum.** On the green view controller's navigation bar, change the title to **Receiving Data/Sum.**

12. Drag two text fields and two labels to the Passing Data/Sum view controller from the Object Library. Add the text "Number 1" and "Number 2" to the labels, and arrange them in the view as shown in Figure 9-29. Drag a label to the **Receiving Data/Sum** view controller from the Object Library. For now, do not change the label's default text.

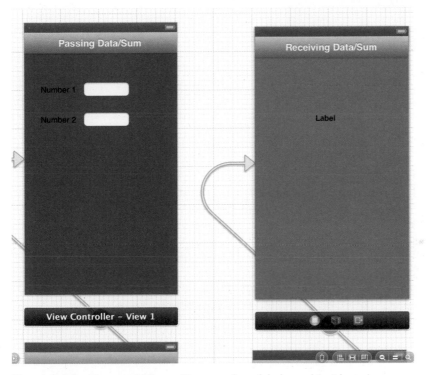

**Figure 9-29** View controllers with new colors, labels, and text boxes

13. Now we need to create the IBOutlets for each of the controls in the view controllers. To get started, display the Assistant Editor pane. The Assistant Editor enables us to see the storyboard while also seeing the code of the view controller files.

14. Create an IBOutlet for the label (output) in the green view controller by control-dragging the label from the green view controller to ViewController2.h, and entering the settings shown in Figure 9-30. We want this label to display the sum of the numbers input in the text fields of the blue view controller. The code generated for the IBOutlet for the label in ViewController2.h is as follows:

```
@property (weak, nonatomic) IBOutlet UILabel *total;
```

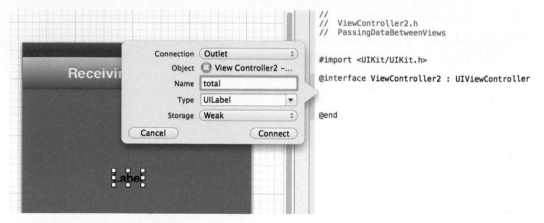

**Figure 9-30** IBOutlet for label
Copyright © 2014 Apple®. All Rights Reserved.

15. If the @synthesize property for the IBOutlet is not autogenerated, then make sure to create it in the ViewController2.m file as shown here:

    @synthesize total;

16. Create IBOutlets for the text fields (num1, num2) in the blue view controller by control-dragging the two text fields from the blue view controller to the ViewController.h.

    The code generated for the IBOutlets for the text fields in the ViewController.h file is as follows:

    @property (weak, nonatomic) IBOutlet UITextField *num1;
    @property (weak, nonatomic) IBOutlet UITextField *num2;

17. If the @synthesize properties for the IBOutlets are not autogenerated, then make sure to create them in the ViewController.m file as shown here:

    @synthesize num1;
    @synthesize num2;

18. Next add a Bar Button Item to the navigation bar on the blue view controller, and then add the text **Add** to the button.

19. Create the segue from the bar button of the blue view controller by control dragging the Add button to the green view controller. Select **push** as the type of connection. At this stage, your app should match Figure 9-31.

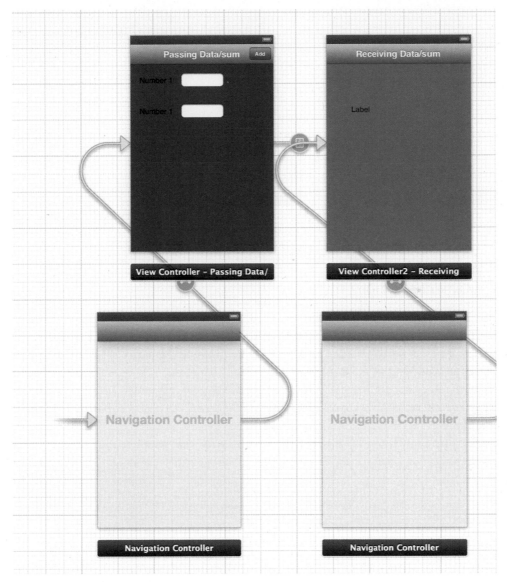

**Figure 9-31** Creating a segue

**20.** Name the segue identifier **sum** by selecting the segue and, in the Attributes Inspector, typing the name (sum) in the Identifier field as shown in Figure 9-32.

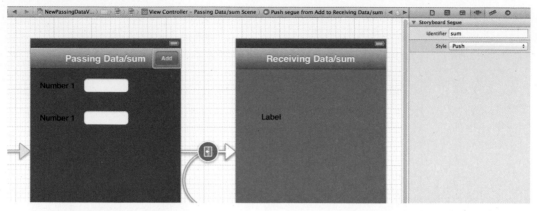

**Figure 9-32**   Naming a segue

21. Import ViewController2 into view 1 by entering the following code in the `ViewController.h` file:

```
#import "ViewController2.h"
```

22. Next, in the `ViewController.m` file, write an `if` statement to make sure you are referring to the correct segue, as there may be multiple segues in a view. The code for this is as follows:

```
-(void) prepareForSegue:(UIStoryboardSegue *)segue
                    sender:(id)sender
{
    if ([segue.identifier isEqualToString:@"sum"]) {
    }
}
```

23. After the code checks to see if the segue is `sum`, we need to write the code for the addition of the two numbers as shown here:

```
int total = [num1.text intValue] + [num2.text intValue];
```

Notice the contents of the text fields are converted to an int value as the value when entered takes a string value and strings cannot be added.

24. We now need to pass the total to the next view controller. We accomplish this by creating an instance of `ViewController2` in the `ViewController.m` file as shown here:

```
ViewController2 *vc2 = [segue destinationViewController];
```

25. Next create a `NSString` property called `receiverSum` in the `ViewController2.h` file. This variable will be used to transfer the sum of the two numbers entered in View 1 to View 2.

```
@property (weak, nonatomic) NSString *receiverSum;
```

**26.** In the `ViewController2.m` file, synthesize the `NSString` variable `receiverSum`, which we created in the `ViewController.h` file, as follows:

`@synthesize receiverSum;`

**27.** Switch back to the ViewController.m file. Since the calculation is an `int` and the receiving variable `receiverSum` is a `NSString` (as declared previously) we have to format the `int` as a string. We do this using the `NSNumber` formatter. We first create an instance of the `NSNumberFormatter` object as seen here:

`NSNumberFormatter *format = [[NSNumberFormatter alloc] init];`

**28.** Next we create an `NSString` called `numberAsString` and store the formatted variable `total` (which is the label we created in View 2) in this string using the instance of the `numberformatter`:

`NSString * numberAsString = [format stringFromNumber:[NSNumber numberWithInt:total]];`

**29.** Next we go back to `ViewController.m` and complete the `prepareForSegue` method. The `prepareForSegue` method is generated when a segue is created using the control-drag method. The `stringAsNumber` variable is passed to the `receiverSum` variable in the `ViewController2` file via the `vc2` instance of the `ViewController2` file as shown in the following code:

`vc2.receiverSum = [NSString stringWithFormat:@"The sum of the 2 numbers is %@", numberAsString];`

**30.** Switch to the ViewController2.m file. Next we need to assign to the total label the value being passed to `ViewController2`, which is stored in `receiverSum`. This requires the following code in the `viewDidLoad` method:

`[total setText:receiverSum];`

**31.** Review the complete code for the `prepareForSegue` method in the `ViewController.m` file, and make sure that yours matches:

```
-(void) prepareForSegue:(UIStoryboardSegue *)segue
sender:(id)sender
{
    if ([segue.identifier isEqualToString:@"sum"]) {
        //do the calculation
        int total = [num1.text intValue] + [num2.text intValue];

        //create a formatter
        NSNumberFormatter *format = [[NSNumberFormatter alloc]
init];

        //format total to a string
        NSString * numberAsString = [format
            stringFromNumber:[NSNumber numberWithInt:total]];

        ViewController2 *vc2 = [segue destinationViewController];
        vc2.receiverSum = [NSString stringWithFormat:@"The sum of
  the 2 numbers is %@", numberAsString];
    }
}
```

The code for `ViewController.h` is shown as follows

```
#import <UIKit/UIKit.h>
#import "ViewController2.h"
@interface ViewController : UIViewController
@property (weak, nonatomic) IBOutlet UITextField *num1;
@property (weak, nonatomic) IBOutlet UITextField *num2;
@end
```

The code for `ViewController.m` is shown as follows

```
#import "ViewController.h"

@interface ViewController ()

@end

@implementation ViewController
@synthesize num1;
@synthesize num2;

- (void)viewDidLoad
{
    [super viewDidLoad];
    // Do any additional setup after loading the view, typically
from a nib.
}

- (void)didReceiveMemoryWarning
{
    [super didReceiveMemoryWarning];
    // Dispose of any resources that can be recreated.
}
-(void) prepareForSegue:(UIStoryboardSegue *)segue
sender:(id)sender
{
    if ([segue.identifier isEqualToString:@"sum"]) {
        //do the calculation
        int total = [num1.text intValue] + [num2.text intValue];

        //create a formatter
        NSNumberFormatter *format = [[NSNumberFormatter alloc]
init];

        //format total to a string
        NSString * numberAsString = [format
                                        stringFromNumber:[NSNumber
numberWithInt:total]];

        ViewController2 *vc2 = [segue destinationViewController];
        vc2.receiverSum = [NSString stringWithFormat:@"The sum of
 the 2 numbers is %@", numberAsString];
    }
}
@end
```

The code for ViewController2.h is shown as follows

```objc
#import <UIKit/UIKit.h>

@interface ViewController2 : UIViewController

@property (weak, nonatomic) IBOutlet UILabel *total;
@property (weak, nonatomic) NSString *receiverSum;

@end
```

The code for ViewController2.m is shown as follows

```objc
#import "ViewController2.h"

@interface ViewController2 ()

@end

@implementation ViewController2
@synthesize receiverSum;
@synthesize total;

- (id)initWithNibName:(NSString *)nibNameOrNil
bundle:(NSBundle *)nibBundleOrNil
{
    self = [super initWithNibName:nibNameOrNil
 bundle:nibBundleOrNil];
    if (self) {
        // Custom initialization
    }
    return self;
}

- (void)viewDidLoad
{
    [super viewDidLoad];
    // Do any additional setup after loading the view.
    [total setText:receiverSum];
}

- (void)didReceiveMemoryWarning
{
    [super didReceiveMemoryWarning];
    // Dispose of any resources that can be recreated.
}

@end
```

**32.** Run the app as shown in Figure 9-33. Enter **78** for Number 1 and **45** for Number 2. Click the **Add** button to display the second view, where the label contains the text "The sum of the 2 numbers is 123".

**Figure 9-33**    Running the app that passes data from one view to another

## HANDS-ON LAB

In this Hands-On Lab, we will create an app that calculates a person's Body Mass Index (BMI). The interface for this app is as shown in Figure 9-34.

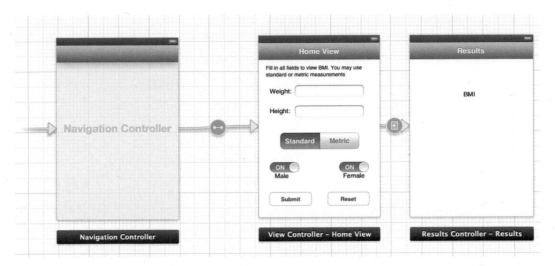

**Figure 9-34** BMI calculator

## PROJECT CREATION

1. Create a new project using the Single View Application template. Remember to select the **Use Storyboards** and the **Use Automatic Reference Counting** check boxes. Name the project **BMICalculator**.

2. Click on the **MainStoryboard.storyboard** file to see the interface in the editor pane.

## ADDING CONTROLS TO THE VIEW CONTROLLER

3. Add a navigation controller to the view controller in the storyboard. Add the title **Home View** to the navigation bar.

4. From the Object Library, drag a label object to the view controller. Double-click the label and type **Fill in the fields to view BMI. You may use standard or metric measurements.** Change the Lines property in the Attributes inspector to 2, if necessary.

5. Drag and drop two labels and two text fields from the Object Library to the view. Position them as shown in Figure 9-34. Add **Weight** and **Height** to the labels, as shown in Figure 9-34.

6. From the Object Library, drag a segmented control to the view. Click on each side of the control, and type **Standard** and **Metric** as shown in Figure 9-34.

7. From the Object Library, drag the following to the view: two labels, two switches, and two buttons. Position them as shown in Figure 9-34. Type **Male** in one label and **Female** in the other, and align each label with a switch as shown in Figure 9-34.

8.  Add **Submit** to one button and **Reset** to the other button, as shown in Figure 9-34.

9.  Add a second view controller to the right of the first one.

10. Add a label to the new view, double-click it, and type **BMI** in it, as shown in Figure 9-34.

## GUI PROGRAMING

11. Click the text field to the right of the "Height" label.

12. Open the Assistant Editor pane.

13. Control-drag the text field from the view controller to the `ViewController.h` file to create an `IBOutlet`. Give this `IBOutlet` the name **height**.

14. Do the same for the text field to the right of the **Weight** label, but use the name **weight** for the IBOutlet.

15. Next, control-drag each of the remaining controls using the following names:

    - Segmented control: `IBOutlet` called **measure**
    - First switch: `IBOutlet` called **male**
    - First switch: `IBAction` called **maleSelected**
    - Second switch: `IBOutlet` called **female**
    - Second switch: `IBAction` called **femaleSelected**
    - Second button: `IBAction` called **resetBtn**

    Next make sure to modify all the `IBOutlet` properties in this lab to retain from weak as seen in the code on page 269. Also remember to synthesize the `IBOutlets` in the ViewController.m file with the following code:

    ```
    @synthesize male;
    @synthesize female;
    @synthesize measure;
    @synthesize height;
    @synthesize weight;
    ```

16. Create the set of ViewController files for the second view controller. Name it **ResultsController**.

17. Associate the second view controller with the newly added Objective-C class files as shown in Figure 9-35.

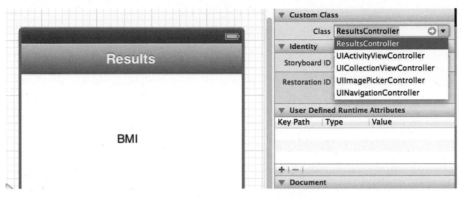

**Figure 9-35** Associating the view controller with the Object-C class files

18. Create a segue between the Submit button and the second view controller, using the push option. As soon as the segue is created a navigation bar will show up on the newly added view controller. Enter "Results" as the title for this navigation bar.:

19. In Attributes Inspector, in the Identifier field, name this segue **sendData**. This will be used later to pass data between views.

20. Create an IBOutlet for the label on the results view controller by control dragging the label to the ResultsViewController.h generating the following code:

    ```
    @property (retain, nonatomic) IBOutlet UILabel *result;
    ```

21. Next create a property for a string variable that will hold the BMI result using a the following code:

    ```
    @property (nonatomic, strong) NSString *calculatedResult;
    ```

22. Remember to synthesize these properties in the ResultViewController.m using the following code:

    ```
    @synthesize result;
    @synthesize calculatedResult;
    ```

## CODING GENDER SELECTION

23. Open the ViewController.m file. Here, we will write the code that ensures that only one gender can be selected at a time. Edit the maleSelected and femaleSelected IBAction methods we created for the maleSelected and femaleSelected switches to look like this:

    ```
    - (IBAction)femaleSelected:(id)sender {
      if (female.on) {
       [male setOn:NO];
      }
      else{
        [male setOn:YES];
      }
    }
    ```

```
-(IBAction)maleSelected:(id)sender {
   if (male.on) {
     [female setOn:NO];
   }
   else{
     [female setOn:YES];
   }
}
```

## CODING THE RESET BUTTON

24. Add the following code for the Reset button. This code clears all controls and restores some defaults.

```
- (IBAction)resetBtn:(id)sender {
   [height setText:@""];
   [weight setText:@""];
   [measure setSelectedSegmentIndex:0];
   [male setOn:NO];
   [female setOn:YES];
}
```

## CODING THE TRANSITION FROM VIEW 1 TO VIEW 2

25. Because we will be passing some data to the ResultViewController, import this class at the top of the ViewController.m file and add the following method to pass data:

```
#import "ResultsController.h"
```

26. Next add the following code to the prepareForSegue method to pass data from ViewController to ResultsViewController:

```
- (void)prepareForSegue:(UIStoryboardSegue *)segue sender:(id)sender {
   double result  = [weight.text doubleValue]/([height.text doubleValue] *
[height.text doubleValue]);
   if(measure.selectedSegmentIndex == 0){
     if (male.isOn) {
       result *= 703;
     }
     else{
       result *= 703;
       }
   }
   else{
           }
           if ([segue.identifier isEqualToString: @"sendData"]){
     ResultsController *resultController = segue.destinationViewController;
     resultController.calculatedResult = [NSString stringWithFormat:@"%.2f",
     result];
     }
}
```

## CODE TO HIDE KEYBOARD

27. The keyboard can get in the way of entering data. We will discuss different mechanisms for hiding the keyboard in chapter 10. For now, select the height text field, and then control-drag it to the interface file to create an IBAction. In the popup window, select an IBAction(IBOutlet will be selected by default), use **hideKeyBoard** as the name, and select **Did End on Exit** as the Event. The following code will be autogenerated in the ViewController.h file:

```
(IBAction)hideKeyboard:(id)sender;
```

28. Create the implementation for the hideKeyboard method in the ViewController.m file, as follows:

```
- (IBAction)hideKeyboard:(id)sender{
    [sender resignFirstResponder];
}
```

29. In the viewDidLoad method of the ViewController.m add the following code:

```
male.on = NO;
    female.on = YES;
```

In the viewDidLoad method of the ResultsViewController.m add the following code:

```
[result setText:calculatedResult];
```

30.    Run the app, enter **123** for the weight, **62** for the height, make sure **Standard** is selected, and then click the **Submit** button. You should see the results shown in Figure 9-36.

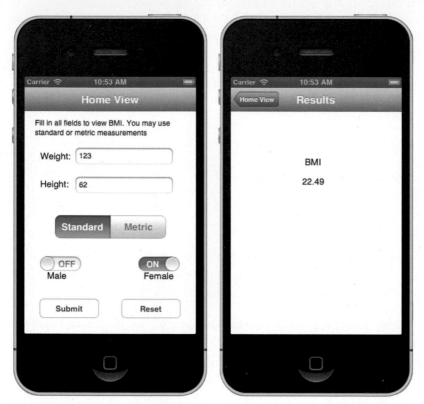

**Figure 9-36**    Running the BMI calculator

The code for the `ViewController.h` file is shown as follows

```
#import <UIKit/UIKit.h>

@interface ViewController : UIViewController
@property (retain, nonatomic) IBOutlet UISwitch *male;

@property (retain, nonatomic) IBOutlet UISwitch *female;
@property (retain, nonatomic) IBOutlet UISegmentedControl
*measure;
@property (retain, nonatomic) IBOutlet UITextField *height;
@property (retain, nonatomic) IBOutlet UITextField *weight;

- (IBAction)femaleSelected:(id)sender;
- (IBAction)maleSelected:(id)sender;
- (IBAction)resetBtn:(id)sender;
-(IBAction)hideKeyboard:(id)sender;

@end
```

The code for the ViewController.m file is shown as follows

```objc
#import "ViewController.h"
#import "ResultsController.h"

@implementation ViewController
@synthesize male;
@synthesize female;
@synthesize measure;
@synthesize height;
@synthesize weight;

- (void)didReceiveMemoryWarning
{
    [super didReceiveMemoryWarning];
    // Release any cached data, images, etc that aren't in use.
}

#pragma mark - View lifecycle

- (void)viewDidLoad
{
    [super viewDidLoad];
    male.on = NO;
    female.on = YES;
    // Do any additional setup after loading the view, typically
from a nib.
}

- (IBAction)femaleSelected:(id)sender {
    if (female.on) {
        [male setOn:NO];
    }
    else{
        [male setOn:YES];
    }
}

- (IBAction)maleSelected:(id)sender {
    if (male.on) {
        [female setOn:NO];
    }
    else{
        [female setOn:YES];
    }
}

- (IBAction)hideKeyboard:(id)sender{
    [sender resignFirstResponder];
}
```

```objc
- (void)prepareForSegue:(UIStoryboardSegue *)segue
sender:(id)sender {
    double result  = [weight.text doubleValue]/([height.text
doubleValue] * [height.text doubleValue]);
    if(measure.selectedSegmentIndex == 0){
        if (male.isOn) {
            result *= 703;
        }
        else{
            result *= 703;
        }
    }
    else{

    }

    if ([segue.identifier isEqualToString:@"sendData"]) {
        ResultsController *resultController =
 segue.destinationViewController;
        resultController.calculatedResult = [NSString
stringWithFormat:@"%.2f", result];
    }
}

- (IBAction)resetBtn:(id)sender {
    [height setText:@""];
    [weight setText:@""];
    [measure setSelectedSegmentIndex:0];
    [male setOn:NO];
    [female setOn:YES];
}
@end
```

The code for the ResultsController.h file is shown as follows

```objc
#import <UIKit/UIKit.h>

@interface ResultsController : UIViewController
@property (retain, nonatomic) IBOutlet UILabel *result;
@property (nonatomic, strong) NSString *calculatedResult;

@end
```

The code for the ResultsController.m file is shown as follows

```objc
#import "ResultsController.h"

@implementation ResultsController
@synthesize result;
@synthesize calculatedResult;

- (id)initWithNibName:(NSString *)nibNameOrNil bundle:(NSBundle *)
nibBundleOrNil
```

```
{
    self = [super initWithNibName:nibNameOrNil
 bundle:nibBundleOrNil];
    if (self) {
        // Custom initialization
    }
    return self;
}

- (void)didReceiveMemoryWarning
{

    // Releases the view if it doesn't have a superview.
    [super didReceiveMemoryWarning];

    // Release any cached data, images, etc that aren't in use.
}

#pragma mark - View lifecycle

// Implement viewDidLoad to do additional setup after loading the
view, typically from a nib.
- (void)viewDidLoad
{
    [super viewDidLoad];
    [result setText:calculatedResult];
}

- (void)viewDidUnload
{
    [self setResult:nil];
    [super viewDidUnload];
    // Release any retained subviews of the main view.
    // e.g. self.myOutlet = nil;
}

-
(BOOL)shouldAutorotateToInterfaceOrientation:(UIInterface
Orientation)interfaceOrientation
{
    // Return YES for supported orientations
    return (interfaceOrientation ==
UIInterfaceOrientationPortrait);
}

@end
```

## Summary

- The UIKit framework supports the user interface in an app and provides all the necessary elements that create and handle user interactions.

- Storyboarding is a feature that allows the developer to see all the views controllers at one time.

- You drag and drop views onto the canvas and then connect them via controls such as the buttons, labels, and text fields.

- The `MainStoryboard.storyboard` file is an interface file similar to the `.xib` file.

- Each view has an associated view controller and `@interface` and `@implementation` classes, along with an `.xib` file.

- A navigation bar supports the transition from one view to another.

- To pass data from one view to another, the `prepareForSegue` method is used.

## Exercises

1. Mark the following statements as true or false. Correct the false statements.

   a. A view is also referred to as a scene, especially when working with storyboards.

   b. A view controller displays data and translates input from the user into action.

   c. Storyboarding is a feature that allows the developer to work with a single view controller.

   d. The transitions in a storyboard are called segues.

   e. When using storyboards, you still need to use `.xib` files.

2. Describe the UIKit framework

3. Describe the main functions of the following objects:

   a. `MainStoryboard.storyboard` file

   b. navigation bar

   c. storyboard

   d. navigation controller

4. What files are automatically generated when a new project is created using storyboards?

5. Explain how to open the Object Library.

6. Explain the following terms:

   a. storyboarding

   b. segue

7. Given a text field named myTextField, a switch named mySwitch, and a label named myLabel, write a line of code that accomplishes each of the following tasks:

    a. Check if the switch is OFF
    b. Set the text of the label to "I love programming"
    c. Set the text of the text field with that of the label
    d. Set the state of switch to ON
    e. Return the state of the switch
    f. Clear the text field
    g. Make the text field noneditable

8. Differentiate between the following

    a. A text field and a label
    b. A segmented control and a switch

9. Given a text field named myTextField, a switch named mySwitch, and a label named myLabel, identify the error in the following code

    a. `[myTextField.text] = @"I am a student";`
    b. `[mySwitch state] = ON;`
    c. `myLabel.Text = @"Full Name";`
    d. `if(mySwitch == ON){ }`
    e. `int num = myTextField.Text`

10. When linking views, what is the difference between applying a push connection and applying a modal connection?

# Programming Exercises

Solve each of these programming questions using storyboards. The design of the user interface is left to your discretion.

1. Create a simple app that allows the user to move between three views. The first view should contain two buttons, which in turn contain the text "Two" and "Three". The second view should contain two buttons: One and Three. The third view contains two buttons: One and Two. When the user clicks on button Two, the second view should appear. When the user clicks on button One, the first view should appear. When the user clicks on button Three, the third view should appear.

2. Create a side-dish-recommender app. The initial view of this app should contain three buttons:

    a. Burger
    b. Pasta
    c. Orange Chicken

When the user clicks one of the buttons, another view should appear that displays a recommended side. For example clicking the Burger button should take the user to a view with the recommended side: fries. Clicking Pasta should display the recommended side dish: breadsticks. Clicking Orange Chicken should display the recommended side dish: potstickers. The second view should have a Back button, which allows the user to go back to the first view.

3.  Create a palindrome-checker app. A palindrome is a word or phrase that reads the same backward and forward. This app should contain two views. The first view should allow the user to enter some text. The app should check to see if the input entered by the user is a palindrome. If it is a palindrome, the app should display a second view with the message "Success!" If it is not a palindrome, the app should display a second view with the message "Try again". The app does not have to check for phrases with spaces.

4.  Create a gift-ideas app. The app should contain three views. The first view should contain two buttons: Male and Female. The second view should contain four buttons: Infant, Adolescent, Adult. The third view should display the gift suggestions listed in Table 9-1.

| First Screen | Second Screen | Suggestions |
| --- | --- | --- |
| Male | Infant | toy trucks, blanket |
| Female | Infant | Lego set, blanket |
| Male | Adolescent | baseball jersey |
| Female | Adolescent | softball jersey |
| Male | Adult | tie, watch |
| Female | Adult | earrings, watch |

**Table 9-1**    Gift suggestions

5.  Create a probability calculator that calculates probability in the following scenario: Suppose there are x orange balls, y white balls, and z green balls in a bag. The probability of removing a orange ball can be given as $x/(y + z + x)$, the probability of removing a white ball is $y/(y + z + x)$ and the probability of removing a green ball is $z/(y + z + x)$. The app should have two views. The first should allow the user to input the number of white, green, and orange balls. The second view should display the probability of picking a ball of each color.

6.  Create a grocery list app containing two screens. In the first screen, the user should be able to enter an item and then touch either the Add button or the View button. If the user enters an item and touches the Add button, the item is added to the list, but the user does not see the entire list. If the user enters an item and clicks the add button and then the View button, the item is added to the list and then the app displays the

entire list so far on the second screen. If the user does not enter any input, and simply touches the View button, the second screen should still display the grocery list thus far.

7. Write an app for a calculator capable of performing the following operations: addition, subtraction, multiplication, division, and factoring. Your app should use controls like text fields, labels, and buttons.

8. Write an app that does the following:
   a. Display a button that the user can touch to generate a random number.

   b. Give the user three chances to guess the random number.

   c. Give the user hints that make it easier to guess the random number each time the user guesses incorrectly. For example, if the user enters a number that is lower than the randomly generated number, it should display "higher," hinting that the user should enter a higher number.

   Your app should use controls like text fields, labels, and buttons.

9. Mr. Nyugen is an art instructor who wants to teach his students about mixing colors. Use storyboards to create an app that simulates the process of mixing paint to create a new color. The app should have three switches for the three primary colors (Red, Blue, and Green) on its initial view. Also include a View button. The user should be able to switch any of the three colors to On or Off, and then click the View button to display a new view with its background set to match the new color that would result if you actually mixed the "On" colors. Here is a summary of the color mixtures:

   - Red is ON + blue is ON + green is ON = white
   - Red is ON + blue is ON + green is OFF = magenta
   - Red is ON + blue is OFF + green is ON = yellow
   - Red is ON + blue is OFF + green is OFF = red
   - Red is OFF + blue is ON + green is ON = cyan
   - Red is OFF + blue is ON + green is OFF = blue
   - Red is OFF + blue is OFF + green is ON = green
   - Red is OFF + blue is OFF + green is OFF = black

# Business Case Study

In this Business Case Study, you will continue working on the pain management journal that allows the user to record pain levels at various times during the day. You started work on this app in Chapter 8. Create a simple storyboard with a single view, and in this view add a text field, a label, and a button. The user should be able to enter the pain level in the text field. Program the button so that when it is touched the pain level is displayed in the label.

# Passing Data Between View Controllers, Delegates, and Protocols

In this chapter you will:

- ◎ Create views without a storyboard
- ◎ Present and view controllers
- ◎ Create view transitions without storyboards
- ◎ Explore the stages of view controller communication
- ◎ Pass data between views using the data member and the `viewWillAppear` method.
- ◎ Use delegates and protocols to pass data between views created using `.xib` files
- ◎ Dismiss the keyboard

In Chapter 9 we explored storyboarding. Storyboards allow us to display all the view controllers in a single space, making it easy to see the transitions and flow of logic. Storyboards are a tool of convenience, but they can make the flow of logic appear to be more complicated than it is, especially if you aren't able to work on a large monitor. In this chapter, we learn to work with transitions without using storyboards. We will also learn how to pass data from view 1 to view 2 using a variable to store the data to be passed. Next, you will learn to pass data from view 2 to view 1 using delegates. Finally, you will learn how to dismiss the keyboard so it doesn't interfere with the view.

## Role of View Controllers

View controllers play a very important role in iOS applications by managing views. They provide a means of transitioning from one view to another and also pass data from one view to another. When a touch event occurs in a view, a message is sent to the view controller of the view. Although the view is where the touch occurred, the view controller is expected to know how to handle the touch.

A view controller can perform multiple actions. For instance it may present another view, go back to the previous view, perform some calculation, display an image, play a sound, or transfer data to another object.

Multiple view controllers collaborate to create an efficient user interface. Although storyboards make it easy to understand these collaborations, it is essential to understand how the .xib files work. One of our first tasks is to learn how to transition from one view to another.

## Presenting and Dismissing View Controllers

When you transition from one view to another, the first view controller is said to **present** the second view controller. In simple words, presenting a view controller means making a view controller visible to the user.

When a view controller is no longer needed, you can close it, or **dismiss it.** When a view controller is dismissed, the previous view controller becomes visible. The view controller that presented a view controller is usually the one to dismiss the same view controller. The code used to dismiss a view controller is as follows:

```
[viewController dismissModalviewControllerAnimated:YES];
- (void)dismissModalViewControllerAnimated:(BOOL)animated
```

When the `dismissModalViewControllerAnimated` method is called on the presented (second) view, the message is sent to the presenter (first) view controller to dismiss the presented view controller.

## Creating Transitions Without Storyboards

No matter how you create an app with multiple view controllers, each view controller has its own set of @interface (.h) and @implementation (.m) files. But whether or not you use storyboards to create the app determines whether the view controller also has a .xib file or a

Storyboard file. As you learned in Chapter 9, when you use storyboards to create an app with multiple view controllers, the interface is stored in the Storyboard file. When you create an app with multiple view controllers *without* using storyboards, the interface is stored in multiple .xib files. Multiple views need transitioning from one view to another.

The steps involved in creating transitions from one view controller to another are described in the following general steps. You'll learn more about the specifics of this process as you begin creating an app with multiple views controllers.

1. Create two view controllers (each with its set of .h, .m, and .xib files).

2. Import the second view controller into the first view controller, so an instance of it can be created and presented.

3. In this first view controller, add a button the user can click to display the second view.

4. Program this button to perform the following tasks:

   a. Create an instance of the second view controller

   b. Set the transition style for the second view controller

   c. Present the second view controller

5. Add a Done button on the second view controller.

6. Program the Done button to dismiss the second view controller, thereby displaying the first view controller.

Now let's learn more about the specifics as we create an app with multiple view controllers without using storyboards.

1. Create a new Xcode project.

2. In the Choose a template for your new project dialog, select **Application** under "iOS," select **Single View Application**, and then click the **Next** button.

3. Type **ViewTransitionWithoutStoryboardExample1** as the Product Name, enter appropriate items in the Organization Name and Company Identifier boxes, make sure **iPhone** is selected in the Devices box, deselect the **Use Storyboards** check box, and select the **Use Automatic Reference Counting** check box.

4. Click the **Next** button, and then save the project in the location of your choice.

5. Add the second view controller by adding a new file of type Objective-C, named **ViewController2**. To add a new file, select **File▶New▶File**. Select **Cocoa Touch** on the left and **Objective-C class** on the right. Click **Next** and in the Choose options for your new file dialog, select a subclass of **UIViewController** and make sure the **With XIB for user interface** check box is selected as shown in Figure 10-1. Click **Next**, then click **Create**.

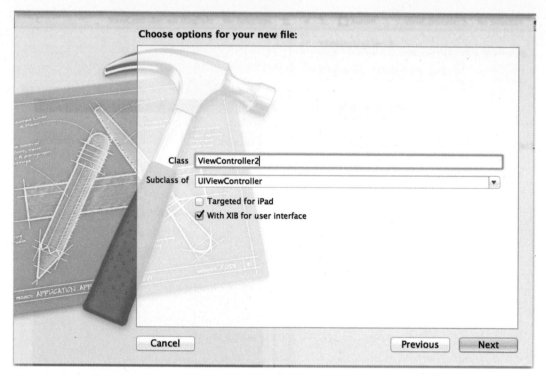

**Figure 10-1**    Choosing options for the Objective-C file

After you add the new file, the Navigation panel should look as shown in Figure 10-2.

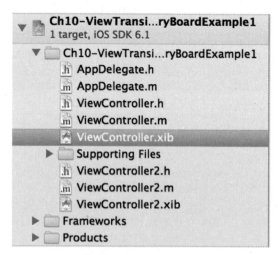

**Figure 10-2**    Navigation panel

6. Add a navigation bar to the first view controller. Use **View 1** as the title of the navigation bar.

7. Add a label and a round rect button to the first view controller as shown in Figure 10-3. Add the text **This is the first View** to the label, and then add the text **Go to View 2** to the button.

**Figure 10-3**   View controller 1

8. Add a navigation bar with the title **View 2** to the second view controller.

9. Add a label and a round rect button to the second view controller as seen in Figure 10-4. Add the text **This is View 2** to the label, and then add the text **Go back to View 1** to the button.

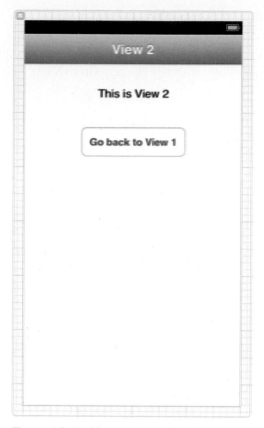

**Figure 10-4**    View controller 2

10.  Import the second view controller into the ViewController.h file by adding the
     following code just below the #import <UIKit/UIKit.h> statement.

     ```
     #import "ViewController2.h"
     ```

11.  On the first view controller, connect the label and the button to the view controller by
     control-dragging and creating an IBOutlet connection called **lbl1** for the label and
     an IBAction called GoToView1:connection for the button as shown in Figure 10-5.
     Code for the first view controller's @interface file is as follows:

     ```
     #import <UIKit/UIKit.h>
     #import "ViewController2.h"


     @interface ViewController : UIViewController
     @property (weak, nonatomic) IBOutlet UILabel *lbl1;
     - (IBAction)GoToView2:(id)sender;

     @end
     ```

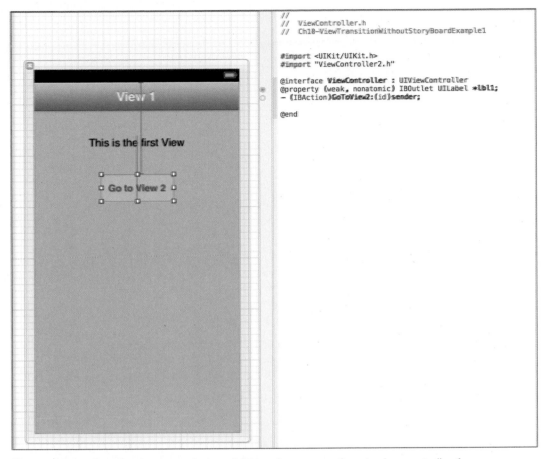

```
//
//  ViewController.h
//  Ch10-ViewTransitionWithoutStoryBoardExample1

#import <UIKit/UIKit.h>
#import "ViewController2.h"

@interface ViewController : UIViewController
@property (weak, nonatomic) IBOutlet UILabel *lbl1;
- (IBAction)GoToView2:(id)sender;

@end
```

**Figure 10-5**    Creating the IBOutlet and IBAction connections to view controller 1

12.  In the second view controller, connect the label and the button to the view controller by Control-dragging and creating an IBOutlet for the label called **lbl2** and an IBAction called GoToView1 for the button as seen in Figure 10-6.

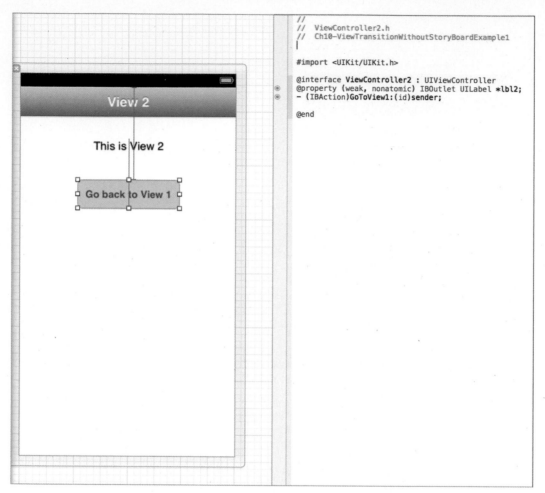

```
//
//  ViewController2.h
//  Ch10-ViewTransitionWithoutStoryBoardExample1
|

#import <UIKit/UIKit.h>

@interface ViewController2 : UIViewController
@property (weak, nonatomic) IBOutlet UILabel *lbl2;
- (IBAction)GoToView1:(id)sender;

@end
```

Figure 10-6    Connecting the IBOutlet and IBAction to view controller 2

Code for the second view controller's @interface file is as follows:

```
#import <UIKit/UIKit.h>

@interface ViewController2 : UIViewController
@property (weak, nonatomic) IBOutlet UILabel *lbl2;
- (IBAction)GoToView1:(id)sender;

@end
```

13. In the ViewController.m file, program the button to make it display the second view controller. Enter the following code in the IBAction method GoToView2, which imports the second view controller, creates an instance of the second view controller, sets the transition style, and then presents the second view controller:

```
-(IBAction)GoToView2:(id)sender {
    //create an instance of the second view controller
    ViewController2 *vc2 = [[ViewController2 alloc] init];

    //set the transition style
    vc2.modalTransitionStyle =
UIModalTransitionStyleCoverVertical;

    //present the view2
        [self presentViewController:vc2 animated:YES completion:Nil];
}
```

14. In the `ViewController2.m` file, program the button to make it hide, or dismiss, the second view controller. Enter the following code in the `GoToView1 IBAction` method:

```
- (IBAction)GoToView1:(id)sender {
    [self dismissViewControllerAnimated:YES completion:Nil];
}
```

15. Run the app. Figure 10-7 shows the two view controllers. Use the **Go to View 2** button to display the second view controller, and then use **Go To View 1** button to return to the first view controller.

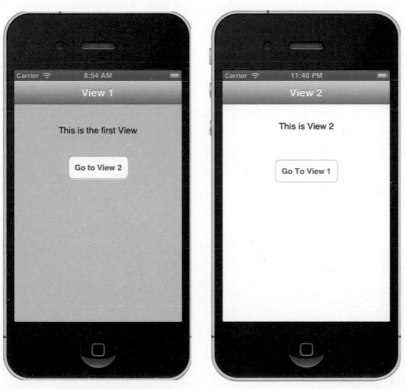

**Figure 10-7**   Running the app

# View Controller Communication

Communication between view controllers—that is, passing data between view controllers—is essential to a fully functioning app. In Chapter 9, you learned how to use storyboards and segues to pass data between view controllers. As you will learn in this section, data flow between view controllers in non-storyboard applications requires a different technique.

In order to understand communications between view controllers, you need to understand the three main phases in a view controller's life cycle:

1. **Instantiation**—In this phase, the view controller is created. It is initiated by another object, usually in order to pass data or to display information.

2. **Lifetime**—This is the longest phase of a view controller's life cycle. During this phase the view controller may perform tasks such as sending notifications, displaying information, passing data, or delegating tasks to other objects.

3. **Destruction**—In this phase, the view controller informs its creator that its task is completed, at which point the creating object dismisses the view controller.

Passing data is one of the most critical tasks a view controller can perform. Using delegates is an efficient way of to accomplish this task. Data can flow in two directions: from the originating view controller to a new view controller and from the new view controller back to the originating view controller. You already have experience with the first option, in which data flows from the first view controller to the second controller. The steps required for this type of data flow are as follows:

1. Declare a variable in the second view controller.

2. Create an instance of the second view controller in the first view controller.

3. Use the variable from the second view controller as a member of the instance of the second view controller to push the data to the second view controller.

The preceding steps can be written in greater detail as follows:

1. A variable is created in view 2:

   ```
   NSString *data;
   ```

2. The second view is instantiated:

   ```
   //instantiate view
   ViewController1 *vc1 = [[ViewController1 alloc]
   init];
   ```

3. Data is passed as a member of the instance created:

   ```
   //push data to View 1
   vc1.data = txt0.text;
   ```

4. In view 2, the contents of the data member are displayed in a label using the ViewWillAppear method:

```
(void) viewWillAppear:(BOOL)animated
{
lbl1.text = data;
}
```

Getting data to flow from the second view controller to the first view controller is more complicated. The preceding steps are not an efficient option. Instead, you need to use delegates to pass data from the second view controller to the first view controller.

## Delegates and Protocols

A **delegate** is an object that acts on behalf of another object. The objects in this case are the view controllers. The delegate-based design pattern is used to enhance the efficiency of an application. In this design pattern, an object plays the role of a delegate by acting on behalf of or coordinating with another object. The object that is not the delegate is called the **delegating object**. The delegating object has to keep track of the delegate and call upon it when needed by sending it a message. When the delegate receives a message from a delegating object, it responds by either presenting another view controller, by displaying data, or by passing data to the delegating object. Figure 10-8 illustrates the relationship between a delegating object and its delegate.

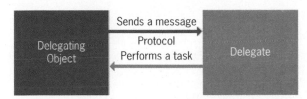

**Figure 10-8**   Delegates and protocols
Credit © 2015 Cengage Learning

Delegates work in conjunction with protocols. A **protocol** is a method that provides a means for programmatically interfacing a delegate with a delegating object. There are two main types of protocols: formal and informal.

**Formal protocols** are used when an object decides to use a delegate to communicate. A formal protocol is created by a protocol declaration in the delegating object. The protocol declaration is then followed by a set of methods associated with the protocol.

**Informal protocols** are usually implemented by a set of objects. We will be working with formal and informal protocols.

Before it can use a delegate to communicate, a view controller must create a protocol . The protocol must contain the method (or methods) that perform the necessary tasks.

The advantage of implementing a delegate is that it hides, or encapsulates, the details of the code, thereby enabling its use in other parts of the app. The steps for implementing a delegate, its accompanying protocol, and how they fit in the view controller life cycle are as follows:

1. **Declare the delegate**—Here the view controller declares itself as the delegate for the view controller being created.

2. **Instantiate the view controller**—In this step, the second view controller is created.

3. **Lifetime of the view controller**—In this step, the view controller is able to respond to an event. When a button is touched, the view controller sends a message to the delegate telling the delegate to perform the tasks defined in the protocol.

4. **Destruction**—When the delegating view controller is done with its tasks, it sends a message to the delegate, at which point the delegate dismisses it.

Figure 10-9 illustrates these steps.

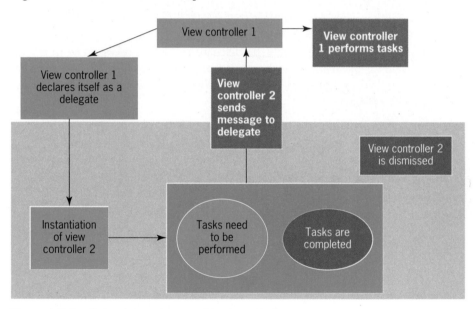

**Figure 10-9**    Delegates and protocol implementation
Credit © 2015 Cengage Learning

## Summary of Steps for Using Protocols and Delegates

The following steps summarize the process of using protocols and delegates. In these steps, view1 is called the "delegate object" and view2 is called the "delegating object."

1. Create two views (each with its set of .h, .m, and .xib files).

2. Import the second view into the first view (in the .h and .m files) so an instance of it can be created and presented and the protocol can be implemented.

3. Design the user interface.

   a. Design the first view to the requirements of the application.

   b. Design the second view to the requirements of the application.

# Coding for View 1

4. Write the code for view 1 required to pass data.

   a. Declare the protocol. In the .h file just below the #import and above the @interface, create the protocol. The protocol consists of a declaration, body, and end.

      i. The protocol declaration starts with the @protocol followed by a unique name of the protocol and the <NSObject>.

      ii. The body of the protocol consists of the methods used by the delegate to perform the tasks for the delegating object.

      iii. The end is a @end statement. For example:

```
//protocol declaration
@protocol ViewController2Delegate < NSObject >

//protocol body, which is a method
-(void) passData:(NSString *)data;

//protocol end
@end
```

   b. Create the delegate property:

```
@property (nonatomic, weak) id
<ViewController2Delegate> delegate;
```

   c. Synthesize the delegate:
```
@synthesize delegate;
```

   d. Just before you dismiss the second view controller, invoke the message from the protocol on the delegate:

```
ViewController2 *vc2 = [[ViewController2 alloc] init];
[self.delegate  passData:itemToPassBack];
```

## Coding for View 2

5.  Write the code for view 2 required to pass data.

a.  Tell view 1 to conform to the protocol by specifying the name of the protocol right in the end of the interface, but first make sure you import the second view controller in the .h file.

```
#import "ViewController2.h"

@interface ViewController: UIViewController
<ViewController1Delegate>
```

b.  Implement the delegate method. In the .m file, create the actual implementation of the method that was declared in the protocol declaration.

```
-(void) passData:(NSString *)item
{
Lbl1.text = item;
}
```

c.  Inform view2 that view1 is the delegate. This is done in view1, right after view2 is instantiated and before it is presented, using the following code:

```
// ViewController2 that ViewController is its delegate
     Vc2.delegate = self;
```

# Using Delegates to Pass Data Between Views

Now let's create a sample app that makes use of delegates to send data from view controller 1 to view controller 2, and then from view controller 2 to view controller 1.

1.  Follow the steps earlier in this chapter to create a new Xcode project with a single view application, without storyboards. You may choose to use the program you just created in the previous example. If you choose to do that you will have to edit the labels and add additional labels as seen in Figure 10-10 and jump to step 3.

2.  Add a second view controller along with the accompanying .h, .m, and .xib files.

3.  Create the user interfaces shown in Figure 10-10.

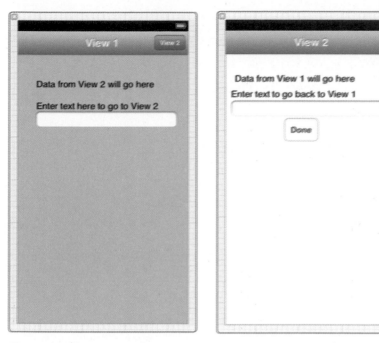

**Figure 10-10**　User Interfaces for view controller 1 and view controller 2

4. Make the appropriate **IBOutlets** and **IBActions** for the labels, text fields, and buttons. One label in each of the two view controllers is used for displaying the data from the other view controller while the text field in each view will be used to enter data to be displayed in the other view controller's label. When you are finished, import the view controller 2 in the **ViewController.h** file.

**In View 1**

- For label 2 create an **IBOutlet** called lbl0.

- For the text field create an **IBOutlet** called txt0.

- For the button create an **IBAction** called view2.

**In View 2**

- For the label 2 create an **IBOutlet** called lbl1.

- For the text field create an **IBOutlet** called txt1.

- For the button create an **IBAction** called Done.

The **@interface** file for view controller 1 is as follows:

```
#import <UIKit/UIKit.h>
#import "ViewController2.h"

@interface ViewController : UIViewController
@property (weak, nonatomic) IBOutlet UITextField *txt0;
```

```
@property (weak, nonatomic) IBOutlet UILabel *lbl0;
- (IBAction)view2:(id)sender;

@end
```

The @interface file for view controller 2 is as follows:

```
#import <UIKit/UIKit.h>

@interface ViewController2: UIViewController
@property (weak, nonatomic) IBOutlet UILabel *lbl1;
@property (weak, nonatomic) IBOutlet UITextField *txt1;
- (IBAction)Done:(id)sender;

@end
```

## Implementing the Flow of Data

Now we are ready to implement the flow of data from the first view controller to the second.

1. In order to transfer data from view controller 1 to view controller 2, we use a variable that will be a data member of the second view controller. We accomplish this by creating a NSString variable by typing in the following code in the ViewController2.h file as shown here:

```
@interface ViewController2: UIViewController
@property (nonatomic, retain) NSString *data;
```

Remember to synthesize all the properties in the ViewController.m and ViewController2.m files.

In ViewController.m file type the following:
```
@synthesize lbl0;
@synthesize txt0;
```

In the ViewController2.m file type the following:
```
@synthesize lbl1;
@synthesize txt1;
@synthesize data;
```

2. The code for presenting view controller 2 is done in the @implementation file of the IBAction method for the button on view controller 1. In order to present view controller 2, do the following:

   a. Create an instance of view controller 2 in the IBAction method called view2 in the ViewController.m file:

   ```
   ViewController2 *vc2 = [[ViewController2 alloc] init];
   ```

b.  Set the transition style as follows:

```
vc2.modalTransitionStyle =
UIModalTransitionStyleCoverVertical;
```

c.  The text entered by the user in the text field in view 1 is stored in the data variable called `data` that we created. The data variable is accessed as a member of the instance of `view2` with the following code:

```
vc2.data = txt0.text;
```

d.  Present it as seen in the following code:

```
[self presentViewController:vc2 animated:YES
completion:Nil];
```

## Complete Code So Far

The complete code for the preceding steps is as follows:

```
- (IBAction)view2:(id)sender {
    //instantiate view
    ViewController2 *vc2 = [[ViewController2 alloc] init];

    //set modal transition
    vc2.modalTransitionStyle =
UIModalTransitionStyleCoverVertical;

    //push data to View2
    vc2.data = txt0.text;

    //present view2
    [self presentViewController:vc2 animated:YES completion:Nil];
}
```

## Writing the `viewDidLoad` Method and Running the App

1.  Write the following `viewDidLoad` method, which takes the contents of the data member of view controller 2 and displays it in the label in view controller 2.

```
- (void) viewDidLoad
{
    lbl1.text = data;
}
```

2.  Run the app. Figure 10-11 shows the two view controllers as the app is running. Note that the flow of data from view controller 2 to the view controller 1 is not yet implemented.

**Figure 10-11**  Running the partially completed app

## Declaring the Protocol and Invoking the Protocol Method

Now we move on to the protocol declaration stage of creating the app.

1. Declare the protocol in the ViewController2.h file, just after the #import statement and before the @interface statement. In this case, we name the protocol ViewControllerDelegate. The method is passData with a parameter of type NSString called data, as shown in the following code:

```
@protocol ViewController2Delegate < NSObject >
-(void) passData:(NSString *)data;
@end
```

2. Create the delegate for the protocol and then synthesize this property. The delegate is created as a property in the interface file of view controller 2, as shown in the following code:

```
@property (nonatomic, weak) id <ViewController2Delegate>
delegate;
```

3. Synthesize the property in the .m file for view controller 2, as shown in the following code:

```
@synthesize delegate;
```

4. Invoke the delegate method in the IBAction method of view controller 2. The contents of the text field are held in a variable and passed to the delegate method as a parameter, as shown in the following code:

```
NSString *itemToPassBack = txt1.text;

    [self.delegate passData:itemToPassBack];
    [self dismissViewControllerAnimated:YES completion:Nil];
```

5. After the import statement in the ViewController.h file, type the name of the delegate protocol using the following code:

```
#import "ViewController2.h"

@interface ViewController : UIViewController
<ViewController2Delegate>
```

6. Implement the delegate method declared in the protocol. This is done in the .m file for view controller 1, as seen in the following code. The name of this method is passData, and we are passing it a parameter that consists of the contents of the text field in view controller 1.

```
-(void) passData:(NSString *)data
{
    lbl0.text = data;
}
```

7. Inform view controller 2, which is the delegating object, about the delegate. This is done in the IBAction method for the button in the ViewController.m file. Insert the code just before the view is presented.

```
// inform ViewController that ViewController is its delegate
    vc2.delegate = self;
```

8. Run the app. Figure 10-12 shows the view controllers.

**Figure 10-12** Running the app

## Complete Code

Code for the ViewController.h file is as follows. Note that the ViewController.h name is autogenerated when we first create the project. Also, although we refer to this view as "view controller 1", there is no "1" in the title.

```objc
#import <UIKit/UIKit.h>
#import "ViewController2.h"

@interface ViewController : UIViewController
<ViewController2Delegate>
@property (weak, nonatomic) IBOutlet UILabel *lbl0;
@property (weak, nonatomic) IBOutlet UITextField *txt0;

- (IBAction)view2:(id)sender;
@end
```

Code for the ViewController.m file is as follows. Note that the ViewController.m name is autogenerated when we first create the project. Also, although we refer to this view as "view controller 1", there is no "1" in the title.

```objc
#import "ViewController.h"

@interface ViewController ()

@end
```

```objc
@implementation ViewController
@synthesize txt0;
@synthesize lbl0;

- (void)viewDidLoad
{
    [super viewDidLoad];
    // Do any additional setup after loading the view, typically
from a nib.
}

- (void)didReceiveMemoryWarning
{
    [super didReceiveMemoryWarning];
    // Dispose of any resources that can be recreated.
}

- (IBAction)view2:(id)sender {
    //instantiate view 2
    ViewController2 *vc2 = [[ViewController2 alloc] init];

    //set modal transition
    vc2.modalTransitionStyle =
UIModalTransitionStyleCoverVertical;

    //push data to view 2
    vc2.data = txt0.text;

    // inform ViewController 2 that ViewController is its delegate
     vc2.delegate = self;

    //present view 2
    [self presentViewController:vc2 animated:YES completion:Nil];

}

-(void) passData:(NSString *)item
{
    lbl0.text = item;
}
@end
```

Code for the ViewController2.h file is as follows

```objc
#import <UIKit/UIKit.h>

@protocol ViewController2Delegate < NSObject >
-(void) passData:(NSString *)data;
@end
```

```
@interface ViewController2 : UIViewController
@property (weak, nonatomic) IBOutlet UILabel *lbl1;
@property (weak, nonatomic) IBOutlet UITextField *txt1;
@property (nonatomic, weak) id <ViewController2Delegate>
delegate;

@property (nonatomic, retain) NSString *data;
- (IBAction)Done:(id)sender;

@end
```

Code for the ViewController2.m file is as follows:

```
#import "ViewController2.h"

@interface ViewController2 ()

@end

@implementation ViewController2
@synthesize lbl1;
@synthesize txt1;
@synthesize data;
@synthesize delegate;


- (id)initWithNibName:(NSString *)nibNameOrNil bundle:(NSBundle *)
nibBundleOrNil
{
    self = [super initWithNibName:nibNameOrNil
bundle:nibBundleOrNil];
    if (self) {
        // Custom initialization
    }
    return self;
}
- (void)viewDidLoad
{
    [super viewDidLoad];
    // Do any additional setup after loading the view from its nib.
    lbl1.text = data;
}
- (void)didReceiveMemoryWarning
{
    [super didReceiveMemoryWarning];
    // Dispose of any resources that can be recreated.
}
```

```
- (IBAction)Done:(id)sender {
    NSString *itemToPassBack = txt1.text;

    [self.delegate passData:itemToPassBack];
    [self dismissViewControllerAnimated:YES completion:Nil];
}
@end
```

# Dismissing Keyboard

Now it's time to think about how to fine-tune an app to make it easier for the user to interact with. In particular, let's consider the keyboard, which, depending on the design of your app's interface, can obscure some controls. To avoid this problem, you need to have a way to hide, or dismiss, the keyboard. There are many ways to do this, but we will focus on the following two ways to dismiss the keyboard:

● The user touches the Return key after entering text in a text field.

● The user touches any open space on the screen, other than on the keyboard.

## Dismiss Keyboard from Within a Text Field

Let's first look at how to program the text field on view 2 so the user can dismiss the keyboard by touching the Return key.

1. On view controller 2, select the text field, and then control drag the text field to the interface file to create an IBAction.

2. In the pop-up window shown in Figure 10-13, select an IBAction (IBOutlet will be selected by default), use **hideKeyBoard** as the name, and select **Did End on Exit** as the Event.

Figure 10-13   Connecting the TextField to dismiss keyboard

3.  Program the method in the implementation file using the following code:

```
- (IBAction)hideKeyBoard:(id)sender {
    [sender resignFirstResponder];
}
```

## Dismiss the Keyboard by Touching Anywhere on the Screen

Now we'll try the second method of dismissing the keyboard by modifying the view
controller to a control so that the user can dismiss the keyboard by touching anywhere in the
open space of the view controller.

1.  Click anywhere on the background of view controller 2 to select view controller 2.

2.  In Identity Inspector, change the setting in the Class box from UIView to
    **UIControl** as shown in Figure 10-14.

**Figure 10-14**   Setting the view controller to a control

3.  In the interface file for view controller 1, create a method and its implementation in
    the implementation file as shown here:

```
- (IBAction)BackGroundTouched:(id)sender {
    [self.txt0 resignFirstResponder];
}
```

4.  In the .xib file of view controller 2, select view controller 2, and click the Connections
    Inspector. Connect the touch down event to the file's owner by selecting the check box
    next to the Touch Down event. In the pop-up dialog, select the **BackGroundTouched**
    method. The connection is made and the File's Owner is listed as **BackGroundTo...**
    as shown in Figure 10-15. "Another way to accomplish the same thing is as follows:
    tap any open space on view 1, control-drag view 1 to the ViewController.h creating an
    IBAction, name the IBAction **BackGroundTouched**, select **Touch Down** as the
    event type, and then, in the ViewController.m file, type the following code:

```
- (IBAction)BackgrounTouched:(id)sender {
    [self.txt0 resignFirstResponder];
}
```

Figure 10-15  Connecting the background to a touch down event

5.  Run the app. Verify that, in view controller 1, touching anywhere on the open space where there are no controls, will dismiss the keyboard. Also verify that, in view controller 2, touching the Return key on the keyboard will dismiss the keyboard.

## HANDS-ON LAB

In this Hands-On Lab, we will create an application that calculates the area and perimeter of a rectangle. The type of operation requested by the user (computation of the area or computation of the perimeter) will be passed from view controller 1 to view controller 2. The area or perimeter is then calculated. After that, the result is sent back to view controller 1 using a delegate and protocol. This way we  will be implementing both mechanisms of data transfer.

### CREATE THE PROJECT

1.  Create a new Xcode project that is a Single View Application, without storyboards, and with ARC and .xib files.

2.  Add a second view controller and its .h and .m files by adding a new Objective-C file with a subclass of UIViewController, and name it **SecondViewController**.

## DESIGN THE USER INTERFACE FOR VIEW CONTROLLER 1

3. Create the user interface for view controller1 as shown in Figure 10-16. It should have two buttons containing the text shown in the figure, and a label under the two buttons whose contents has been deleted. Eventually, the user will be able to click either of the buttons to display a second view controller, where the length and width of the rectangle can be entered and the area or perimeter can be computed. The label in view controller 1 will display the computed result. For now we will leave it blank.

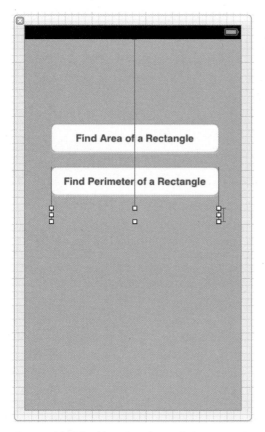

**Figure 10-16**    User interface of view controller 1

4. Connect the label to the `IBOutlet` and then connect the two buttons to the `IBAction` as seen below. Import view controller 2 so we can create an instance of it and present it.

```
#import "SecondViewController.h"
```

```
@interface ViewController : UIViewController
- (IBAction)findArea:(id)sender;
- (IBAction)findPerimeter:(id)sender;
@property (weak, nonatomic) IBOutlet UILabel *displayResultLabel;

@end
```

5. Synthesize the label in the implementation file of the view controller 1 file:

```
@synthesize displayResultLabel;
```

## DESIGN THE USER INTERFACE FOR VIEW CONTROLLER 2

6. Create the interface for view controller 2 as shown in Figure 10-17. Notice that it contains two text fields, three labels, and a button. We will use the label to display a title specific to the task chosen on view 1. So if the user selects "Area of a Rectangle," the label would say "Computing area" and if the user selects "Perimeter of a Rectangle," then the label would say "Computing perimeter."

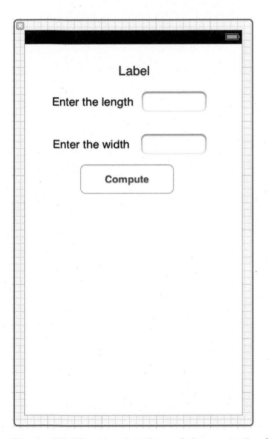

**Figure 10-17**    User interface of view controller 2

7. Connect the text fields and the label to `IBOutlets`, and connect the button to an`IBAction`. Next, create a new property called `typeOfOperation` to hold the type of operation (that is, calculation of area or calculation of perimeter) and a `myStringWithInt` property to hold the string value of the two `int` properties to hold the area and perimeter. The code you write should look like this:

```
@property int area;
@property int perimeter;
@property NSString *typeOfOperation;
@property NSString *myStringWithInt;
@property (weak, nonatomic) IBOutlet UILabel *outLabel;
@property (weak, nonatomic) IBOutlet UITextField
*lengthTxtFld;
@property (weak, nonatomic) IBOutlet UITextField *widthTxtFld;
- (IBAction)compute:(id)sender;
```

8. Synthesize all the properties in the `@implementation` file of view controller 2 as follows:

```
@synthesize lengthTxtFld;
@synthesize widthTxtFld;
@synthesize typeOfOperation;
@synthesize area;
@synthesize perimeter;
@synthesize myStringWithInt;
@synthesize outLabel;
```

## PROTOCOL AND DELEGATE IMPLEMENTATION

9. Create the protocol and the delegate. In this example, view controller 1 (that is, `ViewController`) is the delegate and second view controller (that is, `SecondViewController`) is the delegating view controller. Thus, the protocol declaration is made in the `@interface` for second view controller, along with the method for passing the data. The code you write should look like this:

```
#import <UIKit/UIKit.h>
//protocol declaration
@protocol DataDelegate < NSObject >

//protocol body, which is a method
-(void) passData:(NSString *)data;

//protocol end
@end
@interface SecondViewController : UIViewController
```

10. Create the property for the delegate in the `@interface` for view controller 2 as shown here:

```
@property (nonatomic, weak) id <DataDelegate> delegate;
```

11. Synthesize the property in the @implementation of second view controller as shown here:

```
@synthesize delegate;
```

12. Now we can program the delegate by modifying its @interface file. You need to import view controller 1 for the delegate assignment to work. Change ViewController.h to look like this:

```
#import <UIKit/UIKit.h>
#import "SecondViewController.h"

@interface ViewController : UIViewController <DataDelegate>
```

13. Implement the delegate method in the implementation of view controller 1. Add this code to the bottom of ViewController.m:

```
#pragma mark - DataDelegate

-(void) passData:(NSString *) data
{
displayResultLabel.text = data;
}
```

## CODING THE COMPUTATIONS

14. Now we are ready to code the button that will compute the area. This button will first create an instance of view controller 2, pass the typeOfOperation to it, inform SecondViewController that ViewController is the delegate, and then display SecondViewController. Notice that the label on SecondViewController is set in this method to reflect the type of operation being performed. Add the following code to ViewController.m after the ViewDidLoad method:

```
- (IBAction)findArea:(id)sender {

//create an instance of the SecondViewController
    SecondViewController *svc = [[SecondViewController alloc]
initWithNibName:@"SecondViewController" bundle:nil];

//set the type of operation to computing Area
svc.typeOfOperation = @"Computing Area";

//inform the SecondViewController that ViewController is
 the delegate
    svc.delegate = self;

//present the SecondViewController
    [self presentViewController:svc animated:YES
completion:nil];
}
```

**15.** Now we can code the button that will compute the perimeter. This button will first create an instance of SecondViewController, pass the typeofOperation to the new instance of SecondViewController, inform SecondViewController that ViewController is the delegate, and then display SecondViewController. Notice that the label on SecondViewController is set in this method to reflect the type of operation being performed. Add the following to ViewController.m, right below the findArea method:

```
- (IBAction)findPerimeter:(id)sender {
    //create an instance of the SecondViewController
    SecondViewController *svc = [[SecondViewController
alloc] initWithNibName:@"SecondViewController"
bundle:nil];

//set the label in the SecondView Controller to display
 the typeOfOperation
    svc.typeOfOperation = @"Computing Perimeter";

    //inform the SecondViewController that ViewController
 is the delegate
    svc.delegate = self;

//present the SecondViewController
    [self presentViewController:svc animated:YES
completion:nil];
}
```

## CODING THE COMPUTE BUTTON IN SECONDVIEWCONTROLLER

**16.** In the implementation file of the SecondViewController, the Compute button takes the contents of the text fields and computes either the area or the perimeter based on the typeOfOperator passed to it. The code for the Compute button checks to see what typeOfOperation is passed to it. It then converts the contents of the text field to an integer variable, and then converts that integer to a string so it can be passed to the passData delegate method; this second conversion is necessary because this method only takes an NSString object as a parameter. SecondViewController is then dismissed, so ViewController is displayed. Add the following code to the SecondViewController.m file, below the viewDidLoad method:

```
- (IBAction)compute:(id)sender {
  //if computing area
    if([typeOfOperation isEqualToString:@"Computing
 Area"])
     {
        //compute the area
        area = [lengthTxtFld.text intValue] *
[widthTxtFld.text intValue];

    // store the calculated area as a string
    myStringWithInt = [NSString stringWithFormat:@"The
area is %d", area];
```

```
    //send the delegate method
    [self.delegate passData:myStringWithInt];

    //dismiss the current view controller so the first
one is displayed
        [self dismissViewControllerAnimated:YES
completion:nil];
    }
    else
    {
        //if computing perimeter
        if([typeOfOperation isEqualToString:@"Computing
Perimeter"])
        {
            //compute the perimeter
            perimeter = 2 * ([lengthTxtFld.text intValue] +
[widthTxtFld.txt intValue]);

            // store the calculated perimeter as a string
            myStringWithInt = [NSString
 stringWithFormat:@"The perimeter is %d", perimeter];

            //send the delegate method
            [self.delegate passData:myStringWithInt];

            //dismiss the current view controller so the
first is displayed
            [self dismissViewControllerAnimated:YES
completion:nil];
        }
    }
}
```

17. Now we need to make the label in `SecondViewController` display the type of operation. This is done by setting the label in the `viewDidLoad` method of the `SecondViewController`. Add the following code to the `SecondViewController.m` file in the `viewDidLoad` method:

```
- (void)viewDidLoad
{
    [super viewDidLoad];
    // Do any additional setup after loading the view
 from its nib.
    outLabel.text = typeOfOperation;

}
```

3. Run the app as seen in Figure 10-18.

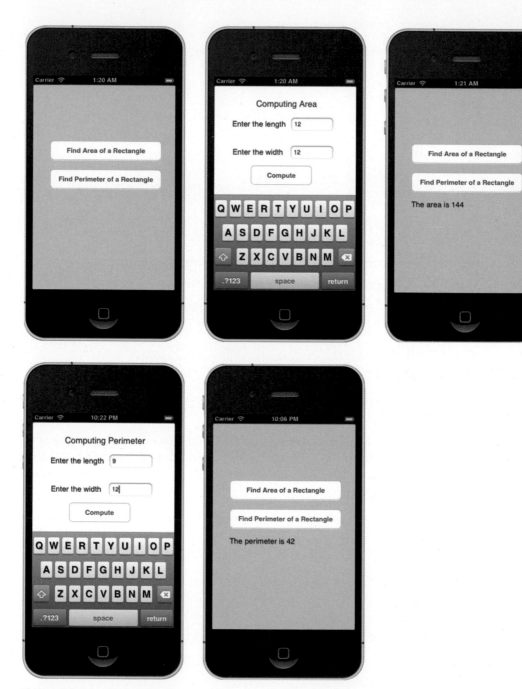

Figure 10-18    Running the app

# Summary

- When a touch event occurs in a view, a message is sent to the view controller of the view. Although the view is where the touch occurred, the View Controller is expected to know how to handle the touch.

- Presenting a view occurs when a view is shown in an application.

- The method used to present the view is `presentViewController:vc2 animated:YES completion:Nil`.

- Each view has an `@interface`, `@implementation` and a `.xib` file.

- Applications created using storyboards do not have `.xib` files for the user interface; instead they have one storyboard file for the user interface.

- In an application that does not use storyboards, each `.xib` file holds the interface for an individual view, which is part of the entire user interface.

- In an application that uses a storyboard, there are no individual `.xib` files; instead, the one storyboard file contains the app's entire user interface.

- The life cycle of a view controller has three phases: instantiation, lifetime, and destruction.

- A view is created by another view by first instantiating it and then presenting it.

- To pass data between views the data is passed as a member of the instance created.

- Delegates and protocols are used to manage and enhance efficiency of applications. There are two objects involved in this mechanism. One object is the delegate, and the other object is called the delegating object.

- When using a delegate to communicate, the view controller will create a protocol so the delegate can implement it in communication.

- When a button is pressed or touched and a task is to be performed, the view controller will send a message to the delegate and the delegate will perform the tasks defined in the protocol.

- One way of dismissing the keyboard is setting the `IBAction` property of a view and resigning the first responder in the event method.

- Another way of dismissing the keyboard is by tapping anywhere other than the keyboard. To make this possible, set the view as a control and program the control to resign the first responder by the method that is triggered by the event of touching the control.

## Exercises

1. Mark the following statements as true or false. If false, explain why.

   a. The only function of a view controller is to provide a means of transitioning from one view to another.

   b. If you are designing an interface using .xib files, each view controller has an @interface, @implementation, and .xib file associated with it.

   c. The object that is not the delegate is called the delegating object.

   d. Delegates provide means of programmatically interfacing a protocol with its delegate.

   e. Protocols and delegates are declared in implementation files.

2. Identify the steps involved in declaring a protocol.

3. Describe the role of view controllers.

4. Explain the three phases in the life cycle of a view controller.

5. Explain the following terms:

   a. Formal protocol

   b. Informal protocols

6. What is a delegate?

7. What are two ways of dismissing the keyboard?

8. Describe how a touch event in a view is handled.

9. What method is used to present a view?

10. List the various types of transitions in presenting a view controller.

## Programming Exercises

1. Create a sleep-tracker app that tracks the number of hours slept the previous night, the number of nights the app has been tracking, and the total hours slept since the app has been tracking. The user must be able to enter the number of hours slept, but the app should track the number of hours entered. Include two view controllers, and use a protocol and a delegate. Use storyboards for this app.

   Possible output for the app could look like this:

   Total nights tracked: 5

   Total hours slept: 40

   Hours slept last night: 6

2. Create a grocery app using labels and text fields. In the first screen, the user should be able to enter an item and press the Submit button, at which point the item should be added to the list of groceries. Include a View List button that the user can press to display the entire grocery list. Ensure that the user can easily switch between the two screens and dismiss the keyboard when necessary.

3. Create a faux horoscope app. One screen should display a list of the horoscope signs to choose from, with a text field where the user can enter one of the signs. After a sign is entered, the app should display a screen that contains information about that sign. Ensure that the app includes only two view controllers and allows the user to dismiss the keyboard as necessary.

4. Create a phone directory app that contains two view controllers. The first should allow the user to enter information for a contact (name, telephone number, address, email address). When the user touches the Submit button, a screen should appear displaying all the newly entered information about the contact. On this second screen, the user should be allowed to edit the contact information.

5. Create a daily-scheduler app. This app should allow a user to organize tasks for the current day by assigning specific amounts of time to each task. The user should be able to enter the title of a task and its duration. On the next screen, the user should be able to see the total hours scheduled for the day. Use `.xib` files and not storyboards to do this.

6. Create an app that calculates the volume of a cylinder and displays it on a second screen. Use `.xib` files to do this.

7. Create a discount calculator app that starts with a screen where the user can press one of four buttons to choose a 25%, 30%, 45%, or 60% discount. After the user selects a discount, a new screen should appear where the user can enter the cost of the item and then touch a Done button, at which point the first screen should reappear, displaying the discount information.

8. Create a sales tax calculator app that allows the user to enter the cost of an item and the sales tax percentage as a decimal. When the user touches the Compute button, a new screen should display the results.

# Business Case Study

In this chapter, you will continue working on the pain management journal app. At this point, the app should contain a simple storyboard with a single view, and in this view you added a text field, a label, and a button. The user can enter the pain level in the text field, and, when the button is touched, the pain level should be displayed in the label.

Now add another view controller, and then add a label to the new view controller. Program the app to pass the data to the newly added view and display the pain level in the label. Also, write the code necessary to allow the user to dismiss the keyboard on the first view controller by the two mechanisms we learned in this chapter; namely pressing the Return key or touching any open space on the view.

*11*

# Table Views

In this chapter you will:

- ◎ Examine table view controllers and their functionalities
- ◎ Differentiate between static and dynamic cells in a table view
- ◎ Explore groups and sections in a table view
- ◎ Learn about the UITableView data source and the delegate
- ◎ Create table views using a .xib file, storyboard, and the Master-Detail Application template
- ◎ Populate a table with data from a NSMutableArray
- ◎ Add new elements to a table view

So far we have implemented view controllers and added controls such as labels, text fields, and buttons. We have been able to display data in labels and text fields. In this chapter we will learn to display data in the form of lists using table views. We will first create a simple table view using .xib files. Next, we will create table views using storyboards. We will then populate table views with data from NSArrays and learn to add, delete, and edit table view data.

## UITable View

A table view, which is a commonly used type of view in iOS programming, looks like a list. A table view is an instance of the UITableView class and a subclass of the UIScrollView. It allows vertical scrolling through a list of items in the table. Each item in a table view is in a placeholder called a UITableViewCell. Due to space restrictions on mobile devices, the UITableView has a single column with multiple rows to represent a list of items. Each row is called a cell. These cells can hold text or images and an optional accessory icon, shown in Figure 11-1, that the user can touch to display a more detailed view of the particular cell.

**Figure 11-1**   Table view

Tables are commonly used to allow the user to navigate through hierarchical data. The topmost level in the hierarchy consists of categories, with the next level down containing subcategories, and the next level down containing subcategories of the subcategories, and so on, drilling down through the main categories. Navigation bars come in handy in drilling down through the levels of the hierarchy.

There are two styles of table views: plain (`UITAbleViewStylePlain`) and grouped (`UITAbleViewStyleGrouped`). The plain table shown in Figure 11-1 has one section, whereas the grouped style shown in Figure 11-2 has multiple rows grouped into sections. Grouping provides a means of separating items of similar type. It also makes it possible to display a clean and neat data entry area for the users, with a title for each section.

**Figure 11-2**   Grouped table view

You can change a table view from plain to grouped by changing the Style setting in the Attributes Inspector, as seen in Figure 11-3. Tables consist of sections and rows. There can be zero or more sections in a table. Each section has a set of rows/cells with optional headers and footers. The sections and rows have index numbers that help identify a section in a table or a row in a section. Any row in a section can be traced by a row index inside of a section index by the following method:`indexPathForRow:inSection`.

Figure 11-3    Table view attributes with Grouped selected

A row in a table view is a cell. A cell is an instance of the UITableViewCell class. When creating cells, you can choose from two types of table prototypes: static and dynamic. If you know ahead of time the number of cells you want your table to contain, you can use the **static** cell format, which is the most commonly used format. In a **dynamic** prototype format, one cell is used as a template for generating other cells. This starting cell has a specific layout that the other cells follow. The main difference between the static and dynamic prototypes is that dynamic prototype cells use the data source at runtime. This is necessary, because the data itself determines the number of necessary cells.

## Delegate and Data Source

Implementing a table view requires a view controller, a data source and a delegate that manages the table. The view controller manages the table view. The delegate follows a standard protocol to manage the selection of cells by the user. The data source follows a standard protocol to manage the data that is displayed in the cells. By using the standard, built-in protocols in the UITableView class, we eliminate the need to write the protocol and delegate for the table; instead the UITableView controller automatically adopts the delegate and data source protocols. In order to adopt the built in delegate and data source protocols, we need to include the following @interface directive:

```
@interface TableViewController: UIViewController
<UITableViewDelegate, UITableViewSource>
```

This directive allows us to use the built-in delegate and data source methods.

When a user taps a cell, the delegate is sent a message that the index of the row was tapped. The delegate uses this information to find the correct data in the data source.

The data source follows the protocol called `UITableViewDataSource`. It has two important methods that have to be implemented so that it can follow the protocol. These are:

- `tableView:numberOfRowsInSection`: Informs the table view of the number of rows in a section.

- `numberOfSectionsInTableView`: Informs the table view of the number of sections in a table view.

Additional methods are optional and support editing the table view. An example of an additional method is the following:

- `tableView:cellForRowAtIndexPath`: Refers to the cell to be displayed in the table view.

The delegate and the data source are often the same object. In our case, the `UITableViewController` class is playing the role of both the data source and the delegate. The delegate follows the `UITableViewDelegate` protocol and all of its methods are optional.

## Creating an App with a Table View

The following is the sequence of steps involved in the creation of a table view:

1. Create and initialize the `UITableView` instance.

2. Set the data source and the delegate, and then send the reload message.

3. Adopt the delegate and the data source.

4. Send the `numberOfSectionsInTableView` message to the data source, informing the table view of the number of sections.

5. For each of the sections, the number of rows is known by the message sent to the table view by the `numberOfRowsInSection` method.

6. The method `cellForRowAtIndexPath` provides information on each individual cell of the table view and returns the `UITableViewcell` object for each row.

Now let's get some practice creating a table view. The `UITableViewController` class will set the delegate and the data source protocols automatically. In this example, we will create a project from the Single View Application template and then add a table view controller to the project. That means we will be using a `UIViewController` object as well as a `UITableViewController` object.

# Creating the Interface

The main purpose of this example is to demonstrate how to add a table view controller to a project. We will create a button on the single view controller and then program it to take us to the table view controller.

1. Create a project named **DisplayTableView** using the **Single View Application** template. Make sure you deselect the **Use Storyboards** check box, and make sure you select the **Automatic Reference Counting** check box.

2. Open the .xib file and drag a button from the Object Library onto the view controller. Edit the text in the button to read **Go to my Table**.

3. Next, we need to add a table view controller to the project. Click **File** on the menu bar, point to **New**, and then click **File**.

4. In the Choose a template for your new file dialog, under iOS, select **Cocoa Touch,** and then select **Objective-C** class.

5. Click **Next** to display the Choose options for your new file dialog. In the Class box, type **TableViewController** and then, in the Subclass box, select **UITableViewController**. Since we are not using storyboards, make sure the With .xib file for user interface check box is selected.

6. Click **Next,** save the files in the project folder, and then click **Create**. The .h, .m, and .xib files of the TableViewController are generated. The TableViewController.h is the header file for the table view controller, TableViewController.m is the implementation file for the table view controller, and the TableViewController.xib is the interface file for the table view controller. When a table view controller is added to a project, its implementation file will have a set of autogenerated methods. Not all of these methods are useful to us. We will modify some of these methods as we learn about various functionalities.

7. Our first task is to get the table view controller to display data in the format of our preference. Click on the TableViewController.xib file. This opens the table view controller in the editor pane.

8. Click the table view controller to display the properties in the utility pane. By default, the table view controller has a plain style, which is what we want.

9. Add a title to the table by dragging a navigation bar from the Object Library to the table view controller and entering the title **My Table**, as seen in Figure 11-4.

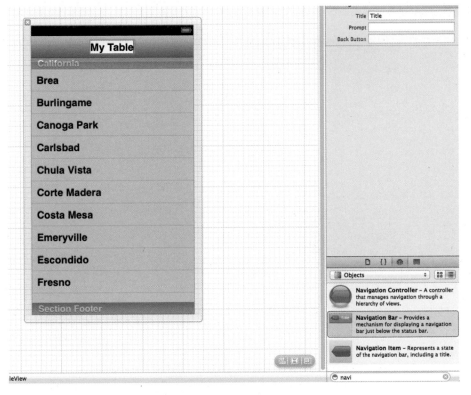

**Figure 11-4**    Adding a navigation bar to add a title to the table

The bar button on the navigation bar will allow the user to get back to the first view controller from the table view controller. This button becomes visible at runtime.

10.    Add a bar button to the navigation bar from the Object Library and change the title to **Done**, as seen in Figure 11-5.

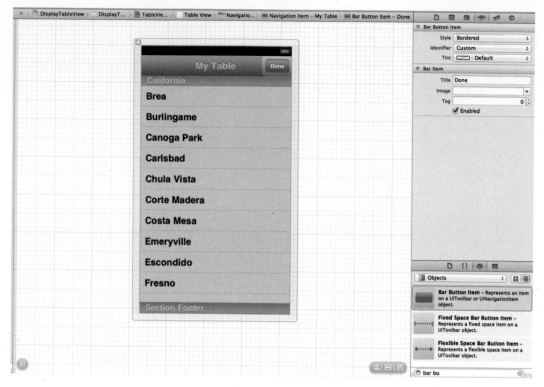

**Figure 11-5** Adding a bar button to the navigation bar on the table view

## Programming the Table View

Now let's move on to programming the table view. When a table view controller is created, a set of methods is automatically created in the table view controller interface and implementation files. These methods help us implement the delegate and protocol methods. They also help with data display, data manipulation, and more. The two most important methods in this set of methods are `numberOfSectionsInTableView` and `numberOfRowsInSection`. By default, the code generated would return 0 sections and 0 rows in each of these sections. In the next two steps, we modify these methods to return the appropriate number of sections and rows in the table depending on the data to be displayed in the table. Note that these methods are autogenerated for us in the implementation file of the table view controller. Each includes a warning preceded by a # sign, which we will delete.

1. Switch to the `TableViewController.m` file. The `numberOfSectionsInTableView` defines the number of sections we would like in the table. In this example we need just one section, so the method will return 1 as seen in the following code

```
- (NSInteger)numberOfSectionsInTableView:(UITableView
*)tableView
{
#warning Potentially incomplete method implementation.
    // Return the number of sections.
    return 1;
}
```

2. Delete the warning message by deleting the entire line starting with the # symbol.

3. The second method, `numberOfRowsInSection`, defines the number of rows in each of the sections we created. We would like to have one row, and so we modify the `return` statement to return 1 instead of a 0, as seen in the following code:

```
- (NSInteger)tableView:(UITableView *)tableView
numberOfRowsInSection:(NSInteger)section
{
#warning Incomplete method implementation.
    // Return the number of rows in the section.
    return 1;
}
```

4. Delete the warning message by deleting the entire line starting with the # symbol.

5. Create an `IBAction` for the Go to my Table button, and then name the `IBAction` method **GoToMyTable** by control-dragging the button to the `ViewController.h` file, as seen in Figure 11-6. This generates the following code, which displays the table view:

```
- (IBAction)GoToMyTable:(id)sender;
```

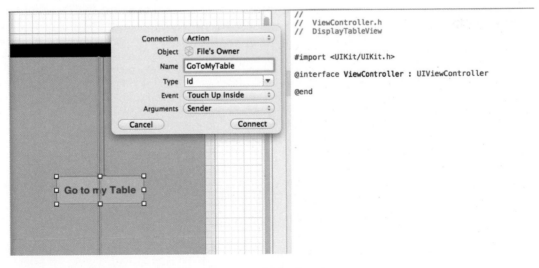

Figure 11-6   Creating an `IBAction` to open a table view

6. Now we need to import the new table view controller into the first view controller header file in order to create a transition from the first view controller to the table view controller. To accomplish this, type the following code in the `ViewController.h` file:

```
#import "TableViewController.h"
```

7. Now we will implement the `GoToMyTable` `IBAction` method in the `ViewController.m` file. In order to do this, we have to create an instance of the table view controller, associate a transition style with it, and then finally present the table view controller. This requires the following code:

```
- (IBAction)GoToMyTable:(id)sender {
    //create an instance of the table view controller
    TableViewController *tvc = [[TableViewController
alloc ] init];

    //assign it a transition style
    tvc.modalTransitionStyle =
UIModalTransitionStyleCrossDissolve;

    //present the table view controller
    [self presentViewController:tvc animated:YES
completion:Nil];

}
```

8. Now that we have a means of going from the view controller to the table view controller, we need to create a transition from the table view controller back to the view controller. We have already created the Done bar button for this, and now it's time to program this Done button. Create an `IBAction` for the Done button by control-dragging it from the table view controller to the header file `TableViewController.h`, and name the `IBAction` **Done**. This generates the following code:

```
- (IBAction)Done:(id)sender;
```

9. Next, implement the **Done** method in the implementation file of the table view controller `TableViewController.m`. The method that dismisses the currently open view controller is invoked. In our case, the currently open view controller would be the table view controller. The code for this is:

```
-(IBAction)Done:(id)sender {
    [self dismissViewControllerAnimated:YES
completion:Nil];
}
```

10. Run the program. You see the screens shown in Figure 11-7. At this point, the table is blank because we have not yet added anything to it.

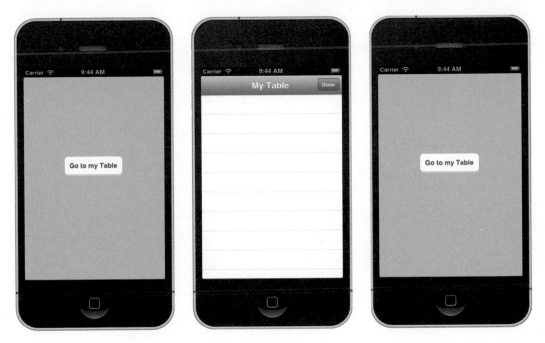

**Figure 11-7**    Running the app with a blank table

So far, all we have done is add a table view controller to an app. In order to show or edit data, we need to add a data source to the table view so there will be actual data displayed in the table view when the app is run. One choice of data source for the table is an NSMutableArray of data.

## Displaying Data in the Table View

We will first learn to populate a table view from an NSArray. The steps involved in using an array as a data source are as follows:

1. Create an array in the table view controller interface file.

2. Create a property for the NSMutableArray in the interface file, and synthesize it in the implementation file.

3. Initialize the array in the viewDidLoad method.

4. Assign the contents of the array to the cell in the cellForRowAtIndex method.

The three essential methods required to create and populate a table are as follows.

- Numbers of sections in a table

```
- (NSInteger)numberOfSectionsInTableView:(UITableView *)tableView
{
    // Return the number of sections.
    return 1;
}
```

- Number of rows in a table

```
- (NSInteger)tableView:(UITableView *)tableView
numberOfRowsInSection:(NSInteger)section
{
    // Return the number of rows in the section.
    return 4;
}
```

- Data in each row

```
- (UITableViewCell *)tableView:(UITableView *)tableView
cellForRowAtIndexPath:(NSIndexPath *)indexPath
{
    static NSString *CellIdentifier = @"Cell";
    UITableViewCell *cell = [tableView
dequeueReusableCellWithIdentifier:CellIdentifier];
    if (cell == nil) {
        cell = [[UITableViewCell alloc]
initWithStyle:UITableViewCellStyleDefault reuseIdentifier:CellIdentifier];
    }

    // Configure the cell...

    return cell;
}
```

Of these three methods, only the first two are required. Although the third method is optional, it is essential for populating a table. In essence, we need to specify the number of sections in the table, the number of rows in the table, and the data that should be displayed in the table.

## Adding a Data Source

Now we are ready to add data stored in an NSArray to My Table.

1. Create an NSArray in the TableViewController.h file as follows:

   NSArray * tableData;

   The TableViewController.h file, with the Done button and the array declaration, should now look like this:

```
#import <UIKit/UIKit.h>

@interface TableViewController : UITableViewController
{
    NSArray *tableData;
}
- (IBAction)Done:(id)sender;

@end
```

2. Create the implementation of the NSArray in the ViewDidLoad method of the TableViewController.m file. The NSArray is populated using the ArrayWithObjects method as seen in the following code:

```
//Implement the array
        tableData = [NSArray arrayWithObjects:@"Persian",
    @"Maine Coon", @"Siamese", @"Bengal", @"Ragdoll",
    @"Scottish Fold", @"British Shorthair", nil];
```

3. Make sure the code in your program looks the same as the following code, so that we can be sure the table view controller knows where the data is coming from. This is done in the cellForRowAtIndexPath method, which is one of the methods that is autogenerated when the table view controller is created. To conserve resources, this method contains code that employs reusable cells, which are cells that disappear from view when the user scrolls up or down. First, a reuse identifier named cell is declared. Then, the dequeueReusableCellWithIdentifier method is invoked to determine if any cells have scrolled off the screen. If none are found (if (cell == nil)) then a new cell is created in the following statement:

```
cell = [[UITableViewCell alloc]
initWithStyle:UITableViewCellStyleDefault
reuseIdentifier:CellIdentifier];
```

In essence, the cellForRowAtIndexPath method in the TableViewController.m file checks to see if the there is a reusable cell available for use. This statement is autogenerated in the cellForRowAtIndexPath method. Note that the entire code for the TableViewController.m is shown below.

4. Assign the array elements to the cells by typing the following code right after the code in the preceding step:

```
// Configure the cell...
    cell.textLabel.text = [tableData
objectAtIndex:[indexPath row]];
```

5. The number of elements in the array dictates the number of rows in the table. Modify the numberOfRowsInSection method to match the following code:

```
- (NSInteger)tableView:(UITableView *)tableView
numberOfRowsInSection:(NSInteger)section
```

```
    {
        // Return the number of rows in the section.

        return [tableData count];

    }
```

## Code for the `TableViewController.m` Files

The entire code for the `TableViewController.m` file is shown as follows:

```objc
#import "TableViewController.h"

@interface TableViewController ()

@end

@implementation TableViewController

- (id)initWithStyle:(UITableViewStyle)style
{
    self = [super initWithStyle:style];
    if (self) {
        // Custom initialization
    }
    return self;
}

- (void)viewDidLoad
{
    [super viewDidLoad];
    tableData = [NSArray arrayWithObjects:@"Persian", @"Maine
Coon", @"Siamese", @"Bengal", @"Ragdoll", @"Scottish Fold",
@"British Shorthair", nil];
}

- (void)didReceiveMemoryWarning
{
    [super didReceiveMemoryWarning];
    // Dispose of any resources that can be recreated.
}

#pragma mark - Table view data source

- (NSInteger)numberOfSectionsInTableView:(UITableView
*)tableView
{
    // Return the number of sections.
    return 1;
}
```

```
- (NSInteger)tableView:(UITableView *)tableView
numberOfRowsInSection:(NSInteger)section
{
    // Return the number of rows in the section.
    return [tableData count];
}

- (UITableViewCell *)tableView:(UITableView *)tableView
cellForRowAtIndexPath:(NSIndexPath *)indexPath
{
    static NSString *CellIdentifier = @"Cell";
    UITableViewCell *cell = [tableView
dequeueReusableCellWithIdentifier:CellIdentifier];
    if (cell == nil) {
        cell = [[UITableViewCell alloc]
initWithStyle:UITableViewCellStyleDefault
reuseIdentifier:CellIdentifier];
    }

    // Configure the cell...
    cell.textLabel.text = [tableData objectAtIndex:[indexPath row]];

    return cell;
}

- (IBAction)Done:(id)sender {
    [self dismissViewControllerAnimated:YES completion:Nil];
}
@end
```

## Running the App

Now we are ready to run the app.

1. Run the app. The results are shown Figure 11-8.

**Figure 11-8**    Running the app

So far we have created an app that displays data in the format of a table. At this point, touching any of the cells does not give us any further information. Now we will look at how to display details for individual cells in a table.

## Creating a Detail View

The cells that provide details usually have a **descriptor**, such as an arrow, indicating that more details on the cell are available. A detail view, with more information about a cell's contents, is created when a user touches a descriptor. The three main types of descriptors, or, as they are also called, accessories, are shown in Figure 11-9.

| Descriptor shape | Name | Explanation |
|---|---|---|
| > | disclosure indicator | A class of the UITableViewCellAccessoryDisclosureIndicator; opens another table view |
| (>) | detail disclosure | A class of the UITableViewCellAccessoryDetailDisclosureButton; may or may not lead to another table view |
| ✓ | checkmark indicator | A class of the UITableViewCellAccesoryCheckmark; allows the user to select a cell |

**Figure 11-9**    Types of descriptors (or accessories)

Table view cells have four optional styles:

- UITableViewCellStyleBasic, the default style, includes a title.

- UITableViewCellStyleSubtitle has a title, subtitle, and an optional left-aligned image.

- UITableViewCellStyleRightDetail has a left-aligned title, a right-aligned subtitle, and does not permit images.

- UITableViewCellStyleLeftDetail has a right-aligned title with indent, a left-aligned subtitle, and does not allow images.

Xcode provides a template that helps the developer create a detail view. This template, called the Master-Detail Application template, provides an initial UITableViewController class, as well as a storyboard for scenes and segues in the user interface. The Master-Detail Application template is an ideal starting point for creating and navigating through a hierarchy of table views.

# Creating a Master-Detail Application Example

1. Create a new project in Xcode. In the Choose a template for your new project dialog, select the **Master-Detail Application** template as seen in Figure 11-10.

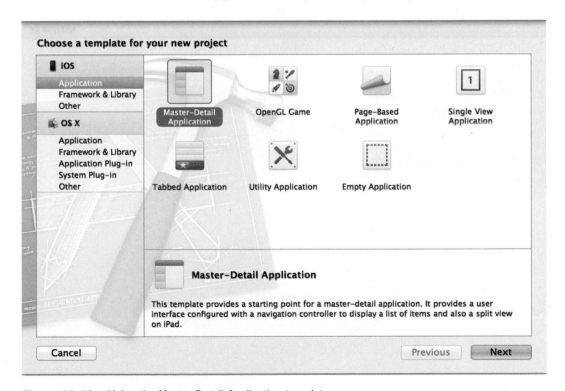

**Figure 11-10**  Using the Master-Detail Application template

2. Click **Next**, and, in the Choose options for your new project dialog, enter the name **MasterDetail** for the product name. Also, make sure to select the **Use Storyboards** and **Use Automatic Reference Counting** check boxes.

3. Click **Next** and save the project in a location of your choice. At this point, the navigator area should look like Figure 11-11. The MainStoryboard.storyboard file holds the interface, whereas the set of MasterViewController.h and MasterViewController.m files are associated with the master view controller. The set of DetailViewController.h and DetailViewController.m files are associated with the detail view controller.

**Figure 11-11**    Files displayed in navigator area

4. Click on the **MainStoryboard.storyboard** file to display two view controllers, as shown in Figure 11-12. Note that the master view controller has a navigation controller embedded in it.

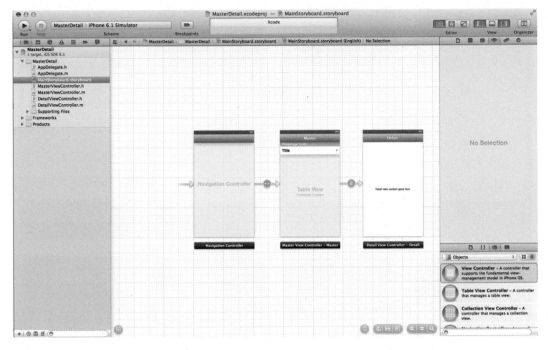

**Figure 11-12**   Interface for a Master-Detail Application example

5.  Run the app without adding any code to the program. You see the first screen shown
    in Figure 11-13. At this point, the user has two options: touch the plus sign button to
    add an item or touch the Edit button to edit an item.

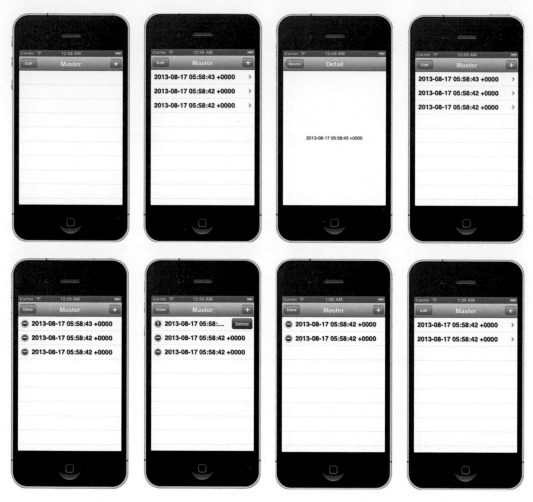

**Figure 11-13**    Running the Master-Detail Application example

6.  Touch the plus sign. Since the app cannot actually add an item at this point, touching the plus sign displays a date/time stamp in the cell.

7.  Touch the plus sign two more times to add two more date/time stamps, as shown in the second screen in Figure 11-13. As you touch on the plus sign button, you can add more date/time stamps to the cells.

8.  Touch the accessory on a cell to view the detail view, as seen in the third screen in Figure 11-13.

9. Touch the **Master** button to return to the master view as seen in the fourth screen in Figure 11-13.

10. Touch the Edit button. This displays the fifth screen shown in Figure 11-13, with a minus sign in a red circle next to each date/time stamp.

11. Touch the red minus sign for the top date/time stamp. The delete button appears, giving you the option of deleting that date/time stamp, as seen in the sixth screen in Figure 11-13.

12. Touch the Delete button. The first date/time stamp is deleted, as seen in the seventh screen in Figure 11-13.

13. Touch the Done button to leave edit mode, as seen in the eighth screen in Figure 11-13.

## Implementing the Master-Detail-Application Template

Now that you've had a chance to see how the Master-Detail Application template allows the user to add, edit, and delete items in the table view, let's go ahead and add a data source to the project we just created.

1. Add a NSMutableArray to hold the data. In the MasterViewController.h file, add the property for the NSMutableArray, as follows:

```
@property (strong, nonatomic) NSMutableArray *myArray;
```

2. Synthesize the property in the implementation file of the MasterViewController.m file as seen here:

```
@synthesize myArray;
```

3. In the implementation file of the MasterViewController.m file, comment out the code for the creation of the _objects NSMutableArray as follows:

```
//NSMutableArray *_objects;
```

The NSMutableArray *_objects code is autogenerated by the Master-Detail Application template, and we will not be using it. If we had not commented it out, it would show errors for the parts of code where the _objects variable was used. After we have created our NSMutableArray, we will replace this array with the _objects NSMutableArray in all the instances throughout the rest of the code.

4. Next, initialize the NSMutableArray in the viewDidLoad method of the implementation file of the Master view controller as seen in the following code:

```
myArray = [[NSMutableArray alloc]
initWithObjects:@"Banana", @"Apple", @"Cherry", nil];
```

5. Since we want our program to be able to insert new items in the table view, we need to modify the `insertNewObject` method to insert an object. In the following code, the template-created code has been deleted, because we are not using the `date` object. Instead, we are writing code that will add the string `"hello"` every time the user touches the plus sign.

```
- (void)insertNewObject:(id)sender
{
    if (!myArray) {
        myArray = [[NSMutableArray alloc] init];
    }
//insert the string "Hello" in the NSMutableArray every
time the + bar button is tapped
    [myArray insertObject:@"Hello" atIndex:0];

//Set the indexpath to the new cell
    NSIndexPath *indexPath = [NSIndexPath
indexPathForRow:0 inSection:0];

//insert the new row
    [self.tableView insertRowsAtIndexPaths:@[indexPath]
withRowAnimation:UITableViewRowAnimationAutomatic];
}
```

6. In the following method, declare the number of sections in the table view:

```
- (NSInteger)numberOfSectionsInTableView:(UITableView
*)tableView
{
    return 1;
}
```

7. Set the number of rows in each section equal to the number of elements in the NSMutableArray, as seen here:

```
- (NSInteger)tableView:(UITableView *)tableView
numberOfRowsInSection:(NSInteger)section
{
    return myArray.count;
}
```

8. Use the `cellForRowAtIndexpath` method to provide the contents for the cell at a specific index. Comment out the NSDate object, and instead populate the cell with the contents of the NSMutableArray at the indexPath:

```
- (UITableViewCell *)tableView:(UITableView *)tableView
cellForRowAtIndexPath:(NSIndexPath *)indexPath
{
    UITableViewCell *cell = [tableView
dequeueReusableCellWithIdentifier:@"Cell"
forIndexPath:indexPath];

    //NSDate *object = _objects[indexPath.row];
```

```
    cell.textLabel.text = [myArray[indexPath.row]
description];
    return cell;
}
```

9. Modify the `commitEditingStyle:forRowAtIndexPath` method to remove the contents of the array at a specific `indexPath`:

```
- (void)tableView:(UITableView *)tableView
commitEditingStyle:(UITableViewCellEditingStyle)editing
Style forRowAtIndexPath:(NSIndexPath *)indexPath
{
    if (editingStyle ==
UITableViewCellEditingStyleDelete) {
        [myArray removeObjectAtIndex:indexPath.row];
        [tableView deleteRowsAtIndexPaths:@[indexPath]
 withRowAnimation:UITableViewRowAnimationFade];
    } else if (editingStyle ==
UITableViewCellEditingStyleInsert) {
    }
}
```

10. The last method we need to modify is the `prepareForSegue` method. This method is used to pass data between views. We will pass our `NSMutableArray` element to the details view, as seen here:

```
- (void)prepareForSegue:(UIStoryboardSegue *)segue
sender:(id)sender
{
    if ([[segue identifier]
isEqualToString:@"showDetail"]) {
        NSIndexPath *indexPath = [self.tableView
 indexPathForSelectedRow];
        //NSDate *object = _objects[indexPath.row];

        [[segue destinationViewController]
setDetailItem:myArray[indexPath.row]];
    }
}
```

Notice that we have not modified the detail view interface or implementation files. Instead, we have only modified the `MasterViewController` interface and implementation file.

## MasterViewController.h file

The entire code for the MasterViewController.h file is as follows:

```
//
//  MasterViewController.h
//  MasterDetail
#import <UIKit/UIKit.h>

@interface MasterViewController : UITableViewController

@property (strong, nonatomic) NSMutableArray *myArray;


@end
```

## MasterViewController.m file

The entire code for the MasterViewController.m file is given here:

```
//
//  MasterViewController.m
//  MasterDetail

#import "MasterViewController.h"

#import "DetailViewController.h"

@interface MasterViewController ()
@end

@implementation MasterViewController
@synthesize myArray;

- (void)awakeFromNib
{
    [super awakeFromNib];
}

- (void)viewDidLoad
{
    [super viewDidLoad];
    // Do any additional setup after loading the view,
 typically from a nib.
    self.navigationItem.leftBarButtonItem =
self.editButtonItem;
    myArray = [[NSMutableArray alloc]
initWithObjects:@"Banana", @"Apple", @"Cherry", nil];

    UIBarButtonItem *addButton = [[UIBarButtonItem alloc]
initWithBarButtonSystemItem:UIBarButtonSystemItemAdd
target:self action:@selector(insertNewObject:)];
    self.navigationItem.rightBarButtonItem = addButton;
}
```

```objc
- (void)didReceiveMemoryWarning
{
    [super didReceiveMemoryWarning];
    // Dispose of any resources that can be recreated.
}

- (void)insertNewObject:(id)sender
{
    if (!myArray) {
        myArray = [[NSMutableArray alloc] init];
    }
    [myArray insertObject:@"Hello" atIndex:0];
    NSIndexPath *indexPath = [NSIndexPath indexPathForRow:0
inSection:0];
    [self.tableView insertRowsAtIndexPaths:@[indexPath]
withRowAnimation:UITableViewRowAnimationAutomatic];
}

#pragma mark - Table View

- (NSInteger)numberOfSectionsInTableView:(UITableView *)tableView
{
    return 1;
}

- (NSInteger)tableView:(UITableView *)tableView
numberOfRowsInSection:(NSInteger)section
{
    return myArray.count;
}

- (UITableViewCell *)tableView:(UITableView *)tableView
cellForRowAtIndexPath:(NSIndexPath *)indexPath
{
    UITableViewCell *cell = [tableView
dequeueReusableCellWithIdentifier:@"Cell"
forIndexPath:indexPath];

    //NSDate *object = _objects[indexPath.row];
    // cell.textLabel.text = [object description];
    cell.textLabel.text = [myArray[indexPath.row]
description];
    return cell;
}

- (BOOL)tableView:(UITableView *)tableView
canEditRowAtIndexPath:(NSIndexPath *)indexPath
{
    // Return NO if you do not want the specified item to be
editable.
    return YES;
}
```

```
- (void)tableView:(UITableView *)tableView
commitEditingStyle:(UITableViewCellEditingStyle)editingStyle
forRowAtIndexPath:(NSIndexPath *)indexPath
{
    if (editingStyle == UITableViewCellEditingStyleDelete) {
        [myArray removeObjectAtIndex:indexPath.row];
        [tableView deleteRowsAtIndexPaths:@[indexPath]
withRowAnimation:UITableViewRowAnimationFade];
    } else if (editingStyle ==
UITableViewCellEditingStyleInsert) {
        // Create a new instance of the appropriate class,
insert it into the array, and add a new row to the table
view.
    }
}


- (void)prepareForSegue:(UIStoryboardSegue *)segue
sender:(id)sender
{
    if ([[segue identifier] isEqualToString:@"showDetail"]) {
        NSIndexPath *indexPath = [self.tableView
indexPathForSelectedRow];
        // NSDate *object = _objects[indexPath.row];
        [[segue destinationViewController]
setDetailItem: myArray[indexPath.row]];
    }
}

@end
```

## Running the App

Now we are ready to run the app.

1.  Run the app. The results are shown in Figure 11-14.

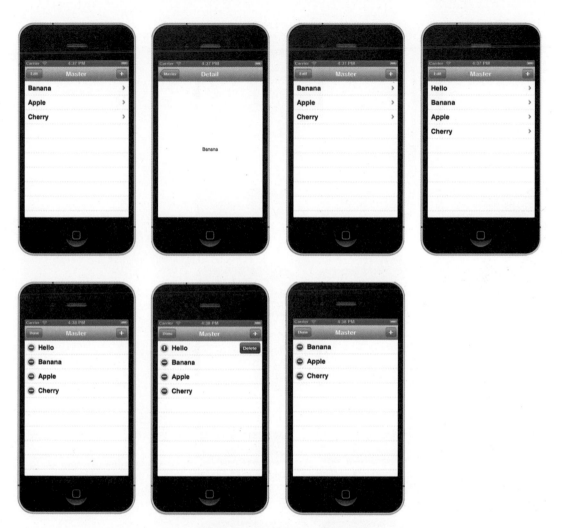

**Figure 11-14**  Running the Master-Detail Application example again

## HANDS-ON LAB

In this Hands-On Lab, you will be building a To Do List app. When you run the app, it will first display a blank table, with an **Add** button in the top-right corner and an Edit button in the top-left corner. When the user touches the **Add** button, the app displays a view with a text field, a Save button and a To Do List bar button.

After the user enters an item in the text field and touches the Add button, the detail accessory appears. The user can touch the accessory to display a view with a detail view When there are items in the list, the Edit button can be used to delete items. Figure 11-15 shows various tasks being performed on the running app.

App is running, with
no list created so far

Creating an item
in the To Do list

After adding first item
to the To Do list

Detail view of the first
item in the To Do List

After adding a second
item in the To Do List;
notice the two accessories.

Editing the To Do list

Deleting item 1 from
the To Do list

After deleting item 1

The To Do list, with
only item 2 remaining

**Figure 11-15**　Running the app in the Hands-On Lab

## CREATE A NEW PROJECT AND DESIGN THE INTERFACE

1. Create a new project in Xcode. In the Choose a template for your new project dialog, select the Master-Detail Application template, and make sure to check the Use Storyboards and Automatic Reference Counting options. Save the project as **handsOnLabCh11**.

2. Click on the `MainStoryboard.storyboard` file in the navigation area, and design the interface as shown in Figure 11-15. Next, drag a view controller onto the interface and combine the table view controller with the view controller. Next drag a view controller from the Object Library to the editor pane, and then drag a label, text field, and a round rect button from the Object Library onto the newly added view controller. Make sure to drag a view controller and not a table view controller. Arrange the controls as shown in Figure 11-15. Modify the text in the button to read **Save** and the text in the label to read **Enter text here**.

3. Add a bar button to the master view controller on the top-right corner and rename this button "Add".

## ADD THE VIEW CONTROLLER FILES

4. Add the interface and the implementation files for the view controller and name them `ViewController`. Next, associate these files with the view controller by first selecting the view controller in the storyboard and then, in the Identity Inspector, select `ViewController` file for the class.

## PROGRAM THE INTERFACE

5. Create a segue from the **Add** button to the newly added view controller by control-dragging the **Add** bar button on the master view controller to the newly added view controller. Select the push option so the navigation bar can be seen on the view controller and also so the back button will be autogenerated.

6. Name this segue **addItem**. As soon as the segue is created, a navigation bar will appear on the newly added view controller. Double-click it in the center and add the title **Add new list item**. Change the title of the navigation bar for the master view controller to **To Do List**.

## CREATE IBOUTLET AND IBACTION CONNECTIONS

7. Control-drag the text field to the `ViewController.h` file to create an IBOutlet, called **itemTextField**. This generates the following code:

```
@property (nonatomic, strong) IBOutlet UITextField
*itemTextField;
```

8. Control-drag the Save button to the `ViewController.h` file to create an IBAction called **add**. The code generated is as follows:

```
-(IBAction)add:(id)sender;
```

9. Control-drag the text field again to the `ViewController.h` file and this time create an **IBAction** for hiding the keyboard. Call this method `textFieldReturn`. The code for the **IBAction** is as follows:

```
-(IBAction)textFieldReturn:(id)sender;
```

10. Click in the center of the view controller and, in the Identity Inspector, select **UIControl** as the class.

11. Write the method to dismiss the keyboard, as done in previous chapters, by converting the view into a control. Control-drag the view to the `ViewController.h` file to create an **IBAction** called `backgroundTouched` as follows:

```
- (IBAction)backgroundTouched:(id)sender;
```

## ADDING A DATA SOURCE

Before we implement all the **IBAction** connections we just created, we need to add a data source to the app. We will be using `NSMutableArrays` to store the items in the list. The reason for the mutable array is that it allows us to add and delete items from it.

12. Create a `NSMutableArray` called `list` in the `ViewController.h` file. The code is as follows:

```
@property (nonatomic, strong) NSMutableArray *list;
```

13. Synthesize it in the `ViewController.m` file along with the **IBOutlet** called `itemTextField` file for the text field on the view controller as follows:

```
@synthesize itemTextField, list;
```

14. Create another `NSMutableArray` in the `MasterViewController.h` file as follows:

```
@property (nonamtoic, strong) NSMutableArray *myArray;
```

15. Synthesize it in the `MasterViewController.m` file as follows:

```
@synthesize myArray;
```

## IMPLEMENT THE IBACTION CONNECTION

16. We're ready to start implementing the **IBAction** connections. Let us first start by implementing the **IBAction** named **add**. In this method, we first check to see if the user has typed anything. If so, then we save the contents of the text field into the `NSMutableArray` called `list`. Next, we close the navigation controller, which will dismiss the current view controller displaying the master view controller. If the user has not typed any text, then nothing is added to the list and the navigation controller is dismissed, revealing the master view controller.

```
- (IBAction)add:(id)sender {
    if ([itemTextField text].length > 0) {
        [list addObject:itemTextField.text];
        [self.navigationController
```

```
popViewControllerAnimated:YES];
    } else {
        [self.navigationController
popViewControllerAnimated:YES];
    }
}
```

17. The next IBAction we need to implement is the textFieldReturn method. This method will hide the keyboard when the user touches the Return key in the keyboard.

```
- (IBAction)textFieldReturn:(id)sender {
    [sender endEditing:YES];
}
```

18. The last method we need to implement for the view controller is the backgroundTouched method. In this method, when the user touches the background, the keyboard will disappear. The necessary code is as follows:

```
- (IBAction)backgroundTouched:(id)sender {
    [itemTextField resignFirstResponder];
}
```

## PROGRAM THE MASTER VIEW CONTROLLER TO DISPLAY DATA

19. Since the Master-Detail Application template is already set up to add and edit a table, we are going to focus on adding new items to the table view in the master view controller. We first need to import the ViewController.h file into the MasterViewController.m file as follows.

```
#import "ViewController.h"
```

20. Now we can create the viewDidLoad method in the MasterViewController.m file. This is the first method that is executed when a view is loaded. In this method, we initialize the NSMutableArray called myArray that will hold the data for the To Do list. Next, we need to deal with some code that was auto generated by the Master-Detail Application template. We will delete all of this code except the code that will display the left bar button, which will perform the edit functionality on the table view. Remember to reload the table view so the updated data can be seen. The necessary code is as follows:

```
- (void)viewDidLoad
{
    [super viewDidLoad];
    myArray = [[NSMutableArray alloc] init];
    self.navigationItem.leftBarButtonItem =
self.editButtonItem;
        [self.tableView reloadData];
}
```

21. The next method we will add to the MasterViewController.m is the viewWillAppear method. This method will help display the data in the table view with updated data each time the view is opened.

347

```
- (void)viewWillAppear:(BOOL)animated {
    [self.tableView reloadData];
}
```

22.  Modify the `numberOfRowsInSection` method to display the number of rows to match the size of `myArray` as seen in the following code:

```
- (NSInteger)tableView:(UITableView *)tableView
numberOfRowsInSection:(NSInteger)section
{
    return myArray.count;
}
```

23.  Next, we need to modify the `cellForRowAtIndexPath` method. This method will populate the cells in the table from `myArray`. The necessary code is as follows:

```
- (UITableViewCell *)tableView:(UITableView *)tableView
cellForRowAtIndexPath:(NSIndexPath *)indexPath
{
    UITableViewCell *cell = [tableView
dequeueReusableCellWithIdentifier:@"Cell"
forIndexPath:indexPath];
    cell.textLabel.text = myArray[indexPath.row];
    cell.accessoryType = UITableViewCellAccessoryDisclosureIndicator;
return cell;
}
```

24.  The next method we will modify is the `commitEditingStyle` method. This method is invoked when the user touches the Edit button on the master view. The only edits we need to make to this method are to replace the autogenerated `NSMutableArray` with the array named `myArray`.

```
- (void)tableView:(UITableView *)tableView
commitEditingStyle:(UITableViewCellEditingStyle)editing
Style forRowAtIndexPath:(NSIndexPath *)indexPath
{
    if (editingStyle ==
UITableViewCellEditingStyleDelete) {
        [myArray removeObjectAtIndex:indexPath.row];
        [tableView deleteRowsAtIndexPaths:@[indexPath]
withRowAnimation:UITableViewRowAnimationFade];
    } else if (editingStyle ==
UITableViewCellEditingStyleInsert) {

    }
}
```

## TRANSFER DATA BETWEEN VIEWS

25.  The transfer of data between the views is done using the `prepareForSegue` method. In this method, a variable of type `indexpath` is used to keep track of the index path. This is where we will implement the segue identifier called `addItem` to separate the segue that goes from the master view to the newly added view controller and the one that goes from the master view to the detail view. The first `if` statement checks the name of the segue; if it is `showDetail`, then the appropriate steps are

taken to display the detail view controller. The code for this does not need to be modified. However, we will add another that checks the name of the segue called addItem to determine if the segue identifier is equal to the string addItem. If this condition is met, then an instance of the newly added view controller is created and the array from this view controller is populated with data from myArray. The necessary code is as follows:

```
- (void)prepareForSegue:(UIStoryboardSegue *)segue
sender:(id)sender
{
    if ([[segue identifier]
isEqualToString:@"showDetail"]) {
        NSIndexPath *indexPath = [self.tableView
indexPathForSelectedRow];
        [[segue destinationViewController]
setDetailItem:myArray[indexPath.row]];
    }
    if ([[segue identifier]
isEqualToString:@"addItem"]) {
        ViewController *vc = (ViewController *)
segue.destinationViewController;
        vc.list = myArray; //pass it the list
    }
}
```

26. Run the app and make sure it works as shown earlier in Figure 11-15.

## SOURCE CODE

The entire code for the ViewController.h file is as follows

```
//
//  ViewController.h
//  handsOnLabCh11

#import <UIKit/UIKit.h>

@interface ViewController : UIViewController
@property (nonatomic, strong) IBOutlet UITextField
*itemTextField;
@property (nonatomic, strong) NSMutableArray *list;
- (IBAction)add:(id)sender;

- (IBAction)textFieldReturn:(id)sender;
- (IBAction)backgroundTouched:(id)sender;
@end
```

The entire code for the ViewController.m is as follows

```
//
//  ViewController.m
//  handsOnLabCh11
```

```objc
#import "ViewController.h"

@interface ViewController ()

@end

@implementation ViewController
@synthesize itemTextField, list;

- (id)initWithNibName:(NSString *)nibNameOrNil
bundle:(NSBundle *)nibBundleOrNil
{
    self = [super initWithNibName:nibNameOrNil
bundle:nibBundleOrNil];
    if (self) {
        // Custom initialization
    }
    return self;
}


- (void)viewDidLoad
{
    [super viewDidLoad];
    // Do any additional setup after loading the view.
}


- (void)didReceiveMemoryWarning
{
    [super didReceiveMemoryWarning];
    // Dispose of any resources that can be recreated.
}
- (IBAction)add:(id)sender {
    if ([itemTextField text].length > 0) {
        [list addObject:itemTextField.text];
        [self.navigationController
popViewControllerAnimated:YES];
    } else {
        [self.navigationController
popViewControllerAnimated:YES];
    }
}


- (IBAction)textFieldReturn:(id)sender {
    [sender endEditing:YES];
}
```

```objc
- (IBAction)backgroundTouched:(id)sender {
    [itemTextField resignFirstResponder];
}

@end
```

The entire code for the `MasterViewController.h` is as follows:

```objc
//
//  MasterViewController.h
//  handsOnLabCh11

#import <UIKit/UIKit.h>

@interface MasterViewController : UITableViewController

@property (nonatomic, strong) NSMutableArray *myArray;

@end
```

The entire code for the `MasterViewController.m` is as follows:

```objc
//
//  MasterViewController.m
//  handsOnLabCh11

#import "MasterViewController.h"

#import "DetailViewController.h"
#import "ViewController.h"

@interface MasterViewController ()
@end

@implementation MasterViewController
@synthesize myArray;

- (void)awakeFromNib
{
    [super awakeFromNib];
}
- (void)viewWillAppear:(BOOL)animated {
    [self.tableView reloadData];
}
- (void)viewDidLoad
{
    [super viewDidLoad];
    myArray = [[NSMutableArray alloc] init];
    self.navigationItem.leftBarButtonItem =
self.editButtonItem;
    [self.tableView reloadData];
}
```

```objc
- (void)didReceiveMemoryWarning
{
    [super didReceiveMemoryWarning];
    // Dispose of any resources that can be recreated.
}
```

```objc
#pragma mark - Table View

- (NSInteger)numberOfSectionsInTableView:(UITableView
*)tableView
{
    return 1;
}

- (NSInteger)tableView:(UITableView *)tableView
numberOfRowsInSection:(NSInteger)section
{
    return myArray.count;
}

- (UITableViewCell *)tableView:(UITableView *)tableView
cellForRowAtIndexPath:(NSIndexPath *)indexPath
{
    UITableViewCell *cell = [tableView
dequeueReusableCellWithIdentifier:@"Cell"
forIndexPath:indexPath];
    cell.textLabel.text = myArray[indexPath.row];
    return cell;
}

- (BOOL)tableView:(UITableView *)tableView
canEditRowAtIndexPath:(NSIndexPath *)indexPath
{
    // Return NO if you do not want the specified item to be
editable.
    return YES;
}

- (void)tableView:(UITableView *)tableView
commitEditingStyle:(UITableViewCellEditingStyle)editingStyle
forRowAtIndexPath:(NSIndexPath *)indexPath
{
    if (editingStyle == UITableViewCellEditingStyleDelete) {
        [myArray removeObjectAtIndex:indexPath.row];
        [tableView deleteRowsAtIndexPaths:@[indexPath]
withRowAnimation:UITableViewRowAnimationFade];
    } else if (editingStyle ==
UITableViewCellEditingStyleInsert) {

    }
}
```

```
- (void)prepareForSegue:(UIStoryboardSegue *)segue
sender:(id)sender
{
    if ([[segue identifier] isEqualToString:@"showDetail"]) {
        NSIndexPath *indexPath = [self.tableView
indexPathForSelectedRow];
        [[segue destinationViewController]
setDetailItem:myArray[indexPath.row]];
    }
    if ([[segue identifier] isEqualToString:@"addItem"]) {
        ViewController *vc = (ViewController *)
segue.destinationViewController;
        vc.list = myArray; //pass it the list
    }
}
@end
```

# Summary

- The table view is a commonly used type of view in iOS programming. It essentially looks like a list.

- Due to space restrictions on mobile devices, the UITable view has a single column with multiple rows to represent a list of items.

- Each row is called a cell and can hold text or an image.

- There are two styles of table views: plain (UITAbleViewStylePlain) and grouped (UITAbleViewStyleGrouped).

- By default, a table view is Plain, but it can be changed from Plain to Grouped in the Attributes Inspector.

- A table view can be static (that is, with a predefined number of cells) or dynamic (in which cells are created dynamically at runtime).

- The UITableView's implementation requires a view controller, a data source, and a delegate that manages the table.

- The data source follows the UITableViewDataSource protocol and has two important methods: numberOfRowsInSection and cellForRowAtIndexPath.

- The cellForRowAtIndexPath method provides information on each individual cell of the table view and returns the UITableViewcell object for each row.

- When populating a table view from an array, the array should be initialized in the viewDidLoad method.

- A detail view is created when a user clicks on the descriptor for any cell to examine the details of that cell. There are three main types of descriptors: disclosure, detail, and checkmark. Descriptors are also called accessories.

- The cells in a table view have four optional styles: `UITableViewCellStyleDefault` is the default style with a title and an optional image. `ITableViewCellStyleSubtitle` has a title, subtitle, and an optional left-aligned image. `UITableViewCellStyleValue1` has a left-aligned title and a right-aligned subtitle and does not permit images. `UITableViewCellStyleValue2` has a left-aligned subtitle, a right-aligned title with indent, and does not allow images.

- The Master-Detail Application template simplifies the process of creating a hierarchy of table views, making it easier to navigate through a hierarchy of views. It provides an initial `UITableViewController` class and the storyboard for scenes and segues in the user interface.

- When you use a `TableViewController`, the delegate and the data source are automatically implemented.

## Exercises

1. Mark the following statements as true or false. Correct the false statement.

   a. The table view is an instance of the `UITableView` class and hence allows vertical scrolling through the list of items in the table.

   b. Any row in a section can be traced by a row index inside of a section index by the `indexPathForRow:inSection` method.

   c. Any section in a table view is a cell.

   d. The `UITableViewController` automatically adopts the delegate and data source protocols.

   e. The detail view is created when a user clicks on any cell descriptor to examine the details of that cell.

   f. UITableViewCellStyleValue2 is an optional cell style that has a left-aligned subtitle and a right-aligned title with indent and allows images.

2. List and briefly describe the two types of table views.

3. When the user taps a cell, how does the delegate find correct data in the data source?

4. Outline the steps involved in creating a table view.

5. List and briefly describe the three main kinds of descriptors.

6. What are the styles of table view cells?

7. What is the difference between plain and grouped table views?

8. What is the purpose of the Master-Detail Application template?

9. What is the method used to select a row in a table

10. Briefly explain the purpose of the following methods:

    a. CellForRowAtIndexPath

    b. prepareForSegue

    c. ViewDidLoad

    d. Count

# Programming Exercises

Use table views and view controllers in each of the following Programming Exercises. In each case, the user interface design is left to your discretion.

1. Modify the grocery list app that you created in Chapter 10 (Programming Exercise 2) to incorporate a table view.

2. Create a phone directory application. The user should be able to see two views. One view should contain a list of all the contacts. When a user selects a contact, a screen containing information about the user (such as name, phone number, and email) should be displayed.

3. Create an app that displays multiplication tables up to times 12. On the first screen, the user should be able to enter the number whose multiplication table she wants to see, at which point the relevant multiplication table should appear as a table view.

4. Create an app that allows the user to add items to a checklist, storing the name and description of the checklist items. Include a checkmark for each item, so the user can view the details of the items.

5. Suppose Big State University has three schools: Business and Technology, Science, and Arts and Letters. The school of Business and Technology is made up of the following departments: Computer Science, Computer Engineering, Economics, Marketing, and Finance. The school of Science has the following departments: Biology, Chemistry, Physics, Biochemistry, and Nursing. The school of Arts and Letters has the following departments: English, Spanish, Dance, and Music. Create an app that shows the various subdivisions. Your first table view should have the name of the schools. Each school should then be linked to another table view with its departments.

6. Jamie has several online accounts and is having a hard time remembering the passwords for these accounts. She wants to be able to save all of her user name and password information in an app on her phone. Build an app for Jamie that has three views. The first view should be a list of all of Jamie's accounts. Take care to display the account name, as well as the user name. When Jamie taps on an account, the app should display the second view, containing the password for that account, in addition to the account name and user name. Use a navigation button to allow new accounts to be added to the list. When Jamie taps on this button, she should see a view where she can enter an

account name, account user name and password for the new account she is adding. The view should also contain a Done and Cancel button. After Jamie enters the necessary information in the text fields in this view and clicks the Done button, the account should be added to the table view and Jamie should be taken back to the first view.

7. Jamal wants an app that lists his subjects in a table view. He wants to be able to view all of his current subjects, as well as his past subjects, although not at the same time. The first view should be a table view with two cells: Current Subjects and Past Subjects. The Current subjects cell will lead Jamal to a view where he can see the classes he is taking. Tapping on the Past Subjects cell shows Jamal the grade he obtained for that subject, in addition to the subject name.

8. Create an app that allows the user to enter notes about the project she is working on. The app should display a table view on the first screen, with an Add button in the navigation bar. When the user clicks the Add button, a new cell is created in the table view. If the cell is the first cell, the title of the cell should be Note 1. If it is the second cell, the title should be Note 2, and so on. Touching any one of the cell descriptors should allow the user to enter some notes.

9. Create a physical therapy app that lists specific exercises to be done in the morning, afternoon, and evening. Create an app that organizes the names of the exercises in alphabetical order, and tracks the time that each is performed, using mostly table views.

## Business Case Study

In this Business Case Study, we continue working on the pain management journal. In Chapter 10, we added functionality to pass data between two views and dismiss the view controller. Now your job is to add table view functionality. Modify the first view so the user can enter the pain journal items, such as the pain level, and the date and time of entry. The first view should also have the ability to view the pain items entered in the journal. When the user selects the view entries option the second view should display a table view with all the journal items entered in the journal. Selecting any one of the items' descriptors should take the user to a detail view where the specific pain entry is displayed along with the time of entry.

# CHAPTER 12

# Tab Bar View and Picker View Controls

In this chapter you will

- ◎ Implement tab bar controllers with and without storyboards
- ◎ Create tab bar applications from the Tabbed Application template
- ◎ Add an additional tab in an application
- ◎ Implement a picker view controller
- ◎ Explore the role of the delegate and data source in a picker view

In the previous chapter we learned about table views and how data can be displayed in the form of a list that the user can edit. Table views are efficient for displaying large lists of data, because they allow the user to display additional information for each item. However, in some cases, you have a list that is too short to justify the use of a table view, or it may not be necessary to include the ability to display additional details about the items in your list. In addition, there may be situations in which you would like to limit data entry to certain options to avoid data-entry errors. In situations such as these, tab bar views can be helpful. In this chapter we will implement tab bar controllers with and without storyboards, and add additional tabs to a tab bar controller. We will also learn how to implement the picker view controller and investigate the role of a delegate and a data source in a picker view.

## Tab Bar View

A tab bar view is a specialized view that displays tabs in a radio style (that is, with tabs in the lower part of the screen set next to each other) and allows for multiple view transitions from each individual tab. Each tab has its own distinct mode of operation. A tab bar view can have multiple tabs that possess control properties and can be used as buttons to transition to other views. Each individual tab leads to a view with varying functionalities.

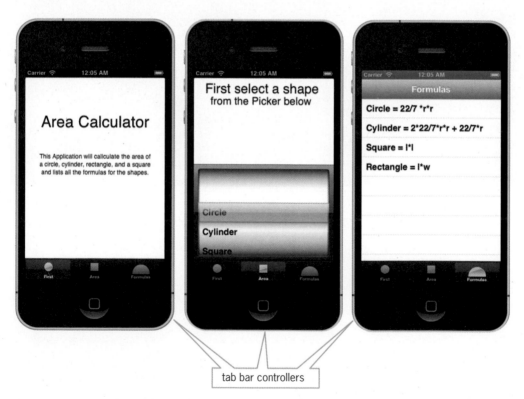

**Figure 12-1**    Tab bar application

As you can see in Figure 12-1, a tab bar controller has tabs in the bottom row of the screen. The user can touch a tab to go to a specific task. The maximum number of tabs a phone can display at a time is five. If you create an app with more than five tabs, the fifth tab displays the word "More." The user can touch it to display additional tabs. The advantage of using a tab bar controller is that no matter what screen the user is on, the option to switch is available at the bottom of the screen. The user does not have to step backward through the app to go to a different view.

The tab bar controller manages the view hierarchies of the app's content view controllers; the content view controllers then manage their distinct view hierarchies. In other words, the tab bar controller is a glorified navigator with the ability to track a new path from any point within the view hierarchy.

The most common way of implementing the tab bar controller is installing it in the main window as the root controller. The root controller is the initial controller, where the tab bar will first appear. This is the approach we will take in this chapter.

The Tabbed Application template, as seen in Figure 12-2, creates a tab bar with two tabs by default. We can then add additional tabs to the tab bar. A tabbed application can be created with or without a storyboard. Note that you can also choose to not use the Tabbed Application template; in that case, you'll need to drag and drop the tab bar control onto the app's first view.

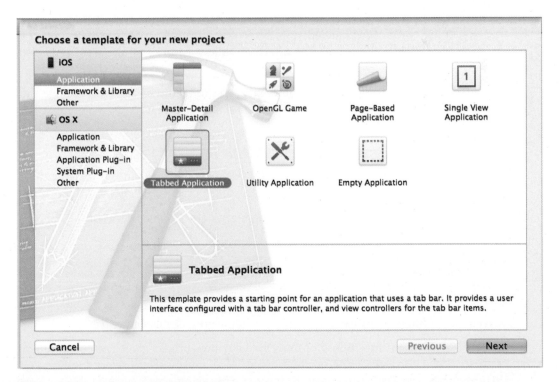

**Figure 12-2**   Tabbed Application template

# Creating a Tab Bar App Using Storyboards

When using storyboards, you can create a tabbed app by dragging and dropping the tab bar view controller from the object library. The tab bar controller is added to the first view. Any additional tabs are added by creating a relationship segue of type view controller. This is unlike in earlier examples, where we created manual segues of type push, modal, or custom, because in this case we are creating a relationship with a view controller. Any view controller relationship created this way will create a tab on the tab bar. You then have to drag and drop the individual tab bar items onto each view, and then set the tab's title and image. The title and the image appear on each individual tab. If you fail to assign a title and image to each tab, Xcode will give it the default name "item," and the tab will not have an image.

The following list summarizes the steps involved in creating a tabbed app using storyboards.

1.  Create a tab bar app using the Tabbed Application template. Make sure to select the Use Storyboards check box.

2.  The template creates a tab bar controller with two view controllers. It sets tab titles to "first and "second" and the images to default images of a circle and square.

3.  To add an additional tab, add a new view controller by dragging a view controller from the object library onto the storyboard.

4.  Connect the new view controller to the tab bar controller by Control-dragging the tab bar controller to the newly added view controller, creating a relationship segue of the type view controller. By default, the interface builder names the tab "item" and does not give it an image.

5.  Select the newly added view controller. Then, in the Identity Inspector, change the default title to something more descriptive, and add an image. The image must be saved as a .png file.

6.  Create the class file to go with the view by adding an Objective-C class.

7.  Connect the class to the view controller by selecting the view, and in the Identity Inspector for the class, select the name of the appropriate class file.

8.  Program the individual views as per the requirements of the application.

## Starting a Tab Bar App Example

Now let's actually create a tab bar app using storyboards.

1.  Create a new project in Xcode. In the Choose a template for your new project dialog, select the **Tabbed Application** template as shown earlier in Figure 12-2.

2.  Click **Next**, and, in the Choose options for your new project dialog, enter the name **TabWithStoryBoard** for the product name. Also, make sure to select the **Use Storyboards** and **Use Automatic Reference Counting** check boxes.

3. Click **Next** and save the project in the location of your choice. At this point, the Navigation panel should look like the one shown in Figure 12-3. As you can see, there is a MainStoryboard.storyboard file, which holds the interface for the app. There is also a set of .h and .m view controller files named FirstViewController and SecondViewController.

**Figure 12-3**   Navigation panel for a tabbed application

4. Click on the **MainStoryboard.storyboard** file to display the interface that was autogenerated by the Tabbed Application template. By default, the Tabbed Application template creates an application with two tabs. Figure 12-4 shows the tab bar controller and the two view controllers, one for each tab. Now we need to add an additional tab, so we will add a new view controller to the project.

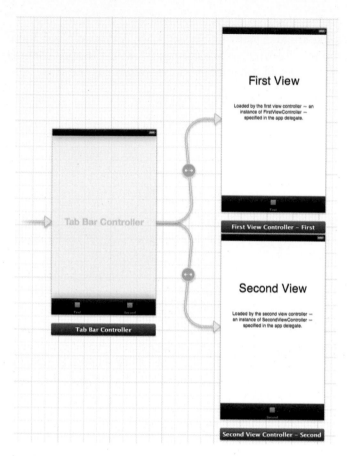

**Figure 12-4**   Interface of the tabbed app

5.  Add a new view controller by dragging it from the Object Library. Because every view controller should have its interface and implementation file, we will now add an Objective-C class file.

6.  In the Xcode File menu, select **File ▶ New ▶ File** and then, in the Choose your template dialog, select **Cocoa Touch** on the left and **Objective-C class** on the right. Click **Next** and, in the Choose options for your new file dialog, select a subclass of **UIViewController** and make sure the **With XIB for user interface check box** is unchecked because we are using storyboards. Name this set of files **ThirdViewController**.

7.  Now we need to associate the newly added view controller with the .h and .m files. Select the view controller, and, in the Identity Inspector, select **ThirdViewController** as the class. See Figure 12-5.

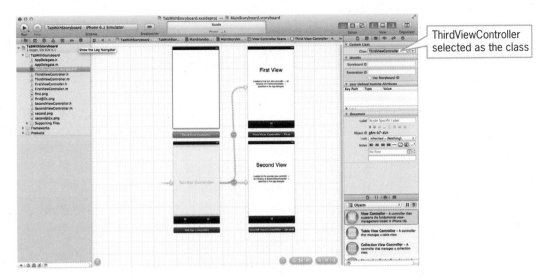

ThirdViewController selected as the class

**Figure 12-5**    Interface after adding an additional view controller

8.  Next we need to connect the third view controller to the tab bar controller and make it the third tab. Select the tab bar controller, and, in the utility pane, click the image indicated in Figure 12-6 to display the Connections Inspector. This displays the setting shown in Figure 12-6, which tells you that the tab bar controller is connected to both the first and second view controllers.

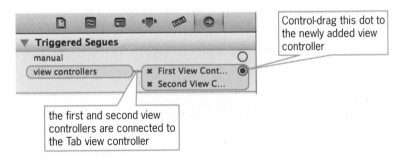

Control-drag this dot to the newly added view controller

the first and second view controllers are connected to the Tab view controller

**Figure 12-6**    Before adding the tab

In the Connections Inspector, select the dot on the right, which represents the connection for the tab bar controller, and then Control-drag this dot to the newly added view controller. This creates a connection and adds a tab to the tab bar controller. Figure 12-7 shows that the tab view controller now has three tabs: First View Controller, Second View Controller, and Third View Controller. (An alternative way of connecting the third view controller to the tab bar controller and assigning it as the third tab is to create a segue from the tab bar controller to the third view controller. You can do this by Control-dragging the tab bar controller to the third view controller; in the dialog that opens, click Relationship Segue and then click view controller as shown in Figure 12-8.)

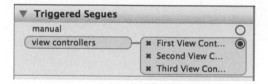

**Figure 12-7**   After adding the tab

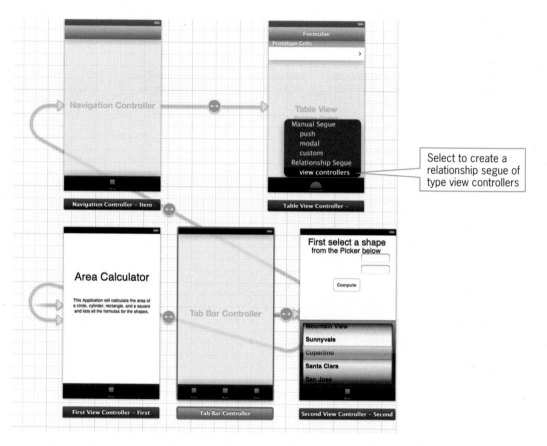

**Figure 12-8**   An alternate way to add a new tab

The new interface with the third view controller connected to the tab bar is shown in Figure 12-9. A tab is now visible on the bottom of the Third View Controller . Although it appears to contain an image in Figure 12-9, when you run the app you will see that the image is missing and the tab currently contains the default title "Item."

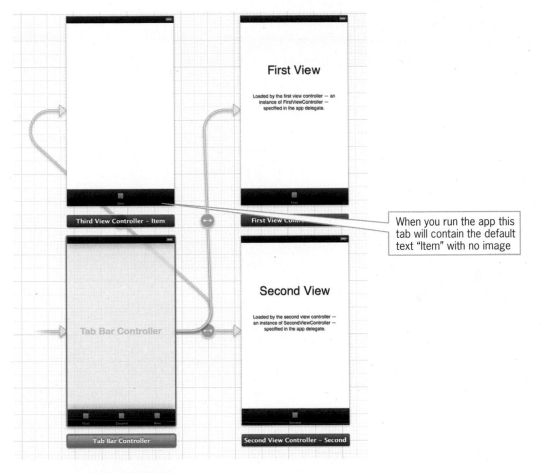

First View

Loaded by the first view controller — an
instance of FirstViewController —
specified in the app delegate.

Third View Controller – Item

First View Con...

When you run the app this
tab will contain the default
text "Item" with no image

Second View

Loaded by the second view controller —
an instance of SecondViewController —
specified in the app delegate.

Tab Bar Controller

Tab Bar Controller

Second View Controller – Second

**Figure 12-9**    Three-tabbed view

## Adding an Image to a Tab

Next we will add an image to the tab. In our example, we will use a default file provided by Apple in the project's Supporting Files folder. However, you need to know how to use your own .png files as images. To do that, you first need to add the image to the project folder, in the form of a .png file, and then assign it to the third tab. The following steps summarize the process of adding your own .png file to a tab as an image. We won't actually be performing these steps now, but you should be familiar with them so you can use your own .png files in the future.

1.   Control-click the project folder in the navigator area, and then select **Add Files to "TabWithStoryboard"** as shown in Figure 12-10. This allows us to add resources such as images, audio, or video files to the project.

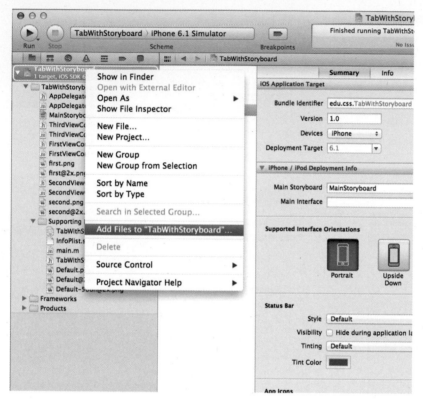

**Figure 12-10** Adding an image to a project

2. In the dialog shown in Figure 12-11, browse to the folder where the `.png` file you want to use is stored. Select the "Copy items into the destination group's folder (if needed)" check box to create a copy of the `.png` file in your project, and then click **Add**. This adds the image files to the project's Supporting Files folder.

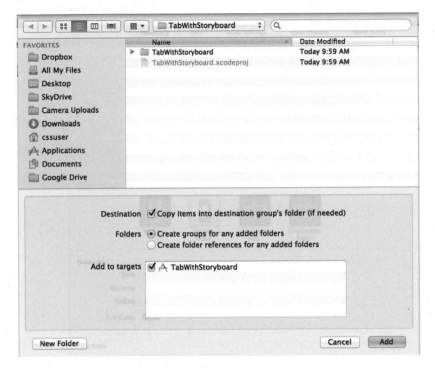

**Figure 12-11** Copying a `.png` file to the project folder

Now we will continue with our example, using the default image from the Supporting Files folder as the tab's image.

1. Select the **MainStoryboard.storyboard** file in the navigator area, select the third view controller in the editor pane, and then click the tab in the bottom of the third view controller, which says "Item". The tab item's attributes are now visible in the Attributes Inspector.

2. In the Attributes Inspector, change the title from "Item" to **Third**.

3. In the Image box, click the down arrow, and then select **Default.png**, as shown in Figure 12-12. This tells Xcode that we want to use the default image of a rectangle from the Supporting Files folder as the tab's image.

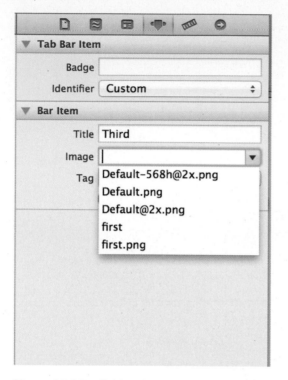

**Figure 12-12**    Setting the image for the tab

4.  Drag and drop a label onto the third view controller, and enter the text **Third View Controller** in the label.

5.  Run the app to see the results shown in Figure 12-13.

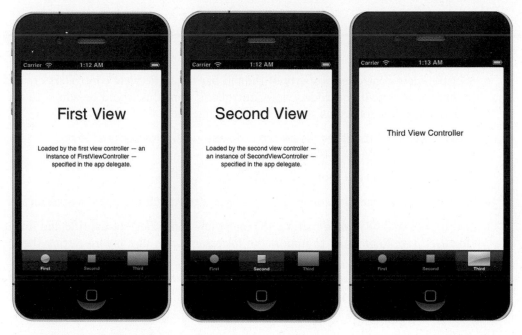

**Figure 12-13**   Running the app

# Creating a Tab Bar Without Storyboards

So far, we've focused on adding a tab bar to an app while using storyboards. Now let's focus on adding a tab bar while using the `.xib` file instead. In this situation, the `AppDelegate.m` file plays a critical role in the workings of the tab bar. The `AppDelegate.m` file is the file where the tab bar controller is created and initialized. The `didFinishLaunchingWithOptions` method of the `AppDelegate.m` file is where all the view controllers are instantiated and assigned to the tab bar.

Some of the most important methods in the implementation of a tabbed app are:

- `viewDidLaunch` in the `AppDelegate.m` file
- `initWithNibName` of the individual view controllers

The following steps summarize the process of adding a tab bar controller to an app without storyboards:

1. Create a new project using the Tabbed Application template.
2. Add a new file of type Objective-C.
3. Open the `.xib` file and drag a button from the Object Library onto the view controller.
4. Import the newly added view controller to the `AppDelegate.m` file.

**5.**  In the `viewDidLaunch` method of the `AppDelegate.m` file, do the following:

a.  Create instances of all the view controllers to be used in the application.

b.  Allocate and initialize the tab bar controller.

c.  Set the view controller property of the tab bar to all the view controllers created in previous step. If you added viewController3, then this would be added to the list of view controllers, as seen in the following code:

```
self.tabBarController.viewControllers = @[viewController1,
viewController2, viewController3];
```

d.  Make the tab bar the root view controller

e.  Design each of the individual view controllers to match the app's requirements.

f.  In the `initWithNibName` method for each view controller, set the title and image for each tab. Remember to import the necessary `.png` files before setting the images.

## Tab Bar and Navigation View Controller Example

Now we're ready to try creating a tab bar app with `.xib` files instead of using a storyboard.

**1.**  Create a new project in Xcode. In the Choose a template for your new project dialog, select the **Tabbed Application** template.

**2.**  Click **Next**, and, in the Choose options for your new project dialog, enter the name **TabWithXib** for the product name. Also, make sure to unselect the **Use Storyboards** check box and check the **Use Automatic Reference Counting** check box.

**3.**  Click **Next** and save the project in a location of your choice. Figure 12-14 shows the navigator area after the project is created. Notice there are two `.xib` files and two sets of corresponding implementation and interface files, one for each `.xib` file. Each `.xib` file will have a view controller with a tab bar at the bottom. In order to add an additional tab bar, we will need to add another set of `.xib` files, along with the accompanying implementation and the interface files.

**Figure 12-14**  Navigator area after the project is created

4. Add another view controller by adding a new file of type Objective-C, and save it as **ThirdViewController**. To add a new file, select **File ▶ New▶ File** and then, in the Choose your template dialog, select **Cocoa Touch** on the left and **Objective-C class** on the right. Click **Next**, and, in the Choose options for your new file dialog, select a subclass of **UIViewController** and make sure **With xib for user interface** is selected.

5. Select the **ThirdViewController.xib** file to ensure that the interface for the third view controller shows in the editor pane.

6. Drag and drop a label from the Object Library to the third view controller. Enter the text **Third View Controller** in the label.

   As mentioned earlier, the AppDelegate.m file is where the tab bar controller is created and initialized. The didFinishLaunchingWithOptions method of the AppDelegate.m file is where all the view controllers are instantiated and assigned to the tab bar. Our first task is to import the third view controller into the AppDelegate.m file, so we can create a view controller instance.

7. Open AppDelegate.m and import ThirdViewController as follows:

   ```
   #import "ThirdViewController.h"
   ```

8. In the didFinishLaunchingWithOptions method, create an instance of ThirdViewController as shown in the following code:

   ```
   //create a ThirdViewController instance
     UIViewController *viewController3 = [[ThirdViewController alloc]
   initWithNibName:@"ThirdViewController" bundle:nil];
   ```

9. Notice the code self.tabBarController.viewControllers = @[viewController1, viewController2]; in the didFinishLaunchingWithOptions method. In this code, the tab bar controller is initialized and the two view controllers are loaded. Now we need to add our view controller to this list. The following code adds a tab to the third view controller and enables the tab bar controller to recognize the third view controller as the third tab. The first line of code shows the code before adding the third view controller and the second line of code shows the code after the third view controller has been added:

```
self.tabBarController.viewControllers = @[viewController1,
viewController2]; // before adding our viewcontroller

//add the ThirdViewController we instantiated to the list of view
controllers in the tab bar
    self.tabBarController.viewControllers = @[viewController1,
viewController2, viewController3];
```

## Complete AppDelegate.m File

The code for the entire AppDelegate.m file is as follows:

```
#import "AppDelegate.h"

#import "FirstViewController.h"

#import "SecondViewController.h"

#import "ThirdViewController.h"

@implementation AppDelegate

- (BOOL)application:(UIApplication *)application
didFinishLaunchingWithOptions:(NSDictionary *)launchOptions
{
    self.window = [[UIWindow alloc] initWithFrame:[[UIScreen
mainScreen] bounds]];
    // Override point for customization after application launch.
    UIViewController *viewController1 = [[FirstViewController
alloc] initWithNibName:@"FirstViewController" bundle:nil];
    UIViewController *viewController2 = [[SecondViewController
alloc] initWithNibName:@"SecondViewController" bundle:nil];
    UIViewController *viewController3 = [[ThirdViewController
alloc] initWithNibName:@"ThirdViewController" bundle:nil];
    self.tabBarController = [[UITabBarController alloc] init];
    self.tabBarController.viewControllers = @[viewController1,
viewController2, viewController3];
    self.window.rootViewController = self.tabBarController;
    [self.window makeKeyAndVisible];
    return YES;
}
@end
```

## Adding Images and Titles

Now we are ready to add images to the new tab in the third view controller. As in the storyboard example that we completed earlier in this chapter, we will use the default image provided by Apple as the image.

1. In the implementation file of the third view controller **if** the **initWithNibName** method. This code assigns the image called **Default** as the tab's image. The **imageNamed** method is where you will enter the name of the image after it has been imported into the project folder.

   ```
   self.tabBarItem.image = [UIImage imageNamed:@"Default"];
   ```

2. Next we need to give the tab a title. This is done by adding the following line of code to the implementation file of the third view controller in the **if** statement of the **initWithNibName** method. This code assigns the name **Third** to the tab for the third view controller.

   ```
   self.tabBarItem.title = @"Third";
   ```

## Complete `ThirdViewController.m` File

The code for the entire `ThirdViewController.m` file is as follows:

```objc
#import "ThirdViewController.h"

@interface ThirdViewController ()

@end

@implementation ThirdViewController

- (id)initWithNibName:(NSString *)nibNameOrNil bundle:(NSBundle
*)nibBundleOrNil
{
    self = [super initWithNibName:nibNameOrNil bundle:nibBundleOrNil];
    if (self) {
        // Custom initialization
        self.tabBarItem.image = [UIImage imageNamed:@"Default"];
        self.tabBarItem.title = @"Third";
    }
    return self;
}

- (void)viewDidLoad
{
    [super viewDidLoad];
    // Do any additional setup after loading the view from its nib.
}
```

```
- (void)didReceiveMemoryWarning
{
    [super didReceiveMemoryWarning];
    // Dispose of any resources that can be recreated.
}
@end
```

## Running the App

Now we are ready to run the new app.

1. Run the app. Figure 12-15 shows the results.

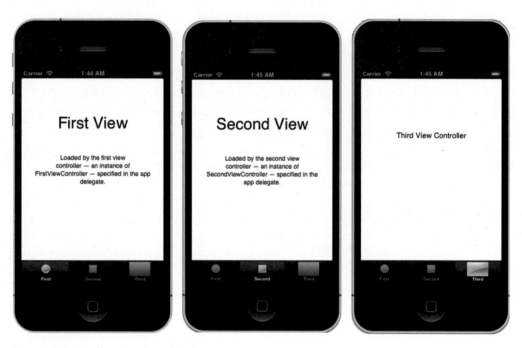

**Figure 12-15**  Running the tabbed app

# Picker View

A **picker view** is a spinning wheel that resembles a slot machine. The user can spin the wheel and select a specific value. A picker restricts the user to specific possibilities, thereby preventing the user input from making erroneous data entries. The picker view class is used to create an instance of the picker view. The selection of a value on the picker is an event. You can program this event to perform specific tasks, such as transitioning to another view, performing a calculation, or displaying data.

A picker view can have multiple wheels, with each wheel is referred to as a **component**. Each component can have multiple rows. Each component of the wheel is stored in an array, with the rows in a component corresponding to the rows of the array. In general, a picker view is similar to a two-dimensional array. Each column is a component and has an index value. Each row in a component also has an index, which is equivalent to the index value of its corresponding array. The tasks performed by the picker require a data source and delegate.

## Using a Delegate and a Data Source with a Picker View

The delegate in the picker view helps create and manage the components, while the data source provides and manages the data. In order for a picker view to utilize the delegate and the data source, it has to adopt the protocols for the delegate and the data source, and also implement the required methods.

Two of the required methods in the implementation of the data source are:

- numberOfComponentsInPickerView

- numberOfRowsInComponent

The numberOfComponentsInPickerView method informs the compiler of the number of wheels in the picker view, while the numberOfRowsInComponent method informs the compiler of the number of elements/rows in the components. (This is also equal to the number of items in the component.)

The required method for the implementation of the delegate is the titleForRow method. This method provides the contents of each row of a given component of the picker view. You must explicitly implement the delegate and the data source in the @interface directive for the view controller the picker view resides in. When a particular row is selected in a given component, the didSelectRow method is implemented to perform tasks that are triggered by the selection of a row. The data for the picker view is usually stored in an array. The initialization of these arrays is done in the viewDidLoad method for the view controller where the picker view resides.

The following steps summarize the process of implementing a picker view:

1. Select the view controller in which you would like to add the picker view.

2. Drag the picker view object from the Object Library to the selected view controller.

3. Connect the picker view to an IBOutlet in the view controller.

4. Explicitly adopt the delegate and the protocol in the @interface directive of the view controller.

5. As we are using an array to populate the components of the picker view, create the array's properties in the @interface file and synthesize them in the @implementation file.

6. Initialize the arrays in the viewDidLoad method.

7. Code the numberOfComponentsInPickerView method to inform the compiler of the number of components in the wheel.

8. Code the numberOfRowsInComponent method to inform the compiler of the number rows in the wheel.

9. Code the titleForRow method to populate the wheel.

10. Code the `didSelectRow` method to perform the given tasks when a value is selected on the wheel.

11. Design and create the rest of the user interface.

## Creating an App with a Picker View

Let's create an app with a picker view.

1. Create a new project in Xcode. In the Choose a template for your new project dialog, select the **Single View Application** template.

2. Click **Next**, and, in the Choose options for your new project dialog, enter the name **PickerView** for the product name. Also, make sure to select the **Use Storyboards** and **Use Automatic Reference Counting** check boxes.

3. Click **Next** and save the project in a location of your choice. Notice that there is one set of `ViewController` implementation and interface files.

4. Now we need to add a picker view to the view controller. Select the **MainStoryboard. storyboard** file in the navigator area. This displays the interface in the editor pane. Drag and drop a picker view from the Object Library on to the view controller.

5. Add three labels to the view controller as seen in Figure 12-16.

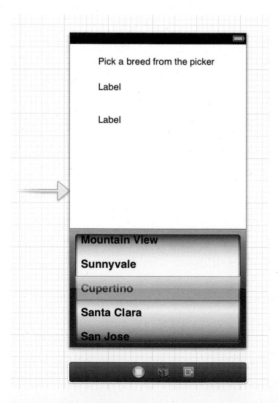

**Figure 12-16** Picker view interface

6. Connect the labels to the IBOutlets and name them **Label1** and **Label2**. This generates the following code in the interface of the view controller.

```
@property (weak, nonatomic) IBOutlet UILabel *Label1;
@property (weak, nonatomic) IBOutlet UILabel *Label2;
```

7. Create an IBOutlet for the picker view and call it **picker**. To accomplish this, Control-drag the picker view to the interface file. This displays the settings seen in Figure 12-17. It also generates the following code in the interface of the view controller.

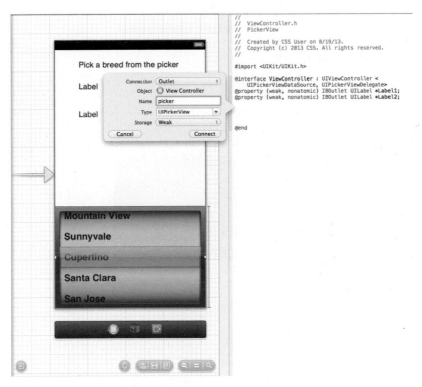

**Figure 12-17**   Creating an IBOutlet for a picker view interface

```
@property (weak, nonatomic) IBOutlet UIPickerView *picker;
```

8. So that we can use the data source and the delegate of the picker view, we need to connect the data source and delegate to the file's owner for the picker view. In order to do this, we must first make sure the document outline is visible by clicking the **Show Document Outline** button in the bottom left corner of the editor pane as shown in Figure 12-18. This opens a vertical area in between the navigator area and the editor area which is the same size as the navigator area. The document outline area shows a hierarchical representation of all the views, the controls within each view, and their connections.

**Figure 12-18**    Show Document Outline button

9.   To connect the data source and the delegate to the file's owner, Control-click the picker view. This displays the settings shown in Figure 12-19.

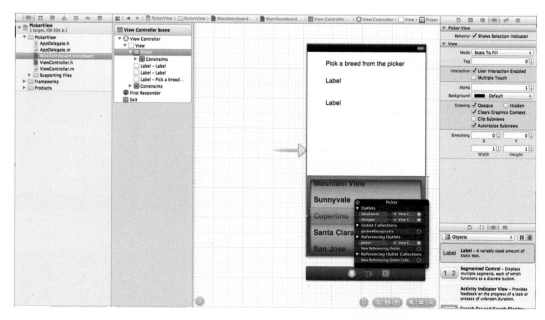

**Figure 12-19**    Setting data source and delegate for the picker view

10.  To the right of the dataSource and delegate, there are two circles. Control-drag each circle to the View Controller in the document outline. This connects the picker view to the view controller, which is the file's owner.

11.  Next, we need to explicitly identify the data source and the delegate as the file's owner by modifying the @interface directive to the data source and the delegate in the ViewController.h file. The following code accomplishes this task:

```
@interface ViewController : UIViewController
<UIPickerViewDataSource, UIPickerViewDelegate>
```

12.  We already created the IBoutlets. Now we need to synthesize the labels and picker view in the ViewController.m files as seen here:

```
@synthesize Label1;
@synthesize Label2;
@synthesize picker;
```

13. We will use data from two different NSArrays: one array to populate the picker and the other array to act as a parallel array, storing data associated with the picker array. Parallel arrays contain the same number of elements array and store related data in each element. Each element of one array has data that is associated with elements from the other array. Create properties for two NSArrays in the ViewController.h file as seen here:

```
@property (strong, nonatomic) NSArray *pickerData;
@property (strong, nonatomic) NSArray *pickerData2;
```

14. Synthesize the arrays in the @implementation file of the view controller as seen here:

```
@synthesize pickerData;
@synthesize pickerData2;
```

15. The arrays need to be initialized in the viewDidLoad method of the ViewController.m file as seen here:

```
- (void)viewDidLoad
{
    [super viewDidLoad];
    //initialize the picker data with cat breed
    pickerData = [[NSArray alloc] initWithObjects:@"Persian",
@"Siamese", @"Rag Doll", @"Turkish Angora",@"Scottish Fold", nil];

    //initialize the pickerData2 with details on the cat breeds
    pickerData2 = [[NSArray alloc] initWithObjects:@"These cats
have long hair", @"These cats have short hair", @"These cats are
larger than average cats", @"These cats are usually white",
@"These cats have folded ears", nil];
}
```

16. In the ViewController.m file, the two methods required for the implementation of the delegate and the data source are numberOfComponentsInPickerView and numberOfRowsInComponent. The numberOfComponentsInPickerView method returns the number of components in the picker view and the numberOfRowsInComponent method returns the number of rows in each component, which is the number of elements in the array. The picker view can have a hierarchy of components. For example, the date picker view can have the day of the month, the date, month, and year as individual components in a hierarchy because they are related. In the following code, we modify the numberOfComponentsInPickerView method to return 1, as we have only one level of hierarchy (that is, only one component).

```
#pragma Picker View methods

-(NSInteger) numberOfComponentsInPickerView:(UIPickerView
*)pickerView
{
    return 1;
}
```

17. Use the following code to modify the numberOfRowsInComponent method to return the count of the number of elements in the array. This will be the same as the number of rows in the picker.

```
-(NSInteger) pickerView:(UIPickerView *)pickerView
numberOfRowsInComponent:(NSInteger)component
{
     return [pickerData count];
}
```

18. The titleForRow method assigns titles for each row in the picker. Type the following code in the ViewController.m file:

```
-(NSString*) pickerView:(UIPickerView *)pickerView titleForRow:
(NSInteger)row forComponent:(NSInteger)component
{

     return [pickerData objectAtIndex:row];
}
```

19. Lastly, we want the labels to display the items selected in the picker. The didSelectRow method is used to display the contents of the picker view in a label, or to respond to a row selection. Type the following code in the ViewController.m file:

```
-(void) pickerView:(UIPickerView *)pickerView didSelectRow:(NSInteger)
row inComponent:(NSInteger)component
{
     Label1.text = [pickerData objectAtIndex:row];
     Label2.text = [pickerData2 objectAtIndex:row];
}
```

## Complete Files

The code for the entire ViewController.h file is as follows:

```
#import <UIKit/UIKit.h>

@interface ViewController : UIViewController
<UIPickerViewDataSource, UIPickerViewDelegate>
@property (weak, nonatomic) IBOutlet UILabel *Label1;
@property (weak, nonatomic) IBOutlet UILabel *Label2;
@property (weak, nonatomic) IBOutlet UIPickerView *picker;

@property (strong, nonatomic) NSArray *pickerData;
@property (strong, nonatomic) NSArray *pickerData2;
@end
```

The code for the entire ViewController.m file is as follows:

```
#import "ViewController.h"

@interface ViewController ()

@end
```

```objc
@implementation ViewController
@synthesize Label1;
@synthesize Label2;
@synthesize picker;
@synthesize pickerData;
@synthesize pickerData2;
- (void)viewDidLoad
{
    [super viewDidLoad];
    // Do any additional setup after loading the view, typically from a nib.
    //initialize the picker data with cat breed
    pickerData = [[NSArray alloc] initWithObjects:@"Persian", @"Siamese",
@"Rag Doll", @" Turkish Angora",@"Scottish fold", nil];

    //initialize the pickerData2 with details on the cat breeds
    pickerData2 = [[NSArray alloc] initWithObjects:@"These cats have
long hair", @"These cats have short hair", @"These cats are larger than
average cats", @" These cats are usually white", @"These cats have
folded ears", nil];
}

- (void)didReceiveMemoryWarning
{
    [super didReceiveMemoryWarning];
    // Dispose of any resources that can be recreated.
}
#pragma Picker View methods
-(NSInteger) numberOfComponentsInPickerView:(UIPickerView *)pickerView
{
    return 1;
}
-(NSInteger) pickerView:(UIPickerView *)pickerView
numberOfRowsInComponent:(NSInteger)component
{
    return [pickerData count];
}

-(NSString*) pickerView:(UIPickerView *)pickerView titleForRow:(NSInteger)
row forComponent:(NSInteger)component
{
    return [pickerData objectAtIndex:row];
}

-(void) pickerView:(UIPickerView *)pickerView didSelectRow:(NSInteger)
row inComponent:(NSInteger)component
{
    Label1.text = [pickerData objectAtIndex:row];
    Label2.text = [pickerData2 objectAtIndex:row];
}
@end
```

**20.** Delete the contents of the labels so when the app runs, nothing will be displayed in the labels. Make sure to delete the contents of the label only, and not the label itself.

**21.** Run the app as shown in Figure 12-20.

**Figure 12-20**   Running the app

## HANDS-ON LAB

In this Hands-On Lab we will create an area calculator with three tabs. The first tab, which provides the information about the app, will be the initial page. The second tab will offer the user a choice of calculating the area of a circle, cylinder, square, or rectangle. The user selects a shape using a picker view; the user is then transitioned to another view where the name of the chosen shape is included in the title. This new view also includes the necessary text fields and labels to prompt the user to enter the necessary measurements (radios, length, width, and so on). It will also contain a Compute button. When the Compute button is touched, the area of the chosen shape will be displayed in a label, as shown in Figure 12-21.

**Figure 12-21** Running the app

1.  Create a new project in Xcode. In the Choose a template for your new project dialog, select the **Tabbed Application** template.

2.  Click **Next**, and, in the Choose options for your new project dialog, enter the name **Ch12-tab-Bar-HandsOn** for the product name. Also, make sure to select the **Use Storyboards** and **Use Automatic Reference Counting** check boxes.

3.  Click **Next** and save the project in a location of your choice. At this point, the project contains a tab bar controller and two view controllers, one for each tab. Modify the first view controller to match the one in Figure 12-21.

4.  Add a new table view controller by dragging a table view controller from the Object Library to the storyboard. Add a set of Objective-C class files with a subclass of `UITableViewController`. Make sure the With xib for user interface check box is unchecked, because we are using storyboards. Name this set of files **TableViewController**.

5.  Associate the newly added view controller with the Objective-C files (`.h` and `.m`) as follows: select the view controller, and then, in the Identity Inspector, select **TableViewController** as the class.

6.  Next we need to connect the table view controller to the tab bar controller and assign it as the third tab, as we did in the first example in this chapter. When you select the tab bar controller, in the utility pane under the Connections Inspector, you will see that the tab bar controller is connected to both the first view controller and the second view controller. Select the dot on the right, which is the connection for the tab bar controller, and Control-drag it to the newly added view. This forms a connection and adds a tab to the tab bar controller.

## ADDING AN IMAGE AND TITLE TO THE TABS

7.  Next we will add an image to the tab, using the Default image file. To select the **MainStoryboard.storyboard** file in the navigator area, select the table view controller in the editor pane, and then click the tab in the bottom of the table view controller that says "Item." In the Attributes Inspector, you now see the attributes of the tab item. Change the title from "Item" to **Formulae** and then select **first@2x.png** as the image. See Figure 12-22.

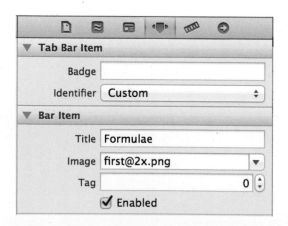

**Figure 12-22**    Setting the title and image of the tab

8. Next select the tab in the second view controller, and change the title to "Area".

## EMBEDDING A NAVIGATION CONTROLLER

9. Embed a navigation controller in the table view controller.

10. Add the title **Formulae** as the navigation bar's title. The new interface, along with the table view controller connected to the tab bar, is shown in Figure 12-23.

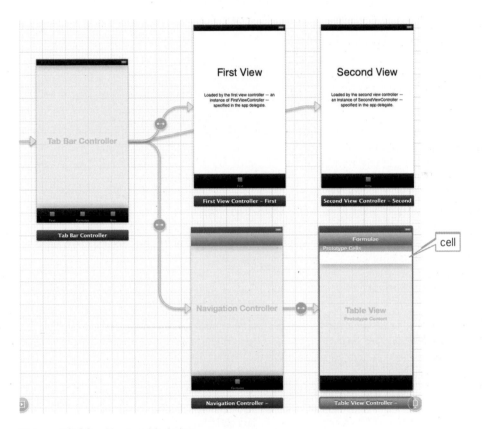

**Figure 12-23**   Newly added view

## TABLE SETUP

11. Make sure the table type is dynamic by checking under the Attributes inspector to see if the content field says **Dynamic Prototypes**. Next select the cell as seen in Figure 12-23 and then enter **Cell** as the Identifier, as shown in Figure 12-24. The Identifier is an attribute of the table view that can be given a title in the Attributes Inspector.

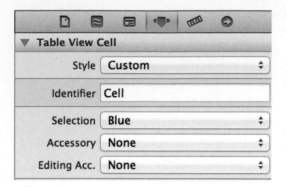

**Figure 12-24**    Setting the name for the table cell to "Cell"

## POPULATING THE TABLE VIEW

12.   In the interface file of the `TableViewController` class create an array named `ShapeList` to hold the names of the shapes and the respective formulae, as seen in the following code:

```
@property (nonatomic, strong) NSArray *ShapeList;
```

13.   Synthesize the array in the implementation of the `TableViewController` class as seen in the following code:

```
@synthesize ShapeList;
```

14.   In the `viewDidLoad` method, allocate and initialize these arrays as shown in the following code:

```
- (void)viewDidLoad
{
    [super viewDidLoad];
    //initialize the Shapelist array to hold the shapes
    ShapeList = [[NSArray alloc] initWithObjects:
@"Circle = 3.141 *r*r", @"Cylinder = 2*3.141*r*r + h(2*3.141*r),
@"Square = l*l", @"Rectangle = l*w", nil];
}
```

15.   Program the `numberOfSectionsInTableView` and the `numberOfRowsInSection` methods associated with table view in the `TableViewController.m` file as shown in the following code:

```
- (NSInteger)numberOfSectionsInTableView:(UITableView *)tableView
{

    // Return the number of sections.
    return 1;
}
```

```
- (NSInteger)tableView:(UITableView *)tableView
numberOfRowsInSection:(NSInteger)section
{

    // Return the number of rows in the section.
    return [ShapeList count];
}
```

16. Program the `cellForRowAtIndexPath` method to display the list of formulas as seen in the following code:

```
- (UITableViewCell *)tableView:(UITableView *)tableView
cellForRowAt
IndexPath:(NSIndexPath *)indexPath
{
    static NSString *CellIdentifier = @"Cell";
    UITableViewCell *cell = [tableView
dequeueReusableCell WithIdentifier:CellIdentifier];

    // Configure the cell...
    if(cell == nil)  {
            cell = [[UITableViewCell alloc] initWithStyle:
UITableViewCellStyleDefault reuseIdentifier:CellIdentifier];
        }
        cell.textLabel.text = [self.ShapeList objectAtIndex:
indexPath.row];
    return cell;
}
```

## CREATING THE INTERFACE

17. Now we are ready to design and program the view that will calculate the area of the shape. In the second view controller, modify the existing title label (which currently reads "Second View") to read **First select a shape from the picker below**. Next, drag two labels, two text fields, a picker, and a button onto the view.

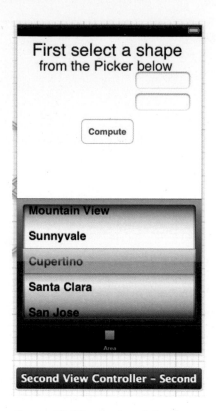

**Figure 12-25**    Design of the view to calculate the area

18.  In the interface of the `SecondViewController` class, add the appropriate properties by creating the `IBOutlets` and `IBActions` for all the labels, text fields, buttons, and also add an array to hold the list of shapes that will be displayed in the picker view. Delete the contents of the labels and position them as seen in Figure 12-25.

```
//label to display the title
@property (weak, nonatomic) IBOutlet UILabel *TitleLabel;

//label for text field
@property (weak, nonatomic) IBOutlet UILabel *subTitleLabel;
//create a picker outlet
@property (strong, nonatomic) IBOutlet UIPickerView *picker;

//create an array to hold the items on the picker view
@property (nonatomic, strong) NSArray *ShapeList;

//text field to input one of  the parameters of the shape
@property (weak, nonatomic) IBOutlet UITextField *AreaTxt2;

//label to display the area. This will be the second label from top
//where the area will be displayed
@property (weak, nonatomic) IBOutlet UILabel *AreaLabel;
```

```
//label for the second text field
@property (weak, nonatomic) IBOutlet UILabel *subTitleLabel2;

//method to calculate the area
- (IBAction)Compute:(id)sender;

//integer variable to track the shape
@property int trackShape;

//text field to input one of the parameters of the shape
@property (weak, nonatomic) IBOutlet UITextField *AreaTxt;

//IBAction to dismiss keyboard
- (IBAction)AreaTxtFld:(id)sender;

//IBAction to dismiss keyboard
- (IBAction)AreaTxtFld2:(id)sender;

@property (weak, nonatomic) IBOutlet UIButton *compute;
```

19. Synthesize all the properties in the SecondViewController.m file as shown here:

```
@synthesize ShapeList;
@synthesize picker;

@synthesize TitleLabel;
@synthesize subTitleLabel;
@synthesize subTitleLabel2;
@synthesize AreaLabel;
@synthesize AreaTxt;
@synthesize AreaTxt2;
@synthesize trackShape;
@synthesize compute;
```

20. In the viewDidLoad method of the SecondViewController.m file, you will need to initialize the array that will hold the shape list to be displayed in the picker view. Initially, when the tab for the area is touched, the view will not display the labels, the text fields, or the compute button. These items should appear only after the user selects a shape. In order to accomplish this, use the hidden property of the text fields and the button to hide them initially. Set up the picker to display the shapes by first implementing the delegate and data source by adding the delegate and the data source to the @interface directive of the SecondViewController.h file as shown here:

```
@interface SecondViewController : UIViewController
<UIPickerViewDataSource, UIPickerViewDelegate>
```

21. Now we need to explicitly connect the delegate and the data source to the picker. To accomplish this, click on the **MainStoryboard.storyboard** file and then Control-drag the picker to the file's owner (that is, the second view controller) in the documentation outline. Then select the delegate and the data source, as we did in the example earlier in this chapter.

22. Implement the methods required by the delegate and the data source for the picker view as shown here:

```
#pragma Picker View methods
//method identifying the number of components in a picker
-(NSInteger) numberOfComponentsInPickerView:(UIPickerView *)pickerView
{
    return 1;
}


//method identifying the number of rows in the component
-(NSInteger) pickerView:(UIPickerView *)pickerView
numberOfRowsInComponent:(NSInteger)component
{
    return [ShapeList count];
}


//method that displays the items in the picker
-(NSString*) pickerView:(UIPickerView *)pickerView
titleForRow: (NSInteger)row
forComponent:(NSInteger)component
{
    return [ShapeList objectAtIndex:row];

}
```

23. When the user selects a shape from the picker, the labels should appear and display the appropriate text. The text fields should also appear, as well as the Compute button. To accomplish this, we need to implement the didSelectRow method, using a switch statement to display the appropriate text in the labels and unhide the appropriate fields.

```
-(void) pickerView:(UIPickerView *)pickerView
didSelectRow:(NSInteger)row inComponent:(NSInteger)component
{
    switch (row) {
        case 0:
            TitleLabel.text = @"You selected a Circle! ";
            subTitleLabel.text =@"Enter the radius here";
            subTitleLabel2.hidden = YES;
            AreaLabel.text = @"";
            AreaTxt.hidden = NO;
            AreaTxt2.hidden = YES;
            compute.hidden = NO;
            trackShape =0;
            break;
        case 1:
            TitleLabel.text = @"You selected a Cylinder! ";
            subTitleLabel.text =@"Enter the radius here";
             subTitleLabel2.hidden = NO;
            subTitleLabel2.text = @"Enter the height here";
            AreaLabel.text = @"";
```

```
                AreaTxt.hidden = NO;
                AreaTxt2.hidden = NO;
                 compute.hidden = NO;
                trackShape =1;
                break;
          case 2:
                TitleLabel.text = @"You selected a Square! ";
                subTitleLabel.text =@"Enter the side here";
                 subTitleLabel2.hidden = YES;
                AreaLabel.text = @"";
                AreaTxt.hidden = NO;
                AreaTxt2.hidden = YES;
                compute.hidden = NO;
                trackShape =2;
                break;
          case 3:
                TitleLabel.text = @"You selected a Rectangle! ";
                subTitleLabel.text =@"Enter the length here";
                 subTitleLabel2.hidden = NO;
                subTitleLabel2.text = @"Enter the width here";
                AreaLabel.text = @"";
                AreaTxt.hidden = NO;
                AreaTxt2.hidden = NO;
                compute.hidden = NO;
                trackShape =3;
                break;

          default:
                break;
      }

  }
```

24. The Compute button calculates the area of the shape selected by the user. A `switch` statement is used to perform the calculation for the selected shape as seen in the following `IBAction` method.

```
- (IBAction)Compute:(id)sender {
    int area;
    switch (trackShape) {
        case 0:
              area = 3.141*[AreaTxt.text intValue]*[AreaTxt.text intValue];
              break;
        case 1:
              area = (2*3.141*[AreaTxt.text intValue] *
[AreaTxt.text intValue]) + [AreaTxt2.text intValue]*
(2*3.141*[AreaTxt.text intValue]);
              break;

        case 2:
              area = [AreaTxt.text intValue] *[AreaTxt.text intValue];
              break;
```

```
        case 3:
            area = [AreaTxt.text intValue] *[AreaTxt2.text intValue];
            break;

    default:
        break;
}
```

```
    AreaLabel.text = [NSString stringWithFormat:@"And the area is
%i", area];
    AreaTxt.text =@"";
    AreaTxt2.text =@"";

    [self.view endEditing:YES];


}
```

## DISMISSING THE KEYBOARD

**25.** In order to dismiss the keyboard, we need to program the IBAction methods for the text fields to resign the first responder. Make sure to connect the IBAction to the text fields for the **Did End On Exit** event as shown here:

```
- (IBAction)AreaTxtFld:(id)sender {
   [self.view resignFirstResponder];

}
- (IBAction)AreaTxtFld2:(id)sender {
   [self.view resignFirstResponder];

}
```

**26.** Finally, in the viewDidLoad method of the SecondViewController.m file, add the following code:

```
- (void)viewDidLoad
{
   [super viewDidLoad];
      // Do any additional setup after loading the view,
      typically from a nib.
   ShapeList = [[NSArray alloc]
initWithObjects:@"Circle",
@"Cylinder", @"Square", @"Rectangle",nil];
   AreaTxt2.hidden = YES;
   AreaTxt.hidden = YES;
   compute.hidden = YES;
}
```

**27.** Run the app and verify that it produces the results shown earlier in Figure 12-21.

# Summary

- A tab bar view is another type of specialized view in iOS programming that displays tabs in a radio-style and allows for multiple view transitions from each individual tab.

- If you are creating an app without using storyboards, the tab bar controller is created in the `didFinishLaunchingWithOptions` method of the `appdelegate.m` file.

- Some of the most important methods in the implementation of the tabbed applications in apps with .xib files are the `viewDidLaunch` method of the `appdelegate.m` file and the `initWithNibName` method of the individual view controllers.

- When using storyboards, you drag and drop the tab bar view controller from the Object Library into the editor pane, You then drag and drop the individual tab bar items onto each view, and set a title and image for each tab.

- A picker view is a spinning wheel that resembles a slot machine. The user can spin the wheel and select a specific value. A picker restricts the user to specific possibilities, thereby preventing the user input from making erroneous data entries.

- The data for the picker view is usually stored in an array. The picker view is similar to a two-dimensional array. Each column is a component and has an index value. Each row in a component also has an index, which is equivalent to the index value of its corresponding array.

- The tasks performed by the picker require a data source and delegate. The delegate in the picker view helps create and manage the components, while the data source provides and manages the data of the picker view.

- Two of the required methods in the implementation of the data source are the `numberOfComponentsInPickerView` and `numberOfRowsInComponent` methods. The first informs the compiler of the number of wheels in the picker view. The second informs the compiler of the number of elements/rows in the components, which is equal to the number of items in the component.

- The `titleForRow` method is the required method for the implementation of the delegate. The `titleForRow` method provides the contents of each row of a given component of the picker view.

# Exercises

1. Mark the following statements as true or false. Correct the false statements.

   a. A tab view control interface can have multiple tabs.

   b. The maximum number of tabs that can be displayed by an app is three.

   c. The most common way of implementing the tab bar controller is installing it in the main window as the root controller.

   d. Tab view image files must be in the `.jpg` format.

   e. The selection of a value on the picker is an event.

   f. The picker can have multiple wheels, with each wheel referred to as a row.

2. Describe what the following methods do:

   a. `didFinishLaunchingWithOptions`

   b. `numberOfSectionsInTableView`

   c. `numberOfComponentsInPickerView`

   d. `numberOfRowsInComponent`

   e. `didSelectRowAtIndexPath`

3. Explain what a tab bar controller is and describe a situation in which a tab bar controller would be useful.

4. What is an advantage of using a tab bar?

5. List the steps involved in creating a tabbed app using storyboards.

6. What is a picker view?

7. What is an advantage of using the picker view?

8. List the steps involved in implementing a picker view.

9. Write Objective-C statements that accomplish the following tasks:

   a. Declare and initialize a `UITabBarController`.

   b. Set the title of a tab to "First".

   c. Set the image of a tab to the image `img.png`.

10. Give two reasons to use a picker view and two limitations to using a picker view.

# Programming Exercises

1. Create a simple birthday-tracker app. This app should have two screens. On the first screen, the user enters a name and a birth date using a picker view. Once the user selects a birth date, another screen appears containing a list of all the names and birthdays entered so far. This screen should have a means of navigating back to the first screen. The user should not be able to submit an entry without a name.

2. Create a date-calculator app that includes a picker with four components. The user should be able to use the picker to select a date, and then click a Choose button to display the number of days until that date arrives (for example, 3 days) or the number of days since the date has passed (for example, -4 days). The interface for this app is shown in Figure 12-26.

**Figure 12-26** Interface for date-calculator app

3. Create a song-journal app. The app should contain three screens. On one screen, the user should be able to enter the name of a song, and then use a picker view to enter a rating for the song on a scale of 1–5. On the second screen, the user should be able to view all entries listed numerically, in descending order by rating, with the most highly rated songs at the top. On the third screen, the user should be able to view all entries listed in the order in which they were entered, with the most recent entry first. Use tab views to create the application, and do not use a storyboard.

4. Modify the app created for Programming Exercise 3 so that the tab for each screen is an image. Also, add another tab that displays a list of all the entries with their respective ratings, in alphabetical order.

5.  Create a sales-tracking app for a hardware store with two screens. In the first screen, the user enters the transaction name (traditionally a transaction ID is used, but for the purpose of this application, we will be using transaction names), name of the component sold, its brand, quantity sold, and the total price. A typical transaction name might be DelOsso or CSS. The second screen displays a list of all the transactions, in the order the transactions were entered. When a user touches a transaction name, the transaction's details should be displayed. Use a tab view with storyboards for this app.

6.  Modify the app described in Programming Exercise 5 to add a third screen (tab) that displays transaction names, organized in descending order by total price, with transactions with the highest total price displayed first.

7.  Create an app with three tabs: tab1, tab2, and tab3. Tab 1 has a button that leads to a new view not under the tab view. Tab 2 has a button that leads to a new set of tabs. Tab 3 has a button that leads to a new view under the tab view, but not the home view of any of the tab views.

8.  Create an app with two tabs. The first tab should contain a list of ten car manufacturers. The second view should contain a list of ten car models. Each individual list in a tab is a fixed list and is not associated with the other.

9.  Create an app for a school's technology library that allows a librarian to keep track of devices reserved for special events. Assume the librarian is choosing from the following devices: iPhone, iPad, projector, camera, and tablet. Use a picker to have the user select a device. After the selection is made, the user should be able to click a button to display the selected device in a new view. Create an additional view to allow the user to add a new device, so that it shows up in the picker. Use tabs to organize your app.

10. Create an app that shows a list of at least five books. Touching a book title should open a view with two tabs. The first tab should show the book's author and the second should show the book's first sentence.

## Business Case Study

In this chapter we will continue working on the pain management app. So far your app has the following:

- Functionality to pass data between two views

- The ability to dismiss the view controller.

- Table view functionality

For now, we will delete the table view functionality and add it back in Chapter 14. Your job in this chapter is to modify the app to implement two tabs. The first tab should provide information about the app. The second tab should allow the user to record a pain level with a picker view. At this point, it may be a good idea to start a new project instead of working on the app from Chapter 11.

# CHAPTER 13

# Creating Multimedia Apps with Images and Sound

In this chapter we will:

- ◎ Add images to views, table views and tabbed applications
- ◎ Play system sound using the AVAudio framework
- ◎ Play videos using the MediaPlayer framework

In the previous chapters we have learned how to display data in views, in the form of lists using tables, in tabbed applications and in picker views. Although we used icons for a tab in a tabbed application, we have mostly dealt with textual data and have not done much with images, sounds, or videos. In this chapter we will learn to add images, sound and video to an application.

**Note:** To complete the examples and exercises in this chapter, you need to download the data files provided for this chapter. Go to the *CengageBrain.com* home page, and search for this book's ISBN (found on the back cover). This will take you to the product page for this book, where you will be able to download the data files.

## Adding Images to an App

Images are a form of data and play a very important role in conveying information in everyday life. They play a critical role in the communication of information. Adding images to an app is accomplished by dragging an image view from the Object Library onto the view.

Let's create an app that displays images of a cat. To complete this app, you will need the Cat1.jpg and Cat2.jpg image files included with the data files for this chapter.

1.  Create a new Xcode project.

2.  In the Choose a template for your new project dialog, select **Application** under "iOS," select **Single View Application**, and then click the **Next** button.

3.  In the Project options dialog, type **Mr. Snuggles** as the Product name, enter appropriate items in the Organization Name and Company identifier boxes, make sure **iPhone** is selected in the Devices box, select the **Use Storyboards** check box, and the **Use Automatic Reference Counting** check box.

4.  Click the **Next** button, and then save the project in the location of your choice.

5.  In the navigator area, on the left, click **MainStoryboard.storyboard**. This opens the Interface Builder, which displays the project's single view controller.

6.  In the Object Library search for **image view**. As you start typing "image view" in the search box of the Object Library, you will see the image view object show up in the Object Library as seen in Figure 13-1.

**Figure 13-1**  Image View object

7.  Drag the image view onto the view controller and then expand the image view to fit the entire view controller as seen in Figure 13-2.

**Figure 13-2**  Image view expanded to fill view controller

8. Any media files for an app must be stored in the Supporting Files folder. So before we can add an image to the app, we need to save the Cat1.jpg and Cat2.jpg files in this folder. Drag the Cat1.jpg and Cat2.jpg files from the folder where you have stored them, and drop them into the Supporting Files folder. Make sure to select the Copy items into destination group's folder (if needed) check box, as shown in Figure 13-3. Click Finish.

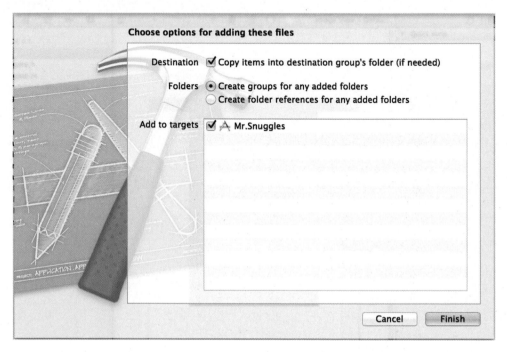

**Figure 13-3**   Copying images into the Supporting Files folder

9. Select the image view and, in the Attributes Inspector, select the **Cat1.jpg** image file, as shown in Figure 13-4. The image of the cat appears in the view controller as shown in Figure 13-5. As you can see, the image looks stretched. We can fix this problem by changing the Mode attribute.

**Figure 13-4**    Image selection

**Figure 13-5**    Cat image looks stretched

Photo courtesy of Arshia Khan.

**10.** Select the image, if necessary, and, in the Attributes Inspector, change the Mode setting from Scale To Fit to **Aspect Fit** as shown in Figure 13-6. The image now looks like the one in Figure 13-7.

**Figure 13-6**   Image mode selection

**Figure 13-7**   Cat image with Aspect Fit selected as the Mode attribute

Photo courtesy of Arshia Khan.

11. Now let's try laying one image on top of another. First, resize the image view to fit the top half of the view controller by dragging one of its sides. Then drag another image view and place it in the lower section of the view controller.

12. In the Attributes Inspector, select the **Cat2.jpg** image file, which you previously dragged into the Supporting Files folder on the second image view. You can look ahead to Figure 13-8 to see where to position this second image.

13. Next, we'll add a label that explains what we see in the photos. Drag a label from the Object Library on to the view controller. Edit the text in the label to read **This is Mr. Snuggles** as shown in Figure 13-8.

**Figure 13-8**   Label added to view controller
Photos courtesy of Arshia Khan.

14. Run the app as shown in Figure 13-9.

**Figure 13-9**   Running the app

Photos courtesy of Arshia Khan.

## Playing Audio

The frameworks primarily responsible for handling audio are:

- Media Player framework: Used to play songs, audio podcasts, and audio books

- AVFoundation framework (AVAudioPlayer): Helps utilize the Objective-C interface to play and record audio

- Audio Toolbox framework: Facilitates handling complex tasks such as synchronization, format conversion, and parsing

- Audio Unit framework: Facilitates audio processing plug-ins

- OpenAL framework: Facilitates audio play back in games

So far we have mainly dealt with UIKit framework, which comes automatically loaded in an app when a project is created in Xcode. To use any additional framework, you first need to add it to the project and import the corresponding framework explicitly. In this chapter, we will work with the AVFoundation framework and learn to play sounds and music using the

AVAudioPlayer class. That means we need to add the AVFoundation framework and then import the AVFoundation/AVFoundation.h file.

The audio formats supported by the AVFoundation framework include IMA4, AAC, and MP3. The AVfoundation framework's AVAudioPlayer class provides a simple Objective-C audio player interface for playing sounds of any duration from files or memory buffers. This class also provides the capability to play multiple sounds. Before an audio player can play audio, you must assign a sound file to the audio player, prepare the audio player and designate an audio player delegate for handling interruptions. Configuring the audio player entails creating a string object that holds the path to the sound file, and creating and initializing a URL to the sound file using the path object.

## Adding Audio to an App

The following steps summarize the process of using the AVAudioPlayer class to play audio in an app:

1. Add the AVFoundation framework to the project.

2. Import the AVFoundation framework into the @interface file.

3. Add the audio file to the Supporting Files folder.

4. Create an instance of the AVAudioPlayer class.

5. If you want the app to be able to handle interruptions, declare a delegate by implementing the following methods:

   - audioPlayerDidFinishPlaying: Returns a message that indicates if the playback completed successfully or not.

   - audioPlayerDecodeErrorDidOccur: Displays a message indicating the type of error that has occurred.

   - audioPlayerBeginInterruption: Handles interruptions such as phone calls.

   - audioPlayerEndInterruption: Continues playback after the interruption is over.

6. Program a button to play or stop the audio using the play and stop methods of the AVAudioPlayer class.

7. Set the volume property of the AVAudioPlayer class to control the volume.

## Creating an App that Plays Audio

Now let's put these steps into practice by creating an app that can play audio. To complete this app, you will need the violin1.mp3 audio file included with the data files for this chapter.

1. Create a new Xcode project.

2. In the Choose a template for your new project dialog, select **Application** under "iOS," select **Single View Application**, and then click the **Next** button.

3. In the Project options dialog, type **Ch13-Audio_Example** as the Product name, enter appropriate items in the Organization Name and Company identifier boxes, make sure **iPhone** is selected in the Devices box, then select the **Use Storyboards** check box, and the **Use Automatic Reference Counting** check box.

4. Click the **Next** button, and then save the project in the location of your choice.

## Add the AVFoundation Framework

5. In the navigator area, select the project folder as shown in Figure in 13-10.

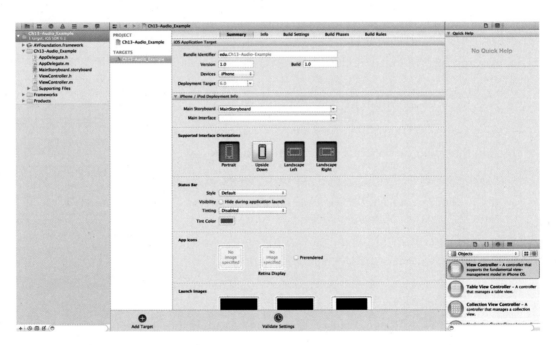

**Figure 13-10**    Select the project folder in the navigator area

6. Click **Build Phases**, as shown Figure 13-11.

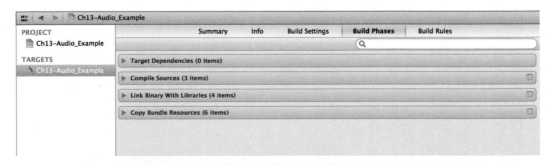

**Figure 13-11**    Adding framework in build phases

7. Click on the small triangle next to **Link Binary With Libraries**. This displays the list of frameworks currently included in the project, seen in Figure 13-12. These frameworks are automatically added by Xcode. You can add additional frameworks to this list by clicking on the plus sign.

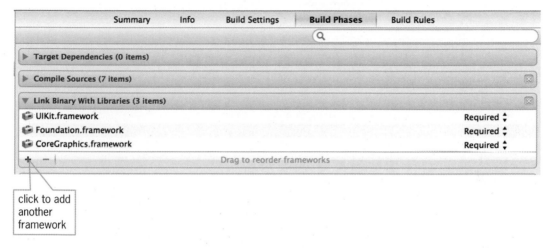

click to add another framework

**Figure 13-12**    Link Binary With Libraries window, with list of frameworks

8. Click the + symbol as shown in Figure 13-12. This opens the Choose frameworks and libraries to add dialog.

9. Type **AV** in the search box. The AVFoundation framework appears, as shown in Figure 13-13. This is the framework we will add to the project.

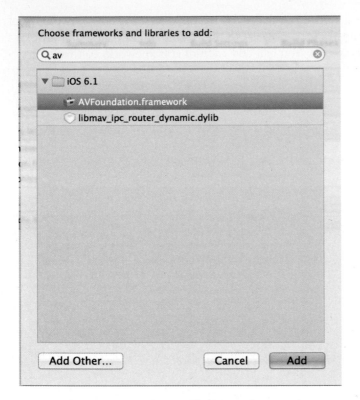

**Figure 13-13**    Displaying the AVFoundation framework

**10.** Click **AVFoundation.framework** and then click the **Add** button. The AVFoundation framework is added to the list of frameworks in the projects, as seen in Figure 13-14.

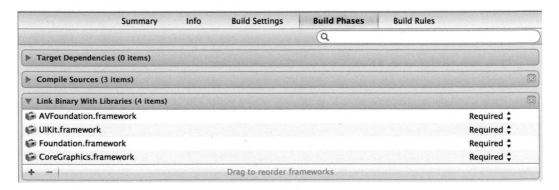

**Figure 13-14**    AVFoundation framework added to the project

11. Next we need to explicitly import the `AVAudioPlayer` class into the interface file of the view controller. There is only one view controller in our project because we create a single view application. The code used to import the AVFoundation framework is as follows:

```
#import <AVFoundation/AVFoundation.h>
```

## Add Music to the Project

12. Next we need to add the violin1.mp3 audio file to the Supporting Files folder. Drag and drop **violin1.mp3** file from the folder where you've stored it into the Supporting Files folder. In the dialog that opens, select the Copy items into destination group's folder (if needed) check box. Click Finish. If you do not select the copy option, the music file will be moved into the Supporting Files folder instead of creating a copy of your music file in the Supporting Files folder.

## Create and Program the Play Button

13. Next we need a control to play the audio. In the navigator area, on the left, click **MainStoryboard.storyboard**. This opens the Interface Builder, which displays the project's single view controller. Drag a round rect button from the Object Library onto the view controller. Change the text on the button to Play.

14. Create an `IBAction` for the button in the `ViewController.h` file, and call it **audioPlay**. This generates the following code:

```
//create an IBAction for the button
- (IBAction)audioPlay:(id)sender;
```

15. We will be using only one button, so the button will initially display the text "Play" and then, when the user clicks it, the button text will display the text "Stop". To accomplish this, create an `IBOutlet` called **playButton** for the button by Control-dragging the button to the `ViewController.h` file, which will produce display the following code:

```
//create an IBOutlet for the button
@property (strong, nonatomic) IBOutlet UIButton *playButton;
```

16. Create an `AVAudioPlayer` object called **player** that will interface with the audioPlay button in the `ViewController.h` file using the following code:

```
//create an audio player object
@property (nonatomic, strong) AVAudioPlayer *player;
```

17. Remember to synthesize all the properties created in the `ViewController.h` file using the following code:

```
@synthesize player;
@synthesize playButton;
```

## Prepare to Program the Play Button

**18.** Before we can program the Play button, we need to do the following:

- Create the path to the music file.

- Inform the compiler of the type of music file.

- Set the file's URL to the music file.

- Initialize the AVAudioPlayer object.

- Implement the delegate in the ViewController.h and .m file.

To accomplish these steps, type the following code in the viewDidLoad method of the ViewController.m file:

```
(void)viewDidLoad
{
    [super viewDidLoad];
// Do any additional setup after loading the view, typically from a
nib.
    //create a string path for the music file
    NSString *stringPath = [[NSBundle mainBundle]
pathForResource:@"violin1" ofType:@"mp3"];
    //create a NSURL for the music file
    NSURL *musicURL = [[NSURL alloc] initFileURLWithPath: string
Path];
    //initialize the player object
    player = [[AVAudioPlayer alloc]
initWithContentsOfURL:musicURL error:nil];
}
```

Note that the delegate is implemented by default when the AVAudioPlayer object is created. Implementation of the delegate provides access to the delegate methods. One such method, audioPlayerDidFinishPlaying, helps detect if the audio successfully played.

## Program the Play Button

**19.** Next we need to program the Play button so that the app starts off with the button text "Play," indicating the app is ready to play music. When the user clicks the Play button, the text should change to "Stop," providing the user the option to stop playing. The AVAudioPlayer class has a property called **playing** that stores the status of the audio player. The playing property is a Boolean variable that provides an indication if the audio player is playing or not by storing a true value for "playing" and a false value for "not playing." In the @implementation file, program the Play button by checking the playing property of the audio player object to test if playing is true. If it is, we want to stop the audio player object from playing and set the button's text to "Stop." If the playing property is false, we want to set the button's text to "Play" and start playing the audio. To accomplish this, type the following code in the ViewController.m file:

```
- (IBAction)audioPlay:(id)sender {
    // if already playing, then stop
    if (self.player.playing) {
        [self.playButton setTitle: @"Play" forState:
UIControlStateHighlighted];
        [self.playButton setTitle: @"Play" forState:
UIControlStateNormal];
        [self.player stop];

        // if stopped, start playing
    } else {
        [self.playButton setTitle: @"Stop" forState:
UIControlStateHighlighted];
        [self.playButton setTitle: @"Stop" forState:
UIControlStateNormal];
        [self.player play];
    }

}
```

## Adding Volume Control to the App

20. The property called **volume** of the AVAudioPlayer class facilitates programmatic control of the volume. We will use a slider control to manage the audio player's volume. Drag a slider (seen in Figure 13-15) from the Object Library to the view controller. Figure 13-16 shows the slider on the view controller.

**Figure 13-15**   Slider in the Object Library

**Figure 13-16**    Adding a slider

21.    We want the slider to adjust the volume as we move it. The position of the slider should also correspond to the position of the slider. In order to do this, we need to make an **IBAction** and an **IBOutlet** for the slider. The **IBAction** will adjust the volume, while the **IBOutlet** will make sure the slider position corresponds to the volume level. Create an **IBOutlet** called **volumeControl** and a **IBAction** called **volumeControlAction** by Control-dragging the slider onto the **@interface** file. This generates the following code:

```
//IBOutlet for the slider
@property (strong, nonatomic) IBOutlet UISlider *volumeControl;

//IBAction for the slider
    -(IBAction)volumeControlAction:(id)sender;
```

22.    Synthesize the **volumeControl** property using the following code in the **ViewController.m** file.

```
@synthesize volumeControl;
```

23.    We'll set the initial volume (the default volume when the app loads) by using the **setVolume** property of the **AVAudioPlayer** class. Add the **setVolume** property for the

audio player object in the viewDidLoad method of the ViewController.m file as seen in the following code:

```
[player setVolume:self.volumeControl.value];
```

24. Program the slider's IBAction in the ViewController.m file by creating an object of the slider and associating the value of this object to the volume property of the audio player object as seen in the following code:

```
- (IBAction)volumeControlAction:(id)sender {
    UISlider *volumeSlider = sender;
    [player setVolume:volumeSlider.value];
}
```

## Adding a Progress Bar

25. It is important to monitor the progress of the audio player by implementing a progress bar. Drag a progress view from the Object Library to the view controller as seen in Figure 13-17.

**Figure 13-17**    Progress view in view controller

26. Next, create an IBOutlet called progressOutlet for the progress view by Control-dragging the progress view on to the ViewController.h file. Create a method to update the progress of the progress bar. This generates the following code:

```
@property (weak, nonatomic) IBOutlet UIProgressView *progressOutlet;
-(void)updateProgress;
```

27. Synthesize the property using the following code in the `ViewController.m` file:

```
@synthesize progressOutlet;
```

28. There are two steps involved in programming the progress view. Step one is to use a timer to control the progress view using the `AVAudioPlayer` method called `scheduledTimerWithTimeInterval`. The second step involves creating a method to update the progress view.

To accomplish the first step, we need to edit the `viewDidLoad` method in the `ViewController.m` file where we use the `NSTimer` method and the `scheduledTimerWithTimeInterval` method to update the progress view. The `scheduledTimerWithTimeInterval` method takes as parameters the frequency of update of the progress view, the target, a means of updating the progress, the user information, and the number of times the method should be repeated.

```
//set progress view
    [NSTimer scheduledTimerWithTimeInterval:.1 target:self
  selector:@selector(updateProgress) userInfo:nil repeats:YES];
```

29. To accomplish the second step in programming the progress view, we need to create a method called `updateProgress`. This method will update the progress view by first creating a `float` variable that will calculate the position of the progress bar in the progress view as a ratio of the current time over the audio's total duration. Next, the method called `progress` of the `AVAudioPlayer` class is used to update the progress bar in the progress view as seen in the following code:

```
-(void) updateProgress
{
    float myprogress = [player currentTime]/[player duration];
    self.progressOutlet.progress = myprogress;
}
```

## ViewController.h File

The code for the `ViewController.h` file is as follows:

```
#import <UIKit/UIKit.h>
#import <AVFoundation/AVFoundation.h>

@interface ViewController : UIViewController

@property (strong, nonatomic) IBOutlet UIButton *playButton;
//create an audio player object
@property (nonatomic, strong) AVAudioPlayer *player;

- (IBAction)audioPlay:(id)sender;
@property (strong, nonatomic) IBOutlet UISlider *volumeControl;
- (IBAction)volumeControlAction:(id)sender;

@property (strong, nonatomic) IBOutlet UIProgressView *progressOutlet;
-(void) updateProgress;
@end
```

**30.** The code for the `ViewController.m` file is as follows:

```objc
#import "ViewController.h"
@interface ViewController ()
@end

@implementation ViewController
@synthesize player;
@synthesize volumeControl;
@synthesize progressOutlet;
@synthesize playButton;

- (void)viewDidLoad
{
    [super viewDidLoad];

    // Do any additional setup after loading the view, typically
from a nib.

    //create a string path for the music file
    NSString *stringPath = [[NSBundle mainBundle]
pathForResource:@"violin1" ofType:@"mp3"];

    //create a NSURL for the music file
    NSURL *musicURL = [[NSURL alloc] initFileURLWithPath:
stringPath];
    //initialize the player object
    player = [[AVAudioPlayer alloc]
initWithContentsOfURL:musicURL error:nil];


    //set volume property to the slider value
    [player setVolume:self.volumeControl.value];

    //set progress view
    [NSTimer scheduledTimerWithTimeInterval:.1 target:self
selector:@selector(updateProgress) userInfo:nil repeats:YES];
}

-(void) updateProgress
{
    float myprogress = [player currentTime]/[player duration];
    self.progressOutlet.progress = myprogress;
}
- (void)didReceiveMemoryWarning
{
    [super didReceiveMemoryWarning];
    // Dispose of any resources that can be recreated.
}

- (IBAction)audioPlay:(id)sender {
```

```
    // if already playing, then stop
    if (self.player.playing) {
        [self.playButton setTitle: @"Play" forState:
UIControlStateHighlighted];
        [self.playButton setTitle: @"Play" forState:
UIControlStateNormal];
        [self.player stop];

        // if stopped, start playing
    } else {
        [self.playButton setTitle: @"Stop" forState:
UIControlStateHighlighted];
        [self.playButton setTitle: @"Stop" forState:
UIControlStateNormal];
        [self.player play];
    }

}
- (IBAction)volumeControlAction:(id)sender {
    UISlider *volumeSlider = sender;
    [player setVolume:volumeSlider.value];
}
@end
```

## Running the App

**31.** Run the app as shown in Figure 13-18.

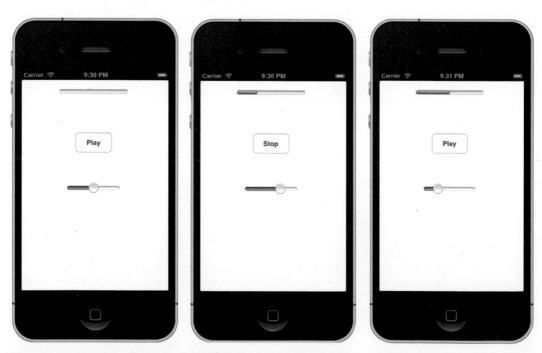

**Figure 13-18**    Running the audio player app

# Playing Video

So far, we've learned how to add images and audio to an app. Now we'll work with the most eye-catching part of any multimedia app—video. An instance of the MPMoviePlayerControl class is used to handle movie playback, either from a file or a network stream. The video is displayed in a view that is owned by the instance of the MPMoviePlayerController, which facilitates the programmatic control of movie playback. The various methods of the MPMoviePlayerControl class make it easy to programmatically incorporate basic functionality of movie playing, such as starting, stopping, and pausing. Before we can incorporate video into an app, we must first copy the video file into the Supporting Files folder. By simply changing the contentURL property of the MPMoviePlayerControl class, you can play a different movie using the same player object. Note, however, that playing simultaneous videos is not possible. Video formats supported by MediaPlayer framework include .mp4, .3gp, .mov, and .mpv.

## Adding Video to an App

The following steps summarize the process of adding video to an app:

1. Add the MediaPlayer framework to the project.

2. Import the MediaPlayer framework into the @interface file.

3. Add the video file to the Supporting Files folder.

4. Create the path to the video file and inform the compiler of the type of video file.

5. Set the file's URL to the video file.

6. Create an instance of the MPMoviePlayerController class.

7. Select the playback mode to either full screen or embedded in a view.

8. Set the delegate.

9. Program the Play/Stop button using the play and stop methods of the MPMoviePlayerController class.

## Creating an App that Plays Video

Now we will create a simple application that will play videos. To complete this app, you need the snuggles-Clip1.mov video file included with the data files for this chapter.

1. Create a new Xcode project.

2. In the Choose a template for your new project dialog, select **Application** under "iOS," select **Single View Application**, and then click the **Next** button.

3. In the Project options dialog, type **Ch13-VideoPlaying** as the Product name, enter appropriate items in the Organization Name and Company identifier boxes, make sure **iPhone** is selected in the Devices box, and then select the **Use Storyboards** and the **Use Automatic Reference Counting** check box.

4. Click the **Next** button, and then save the project in the location of your choice.

## Add MediaPlayer framework

5. The MediaPlayer framework is required to play a video, so we need to add it to the project. Click **Build Phases** as we did in the previous example, and then click the triangle next to **Link Binary With Libraries**. This displays a list of the three frameworks that are currently in the project.

6. Click the + symbol, and type **media** as shown in Figure 13-19.

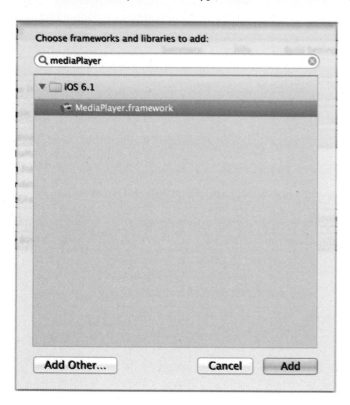

**Figure 13-19**    Adding the MediaPlayer framework

7. Select **MediaPlayer.framework** and then click **Add**. The MediaPlayer framework is added to the list of frameworks in the project, as seen in Figure 13-20.

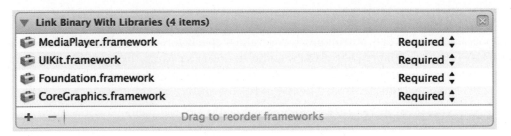

**Figure 13-20** The MediaPlayer framework added to the project

8. Next we need to explicitly import the MediaPlayer framework into the `ViewController.h` file. There is only one view controller in our project because we created a single view application. The code used to import the MediaPlayer framework is as follows:

```
#import <MediaPlayer/MediaPlayer.h>
```

## Create and Program a Play Button

9. Next, we need to add a button to play the video. Drag a round rect button on to the view controller and edit the text in the button to say "Play".

10. Create an `IBAction` called `PlayVideo` for the round rect button by Control-dragging the button to the `ViewController.h` file. This generates the following code:

```
- (IBAction)PlayVideo:(id)sender;
```

11. Create the `MPMoviePlayerController` object by creating a property in the `ViewController.h` file, as seen in the following code:

```
@property (nonatomic, strong) MPMoviePlayerController *moviePlayer;
```

12. Synthesize the `MPMoviePlayerController` object in the `ViewController.m` files as seen in the following code:

```
@synthesize moviePlayer;
```

13. Drag the **snuggles-Clip1.mov** file from the folder where you stored it into the Supporting Files folder. Again, remember to select the Copy items into the destination group's folder check box. Note that the extension of the type of video file will be entered in the method that provides the path to the video file as seen in the following code:

```
NSString *videoPath = [[NSBundle mainBundle]
pathForResource:@"snuggles-Clip1" ofType:@"mov"];
```

Here the type of video file is "mov."

## Program the Play Button

**14.** Programming the Play button involves several steps. Before creating an instance of the MPMoviePlayerController class, we need to create a path to the video file. This path should point to the mainBundle folder where the video file is stored and also identifies the file's name and extension. The MPMoviePlayerController class is part of the MediaPlayer framework. To accomplish this step, type the following code in the ViewController.m file:

```
- (IBAction)PlayVideo:(id)sender {
    //create a path to the movie file
    NSString *videoPath = [[NSBundle mainBundle]
pathForResource:@"snuggles-Clip1" ofType:@"mov"];
```

Create an instance of the MPMoviePlayerController class and initialize the path to the video file, which is then passed as a parameter to the MPMoviePlayerController object, as seen in the following code:

```
    //instantiate the movie player object with the path to the
movie player as a parameter
    moviePlayer = [[MPMoviePlayerController alloc]
initWithContentURL:[NSURL fileURLWithPath:videoPath]];
```

**15.** Create a subview to the view for the movie player. The subview will be responsible for playing the movie.

```
//Create and add a moviePlayer subview
[self.view addSubview:moviePlayer.view];
```

**16.** Set the fullscreen property of the moviePlayer class to YES (that is, true) so the movie is shown on the entire screen.

```
    //set the fullscreen property of the moviePlayer to view in
full screen
    moviePlayer.fullscreen = YES;
```

**17.** Add wireless access functionality to the video player as seen in the following code:

```
//Allow for wireless access to the movie player
  moviePlayer.allowsAirPlay = YES;
```

**18.** Invoke the play method of the MPMoviePlayerController to play the movie as seen in the following code:

```
    //Invoke the play method of the moviePlayer class to play the
movie
    [moviePlayer play];

}
```

The complete code for the ViewController.h file is:

```
#import <UIKit/UIKit.h>
#import <MediaPlayer/MediaPlayer.h>

@interface ViewController : UIViewController
- (IBAction)PlayVideo:(id)sender;
@property(nonatomic, strong) MPMoviePlayerController *moviePlayer;

@end
```

The complete code for the ViewController.m file is:

```
#import "ViewController.h"

@interface ViewController ()

@end

@implementation ViewController
@synthesize moviePlayer;

- (void)viewDidLoad
{
    [super viewDidLoad];
    // Do any additional setup after loading the view, typically
from a nib.
}

- (void)didReceiveMemoryWarning
{
    [super didReceiveMemoryWarning];
    // Dispose of any resources that can be recreated.
}

- (IBAction)PlayVideo:(id)sender {
    NSString *videoPath = [[NSBundle mainBundle]
pathForResource:@"snuggles-Clip1" ofType:@"mov"];
    moviePlayer = [[MPMoviePlayerController alloc]
initWithContentURL:[NSURL fileURLWithPath:videoPath]];
    [self.view addSubview:moviePlayer.view];
    moviePlayer.fullscreen = YES;
    moviePlayer.allowsAirPlay = YES;
    [moviePlayer play];
}
@end
```

19. Run the application as seen below in Figure 13-21.

**Figure 13-21**    Running the video player app
© iStockphoto/Milax

## HANDS-ON LAB

In this hands-on lab, we will not only demonstrate the ability to play audio and video and display images, but also implement the tab view and the picker view. To complete this app, you will need the following media files, which are included in the data files for this chapter: img1.jpg, Danish2.mp3, violin1.mp3, snuggles-Clip1. mov, Danish4.mov.

Create an app with the following three tabs:

- Tab1: Contains the main page, with an image and a title
- Tab2: Contains an audio player that allows the user to select a song from a picker view
- Tab3: Contains a video player that allows the user to select a movie from a picker view

The running of the app is shown in Figure 13-22.

**Figure 13-22**   Running the Hands-On Lab app
© iStockphoto/Milax

## CREATING THE PROJECT

1. Create a new project in Xcode. In the Choose a template for your new project dialog, select the **Tabbed Application** template.

2. Click **Next**, and, in the Choose options for your new project dialog, enter the name **Ch13_HandsOnLab** for the product name. Also, make sure to select the **Use Storyboards** and **Use Automatic Reference Counting** check boxes.

3. Click **Next** and save the project in a location of your choice. By default, the Tabbed application template creates an application with two tabs.

4. Click on the **MainStoryboard.storyboard** file to display the interface that was generated by the tabbed application template. You see a tab bar controller and two view controllers, one for each tab. We need a third tab, so we'll have to add it.

## CREATE A THIRD TAB

5. Add a new view controller to the project.

6. Now we need to add a set of Objective-C class files. In the Xcode menu, select **File ▶ New ▶ File** and then, in the Choose your template dialog, select **Cocoa Touch** on the left and **Objective-C class** on the right.

7. Click **Next** and, in the Choose options for your new file dialog, select a subclass of **UIViewController** and make sure the With XIB for user interface check box is unchecked, as we are using storyboards. Name this set of files **ThirdViewController**.

8. Next we need to associate the third view controller with the Objective-C files (.h and .m). Select the third view controller and, in the Identity Inspector, select **ThirdViewController** as the class.

9. Now we need to connect the third view controller to the tab bar controller and then create a segue from the tab bar controller to the third view controller. To accomplish this, Control-drag the tab bar controller to the third view controller and, in the dialog that opens, select **Relationship Segue ▶ view controllers**.

10. This third tab does not have an image, although you see a square and the word "Item." Add an image to the tab, as shown in Figure 13-22, using the **first** file provided by Apple.

## ADDING FRAMEWORKS FOR AUDIO AND MEDIA

11. Add the AVAudioPlayer and MediaPlayer frameworks, as explained earlier in this chapter.

## CUSTOMIZE THE THREE TABS

Now we will customize the three tabs as seen in Figure 13-23.

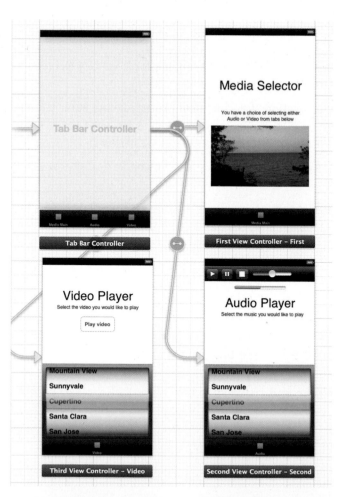

**Figure 13-23**   Storyboard for the Hands on Lab

Photo courtesy of Arshia Khan.

12. Modify the first tab by following these steps:

   a. Change the tab's title to **Media Main**

   b. Change controller's title to **Media Selector**.

   c. Change the second title to **You have a choice of selecting either Audio or Video from the tabs below**.

   d. Add an image view to the first view controller, and then drag the img1.jpg file to the Supporting Files folder.

   e. In the Attributes Inspector, select the newly added image as the image for the image view. The interface should now look similar to Figure 13-24.

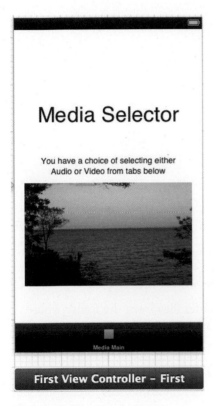

**Figure 13-24** Tab 1 design
Photo courtesy of Arshia Khan.

13. The second view controller already has a main title and a subtitle. Complete the design of the second view controller, as seen in Figure 13-25, by following these steps:

**Figure 13-25**    Tab 2 design

a. Change the title of the tab to **Audio**.

b. Change the main title to **Audio Player**.

c. Change the subtitle to **Select the music you would like to play**.

d. Drag the **Danish2.mp3**, and **violin1.mp3** audio files from the folder where you've stored them into the Supporting Files folder.

e. Add a picker view.

f. Set the data source and the delegate of the picker view by Control-dragging the picker view to the view controller. You learned how to do this in Chapter 12.

g. Add a toolbar at the top of the second view controller by dragging a toolbar object from the Object Library to the second view controller.

h. Add the Play, Pause, and Stop buttons to the toolbar by dragging two bar buttons on to the tool bar. The tool bar already has a bar button. Select this bar button and, in the Attributes Inspector, select **Play** as the Identifier property. Select the other two bar buttons individually and set their Identifier properties as **Pause** and **Stop.**

i. Add a progress bar just below the toolbar.

j. Add a slider to the toolbar for volume control.

## PROGRAM THE SECOND VIEW CONTROLLER IN THE SECONDVIEWCONTROLLER.H FILE

14. Import the AVFramework into the SecondViewController.h file using the import statement as follows:

   `#import <AVFoundation/AVFoundation.h>`

## ADD DATA TO THE PICKER VIEW

15. Connect the data source and delegate of the picker view by right-clicking the picker view. In the dialog that opens, Control-drag the circles next to the data source and delegate to the file's owner, as explained in in Chapter 12. Then explicitly define the data source and delegate as the file's owner by modifying the @interface directive as shown in the following code:
   `@interface ViewController : UIViewController <UIPickerViewDataSource, UIPickerViewDelegate>`

16. Create an NSArray property called **musicPicker** to hold the items for the picker view.

17. Create an IBOutlet called **pickerOutlet** for the picker view.

18. Create a property called **musicPlayer** for the AVAudioPlayer class, so an instance of it can be created to play audio.

19. Create an IBOutlet called **volumeControl** and an IBAction called **volumeControlAction** for the slider to control volume. If you have trouble creating an IBOutlet for the slider when the slider is on the toolbar, place the slider in the middle of the view controller (not on the toolbar), create the UISlider outlet, and then move the slider to the toolbar.

20. Create an IBOutlet called **progressOutlet** for the progress view so an instance of it can be created to monitor the progress of the audio player.

21. Create a method called **updateProgress** that will update the progress of the progress view.

22. Create an IBAction called **playButton** for the Play bar button that will play the audio.

23. Create an IBAction called **stopButton** for the Stop bar button

24. Create an IBAction called **pauseButton** for the Pause bar button

## SECONDVIEWCONTROLLER.H FILE

The code created in Steps 15 to 24 is as follows:

```
#import <AVFoundation/AVFoundation.h>
//Explicitly define the data source and delegate for the Picker view
@interface SecondViewController : UIViewController <UIPickerViewDataSource,
UIPickerViewDelegate>
//Array to hold the song names
@property (strong, nonatomic) NSArray *musicPicker;

//picker view outlet
@property (strong, nonatomic) IBOutlet UIPickerView *pickerOutlet;
```

```
//create an audio player object
@property (nonatomic, retain) AVAudioPlayer *musicPlayer;

//Volume control outlet - need this to find the value of the control
@property (strong, nonatomic) IBOutlet UISlider *volumeControl;
//Volume control IBAction method
- (IBAction)volumeControlAction:(id)sender;

//progress view outlet to monitor the progress of the playing
@property (strong, nonatomic) IBOutlet UIProgressView *progressOutlet;
//Update method will monitor the progress of the audio playing
-(void) updateProgress;
//play button IBAction method
- (IBAction)playButton:(id)sender;

//Stop IBAction button
- (IBAction)stopButton:(id)sender;

//pause IBAction button
- (IBAction)pauseButton:(id)sender;
@property (strong, nonatomic) IBOutlet UIBarButtonItem *pauseButton;

@end
```

## SYNTHESIZE ALL THE PROPERTIES

25.   Synthesize all the properties that were created in the @interface file as seen below.

```
@synthesize musicPicker;
@synthesize pickerOutlet;
@synthesize musicPlayer;
@synthesize volumeControl;
@synthesize progressOutlet;
```

26.   In the viewDidLoad method, do the following:

a.   Initialize the NSArray to the items for the picker view.

b.   Set the volume to the value of the slider, and set the progress to be updated every 0.1 seconds.

c.   Invoke the update method to update the progress view as seen in the following code:

```
- (void)viewDidLoad
{
    [super viewDidLoad];
    // Do any additional setup after loading the view, typically
from a nib.
```

```
    //initialize the picker with list of songs
    self.musicPicker = [[NSArray alloc] initWithObjects:@"song 1",
@"song 2", nil];
    //set volume property to the slider value
    [musicPlayer setVolume:self.volumeControl.value];

    //set progress view
    [NSTimer scheduledTimerWithTimeInterval:.1 target:self selector:
@selector(updateProgress) userInfo:nil repeats:YES];

}
```

27. Implement the methods for the picker view. The methods required by the delegate are numberOfComponentsInPickerView and numberOfRowsInComponent. These methods inform the compiler of the number of components and rows in the picker view. The relevant code is as follows:

```
-(NSInteger) numberOfComponentsInPickerView:(UIPickerView *)pickerView
{
    return 1;
}
-(NSInteger) pickerView:(UIPickerView *)pickerView
numberOfRowsInComponent:(NSInteger)component
{
    return [musicPicker count];
}
```

28. To display the items from the NSArray in the picker view, use the titleForRow method.

```
-(NSString*) pickerView:(UIPickerView *)pickerView
titleForRow:(NSInteger)row forComponent:(NSInteger)component
{
    return [musicPicker objectAtIndex:row];
}
```

29. When the user selects a row in the picker, the didSelectRow method must perform the necessary action. To accomplish this, complete the following steps:

a. Use the row number of the picker view in an if statement to select the appropriate song.

b. Create the path to the audio files **Danish2.mp3** and **violin1.mps**. This instantiates the URL, which in turn is used to instantiate the AVAudioPlayer object.

c. Implement the setVolume property of the AVAudioPlayer object. Code for the steps 30a through 30c is as follow:

```
-(void) pickerView:(UIPickerView *)pickerView didSelectRow:(NSInteger)
row inComponent:(NSInteger)component
```

430

```
{
     if (row ==0) {
          NSString *stringPath = [[NSBundle mainBundle] pathForResource:
@"Danish2" ofType:@"mp3"];

          //create a NSURL for the music file
          NSURL *musicURL = [[NSURL alloc] initFileURLWithPath:
stringPath];
          //initialize the player object
          musicPlayer = [[AVAudioPlayer alloc]
initWithContentsOfURL:musicURL error:nil];
          //set volume property to the slider value
          [musicPlayer setVolume:self.volumeControl.value];
          //set progress view
          [NSTimer scheduledTimerWithTimeInterval:.1 target:self
selector:@selector(updateProgress) userInfo:nil repeats:YES];
     }
     else
     {
          NSString *stringPath = [[NSBundle mainBundle]
pathForResource:@" violin1" ofType:@"mp3"];
          //create a NSURL for the music file
          NSURL *musicURL = [[NSURL alloc] initFileURLWithPath:
stringPath];
          //initialize the player object
          musicPlayer = [[AVAudioPlayer alloc]
initWithContentsOfURL:musicURL error:nil];
          //set volume property to the slider value
          [musicPlayer setVolume:self.volumeControl.value];
          //set progress view
          [NSTimer scheduledTimerWithTimeInterval:.1 target:self
selector:@selector(updateProgress) userInfo:nil repeats:YES];

     }
}
```

30. Program the updateProgress method so the current time and the duration methods are invoked for the musicplayer object, as seen in this code:

```
-(void) updateProgress
{
     float myprogress = [musicPlayer currentTime]/[musicPlayer duration];
     self.progressOutlet.progress = myprogress;
}
```

31. Program the volume control IBAction so the slider is used as the sender

```
- (IBAction)volumeControlAction:(id)sender
{
    UISlider *volumeSlider = sender;
    [musicPlayer setVolume:volumeSlider.value];
}
```

32. Program the Play, Pause and Stop buttons to implement the play, pause, and stop properties, as seen in the following code:

```
- (IBAction)playButton:(id)sender
{
    // if already playing, then stop
    if (!self.musicPlayer.playing) {
        [self.musicPlayer play];
    }
}
- (IBAction)pauseButton:(id)sender {
    // if already playing, then stop
    if (self.musicPlayer.playing) {
        [self.musicPlayer pause];
    }
}
- (IBAction)stopButton:(id)sender {
    // if already playing, then stop
    if (self.musicPlayer.playing) {
        [self.musicPlayer stop];
    }

}
```

## DESIGNING THE THIRD VIEW CONTROLLER

Now we are ready to complete the following steps to make the third view controller match Figure 13-26.

**Figure 13-26**   Third view controller design

33. Set the title of the tab to **Video**.

34. Add two labels for the main title and subtitle.

35. Add **Video Player** as the main title.

36. Add **Select the video you would like to play** as the subtitle.

37. Drag the **snuggles-Clip1.mov** and the **Danish4.MOV** files from the folder where you stored them into the Supporting Files folder.

38. Add a round rect button and add **Play video** as the text.

39. Add a picker view.

## PROGRAMMING THE THIRD VIEW CONTROLLER IN THE THIRDVIEWCONTROLLER.H FILE

40. Set the data source and the delegate of the picker view by Control-dragging the picker view to the view controller.

41. Import the MediaPlayer framework into the `ThirdViewController.h` file using the `import` statement.

    `#import <MediaPlayer/MediaPlayer.h>`

## ADDING DATA TO THE PICKER VIEW

42. Create an `NSArray` property called `moviePicker` to hold the items for the picker view.

43. Create an `IBOutlet` called `moviePickerOutlet` for the picker view.

44. Create a property for the `MPMoviePlayerController` class called `moviePlayer`, so an instance of it can be created to play video as seen below.

45. Create an `IBAction` called `PlayVideo` for the Play button.

    The `ThirdViewController.h` file is shown as follows:

    ```
    #import <MediaPlayer/MediaPlayer.h>

    @interface ThirdViewController : UIViewController
    //Array to hold the song names
    @property (strong, nonatomic) NSArray *moviePicker;

    //create an IBOutlet for the pickerview
    @property (strong, nonatomic) IBOutlet UIPickerView *moviePickerOutlet;

    //Create a property for the MPMoviePlayerController class
    @property (nonatomic, strong) MPMoviePlayerController *moviePlayer;

    //Create an IBACtion for the Play button
    - (IBAction)PlayVideo:(id)sender;
    @end
    ```

## PROGRAMMING THE THIRD VIEW CONTROLLER IN THE THIRDVIEWCONTROLLER.H FILE

46. Synthesize the respective properties that were created in the `@interface` file, as seen here:

    ```
    @synthesize moviePicker;
    @synthesize moviePickerOutlet;
    @synthesize moviePlayer;
    ```

**47.** In the `viewDidLoad` method, initialize the `NSArray` with the elements/movie for the picker view as seen in the following code:

```
- (void)viewDidLoad
{
    [super viewDidLoad];
    // Do any additional setup after loading the view.
    //initialize the picker with list of songs
    moviePicker = [[NSArray alloc] initWithObjects:@"Movie 1",
@"Movie 2", nil];
}
```

**48.** Implement the respective picker view methods to inform the compiler of the number of components and the items in the picker view as seen in the following code:

```
-(NSInteger) numberOfComponentsInPickerView:(UIPickerView *)pickerView
{
    return 1;
}
-(NSInteger) pickerView:(UIPickerView *)pickerView
numberOfRowsInComponent:(NSInteger)component
{
    return [moviePicker count];
}
```

**49.** Program the `titleForRow` method to display the elements of the array as the items in the picker view, as seen here:

```
-(NSString*) pickerView:(UIPickerView *)pickerView
titleForRow:(NSInteger)row forComponent:(NSInteger)component

{

    return [moviePicker objectAtIndex:row];
}
```

**50.** In the `didSelectRow` method, set the path to the video file and the URL for the video files, and then instantiate the `moviePlayer` object, as seen in the following code. Use the **snuggles-Clip1.mov** and **Danish4.MOV** video files.

```
-(void) pickerView:(UIPickerView *)pickerView
didSelectRow:(NSInteger)row inComponent:(NSInteger)component
{
    if (row == 0) {
        NSString *videoPath = [[NSBundle mainBundle]
pathForResource:@"snuggles-Clip1" ofType:@"mov"];
        //instantiate the movie player object
        moviePlayer = [[MPMoviePlayerController alloc]
initWithContentURL:[NSURL fileURLWithPath:videoPath]];
    }
    else
```

```
    {
        NSString *videoPath = [[NSBundle mainBundle]
pathForResource:@"Danish4" ofType:@"MOV"];
        //instantiate the movie player object
        moviePlayer = [[MPMoviePlayerController alloc]
initWithContentURL:[NSURL fileURLWithPath:videoPath]];

    }
}
```

51. Program the IBAction for the Play button so the movie player's play property is
    implemented to play the video and the fullscreen property is implemented to play in
    fullscreen mode, as seen here:

```
- (IBAction)PlayVideo:(id)sender
{
    [self.view addSubview:moviePlayer.view];

    moviePlayer.fullscreen = YES;

    moviePlayer.allowsAirPlay = YES;

    [moviePlayer play];
}
```

52. Run the app.

# Summary

- Images are a form of data and play a very important role in conveying information in
  everyday life.

- To add an image to an app, drag and drop an image view from the Object Library to the
  view controller, and then set the image property under the Attributes Inspector for the
  image to be displayed in it.

- The Aspect Fit option helps fit the image with the appropriate aspect in the image view. This
  prevents the image from stretching and making the image appear disproportionate.

- There are multiple ways of playing sounds in iOS, including iPod library access, audio
  queue services, the OpenAL framework, and the AVFoundation framework.

- Audio-related tasks include playing, recording, synchronizing, parsing, format
  conversions, and plugins.

- The following frameworks support audio: Media Player, AVFoundation, Audio Toolbox,
  Audio Unit, and OpenAL.

- The UIKit framework is automatically added to the project. Any other frameworks required to play audio or video must be manually added to the project and then imported into the files.

- Audio formats supported by the AVFoundation framework include IMA4, AAC, and MP3.

- Interruptions, such as phone calls during audio playback or recording, are handled by the delegate methods of the AVAudioPlayer and the AVAudiorecorder classes.

- The AVAudioPlayer class provides a simple Objective-C interface for playing audio of any duration from files or memory buffers and even supports multiple file playback.

- To configure the audio player, you must assign an audio file to the audio player, prepare the audio player by acquiring the required hardware resources, and, finally, assign an audio player delegate for handling interruptions.

- The configuration of the AVAudioPlayer involves creating a string object that holds the path to the sound file, and also creating and initializing a URL to the sound file using the path object.

- The framework that supports the video play back is MediaPlayer.

- The MPMoviePlayerController class handles movie playback from a file or a network stream.

- The play, pause, and stop methods associated with the MPMediaPlayerController class support playing, pausing, and stopping movies.

## Exercises

1. What are images?

2. Which framework is used for playing audio? Which framework is used to play video?

3. Name four methods associated with sound files in iOS and state their purpose.

4. Write code to create a path to a video file named snuggles-Clip1.mov.

5. Briefly describe the MPMoviePlayerController class.

6. Briefly list the steps that you must perform before programming a Play button.

7. Write Objective-C statements that accomplish the following tasks:

   a. Create an audio player object called myPlayer.

   b. Pause the audio player.

   c. Stop the audio player.

   d. Set the volume value of the object player to six.

8. List the frameworks primarily responsible for handling audio.

9. List the steps involved in playing video in an app.

10. Please mark the following as true or false. Correct the false statements.

    a. iOS allows multiple audio files to be processed simultaneously.

    b. iOS audio and video files can only be processed when stored in a particular folder.

    c. The `AVAudioPlayer` class contains methods that handle the sound of video files.

    d. The configuration of the AVAudioPlayer involves creating a string object that holds the path to the sound file, and also creating and initializing a URL to the sound file using the path object.

# Programming Exercises

To complete these Programming Exercises, you can use the media files included with the data files provided for this chapter, or you can download some media files of your choice from copyright-free sites on the web, or you can create your own media files using an iPhone, iPad, or other device. If you do use your own files, remember that you will be sharing your app with your instructor, and possibly with your classmates. So take care not to include files that reveal private information or that are inappropriate in any way.

1. Create an app with a table view. Each row of the table view should contain the name of an animal and the image of that animal.

2. Create an app with a list view of audio or video file icons. The user should be able to click an icon to play the corresponding audio or video file.

3. Create an app that contains at least six clickable images in a grid. Clicking an image should play a sound.

4. Create an arithmetic app. The app should randomly generate two numbers and an operator, and then prompt the user for the answer. If the answer is correct, the app should display an image of a happy face and play a sound. Otherwise, it should display a sad face and play a different sound.

5. Create an app that contains a list view with nine images. Clicking an image should display a larger view of the image.

6. Create an app with a picker view that contains a list of seven different major world regions. Clicking a region's name should display a map of that region. You will probably find it easiest to use the map images provided for this Programming Exercise, which are included in the data files for this chapter. The data files include maps for the following regions: Africa, Asia, Australia, Europe, the Middle East, North America, and South America.

7. Modify Exercise 5 to make it a tabbed app. One tab should display the list view described in Exercise 5. The second tab should display a list videos. When the user selects any of these videos, the selected clip should play.

## Business Case Study

In this Business Case Study, we will continue our work on the pain management app. Add images of sad, crying, and happy faces for the various levels of pain to the first tab. Create your own image files, or, if you prefer, you can use the image files included with the data files for this chapter. Add appropriate audio programming so that the app makes a sound each time a pain level is selected from the picker. For the sound, you can create your own audio file, or you can use the file included with the data files for this chapter.

# 14

# Data Persistence

In this chapter you will:

◎ Use the NSUserDefaults class to allow the user to set and save default settings

◎ Use property lists to store configuration information

◎ Use archiving to store data in a file system

◎ Use SQLite to store data in a database

The apps we created so far are incapable of retaining data after the app stops running. In other words, the apps lacked data persistence. Each time one of our apps started, it launched with the same data. Any edits to the data (for example, a list of songs added to a music app) were available only when the app was running and were not available the next time the app started. The data did not persist because it was not stored. In this chapter we look at the various means of storing data in an app.

## Data Persistence Mechanisms

**Data persistence** is the ability to save data in an app so the data does not revert to its initial values each time the app launches. There are many ways of saving data so it persists, and most apps use some means of data persistence. The type and size of data usually dictates the appropriate mechanism for an app. Some commonly used data persistence mechanisms are listed in Table 14-1.

| Mechanism | Size | Type of data |
|---|---|---|
| NSUserDefaults class | small | basic |
| Property List (plist) | small | basic |
| Archiving file | medium | basic and complex |
| SQLite3 database | large | complex |

**Table 14-1**    Data persistence mechanisms

In this chapter, we will learn how to implement the mechanisms listed in Table 14-1.

## NSUserDefaults Class

Occasionally a user may want to set and save her own default settings for an app. This can be accomplished using the NSUserDefaults class, which inherits from the NSObject class. The NSUserDefaults class offers a programmatic interface to an app's user preferences. When a user customizes an app, the user preferences are stored in the NSUserDefaults object. This very simple means of achieving data persistence can be used to store small, basic data such as integers, floats, doubles, and Booleans, in addition to NSData, NSDate, NSString, NSNumber, NSArray, and NSDictionary objects. The data returned by the NSUSerDefaults object is immutable even if it was mutable before it was stored in the NSUserDefaults object.

An example of implementing the NSUserDefaults occurs when an app offers the user a choice of fonts, in which case the fonts would be saved in the NSUserDefaults database as parameters. Parameters stored in this database are often referred to as defaults; the app customizes itself based on these defaults at each launch.

The NSUserDefaults class is useful for storing a single data element. It is relatively easy to use, because it involves very little code. For that reason, it is often misused by developers to store information other than user preferences. The process of using the NSUSerDefaults class to store data is also informally referred to as key-value pair storage, because the data is stored in pairs consisting of a key and its corresponding value.

An object of the NSUserDefaults class is created in the viewDidLoad method as follows:

```
//Create an instance of the NSUserDefaults
    NSUserDefaults *ud = [NSUserDefaults standardUserDefaults];
```

Methods commonly used to set the values of the key-value pair include the following:

- -setBool:forkey:
- -setFloat:forkey:
- -setInteger:forkey:
- -setObject:forkey:
- -setDouble:forkey:

As the values of the data variables change, a built-in synchronize method is automatically invoked to update data frequently. The developer may choose to manually synchronize the defaults as well to ensure the updated values are saved.

## Writing Data to a NSUserDefaults Object

The following steps summarize the process of writing data to a NSUserDefaults object.

1. Instantiate an NSUserDefaults object.

2. Use one of the set methods of the NSUserDefaults class to populate the key value pairs of the NSUserDefaults object.

3. Synchronize the NSUserDefaults instance to update the data.

4. To retain data, read the saved data in the viewDidLoad method.

## Creating a NSUserDefaults Example App

Now let's create an example app in which a string is saved using the NSUserDefaults class.

1. Create a project named **NSUserDefaultsExample** using the **Single View Application** template. Make sure you select the **Use Storyboards** and the **Use Automatic Reference Counting** check boxes.

2. Create the user interface shown in Figure 14-1 by dragging a label, text field, and a round rect button from the Object Library onto the view controller. This app has a text field (where the user will type text that will be saved as a string), a label (where the app will display the saved string), and a button to save the string entered by the user.

**Figure 14-1**    NSUserDefaults Example

3.  Change the default text in the label to **My saved data** and the button title to **Save data**.

4.  Create an `IBOutlet` for the label by Control-dragging the label to the `ViewController.h` file. Call this `IBOutlet savedText`. This generates the following code:

    ```
    @property (strong, nonatomic) IBOutlet UILabel *savedText;
    ```

5.  Create an `IBOutlet` for the text field and call it `usersText`. This generates the following code:

    ```
    @property (strong, nonatomic) IBOutlet UITextField *usersText;
    ```

6.  Next create an `IBAction` for the button and call it `saveText`. This generates the following code:

    ```
    - (IBAction)saveText:(id)sender;
    ```

    At this point, the `@interface` file looks like this:

    ```
    #import <UIKit/UIKit.h>

    @interface ViewController : UIViewController
    @property (strong, nonatomic) IBOutlet UITextField *usersText;
    @property (strong, nonatomic) IBOutlet UILabel *savedText;
    - (IBAction)saveText:(id)sender;
    @end
    ```

**7.** Next, synthesize the IBOutlets for the text field and the label with the following code in the ViewController.m file:

```
@synthesize usersText;
@synthesize savedText;
```

**8.** Because we want the string entered by the user to persist after the app stops running, we will save it in the NSUserDefaults object. To illustrate that data persistence has been achieved, we will then reload the string in the viewDidLoad method. In the saveText IBAction method, which is located in the ViewController.m file, program the button to save the data in the NSUserDefaults object, using the following code. Note that this code includes line numbers to make it easier to discuss the code in subsequent steps. Keep in mind that you should not include the line numbers in the code you type:

```
1   -
2   (IBAction)saveText:(id)sender {
3       //save the string to the NSUserDefaults
4       //create an NSString object to hold the string to be saved
5       NSString *saveString = usersText.text;
6
7       //Create an instance of the NSUserDefaults
8       NSUserDefaults *ud = [NSUserDefaults standardUserDefaults];
9
10      //save the string to the NSUserDefaults
11      [ud setObject:saveString forKey:@"myString"];
12
13      //synchronize the NSUserDefaults to make sure the data is
14  updated
15      [ud synchronize];
16  }
```

In the saveText method, a NSString object is first created in line 4. This string variable will hold the text entered by the user. Line 7 instantiates the NSUserDefaults object, and line 10 sets its object to the string that holds the user's text. Lastly, the synchronize method is invoked in line 14 on the NSUserdefaults instance to make sure the data is saved, even though the NSUserDefaults database is periodically updated automatically.

**9.** To demonstrate the app's data persistence, we program the viewDidLoad method in the ViewController.m file to display the saved string. We do this by first creating an instance of the NSUserDefaults object (line 9 in the following code) and then setting the label text to the object retrieved from the NSUserDefaults object (line 11 in the following code). The complete viewDidLoad method is as follows:

```
1   - (void)viewDidLoad
2   {
3       [super viewDidLoad];
4       // Do any additional setup after loading the view, typically
5   from a nib.
6       //display the saved string in the label when the app is
7   launched
```

```
8      //start by creating an instance of the NSUserDefaults
9      NSUserDefaults *ud = [NSUserDefaults standardUserDefaults];
10     //set the label to the saved string
11     [savedText setText:[ud objectForKey:@"myString"]];
12
13 }
```

The code for the ViewController.m file is as follows:

```
#import "ViewController.h"

@interface ViewController ()

@end

@implementation ViewController
@synthesize usersText;
@synthesize savedText;

- (void)viewDidLoad
{
    [super viewDidLoad];
    // Display the saved string in the label when the app is
launched
    //start by creating an instance of the NSUserDefaults
    NSUserDefaults *ud = [NSUserDefaults standardUserDefaults];
    //set the label to the saved string
    [savedText setText:[ud objectForKey:@"myString"]];

}

- (void)didReceiveMemoryWarning
{
    [super didReceiveMemoryWarning];
    // Dispose of any resources that can be recreated.
}

- (IBAction)saveText:(id)sender {
    //save the string to the NSUserDefaults
    //create an NSString object to hold the string to be saved
    NSString *saveString = usersText.text;

    //Create an instance of the NSUserDefaults
    NSUserDefaults *ud = [NSUserDefaults standardUserDefaults];

    //saved the string to the NSUserDefaults
    [ud setObject:saveString forKey:@"myString"];

    //synchronize the NSUserDefaults to make sure the data is
updated
    [ud synchronize];
}
@end
```

**10.** Run the app as seen in Figure 14-2.

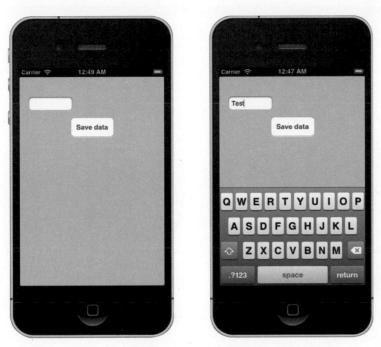

**Figure 14-2** First run of the NSUserDefaults example app

**11.** Type the text **Test** in the text field, and then touch the **Save data** button.

**12.** Quit the app and rerun it. The initial view now looks like Figure 14-3, with the stored string "Text" visible next to the text box.

**Figure 14-3**    "Test" next to the text box demonstrates data persistence

A second way of achieving data persistence is by using property lists.

## Property Lists

**Property lists**, which are also called **plists**, are files that hold configuration information for an app. Within a plist, information is organized as key-value pairs. Plists are usually used to store basic data types such as `float`, `int`, `double`, `strings`, `dates`, and Boolean values, as well as objects. (Note that some data types, such as `NSColor` and `NSFont`, cannot be stored in plists.)

Plists convert data into binary, XML, or ASCII formats in order to store them. Each of these formats has advantages over the other. For instance, binary data is the most compact of the three, while the XML is the most portable, widely used and editable format. If storage size is an issue then the binary format is recommended.

The `NSUSerDefaults` class uses plists to organize, structure, store, and access data. Property lists are typically used to retain small amounts of data—that is, less than a few hundred kilobytes. Large amounts of data cannot be handled by property lists.

The following steps summarize the process of using plists to achieve data persistence.

1.  Manually create a plist.

2.  Create a file path to the plist.

3.  Create a mutable array/dictionary to hold the data elements.

4. Store the data in the new array/dictionary.

5. Write this array/dictionary to the file path created in Step 2.

6. To retain data, read the saved data in the viewDidLoad method.

## Creating a Plist Example App

Let's create an app that uses a plist to store a student's name.

1. Create a project named **PListExample** using the **Single View Application** template. Make sure you select the **Use Storyboards** and the **Use Automatic Reference Counting** check boxes.

2. A plist called **PListExample-Info.plist** is created by default when the project is first created. This plist holds essential configuration information for the app. Now we will add a new plist for storing the name and course information. In the navigator area, Control-click the Supporting Files folder, and then select **New File.** This opens the Choose a template for your new file dialog.

3. Under "iOS," click **Resource**, and then click **Property List**, as shown in Figure 14-4.

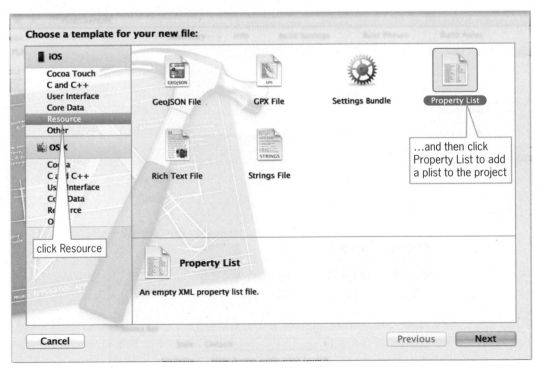

**Figure 14-4** Adding a plist to the project

4. Click **Next,** select a location to save the file, name the new file **myPlist** and then click **Create**.

# Adding Items to a Property List

5. Now we can add items to the plist. To get started, select the plist in the navigator area. This opens the plist in the editor pane, as seen in Figure 14-5. The plist consists of a table with columns labeled "Key," "Type," and "Value." The row that appears in the plist by default is called the Root row. It contains "Root" in the Key column and "Dictionary" in the Type column.

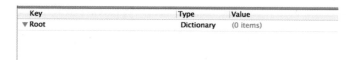

**Figure 14-5**   New plist displayed in the editor pane

6. We need to add a new row that will contain a variable to hold the data to be stored. To begin adding a new row, right-click on the root row to display the menu shown in Figure 14-6.

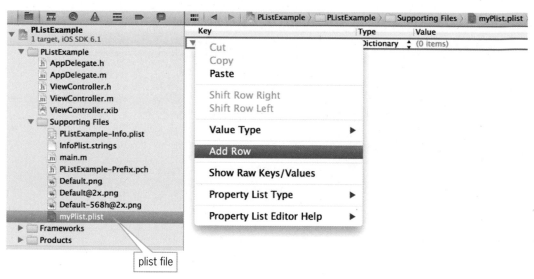

**Figure 14-6**   Adding a new row for data entry to the plist

7. Click **Add Row**. A new row appears in the table. In the **Key** column, type **Name**, which is the name of the variable. In the Type column, select **String**, and in the Value column type **Arshia**. When you are finished, your plist should look like the one shown in Figure 14-7. Note that to add additional rows, you can click the plus icon indicated in Figure 14-7.

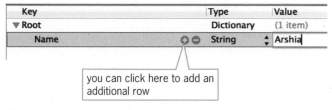

| Key | Type | Value |
|---|---|---|
| ▼ Root | Dictionary | (1 item) |
| Name | String | Arshia |

you can click here to add an additional row

**Figure 14-7**  New row added to plist

## Designing the Interface

8. Create a user interface that matches the one shown in Figure 14-8 by dragging a label, text field, and a round rect button from the Object Library onto the view controller. The user will type a name in the text box, and then click the button to save the name and display it in the label.

9. Delete the default text in the label and enter **My saved data**. Change the button title to **Save Name**.

My saved data

Save Name

**Figure 14-8**  Interface for the plist example

10. Create an IBOutlet for the label by Control-dragging the label to the ViewController.h file. Call this IBOutlet nameLabel. The autogenerated code is as follows:

```
@property (strong, nonatomic) IBOutlet UILabel *nameLabel;
```

449

**11.** Create an `IBOutlet` for the text field and call it `name`. The autogenerated code is as follows:

```
@property (strong, nonatomic) IBOutlet UITextField *name;
```

**12.** Create an `IBAction` for the button, and call it `saveName`. The autogenerated code is as follows:

```
- (IBAction)saveName:(id)sender;
```

**13.** We need the `writeToPlist` method to write data to the plist, the `readFromPlist` method to read from the plist, and the `filePath` method to track the path to the plist. Create these methods by typing the following code in the `ViewController.h` file.

```
-(NSString *) filePath;
-(void) writeToPlist;
-(void) readFromPlist;
```

At this point, the code for the interface file should look like this:

```
#import <UIKit/UIKit.h>

@interface ViewController : UIViewController
@property (weak, nonatomic) IBOutlet UILabel *nameLabel;

@property (weak, nonatomic) IBOutlet UITextField *name;
@property (weak, nonatomic) IBOutlet UIButton *saveName;

-(NSString *) filePath;
-(void) writeToPlist;
-(void) readFromPlist;
@end
```

**14.** Synthesize the labels and the text fields with the following code in the `ViewController.m` file:

```
@synthesize nameLabel;
@synthesize name;
```

**15.** Now we need to program the Save Name button to save the name in the plist. To accomplish this, we need a method that finds the file's path, and another method that writes the name to the plist. We start with the `filePath` method, which finds the file's path:

```
1  -(NSString *) filePath
2  {
3      //NSArray that will hold the path to the directory where the
4  plist is
5      NSArray *pathToPlist =
6  NSSearchPathForDirectoriesInDomains(NSDocumentDirectory,NSUserDom
7  ainMask, YES);
8
```

```
 9      //An NSString that holds the path to the plist file using the
10   directory found above
11      NSString *documentsDirectory = [pathToPlist objectAtIndex:0];
12
13      //return the path to the myPlist
14      return [documentsDirectory
15   stringByAppendingPathComponent:@"myPlist.plist"];
16   }
```

The `filePath` method first creates a `NSArray` (line 5) to store the path to the directory where the app documents are stored. This directory is where the plist will be stored. A `NSString` variable (line 11) is used to pull the first element of the directory to the documents. Lastly, line 14 returns the path to the documents directory concatenated with the name of the plist file.

16. Next we need a method to write to the plist so we can write the user-entered values to the plist. As you can see in the following code, this method first creates a `NSMutableDictionary` (line 6) and populates it with the contents of the text field. A `NSString` variable (line 12) is used to store the contents of the text field, which is then used to set the value in the plist (line 15). Line 18 invokes the `writeToFile` method that uses the `filePath` method to write to the `myPlist` we created. Lastly, the label is set to the user-entered value from the text field (line 21).

```
 1
 2   //Method to write to the plist
 3   -(void) writeToPlist
 4   {
 5      //create a NSMutable dictionary that will hold the plist
 6   values
 7      NSMutableDictionary *myPlistDict = [[NSMutableDictionary
 8   alloc]init];
 9
10      //create a NSString that will hold the contents of the text
11   field
12      NSString *value = name.text;
13      //set the plist to the NSString that is holding the contents
14   of the text field
15      [myPlistDict setValue:value forKey:@"Name"];
16      //invoke the writeToFile method to write the contents to the
17   plist
18      [myPlistDict writeToFile:[self filePath] atomically:YES];
19      //set the label to the contents of the text field for the
20   user to see what is being written
21      [nameLabel setText:name.text];
22   }
```

17. Next we need to program the Save button, which will save the user-entered text in the plist first by invoking the `writeToPlist` method. This requires the following code:

```
1   - (IBAction)saveName:(id)sender {
2       //invoke the writeToPlist method to write the contents of the text
```

```
3  field to the plist
4       [self writeToPlist];
5
6
7 }
```

18. Next we need to write a method that can read from the plist, so we can retrieve the data that we stored in the plist. The following readFromPlist method reads from the plist and displays the value in the label. In this method, a NSString variable is created to store the path to the myPlist file (line 6) by invoking the filePath method. Then it checks to see if the path to the file exists and if it is correct (line 9). If so, a NSMutableDictionary is created to hold values from the plist (line 14). Lastly, the contents of the label are populated with the contents of the NSMutableDictionary (line 19). The code for the readFromPlist method is as follows:

```
1  -(void) readFromPlist
2  {
3
4      //create a NSString that will hold the path to the file by
5  invoking the filePath method
6          NSString *pathToFile = [self filePath];
7
8      //test to see if the plist already exists
9          if([[NSFileManager defaultManager]
10 fileExistsAtPath:pathToFile])
11         {
12             //create a NSMutable dictionary set to the path to the
13 plist to hold the contents of the plist
14             NSMutableDictionary *myPListDict = [[NSMutableDictionary
15 alloc] initWithContentsOfFile:pathToFile];
16
17             //set the label to the contents of the plist at the Name
18 key
19             [nameLabel setText:[myPListDict objectForKey:@"Name"]];
20
21
22         }
23 }
```

19. Lastly, to demonstrate the persistence of the data, we want the most recently saved text to appear in the label the next time the app is launched. To accomplish this, we need to invoke the readFromPlist method in the viewDidLoad method, as seen in the following code:

```
1  - (void)viewDidLoad
2  {
3      [super viewDidLoad];

4      //invoke the readFromPlist method to read the contents of the plist
   into the label
5      [self readFromPlist];
6  }
```

**20.** Run the app as shown in Figure 14-9. Data is entered and the app is relaunched in Figure 14-10.

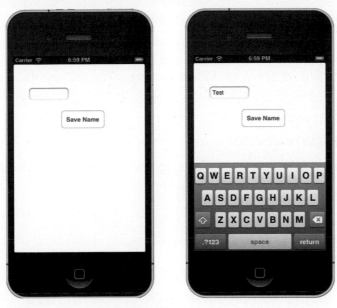

**Figure 14-9** Running the plist app

**Figure 14-10** Data persistence demonstrated in plist app

# Archiving

Archiving is another mechanism for achieving data persistence in which data is stored in a file system. The NSCoding and NSCopying protocols make archiving possible.

The NSCoding protocol requires a method for encoding data into an archive and another for decoding an archive. Implementation of NSCoding protocol requires the creation of an instance of the NSCoder class, and utilizes the key-value pair concept. The NSCopying protocol helps with encoded objects and is implemented by instantiating the NSCopy object.

The following steps summarize the process of archiving data:

1. Create an instance of a NSMutableData class to hold the encoded data.

2. Create an NSKeyedArchiver object to save the data from the NSMutableData object.

3. Use the key-value pair to archive the data.

4. Write the archived data to the file system.

5. The NSKeyedUnArchiver object is used to unarchive the data.

6. Retrieve the archived data.

## Creating an Archiving Example App

Let us look at a simple example in which we use archiving to save an NSString object.

1. Create a project named **Archive** using the **Single View Application** template. Make sure you select the **Use Storyboards** and the **Use Automatic Reference Counting** check boxes.

2. Create the user interface shown in Figure 14-11 by dragging a label, text field, and a round rect button from the Object Library onto the view controller. The user will type a name in the text box and then click the button to save the name to a file as a string. The label will then display the name.

3. Delete the default text in the label, and change the button title to **Save**.

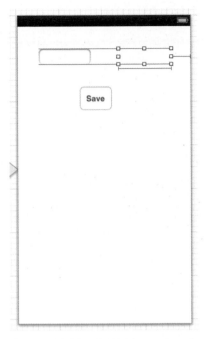

**Figure 14-11**  Archiving app interface

4. Create an IBOutlet for the label by Control-dragging the label to the ViewController.h file. Call this IBOutlet **nameLabel**. The autogenerated code is as follows:

```
@property (strong, nonatomic) IBOutlet UILabel *nameLabel;
```

5. Next, create an IBOutlet for the text field and call it **Name**. The autogenerated code is as follows:

```
@property (strong, nonatomic) IBOutlet UITextField *Name;
```

6. Next, create an IBAction for the button and call it **save**. The autogenerated code is as follows:

```
- (IBAction)save:(id)sender;
```

7. We want the app to save data to the documents directory. To make this possible, we first need to create a method in the ViewController.h file to find the path. The necessary method declaration is as follows:

```
-(NSString *) filePath
```

The code in the ViewController.h file should look like this:

```
#import <UIKit/UIKit.h>

@interface ViewController : UIViewController <NSCoding>
@property (strong, nonatomic) IBOutlet UITextField *Name;
```

```
@property (strong, nonatomic) IBOutlet UILabel *nameLabel;
- (IBAction)save:(id)sender;

-(NSString *) filePath;
@end
```

8. Next, synthesize the text field and the label in the `ViewController.m` file with the following code.

```
@synthesize nameLabel;
@synthesize Name;
```

9. In the following implementation of the `filePath` method, a `NSArray` (line 4) is created to store the path to the directory where the app documents are stored. The archived file is then stored in that directory. The path is stored as the first element in the array (line 10), and then the name of the archive file is appended to this path using the `stringByAppendingPathComponent` method (line 16). A `NSString` variable (line 10) is used to pull the first element of the directory to the archived file. Lastly, line 19 returns the path to the archived file.

```
1  -(NSString *) filePath
2  {
3      //NSArray that will hold the path to the documents directory
4      NSArray *pathToPlist =
5  NSSearchPathForDirectoriesInDomains(NSDocumentDirectory,NSUserDom
6  ainMask, YES);
7
8      //An NSString that holds the path to the plist file using the
9  directory found above
10     NSString *documentsdir = pathToPlist[0];
11
12     //build the path to the data file by appending the name of
13 the archiving file
14     NSString *dataFilePath = [[NSString alloc]
15 initWithString:[documentsdir
16 stringByAppendingPathComponent:@"myFile.archive"]];
17
18     //return the path to the myPlist
19     return dataFilePath;
20 }
```

10. We want the user to be able to click the Save button to save the data, so we must implement the following code to archive the user-entered data in the Save button. In the `IBAction` method for the Save button, create an `NSMutableArray` created (line 4) to hold the data, then add the user-entered text to this array (line 10). Next, archive the array by invoking the `NSKeyedArchiver` method (line 13).

```
1   - (IBAction)save:(id)sender {
2
3      //Create an NSMutableArray to hold the data
4      NSMutableArray *myArray = [[NSMutableArray alloc] init];
```

```
 5
 6   //Add the user entered text from the text field to the array
 7   created above
 8       [myArray addObject:Name.text];
 9
10   //archive the array
11       [NSKeyedArchiver archiveRootObject:myArray toFile:[self
12   filePath]];
13   }
```

11. Now we need to complete the part of the app that demonstrates persistence by retrieving the data from the archived file and displaying it in the label. This is done in the following viewDidLoad method. First, the path to the archived file is extracted by invoking the filePath method (line 6). Next, an if statement (line 10) checks to see if the archived file exists, and, if it does, then an NSMutableArray is created (line 14) to store the data extracted from the file. The data is unarchived, or retrieved, from the archive file and stored in the array (line 17). Next, the label is populated with the retrieved data (line 21).

```
 1   - (void)viewDidLoad
 2   {
 3       [super viewDidLoad];
 4
 5   //get the path to the file by invoking the filePath method
 6       NSString * pathToFile = [self filePath];
 7
 8   // Check to see if the archive file was created
 9
10       if([[NSFileManager defaultManager]
11   fileExistsAtPath:pathToFile])
12       {
13   //create an NSMutableArray
14           NSMutableArray *myArray;
15
16   //unarchive the data and store it in the above array
17           myArray = [NSKeyedUnarchiver
18   unarchiveObjectWithFile:[self filePath]];
19
20   //display the archived data into the label
21           nameLabel.text = myArray[0];
22
23       }
24   }
```

12. Run the app. Figure 14-12 shows the data entered by the user in the text field. Figure 14-13 shows the data retrieved in the second launch of the app.

**Figure 14-12**    First launch showing the user-entered data

**Figure 14-13**    Second launch showing the retrieved data

# SQLite

SQLite is a software library that can be used to implement a relational database in an iOS app. The iOS SDK supports SQLite through the C programming language. To access data stored in a SQLite database, we write statements, known as **queries**. SQLite commands are based on the Structured Query language (or SQL). Some commonly used SQL commands that work with SQLite are:

- **sqlite3_open()**: Opens a database using the path to the documents directory and the name of the database as a parameter.
- **sqlite3_close()**: Closes an open database.
- **sqlite3_prepare_v2()**: Prepares a SQL statement for execution.
- **sqlite3_step()**: Executes a SQL statement and steps through the database to retrieve elements.
- **sqlite3_exec()**: Executes a SQL command.

The following steps summarize the process of creating a SQLite database in an iOS app:

1. Add the `sqlite3` library to the project.
2. Find a path to the documents directory and attach the name of the database to this path.
3. Open the database using the `sqlite3_open` method.
4. Create a SQL command that opens the database and creates a table.
5. Create a method that updates the database by inserting items in the database table.
6. Create a method that reads data from the database by first preparing the `Select sql` command and then stepping through each row of the table and storing the items from the table in a string.

## Creating a SQLite Example

Let us create a simple app that stores an `NSString` in a database and then retrieves it.

1. Create a project named **SQLiteExample_SingleView** using the **Single View Application** template. Make sure you select the **Use Storyboards** check box and **Use Automatic Reference Counting** check box.
2. Before we can implement SQLite3, we need to add its library to the project. To add the sqlite3 library, click **SQLiteExample_SingleView** at the top of the navigator area.
3. Click the **Build Phases** tab to display the information shown in Figure 14-14.

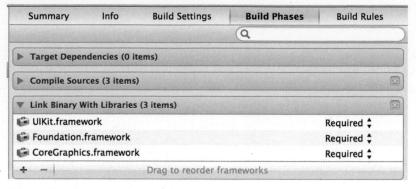

Figure 14-14    Build Phases tab

4. Click **Link Binary With Libraries**. This displays the project's three default frameworks, as seen in Figure 14-15.

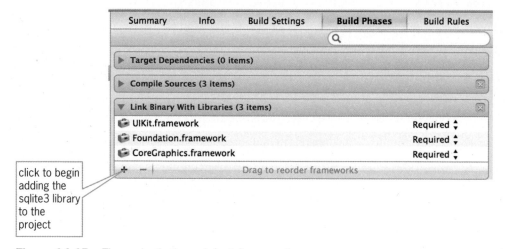

click to begin adding the sqlite3 library to the project

Figure 14-15    The project's three default frameworks

5. Click the + sign as shown in Figure 14-15, type **libs** in the search bar, select **libsqlite 3.0.dylib** in the list, and then click **Add** as shown in Figure 14-16.

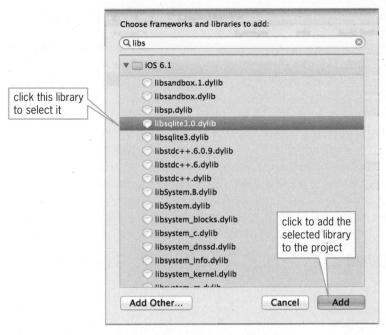

click this library to select it

click to add the selected library to the project

**Figure 14-16**   Adding the sqlite3 library to the project

Figure 14-17 shows the library added to the frameworks library. Figure 14-18 shows the library in the navigator area.

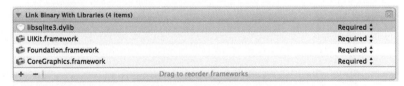

**Figure 14-17**   The sqlite3 library in the Link Binary With Libraries list

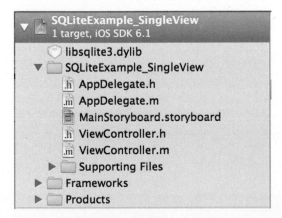

**Figure 14-18**   The sqlite3 library added to the project

6. Add the `import` statement to the `ViewController.h` file to import the sqlite3 library as follows:

```
#import "sqlite3.h"
```

7. Create the user interface shown in Figure 14-19 by dragging a label, text field, and two round rect buttons from the Object Library onto the view controller. Note that, unlike the previous apps, this app has two buttons. In this app, the user will type text in the text box, and then click one button save the text to the database and another to retrieve the saved text from the database and display it in the label. Change the default text in the label to **Data saved will appear here.** Make sure to stretch the label to fit the width of the screen to make room for the date stamp to appear next to the name. Change the left button's title to **Save to Database** and the right button's title to **Show Data**. Edit the placeholder text in the text field to read **Enter text here**.

**Figure 14-19**    User interface for the sqlite3 project

8. Create an `IBOutlet` for the text field in the `ViewController.h` file and call it **myText**. This generates the following code:

```
@property (strong, nonatomic) IBOutlet UITextField *myText;
```

9. Create an `IBOutlet` for the label in the `ViewController.h` file and call it **savedText**. This generates the following code:

```
@property (strong, nonatomic) IBOutlet UILabel *savedText;
```

10. Create an IBAction for the button titled **Save to Database** in the ViewController.h file and call it **Save**. This generates the following code:

```
- (IBAction)Save:(id)sender;
```

11. Create another IBAction for the button titled **Show Data** in the ViewController.h file and call it **showData**. This generates the following code:

```
- (IBAction)showData:(id)sender;
```

12. Create an instance variable for the database in the ViewController.h file using the following code in curly braces right after the @interface directive:

```
{
sqlite3 *db;
}
```

13. Create the following method declaration for a method that extracts the path to the database in the ViewController.h file:

```
-(NSString *) filePath;
```

14. Create the following method declaration to open the database in the ViewController.h file:

```
-(void) openDB;
```

15. Create the following method declaration to create a table in the ViewController.h file:

```
#import <UIKit/UIKit.h>
#import "sqlite3.h"
-(void) createTable: (NSString *) tableName
     withPrimaryKey: (NSString *) key
           withName: (NSString *) Name;
```

The code for the ViewController.h file with all the method declarations is as follows:

```
@interface ViewController : UIViewController
{
    sqlite3 *db;
}
@property (strong, nonatomic) IBOutlet UITextField *myText;
@property (strong, nonatomic) IBOutlet UILabel *savedText;

- (IBAction)Save:(id)sender;
- (IBAction)showData:(id)sender;

//method to find the path to the database
-(NSString *) filePath;

//method to open the database
-(void) openDB;
```

```
//method to create a table
-(void) createTable: (NSString *) tableName
     withPrimaryKey: (NSString *) key
           withName: (NSString *) Name;
```

@end

16. Create a NSString variable to hold the string typed by the user using the following code:

@property (nonatomic, strong) NSString *mydata;

17. Next create a NSMutableArray to hold the data being saved in the database using the following code:

@property (nonatomic, strong) NSMutableArray *dataElements;

18. In the ViewController.m file, synthesize the IBOutlets, NSMutableArray, and NSString using the following code:

```
@synthesize myText;
@synthesize savedText;
@synthesize dataElements;
@synthesize mydata;
```

19. In the ViewController.m file, implement the method that finds the path to the database. In this method, an array is first created (line 6) to hold the path to the documents folder where the database will be stored. Next, the path to the documents folder is found (line 11) and finally the database name is appended (line 16) to it.

```
1  //method to find the path to the database
2  -(NSString *) filePath
3  {
4      //NSArray that will hold the path to the documents
5  directory where the database is stored
6      NSArray *pathToPlist =
7  NSSearchPathForDirectoriesInDomains(NSDocumentDirectory,NSUserDom
8  ainMask, YES);
9
10     //The path is transferred to a NSString from the NSArray
11     NSString *documentsDirectory = [pathToPlist objectAtIndex:0];
12
13     //return the path to the database after appending the name of
14  the dataset to the path
15     return [documentsDirectory
16  stringByAppendingPathComponent:@"db.sql"];
17 }
```

20. In the ViewController.m file, implement the method that opens the database. In this method, the sqlite3_open method (line 7) is invoked by passing the path to the database as a parameter, while simultaneously checking to see if the method responsible for opening the database was executed. If the database was not open, then a "database failed to open message" is generated using the NSAssert method

in line 9. Otherwise, a NSLog statement is used to indicate that the database was opened (line 13). Note that this NSLog is included in this app to make debugging easier.

```
1   //method to open the database
2   -(void) openDB
3   {
4       //Use the sqlite3_open method to open the database and
5   simultaneously check to see if the database is open and if it is
6   not then NSAssert that the database failed to open
7       if (sqlite3_open([[self filePath] UTF8String], &db)) {
8           sqlite3_close(db);
9           NSAssert(0, @"Database failed to open");
10      }
11      //otherwise the database is open
12      else
13          NSLog(@"Database opened");
14  }
```

21. Implement the createTable method as shown in the following code. The sql command is created using the stringWithFormat method (line 10). The sqlite3_exec method is invoked (line 16) with the sql command and an error message as parameters. This error message is declared on line 7. If the sql command (line 16) is not executed successfully, then "Could not create table" is generated and the database is closed (line 19).

```
1   //method to create a table
2   -(void) createTable: (NSString *) tableName
3       withPrimaryKey: (NSString *) key
4           withName: (NSString *) Name
5   {
6       //create a char to hold the error
7       char *err;
8
9       //format a sql command to create a database with 2 fields
10      NSString *sql = [NSString stringWithFormat:@"CREATE TABLE IF
11  NOT EXISTS '%@'('%@' ""TEXT PRIMARY KEY, '%@'   TEXT);",
12  tableName, key, Name];
13
14      //If the command to create the table is not executed then
15  display an error message
16      if (sqlite3_exec(db, [sql UTF8String], NULL, NULL, &err)
17          != SQLITE_OK)
18      {
19          sqlite3_close(db);
20          NSAssert(0, @"Could not create table");
21      }
22      else
23          NSLog(@"Table created");
24  }
```

22. Now that the database has been opened and a table has been created, we need to program the **Save to Database** button in the `ViewController.m` file to update the table. This will have the effect of saving the data entered by the user. In this method, we first save the text entered by the user (line 2), with the current date used as the primary key (line 3), then the `sql` command that inserts values in the table, which is created using the `stringWithFormat` method (line 6) is executed by the `sqlite3_exec` method (line 14). If the command was not successfully executed, line 19 will close the database, and line 20 will generate a message indicating that the database was not opened.

```
1   - (IBAction)Save:(id)sender {
2       NSString * Name = myText.text;
3       NSDate *key = [NSDate date];
4
5       //create an sql query
6       NSString *sql = [NSString stringWithFormat:@"INSERT INTO
7   MyTable ('theDate', 'Name') VALUES ('%@', '%@')", key, Name];
8
9       //char to hold the error
10      char *err;
11
12      //execute the sql command and test to see if the command was
13  successfully executed
14      if(sqlite3_exec(db, [sql UTF8String], NULL, NULL, &err)
15  !=SQLITE_OK)
16      {
17          //close the database if the command was not successfully
18  executed
19          sqlite3_close(db);
20          NSAssert(0, @"Could not update table");
21      }
22      else
23      {
24          NSLog(@"Table has been updated");
25      }
26      //set the textfield in the user interface to blank when the
27  user taps the save button
28      myText.text = @"";
29
30  }
```

23. Program the Show Data button to display the data saved in the database. In the following code, we first create a SQL query statement (line 4) to select items from the database. This SQL statement is stored in an `NSString`, then this query is prepared to be executed using the `sqlite3_prepare_v2` method (line 9). This method takes several parameters, one of which is a SQL statement that is declared as statement of type `sqlite3_stmt` (line 6). If this preparation of the query is done successfully, then the program steps through the database, one row at a time, using the `sqlite3_step` method (line 13). At each step, the contents of the table fields are stored variables (line 16). All of these variables are then concatenated and displayed in the label in the user interface (line 36).

```
1   - (IBAction)showData:(id)sender {
2
3       //to load the data from the database format a select command
4       NSString *sql = [NSString stringWithFormat:@"SELECT * FROM
5   MyTable"];
6       sqlite3_stmt *statement;
7
8       //prepare the sql query to run
9       if (sqlite3_prepare v2(db, [sql UTF8String], -1, &statement,
10  nil) == SQLITE_OK) {
11
12          //Step through the database one row at a time
13          while (sqlite3_step(statement) ==SQLITE_ROW) {
14
15              //store the first statement into the date field
16              char *myDate = (char *)
17  sqlite3_column_text(statement, 0);
18              //convert this to a NSString format
19              NSString *myDateStr = [[NSString alloc]
20  initWithUTF8String:myDate];
21
22              //store the first statement into the Name field
23              char *myName = (char *)
24  sqlite3_column_text(statement, 1);
25              //convert this to a NSString format
26              NSString *myNameStr = [[NSString alloc]
27  initWithUTF8String:myName];
28
29              //store all the fields in a row into a string
30              NSString *str = [[NSString alloc] initWithFormat:@"%@
31  - %@ ", myDateStr, myNameStr];
32
33              //write the string to the label on the user interface
34              [dataElements addObject:str];
35              mydata = str;
36              savedText.text = mydata;
37
38          }
39      }
40  }
```

24. Now that all the methods required to implement the database are created, we need to invoke them in the viewDidLoad method. When the app starts, the viewDidLoad method is run. Within this method, the database is opened by the opendatabase method (line 6). The table is then created by the createTable method (line 9).

```
1   - (void)viewDidLoad
2   {
3       [super viewDidLoad];
4
5       //invoke the method to open the database
6       [self openDB];
7
```

```
 8          //invoke the method to create a table
 9          [self createTable:@"MyTable" withPrimaryKey:@"theDate"
10   withName:@"Name"];
11   }
```

25.    Run the app as seen in Figure 14-20. Enter a name, click the Save to Database button to save it in the database, and then click the Show Data button to display the saved data in the label.

**Figure 14-20**    Running the sqlite example

## HANDS-ON LAB

In this Hands-On Lab we create a blood sugar tracker. The data will consist of blood sugar levels, comments about each level, and the date each level was recorded. This app will have two text fields, two labels and two buttons. The user will enter a blood sugar level in one text field, and any comments in the second text box. The user can then click one button to save the data in a SQLite database and a second button to display all the recorded data in a table format. The date for each level will be autogenerated. The user interface for this app is shown in Figure 14-21.

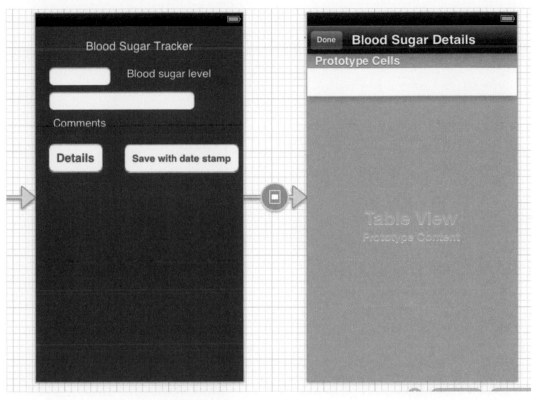

**Figure 14-21**    User interface for the blood level tracker app

This app requires a new template called the Utility Application template. This template has two view controllers as seen in Figure 14-22—the main view controller (which is the initial view controller) and the flipside view controller. Note the information button (with the lower case "i") in the bottom-right corner of the main view controller. Touching the information button changes, or flips, the view to the flipside view controller. The template includes a navigation bar with the Done button on the flipside view controller. Touching the Done button returns the user to the main view. The Utility Application template provides the essential interface for this app.

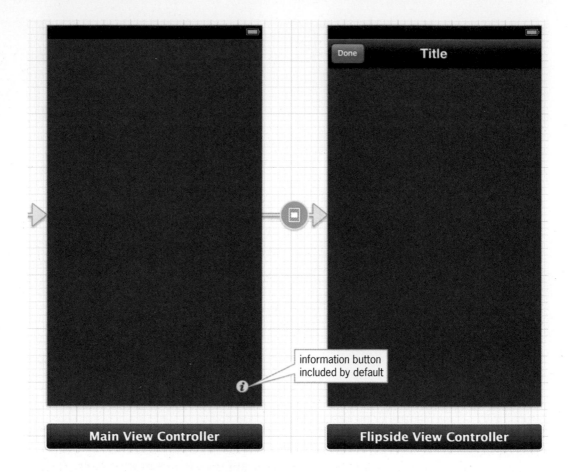

information button
included by default

**Main View Controller**

**Flipside View Controller**

**Figure 14-22**    The Utility Application template

## DESIGN THE USER INTERFACE

1. The first step in creating this app is to create the user interface shown earlier in Figure 14-21. Start by creating a new project using the Utility Application template as seen in Figure 14-23. Make sure to select **Use Storyboards** and **Use Automatic Reference Counting** check boxes and save it as BloodSugarTracker.

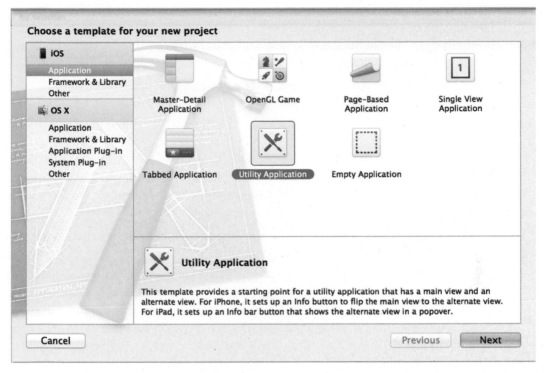

**Figure 14-23**  Implementing the Utility Application template

2. Now we need to change the information button on the main or first view controller to a round rect button. To accomplish this, select the information button, and then, in the Attributes Inspector, change the type field to **Rounded Rect**, as shown in Figure 14-24.

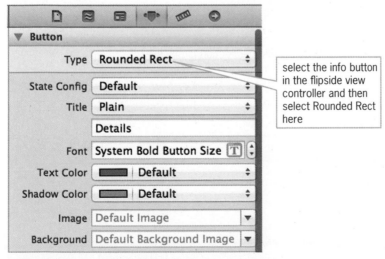

**Figure 14-24**  Modifying the information button on the flipside view

3.  In the main view controller, change the text in the information button to **Details**. Modify the size of the button to accommodate the text "Details" and move the button towards the center of the screen as seen earlier in Figure 14-21. Modify the background color of the main view controller to a royal blue as shown in Figure 14-21.

4.  Drag two text fields, two labels, and one button onto the main view controller. Drag an additional label to the main view controller and edit the text to say "Blood Sugar Tracker" for the title of this view controller. Increase the font size of the "Blood Sugar Tracker" label and change the font color to white.

5.  On the flipside view controller, change the title of the navigation bar to **Blood Sugar Details**. On the main view controller, change the first label text to **Blood sugar level**, the second label text to **Comments** and the button text to **Save with date stamp**. Then size the text boxes as seen earlier in Figure 14-21.

6.  Drag a table view (make sure you are not dragging a table view controller) from the Object Library onto the flipside view controller.

7.  Select the table view and, in the Connections Inspector, Control-drag the circles next to "dataSource" and "delegate" to the file's owner one at a time, as we have done in previous chapters. Figure 14-25 shows the dataSource and delegate before the connections are made. After the connections are made, your screen should match Figure 14-26.

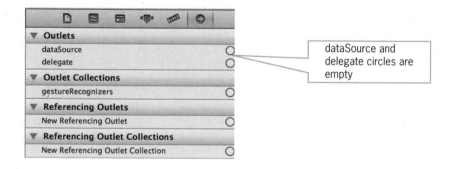

**Figure 14-25**    DataSource and delegate before the connection is made

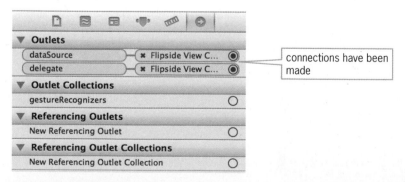

**Figure 14-26**    DataSource and delegate after creating the connection to the file's owner

8. Next, drag a table view cell from the Object Library onto the flipside view controller, as seen in Figure 14-27.

**Figure 14-27** Table view cell added

9. Select the table view cell on the flipside view controller and, in the Attributes Inspector, change the Identifier field to **Cell** as seen in Figure 14-28.

| ▼ Table View Cell | | |
|---|---|---|
| Style | Custom | ▲▼ |
| Identifier | Cell | |
| Selection | Blue | ▲▼ |
| Accessory | None | ▲▼ |
| Editing Acc. | None | ▲▼ |
| Indentation | 0 ▲▼ | 10 ▲▼ |
| | Level | Width |
| | ☑ Indent While Editing | |
| | ☐ Shows Re−order Controls | |

**Figure 14-28** Identifier changed to "Cell"

## ADD THE SQLITE DATABASE LIBRARY

10. Add the sqlite3 library to the project as we did earlier in the chapter.

11. Add the `import` statement to the `MainViewController.h` file and the `FlipsideViewController.h` file using the following code:

```
#import "sqlite3.h"
```

## PROGRAMMING THE MAINVIEWCONTROLLER.H FILE

12. Create an instance of the `sqlite3` class and call it `db1` using the following code in curly braces immediately after the `@interface` directive:

```
sqlite3 *db1;
```

13. Now we need to create the `IBOutlets` and the `IBActions` for all the user interface elements in the main view, except for the Details button, which is preprogrammed by the Utility Application template. First, create the `IBOutlet` for the Blood sugar level text field, and call it `bloodSugar`. This generates the following code:

```
@property (strong, nonatomic) IBOutlet UITextField *bloodSugar;
```

14. Create the `IBOutlet` for the Comments text field and call it `bloodSugarComments`. This generates the following code:

```
@property (strong, nonatomic) IBOutlet UITextField *bloodSugarComments;
```

15. Create the `IBAction` for the Save with date stamp button and call it **Save**. This generates the following code:

```
- (IBAction)Save:(id)sender;
```

16. Create a method declaration for a method that will find the path to the database:

```
-(NSString *) filePath;
```

17. Create a method declaration to open the database:

```
-(void) openDB;
```

18. Create a method declaration to create a table with the following three fields: `BloodSugar`, `Comments`, and `PrimaryKey`. Note that we will use the date as the primary key.

```
-(void) createTable: (NSString *) tableName
    withBloodSugar: (NSString *) bSugar
      withComments:(NSString *) comments
    withPrimaryKey: (NSString *) key;
```

At this point, the code for the `MainViewCntroller.h` file should look like this:

```
#import "FlipsideViewController.h"
#import "sqlite3.h"

@interface MainViewController : UIViewController
<FlipsideViewControllerDelegate>
{
    sqlite3 *db1;
}
//textfield to enter blood sugar level
@property (strong, nonatomic) IBOutlet UITextField *bloodSugar;

//comments for blood sugar
@property (strong, nonatomic) IBOutlet UITextField *bloodSugarComments;

//save the record
- (IBAction)Save:(id)sender;

//method to find the path to the database
-(NSString *) filePath;

//method to open the database
-(void) openDB;

//method to create a table
-(void) createTable: (NSString *) tableName
    withBloodSugar: (NSString *) bSugar
      withComments:(NSString *) comments
    withPrimaryKey: (NSString *) key;
@end
```

## PROGRAM THE MAINVIEWCONTROLLER.M FILE

19. Synthesize all the properties from the `MainViewController.h` file, as follows:

```
@synthesize bloodSugar;
@synthesize bloodSugarComments;
```

20. Now we need to implement the database methods that will find the file path to the database, open the database, create a table, and save the database. To get started, create the method that finds the file path to the database, as follows:

```
#pragma SQLite database methods
//method to find the path to the database
-(NSString *) filePath
{
    //NSArray that will hold the path to the directory where the
database is stored
    NSArray *pathToPlist = NSSearchPathForDirectoriesInDomains
(NSDocumentDirectory,NSUserDomainMask, YES);
```

```
    //An NSString that holds the path to the database using the
directory found above
    NSString *documentsDirectory = [pathToPlist objectAtIndex:0];

    //return the path to the database
    return [documentsDirectory
stringByAppendingPathComponent:@"db1.sql"];
}
```

21. Create the method that opens the database, as follows:

```
//method to open the database
-(void) openDB
{
    //Use the sqlite3_open method to open the database and
simultaneously check to see if the database is open and if it is
not then NSAssert that the database failed to open
    if (sqlite3_open([[self filePath] UTF8String], &db1)) {
        sqlite3_close(db1);
        NSAssert(0, @"Database failed to open");
    }
    //otherwise the database is open
    else
        NSLog(@"Database opened");
}
```

22. Create the method that creates a table, as follows:

```
//method to create a table
-(void) createTable: (NSString *) tableName
    withBloodSugar: (NSString *) bSugar
      withComments:(NSString *) comments
    withPrimaryKey: (NSString *) key
{
    //create a char to hold the error
    char *err;

    //format a sql command to create a database with 2 fields
    NSString *sql = [NSString stringWithFormat:@"CREATE TABLE IF
NOT EXISTS '%@' ('%@'  TEXT, '%@'  TEXT, '%@' ""TEXT PRIMARY
KEY);", tableName, bSugar, comments, key];

    //If the command to create the table is not executed then
display an error message
    if (sqlite3_exec(db1, [sql UTF8String], NULL, NULL, &err)
        != SQLITE_OK)
    {
        sqlite3_close(db1);
        NSAssert(0, @"Could not create table");
    }
    else
        NSLog(@"Table created");
}
```

**23.** Create the method that saves the data to the database, as follows:

```
//save the record
- (IBAction)Save:(id)sender {
    NSString * bSugar = bloodSugar.text;
    NSDate *theDate = [NSDate date];
    NSString *bSComments = bloodSugarComments.text;

    //create an sql query
    NSString *sql = [NSString stringWithFormat:@"INSERT INTO
MyTable('bloodSugar', 'Comments', 'theDate') VALUES ('%@', '%@',
'%@')", bSugar, bSComments, theDate];

    //char to hold the error
    char *err;

    //execute the sql command and test to see if the command was
successfully executed
    if(sqlite3_exec(db1, [sql UTF8String], NULL, NULL, &err)
!=SQLITE_OK)
    {
        //close the database if the command was not successfully
executed
        sqlite3_close(db1);
        NSAssert(0, @"Could not update table");
    }
    else
    {
        NSLog(@"Table has been updated");
    }
    //set the text field in the user interface to blank when the
user taps the save button
    bloodSugar.text - @"";
    bloodSugarComments.text = @"";

}
```

**24.** In the `viewDidLoad` method, invoke the method that opens the database. Next, invoke the method that creates a table named `MyTable`. The new table should contain the following fields `bloodSugar`, `Comments`, and `theDate`. There is no need to modify any of the Flipside view code.

```
- (void)viewDidLoad
{
    [super viewDidLoad];
    // Do any additional setup after loading the view, typically
from a nib.

    //invoke the method to open the database
    [self openDB];
```

```
//invoke the method to create a table
[self createTable:@"MyTable" withBloodSugar:@"bloodSugar"
withComments:@"Comments" withPrimaryKey:@"theDate"];
}
```

The code for the `MainViewController.m` file should look like the following:

```
#import "MainViewController.h"

@interface MainViewController ()

@end

@implementation MainViewController
@synthesize bloodSugar;
@synthesize bloodSugarComments;

- (void)viewDidLoad
{
    [super viewDidLoad];
    // Do any additional setup after loading the view, typically
from a nib.
    //invoke the method to open the database
    [self openDB];
    //invoke the method to create a table
    [self createTable:@"MyTable" withBloodSugar:@"bloodSugar"
withComments:@"Comments" withPrimaryKey:@"theDate"];
}

- (void)didReceiveMemoryWarning
{
    [super didReceiveMemoryWarning];
    // Dispose of any resources that can be recreated.
}

#pragma mark - Flipside View

- (void)flipsideViewControllerDidFinish:(FlipsideViewController
*)controller
{
    [self dismissViewControllerAnimated:YES completion:nil];
}

- (void)prepareForSegue:(UIStoryboardSegue *)segue sender:(id)sender
{
    if ([[segue identifier] isEqualToString:@"showAlternate"]) {
        [[segue destinationViewController] setDelegate:self];
    }
}
```

```
#pragma SQLite database methods

//method to find the path to the database
-(NSString *) filePath
{
    //NSArray that will hold the path to the directory where the
database is stored
    NSArray *pathToPlist = NSSearchPathForDirectoriesInDomains
(NSDocumentDirectory,NSUserDomainMask, YES);

    //An NSString that holds the path to the database using the
directory found above
    NSString *documentsDirectory = [pathToPlist objectAtIndex:0];

    //return the path to the database
    return [documentsDirectory \
stringByAppendingPathComponent:@"db1.sql"];
}

//method to open the database
-(void) openDB
{
    //Use the sqlite3_open method to open the database and
simultaneously check to see if the database is open and if it is
not then NSAssert that the database failed to open
    if (sqlite3_open([[self filePath] UTF8String], &db1)) {
        sqlite3_close(db1);
        NSAssert(0, @"Database failed to open");
    }
    //otherwise the database is open
    else
        NSLog(@"Database opened");
}

//method to create a table
-(void) createTable: (NSString *) tableName
    withBloodSugar: (NSString *) bSugar
      withComments:(NSString *) comments
    withPrimaryKey: (NSString *) key
{
    //create a char to hold the error
    char *err;

    //format a sql command to create a database with 2 fields
    NSString *sql = [NSString stringWithFormat:@"CREATE TABLE IF
NOT EXISTS '%@' ('%@'  TEXT, '%@'  TEXT, '%@' ""TEXT PRIMARY
KEY);", tableName, bSugar, comments, key];

    //If the command to create the table is not executed then
display an error message
    if (sqlite3_exec(db1, [sql UTF8String], NULL, NULL, &err)
        != SQLITE_OK)
```

```objectivec
        {
            sqlite3_close(db1);
            NSAssert(0, @"Could not create table");
        }
        else
            NSLog(@"Table created");
    }
    //save the record
    - (IBAction)Save:(id)sender {
        NSString * bSugar = bloodSugar.text;
        NSDate *theDate = [NSDate date];
        NSString *bSComments = bloodSugarComments.text;

        //create an sql query
        NSString *sql = [NSString stringWithFormat:@"INSERT INTO
MyTable('bloodSugar', 'Comments', 'theDate') VALUES ('%@', '%@',
'%@')", bSugar, bSComments, theDate];

        //char to hold the error
        char *err;

        //execute the sql command and test to see if the command was
successfully executed
        if(sqlite3_exec(db1, [sql UTF8String], NULL, NULL, &err)
!=SQLITE_OK)
        {
            //close the database if the command was not successfully
executed
            sqlite3_close(db1);
            NSAssert(0, @"Could not update table");
        }
        else
        {
            NSLog(@"Table has been updated");
        }
        //set the text field in the user interface to blank when the
user taps the save button
        bloodSugar.text = @"";
        bloodSugarComments.text = @"";
    }
    @end
```

## WRITING THE CODE FOR THE FLIPSIDEVIEWCONTROLLER.H FILE

25. Within the curly braces immediately after the @interface directive, create an instance of the sqlite3 object and call it db1, as follows:

```objectivec
{
sqlite3 *db1;
}
```

26. Create a property for a NSMutableArray that we will use to retrieve the data from the sqlite3 database:

```
@property (nonatomic, retain) NSMutableArray *data;
```

27. Create a method declaration for a method that will find the path to the database:

```
-(NSString *) filePath;
```

28. Create a method declaration to open the database:

```
-(void) openDB;
```

At this point, the code for your FlipsideViewController.h should match the following:

```
#import <UIKit/UIKit.h>
#import "sqlite3.h"

@class FlipsideViewController;

@protocol FlipsideViewControllerDelegate
- (void)flipsideViewControllerDidFinish:(FlipsideViewController
*)controller;
@end

@interface FlipsideViewController : UIViewController
{
    sqlite3 *db1;
}

@property (weak, nonatomic) id <FlipsideViewControllerDelegate>
delegate;

@property (nonatomic, retain) NSMutableArray *data;

- (IBAction)done:(id)sender;

//method to find the path to the database
-(NSString *) filePath;

//method to open the database
-(void) openDB;
@end
```

## WRITING THE CODE FOR THE FLIPSIDEVIEWCONTROLLER.M FILE

29. Synthesize the NSMutableArray we created in the FlipsideViewController.h file using the following code:

```
@synthesize data;
```

30. Next, we need to implement the sqlite3 database methods to find the file path to the database, and then open the database. The method to find the file path to the database is as follows:

```
#pragma mark sqlite3 methods
//method to find the path to the database
-(NSString *) filePath
{
    //NSArray that will hold the path to the directory where the
database is stored
    NSArray *pathToPlist = NSSearchPathForDirectoriesInDomains
(NSDocumentDirectory,NSUserDomainMask, YES);

    //An NSString that holds the path to the database using the
directory found above
    NSString *documentsDirectory = [pathToPlist objectAtIndex:0];

    //return the path to the database
    return [documentsDirectory
stringByAppendingPathComponent:@"db1.sql"];
}
```

31. The method to open the database is as follows:

```
//method to open the database
-(void) openDB
{
    //Use the sqlite3_open method to open the database and
simultaneously check to see if the database is open and if it is
not then NSAssert that the database failed to open
    if (sqlite3_open([[self filePath] UTF8String], &db1)) {
        sqlite3_close(db1);
        NSAssert(0, @"Database failed to open");
    }
    //otherwise the database is open
    else
        NSLog(@"Database opened");
}
```

32. Next, we need to implement the methods for the table view. Specifically, we needs methods that specify the number of sections in the table, the table's title, and the number of rows in the table view. Finally, we need to use the `CellForRowAtIndexPath` method to display the data from the `NSMutable` array in the table. To get started, the method to define the number of sections in the table is as follows:

```
#pragma table methods
//Number of sections in the table
- (NSInteger)numberOfSectionsInTableView:(UITableView *)tableView
{
    return 1;
}
```

33. The method to assign a title to the table view is as follows:

```
//Customize the title and header for sections
-(NSString *) tableView:(UITableView *) tableView
titleForHeaderInSection:(NSInteger)section
{
    NSString *theTitle = [[NSString alloc] initWithFormat:@"Blood
Sugar Tracking Details"];
    return theTitle;
}
```

34. The method to define the number of rows in the table view is as follows:

```
// Customize the number of rows in the table view.
- (NSInteger)tableView:(UITableView *)tableView
numberOfRowsInSection:(NSInteger)section {
    return [data count];
}
```

35. The method to display data in the table view is as follows:

```
// Customize the appearance of table view cells.
- (UITableViewCell *)tableView:(UITableView *)tableView
cellForRowAtIndexPath:(NSIndexPath *)indexPath {

    static NSString *CellIdentifier = @"Cell";

    UITableViewCell *cell = [tableView
dequeueReusableCellWithIdentifier:CellIdentifier
forIndexPath:indexPath];


    // Set up the cell...
    cell.textLabel.text = [data objectAtIndex:indexPath.row];
    return cell;
}
```

## WRITING THE VIEWDIDLOAD METHOD

36. Initialize the NSMutableArray, as follows:

```
data = [[NSMutableArray alloc] init];
```

37. Open the database, as follows:

```
[self openDB];
```

**38.** Create a `sql` statement that retrieves the data from each column, one row at a time, and saves the retrieved data in an `NSString`.

```
NSString *sql = [NSString stringWithFormat:@"SELECT * FROM
MyTable"];
    sqlite3_stmt *statement;
    if (sqlite3_prepare_v2(db1, [sql UTF8String], -1, &statement,
nil) ==SQLITE_OK) {

        //Step through the database one row at a time
        while (sqlite3_step(statement) ==SQLITE_ROW) {
```

**39.** Concatenate all the `NSStrings` to form one string that is displayed in each row of the table:

```
//store the first statement into the Name field
        char *myBloodSugar = (char *)
sqlite3_column_text(statement, 0);
        //convert this to a NSString format
        NSString *myBloodSugarStr = [[NSString alloc]
initWithUTF8String:myBloodSugar];

        //store the first statement into the date field
        char *myComments = (char *)
sqlite3_column_text(statement, 1);
        //convert this to a NSString format
        NSString *myCommentsStr = [[NSString alloc]
initWithUTF8String:myComments];

        //store the first statement into the date field
        char *myDate = (char *)
sqlite3_column_text(statement, 2);
        //convert this to a NSString format
        NSString *myDateStr = [[NSString alloc]
initWithUTF8String:myDate];

        //store all the fields in arow into a string
        NSString *str = [[NSString alloc] initWithFormat:@"%@
- %@ - %@ ", myBloodSugarStr, myCommentsStr, myDateStr];

        //write the string to the label on the user interface
        [data addObject:str];
    }
}
```

Your `FlipsideViewController.m` file should look like this:

```
#import "FlipsideViewController.h"

@interface FlipsideViewController ()

@end
```

```
@implementation FlipsideViewController
@synthesize data;

- (void)viewDidLoad
{
    [super viewDidLoad];
    // Do any additional setup after loading the view, typically
from a nib.

    //initialize the NSMutableArray
    data = [[NSMutableArray alloc] init];

    //open database
    [self openDB];

    //create a sql statement
    NSString *sql = [NSString stringWithFormat:@"SELECT * FROM
MyTable"];
    sqlite3_stmt *statement;
    //prepare the sql query to run
    if (sqlite3_prepare_v2(db1, [sql UTF8String], -1, &statement,
nil) ==SQLITE_OK) {

        //Step through the database one row at a time
        while (sqlite3_step(statement) ==SQLITE_ROW) {


            //store the first statement into the Name field
            char *myBloodSugar = (char *)
sqlite3_column_text(statement, 0);
            //convert this to a NSString format
            NSString *myBloodSugarStr = [[NSString alloc]
initWithUTF8String:myBloodSugar];

            //store the first statement into the date field
            char *myComments = (char *)
sqlite3_column_text(statement, 1);
            //convert this to a NSString format
            NSString *myCommentsStr = [[NSString alloc]
initWithUTF8String:myComments];

            //store the first statement into the date field
            char *myDate = (char *)
sqlite3_column_text(statement, 2);
            //convert this to a NSString format
            NSString *myDateStr = [[NSString alloc]
initWithUTF8String:myDate];

            //store all the fields in a row as a string
            NSString *str = [[NSString alloc] initWithFormat:@"%@
- %@ - %@ ", myBloodSugarStr, myCommentsStr, myDateStr];
```

```
                    //write the string to the label on the user interface
                    [data addObject:str];


        }
    }


}


- (void)didReceiveMemoryWarning
{
    [super didReceiveMemoryWarning];
    // Dispose of any resources that can be recreated.
}


#pragma mark - Actions

- (IBAction)done:(id)sender
{
    [self.delegate flipsideViewControllerDidFinish:self];
}


#pragma mark sqlite3 methods
//method to find the path to the database
-(NSString *) filePath
{
    //NSArray that will hold the path to the directory where the
database is stored
    NSArray *pathToPlist = NSSearchPathForDirectoriesInDomains
(NSDocumentDirectory,NSUserDomainMask, YES);

    //An NSString that holds the path to the database using the
directory found above
    NSString *documentsDirectory = [pathToPlist objectAtIndex:0];

    //return the path to the database
    return [documentsDirectory
stringByAppendingPathComponent:@"db1.sql"];
}


//method to open the database
-(void) openDB
{
    //Use the sqlite3_open method to open the database and
simultaneously check to see if the database is open and if it is
not then NSAssert that the database failed to open
```

```
    if (sqlite3_open([[self filePath] UTF8String], &db1)) {
        sqlite3_close(db1);
        NSAssert(0, @"Database failed to open");
    }
    //otherwise the database is open
    else
        NSLog(@"Database opened");
}

#pragma table methods
//Number of sections in the table
- (NSInteger)numberOfSectionsInTableView:(UITableView *)tableView
{
    return 1;
}

//Customize the title and header for sections
-(NSString *) tableView:(UITableView *) tableView
titleForHeaderInSection:(NSInteger)section
{
    NSString *theTitle = [[NSString alloc] initWithFormat:@"Blood
Sugar Tracking Details"];
    return theTitle;
}

// Customize the number of rows in the table view.
- (NSInteger)tableView:(UITableView *)tableView
numberOfRowsInSection:(NSInteger)section {
    return [data count];
}

// Customize the appearance of table view cells.
- (UITableViewCell *)tableView:(UITableView *)tableView
cellForRowAtIndexPath:(NSIndexPath *)indexPath {

    static NSString *CellIdentifier = @"Cell";

    UITableViewCell *cell = [tableView
dequeueReusableCellWithIdentifier:CellIdentifier
forIndexPath:indexPath];


    // Set up the cell...
    cell.textLabel.text = [data objectAtIndex:indexPath.row];
    return cell;
}

@end
```

## RUNNING THE COMPLETED APP

40.    Run the app as seen in Figure 14-29.

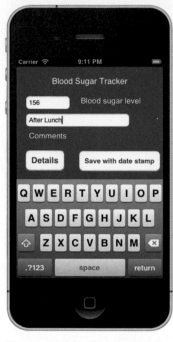  

Figure 14-29    Running the Hands-On Lab app

# Summary

- Data persistence is the ability to save data in an app so that the data is available the next time the app is launched.

- The type and size of data usually dictates the type of mechanism utilized to achieve data persistence.

- The most commonly used data persistence mechanisms are:

    - `NSUSerDefaults`

    - Property lists (or plists)

    - Archiving

    - SQLite

- The NSUserDefaults class offers a programmatic interface to an app's user preferences. When a user customizes an app, the user preferences are stored in the NSUserDefaults object. The steps involved in implementing the NSUserDefaults mechanism are: instantiate the NSUserDefaults object, populate this object with the data you want to save, synchronize it, and then use the viewDidLoad method to retrieve the saved data.

- Property lists, also called plists, are files used to store data that is organized as key-value pairs. They are typically used to store small amounts of data.

- The steps involved in implementing plists are: create the plist, create a file path to the plist, store data in the plist, create an array to hold the data, and then read the saved data into the array.

- Archiving is a mechanism by which data is stored in a file system. In archiving, data must conform to the NSCoding and NSCopying protocols.

- The steps required to archive data are: create an instance of a NSMutableData array to hold the encoded data, create an NSKeyedArchiver method to save the data from the NSMutableData array, implement the key-value pair to archive the data, save the archived data to the file system, and then use the NSKeyedUnArchiver method to unarchive the data and decode the object.

- SQLite is a software library that can be used to implement a relational database in an iOS app. To access data stored in a SQLite database, we write SQLite statements, known as queries. SQLite commands are based on the Structured Query language (or SQL).

- The steps required to implement a SQLite database are: add the sqlite3 library to the project, find the file path to the SQLite database, open the database, create a table with the necessary fields, create a method to save the data, and then create a method to retrieve the data.

489

## Exercises

1. Mark the following statements as true or false. Correct the false statements.

   a. Data persistence ensures that the data does not revert to the original setting at each launch.

   b. The data returned by a NSUserDefaults object is mutable even if it was immutable to start with before it was stored in the NSUserDefaults object.

   c. NSUserDefault class is useful for storing multiple pieces of data.

   d. XML is the most portable, widely used, and editable format.

   e. Large amounts of data cannot be handled by property lists.

   f. The NSColor and NSFont objects cannot be stored in a plist.

2. Categorize each of these mechanisms by the kind of data they store (small, medium, or large):

   a. NSUSerDefaults

   b. archiving

   c. property lists (plists)

   d. SQLite3

3. Give an example of the kind of data that can be stored using NSUserDefaults.

4. Describe the steps involved in using the NSUSerDefaults class to save data.

5. Describe the steps involved in writing to a plist.

6. Describe the steps involved in archiving.

7. Explain the importance of the NSCoding protocol when archiving.

8. Describe the functions of the following SQLite commands:

   a. sqlite3_open()

   b. sqlite3_close()

   c. sqlite3_prepare_v2()

   d. sqlite3_step()

   e. sqlite3_exec()

9. What are the most commonly used data persistence mechanisms?

10. Describe the steps involved in creating a sqlite database.

## Programming Exercises

1. Create an app that remembers the user's name. When the user opens the app for the first time, the app should ask the user for his or her name. Afterwards, every time the app is launched, it should display the name of the most recent user. Use the NSUSerDefaults class to complete this app.

2. Create the app described in Programming Exercise 1 using archiving instead of the NSUSerDefaults class.

3. Modify the app described in the Programming Exercise 2 to allow the user to change the view's background color. The user should be given three color choices (red, green and blue). When the user touches the Enter button, the color and name should be saved. Every time the app is launched, it should display the previously chosen background color as well as the previous user's name.

4. Create a grocery list that displays the entries made by the previous user every time the app is launched.

5. Modify the app described in Programming Exercise 4 so that the first time that the user launches the app, he or she is asked to enter a grocery budget. Henceforth, every time that the app is launched, the groceries budget should be displayed, along with the list of groceries entered the last time the app was launched. The user should be allowed to change the budget.

6. Modify the app created in Programming Exercise 5 so that it allows the user to enter his or her name, and then displays the user's name when it is relaunched. Further, when the app is first launched, it should also ask the user to select a background color for the app as in Programming Exercise 2. When the app is relaunched, the background color should match the color selected on the previous run.

7. Create a math test app that displays five questions that the user is required to answer. Before a user exits the app, it should record the number of questions that the user answered correctly. The app should also allow the user to display statistics, such as the number of questions answered correctly in previous attempts.

8. Modify the app described in Programming Exercise 7 so that it allows the user to enter his or her name, and then displays the user's name when the app is re-launched. The app should have the added convenience of allowing a user to change his or her name. When the statistics screen displays, the user should be able to view the previous user's name and the number of questions answered correctly.

## Business case study

In Chapter 13 we added three images for the pain levels and added a sound each time the user selects a pain level. In this chapter we will use SQLite to incorporate some data persistence features.

Modify the first view so the user can enter the pain journal items, such as the pain level, and the date and time of entry. The first view should also have the ability to display the pain items entered in the journal. When the user selects the Pain Level tab, the second view should display a picker view where the user can select a pain level. When the user selects the History tab, the second view should display all the pain levels entered so far in a table view format. Save the data in a SQLite database.

# Xcode Debugger

A debugger is a tool that helps you monitor a program while it is running by stepping through the program one step at a time. Using the Xcode debugger, you can step through the program and examine the contents of variables at certain points in the program called break points. To use the Xcode debugger, you insert one or more breakpoints (as described in the steps later in this appendix) and then activate the debugger.

Activating the debugger displays the debug area, shown in Figure A-1, which contains two components: the **debug bar**, which contains the debugger controls, and the **content pane**, where the information about selected items is displayed. You can step through the code in a program line by line using the buttons on the debug bar shown in Figure A-2. When code execution reaches a break point, you have the option of clicking the Step Over button, the Step Into button, or the Step Out button on the debug bar:

- **Step Over**: Executes one step. However, if the step invokes a function, then the function is executed all at once, as one step.

- **Step Into**: Executes one step. However, if the step invokes a function, then the function is also executed a step at a time.

- **Step Out**: Finishes the execution of the current function and goes to the main program or, if the execution is in the main program, the execution of the main function is completed in one step.

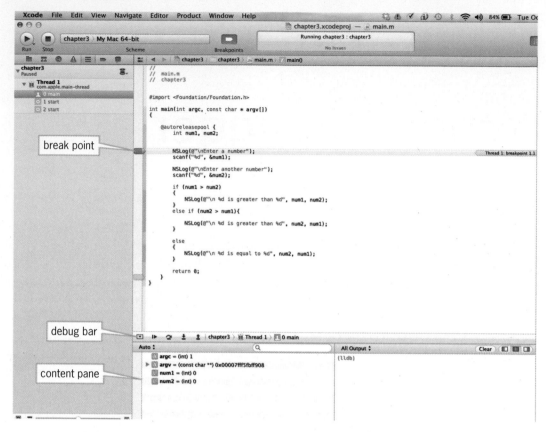

**Figure A-1**   Debugger activated in Xcode
Copyright © 2014 Apple®. All Rights Reserved

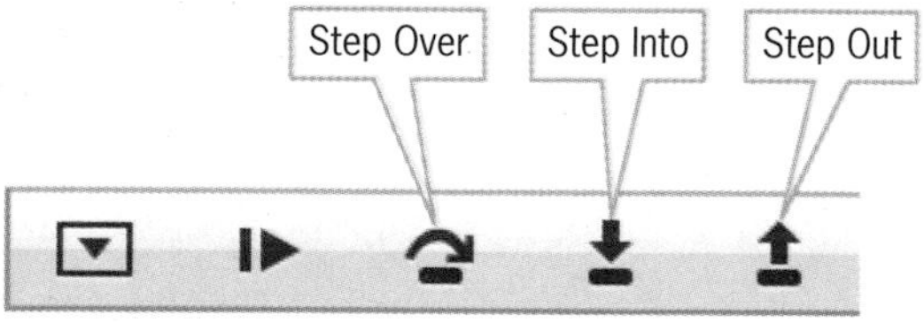

**Figure A-2**   Debug bar

Now we're ready to try debugging a program. First, we need to set up the debugger.

1.  Select **Xcode ▶ Behaviors ▶ Edit Behaviors**, as shown in Figure A-3.

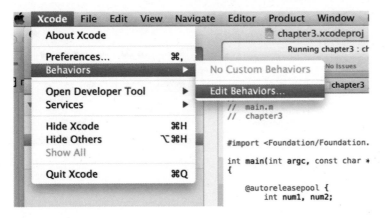

**Figure A-3**   Setting up the debugger

2.  Next, we need to tell the debugger to show the contents of the variables during program execution. In the Behaviors dialog, locate the **Running** heading on the left. Under "Running," select **Starts** and then select the check box next to "Show debugger with." Also, select **Variables & Console View**, as shown in Figure A-4.

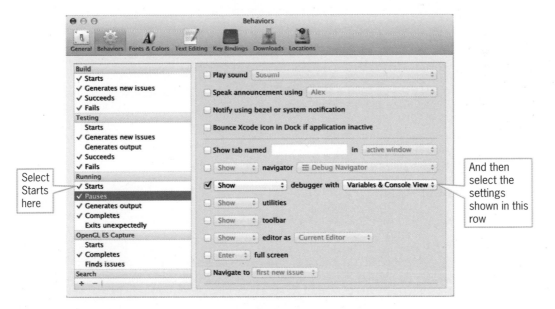

**Figure A-4**   Setting up the debugger to display the contents of variables

3.  Do the same for **Pauses** and **Generates output** as well, which are listed just below "Starts."

4. Now we need to create a program to debug. Create an Objective-C project called **AppendixExample** by selecting **OS X Application** and then selecting **Command Line Tool**, as shown in Figure A-5.

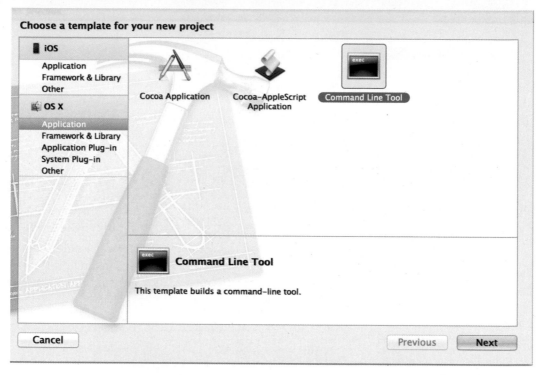

**Figure A-5**   Creating a new Objective-C project

5. Type the following code into the program:

```
1  #import <Foundation/Foundation.h>
2  int add (int n1, int n2);
3  int main (int argc, const char * argv[])
4  {
5      @autoreleasepool {
6          int num1, result;
7          NSLog (@"Enter first number to be added");
8          scanf ("%d",&result);
9          for (int i = 0; i < 4; i++) {
10             NSLog (@"Enter another number to be added");
11             scanf ("%d",&num1);
12             result = add (result, num1);
13         }
14         NSLog (@"\nThe sum of the 5 numbers is %d", result);
15     }
16     return 0;
17 }
```

```
18  int add (int n1, int n2)
19  {
20      int sum;
21      sum = n1+n2;
22      return sum;
23  }
```

6. Create a breakpoint by clicking to the left of line 6, in the space between the code and the navigator area.

7. If necessary, activate the debugger by selecting **Product ▶ Debug ▶ Activate Breakpoints**, as shown in Figure A-6, or by clicking the **Breakpoints** button, as shown in Figure A-7.

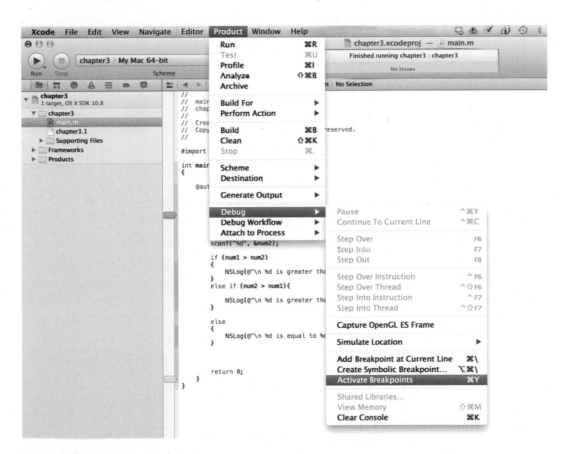

**Figure A-6**   Activating the debugger

**Figure A-7**   Breakpoint button

8.   Run the app. At this point, your Xcode window should look like Figure A-8.

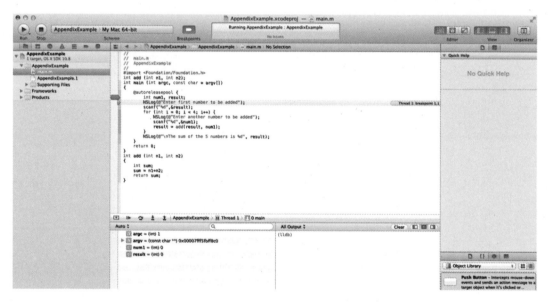

**Figure A-8**   Running the app in debug mode

9.   Now we will demonstrate the debugger using the Step Over option. Click the **Step Over** button.

10.   You are prompted to enter a number, so enter a number click Step Over one more time before you enter a number.

11.   Click the **Step Over** button to execute the next step.

12.   You are prompted for another number, so enter another number click Step Over one more time before you enter another number.

13.   Click the **Step Over** button to go to the next line. At this point execution is at line 9, as shown in Figure A-9. Notice the contents of the variables in the lower-left corner. At this point, num1 = 45 and result = 90.

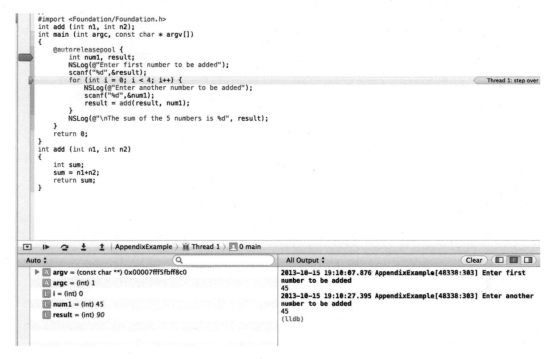

```
#import <Foundation/Foundation.h>
int add (int n1, int n2);
int main (int argc, const char * argv[])
{
    @autoreleasepool {
        int num1, result;
        NSLog(@"Enter first number to be added");
        scanf("%d",&result);
        for (int i = 0; i < 4; i++) {                                    Thread 1: step over
            NSLog(@"Enter another number to be added");
            scanf("%d",&num1);
            result = add(result, num1);
        }
        NSLog(@"\nThe sum of the 5 numbers is %d", result);
    }
    return 0;
}
int add (int n1, int n2)
{
    int sum;
    sum = n1+n2;
    return sum;
}
```

499

```
☐   I▶   ⟳   ↧   ↥   | AppendixExample ⟩ 📚 Thread 1 ⟩ 🔲 0 main

Auto ⬍                        (🔍                    )  All Output ⬍                              Clear  ⬜ ⬛ ⬜
  ▶ Ⓐ argv = (const char **) 0x00007fff5fbff8c0    2013-10-15 19:10:07.876 AppendixExample[48338:303] Enter first
    Ⓐ argc = (int) 1                               number to be added
    Ⓛ i = (int) 0                                  45
                                                   2013-10-15 19:10:27.395 AppendixExample[48338:303] Enter another
    Ⓛ num1 = (int) 45                              number to be added
    Ⓛ result = (int) 90                            45
                                                   (lldb)
```

Figure A-9   Content pane displaying variable contents

14. Click the **Step Over** button a few more times until the `for` loop is executed and the contents of the variables match the variables shown in Figure A-10. At this point `i = 1`, `num1 = 34` and `result = 124`.

```
☐   I▶   ⟳   ↧   ↥   | AppendixExample ⟩ 📚 Thread 1 ⟩ 🔲 0 main

Auto ⬍                        (🔍                    )  All Output ⬍                              Clear  ⬜ ⬛ ⬜
  ▶ Ⓐ argv = (const char **) 0x00007fff5fbff8c0    2013-10-15 19:10:07.876 AppendixExample[48338:303] Enter first
    Ⓐ argc = (int) 1                               number to be added
    Ⓛ i = (int) 1                                  45
                                                   2013-10-15 19:10:27.395 AppendixExample[48338:303] Enter another
    Ⓛ num1 = (int) 34                              number to be added
    Ⓛ result = (int) 124                           45
                                                   2013-10-15 19:21:35.185 AppendixExample[48338:303] Enter another
                                                   number to be added
                                                   34
                                                   (lldb) |
```

Figure A-10   Content pane displaying new variable contents

15. Because we are using the Step Over button, execution treats the entire function as one step. Since this function is very simple and only adds the two numbers that are passed to it, the use of Step Over is justified. If you are debugging a long program containing a complicated function, you may want to use the Step Into functionality instead, so you can execute each individual line of code in the function. To get some practice, we'll try using the Step Into button now, on our third pass through the `for` loop. Click the **Step Into** button a few times until the execution enters the `add` function.

**16.** Continue clicking the **Step Into** button to complete the function. Keep in mind that you can always exit a function by clicking the Step Out button, in which case execution jumps out of the function and back to the main function. See Figure A-11.

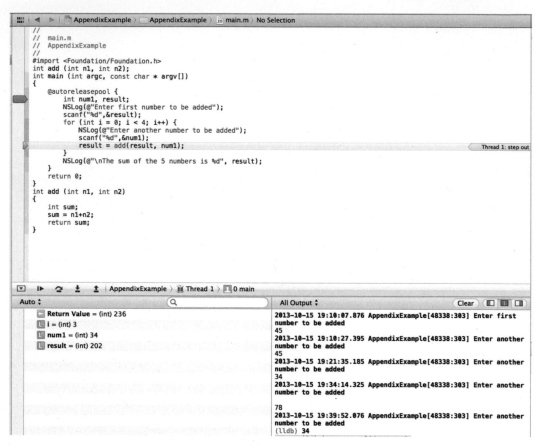

```
//
//  main.m
//  AppendixExample
//
#import <Foundation/Foundation.h>
int add (int n1, int n2);
int main (int argc, const char * argv[])
{
    @autoreleasepool {
        int num1, result;
        NSLog(@"Enter first number to be added");
        scanf("%d",&result);
        for (int i = 0; i < 4; i++) {
            NSLog(@"Enter another number to be added");
            scanf("%d",&num1);
            result = add(result, num1);                          Thread 1: step out
        }
        NSLog(@"\nThe sum of the 5 numbers is %d", result);
    }
    return 0;
}
int add (int n1, int n2)
{
    int sum;
    sum = n1+n2;
    return sum;
}
```

AppendixExample > Thread 1 > 0 main

Auto

Return Value = (int) 236
i = (int) 3
num1 = (int) 34
result = (int) 202

All Output        Clear

```
2013-10-15 19:10:07.876 AppendixExample[48338:303] Enter first
number to be added
45
2013-10-15 19:10:27.395 AppendixExample[48338:303] Enter another
number to be added
45
2013-10-15 19:21:35.185 AppendixExample[48338:303] Enter another
number to be added
34
2013-10-15 19:34:14.325 AppendixExample[48338:303] Enter another
number to be added

78
2013-10-15 19:39:52.076 AppendixExample[48338:303] Enter another
number to be added
(lldb) 34
```

**Figure A-11**    Demonstrating step out

# Index

Note: Page numbers in **boldface** type indicate where key terms are defined.